Miles Davis
A Critical Biography

ALSO BY IAN CARR
Music Outside

Miles Davis

A Critical Biography

Ian Carr

Quartet Books
London   Melbourne   New York

First published by Quartet Books Limited 1982
A member of the Namara Group
27/29 Goodge Street, London W1P 1FD

Copyright © Ian Carr 1982
Discography copyright © Brian Priestley 1982

British Library Cataloguing in Publication Data

Carr, Ian
  1. Davis, Miles
  2. Jazz musicians – United States – Biography
  I. Title
  788'.1'0924   ML 419.D39

  ISBN 0-7043-2273-0

Printed in Great Britain by
Mackays of Chatham Limited

Music

Contents

List of Illustrations   vii
Acknowledgements   ix

1 – Miles Dewey Davis III   1
2 – Bird Land   12
3 – The Birth of the Cool   31
4 – Cold Turkey   41
5 – The First Great Quintet   53
6 – Miles Ahead   68
7 – The First Great Sextet   82
8 – Porgy and Bess   95
9 – Is It Jazz?   104
10 – After Coltrane   117
11 – In and Out of the Doldrums   129
12 – Miles in the Sky   148
13 – Play What's *Not* There!   165
14 – Miles Runs the Voodoo Down   179
15 – Jazz Into Rock *Will* Go   189
16 – Live–Evil   205
17 – Manhattan Jungle Symphony   217
18 – Postscript   230

References   237
Bibliography   247
Appendix A: Musical Examples   251
Appendix B: Notes on Repertoire   265
Appendix C: Discography   267
Index   303

Copyright credits for Musical Examples in Appendix A

Illustrations

Paris Jazz Fair, 1949 (*New York Times*)
Paris Jazz Fair, 1949 (*Max Jones*)
Miles and John Coltrane (*Courtesy of CBS Records, photo: Al Avakian*)
Miles and Red Garland (*Courtesy of CBS Records, photo: Al Avakian*)
Miles and Gil Evans (*Courtesy of CBS Records, photo: Don Hunstein*)
Miles and Gil recording *Miles Ahead*, (a) and (b) (*Courtesy of CBS Records, photo: Don Hunstein*)
Miles and Gil recording *Porgy and Bess*, (a) and (b) (*Courtesy of CBS Records, photo: Vernon Smith*)
Miles, 1958 (*Courtesy of CBS Records, photo: Vernon Smith*)
Miles and Bill Evans (*Courtesy of CBS Records, photo: Don Hunstein*)
John Coltrane, Cannonball Adderley, Miles, Bill Evans (*Courtesy of CBS Records, photo: Don Hunstein*)
Jimmy Cobb, Wynton Kelly, Paul Chambers (*Valerie Wilmer*)
Miles, 1967 (*Valerie Wilmer*)
Dave Holland, Jack DeJohnette, Miles (*Valerie Wilmer*)
Miles and Teo Macero, (a), (b) and (c) (*Courtesy of CBS Records*)
Miles with Clive Davis (*Courtesy of CBS Records*)
Miles in the early 1970s, (a) and (b) (*Courtesy of CBS Records, photo: Don Hunstein*)
Selection of album covers (*Courtesy of CBS Records*)
Miles in 1974 (*Courtesy of CBS Records*)
Cover of *Directions* (*Courtesy of CBS Records*)

Acknowledgements

I am grateful to the following musicians for talking to me at length: Gil Coggins, Clark Terry, Dave Holland, Herbie Hancock, Joe Zawinul, Jimmy Cobb, Teo Macero, Jimmy Garrison, Red Rodney, Horace Silver, Paul Buckmaster, Derek Wadsworth, Harry Klein, Vic Ash, Sonny and Linda Sharrock.

I am also grateful to Keith Jarrett and Dave Liebman for information and insights and to Gil and Anita Evans for an evening I spent in their company in New York, 1975. Special thanks to Brian Priestley for compiling the discography, and for reading through and checking my manuscript, but I take full responsibility for any errors.

For various help and encouragement, I'm grateful to the following people: Ray Coleman – editor-in-chief of *Melody Maker*; Trevor Timmers; Charles Fox; George Foster; Valerie Wilmer; David Apps; Alun Morgan; Tony Hall; Peter Philbin of CBS New York; Hugh Attwooll; Simon Frodsham; Jonathan Morrish and Terry Lott of CBS London; Barbara Carr and Mary Lou of ABC Records; Arthur Levy and Stanley Meises of Atlantic Records; David Marsh and Chet Flippo of *Rolling Stone* magazine; Nik Cohn; Gary Giddins; Stanley Dance; Max Jones; John Chilton; Keith Winter and Jeff Pressing of La Trobe University, Australia; Vera Brandes; Frank Modica; Don Friedman; Tony Middleton of Dobell's Jazz Record Shop, London; Keith Goodwin; Michael Rusenberg.

I am also grateful for the insights of several critics, in particular: Leonard Feather; Nat Hentoff; Ralph J. Gleason; Max Harrison; Martin Williams; Michael James; LeRoi Jones.

1
Miles Dewey Davis III

'I just got on to the trumpet and studied and played.'[1]

Miles Davis

Miles Davis was born in Alton, Illinois, on 25 May 1926, and a year later his family moved south to East St Louis, a small town on the east side of the Mississippi River. There was an older sister, Dorothy, and in 1929 his brother, Vernon, was born. The family was middle-class and prosperous, having established itself in just two generations since Lincoln and Congress abolished slavery in America. The men of the family were proud, intelligent and self-willed, and the name 'Miles' was passed on from generation to generation.

In the days of slavery the Davis family had been musicians and had performed classical string music for the plantation owners. But after Emancipation this musical tradition was broken. For several decades there were only two courses open to Negro musicians: either to be an entertainer for white folks, or to play in clip-joints, brothels or bars. Neither alternative was acceptable to the aristocratic Davis men. Miles's father (Miles II) wanted to be a musician himself but was emphatically dissuaded: 'My father, Miles I, was born six years after the Emancipation and forbade me to play music because the only place a Negro could play then was in barrel-houses. My father was the most efficient double entry column book-keeper in Arkansas before the coming of the adding machine and white men came to his home under cover of night for him to fix their books.'[2]

It was no illegal 'fixing', but at that time no white man wanted it known that his accounts were being done by a Negro. Miles I was eventually able to buy a thousand acres of land in Arkansas and send his son, Miles II, to Northwestern College to study dentistry. Miles II worked hard and when the family moved to East St Louis he had a thriving practice and became a substantial landowner, buying a 200-acre ranch on which he raised pedigree hogs and kept horses. This enabled his son, Miles III, to grow up in the open country and to enjoy the pursuits of riding, hunting and fishing.

1

According to his father, he liked long country walks and was an excellent horseman – 'if he was ever thrown he'd remount immediately and master his mount'.[3]

The young Miles had the ingredients for a secure and happy boyhood – parents who cared about him and a father with professional status, wealth and property. However, this meant little if you were black and lived in a city as racist as East St Louis. The Davis family moved into an all-white neighbourhood – a bold and provocative gesture typical of them. But although East St Louis was in the officially mid-west state of Illinois, it was in *southern* Illinois and racism was still prevalent (many blacks had been murdered there in the infamous and bloody riots of 1917). One of Miles's earliest memories is of being chased down a street by a white man shouting 'Nigger! Nigger!' Miles, a sensitive boy, never forgot it.

In physique, Miles Davis took after his father, having the same slight, though wiry frame. He inherited his mother's good looks – the large, luminous eyes, the straight, finely chiselled nose, and the delicate jawline. His early relationship with her was deeply affected by the racial and social situation. As the wife of a dental surgeon, Miles's mother was aware that her family had an important place in local society, and she strove to uphold that position. After Emancipation, it was the professional men and ministers of the church who were the heads of the new black society, and they were at pains to get rid of any customs, habits or mannerisms that were too negroid or which harked back to slavery. It often happened that leading Negro citizens became the most fanatical imitators of white society.

The music in the Davis household was limited to the genteel western variety. Miles's older sister, Dorothy, played the piano, and he used to peep through the door and watch when she had her piano lessons. His mother played the violin and wanted Miles to take it up. But another side of her musical ability, which she did not reveal to Miles for many years, was always suppressed; she could play the piano and knew the blues. In 1958 he said, 'I didn't know until after I'd gone back there for a visit a few years ago, that my mother ever knew one note of the piano. But she sat down one day and played some funky blues. Turned out that my grandmother used to teach organ.'[4] So complete was the censorship that even the knowledge of his grandmother's musical proclivities had been kept secret.

As befitted their social position, the Davis family went to church, but Miles was already showing signs of that sharp intelligence and individualism which were to illuminate and shape his adult life. He had already begun asking awkward questions and expecting honest answers: 'I went to church when I was very young, but when I was about six, I asked my mother why the church kept calling me a sinner when I hadn't done anything wrong. When I didn't get a good

2

answer, I stopped going to church.'[5]

Miles's mother was also active in community life. Later on she was to work with such organizations as the Urban League, the aims of which were: 'To eliminate racial segregation and discrimination in the US, and to help black citizens and other economically and socially disadvantaged groups to share equally in every aspect of American life.'

Although intensely conscious of his social position, Miles's father did not attempt to blot out the past with the same fanaticism as his wife, nor did he try to ape all the customs of white society; he was proud of his own father and reminisced about his forebears. He also instilled into Miles junior the necessity for self-sufficiency, insisting there was no excuse for being poor. As a result, Miles was, from an early age, money-conscious and frugal. By the time he was ten he was doing a paper-round. 'I got a paper route and it got bigger than I could handle because my customers liked me so much. I just delivered papers the best I could, and minded my business... I saved most of what I made except for buying records.'[6]

When he reached his teens, Miles had become aware that his mother and father were not getting along well. (They were eventually divorced.) One confrontation occurred on Miles's thirteenth birthday. His mother wanted to give him a violin as a birthday present, but, Miles recalled with irony: 'My father gave me a trumpet because he loved my mother so much!'[7] The choice represented two cultural polarities: the violin was representative of western 'serious' music, and the trumpet (after Buddy Bolden, Louis Armstrong and Roy Eldridge) had come to symbolize the essence of jazz –a music with non-western roots. Miles's mother deeply resented this choice. Furthermore, his father had not only chosen the instrument, he'd also chosen the teacher. Buchanan, a patient of Miles senior, worked for the local education authority as a peripatetic teacher and was an excellent trumpeter. Miles started playing the trumpet at grade school and from Buchanan, as well as technical lessons, he learned something of the romantic myths and folklore of jazz: 'He used to tell us all about jam sessions on the Showboat, about trumpet players like Bobby Hackett and Hal Baker.'[8]

From the start, Miles began to find out things for himself. To achieve breath control, good intonation and a clear sound, it is essential for trumpet players to practise holding long notes, and when Miles first began lessons at school, once a week the class would hold long notes. There was a certain spirit of competition in this activity: 'Everybody would fight to play best. Lucky for me, I learned to play the chromatic scale right away. A friend of my father's brought me a book one night and showed me how to do it so I wouldn't have to sit there and hold that note all the time... The next day in school I was the belle of the ball!'[9]

3

When Miles went to high school, he received daily lessons from Buchanan, and also joined the school band. The teacher gave him some advice which profoundly influenced Miles's whole approach to the trumpet. He was told not to play with vibrato: 'Buchanan didn't believe in it. He said that all the white guys used it, and the best guys were the black guys who played straight sounds.'[10] He also warned Miles: 'You're gonna get old anyway and start shaking.' From that time on, the young Miles tried to play 'fast and light and no vibrato.'[11]

The high school was racially mixed, but Miles had no real friends among the white pupils. He made rapid progress on the trumpet, but came up against racial prejudice. According to his father: 'In school competitions he was always the best, but the blue-eyed boys always won first and second prizes. Miles had always to settle for third. The officials, Miles and everybody else knew he should have had first prize. You can't treat a kid like that and tell him to come out and say the water wasn't dirty.'[12] The injustice made a deep impression on Miles. Years later, he recalled: 'It made me so mad I made up my mind to outdo anybody white on my horn. If I hadn't met that prejudice, I probably wouldn't have had as much drive in my work.'[13]

The high school band rehearsed twice a week and tried to sound like Count Basie, and soon Miles was also playing at weekends with drums, piano and an alto saxophonist who 'sounded like Guy Lombardo's first alto'. He was rising steeply in the estimation of his teacher, Buchanan, who talked of him in glowing terms. The teacher was a drinking companion of trumpeter Clark Terry who was six years older than Miles and who lived across the river in St Louis. According to Terry, Buchanan was tremendously proud of Miles and used to say: 'Man, I gotta little cat over there! You gotta come and hear him! He's playing his ass off!' He enthused so much that eventually Terry went over to hear Miles play and was deeply impressed. If Clark Terry appreciated Miles's playing, Miles had an even greater respect for the older man, and said of Terry: 'I started to play like him. I idolized him.'[14]

Shortly after this, Miles met up with his hero again, but was rebuffed. Terry was playing with a band which was hired by the Parks Commission to play at an outdoor athletic and band competition between various Illinois high schools. Miles was competing with the East St Louis high school band and tried to chat to Clark Terry who was busy eyeing up the numerous pretty girls. Terry recalls: 'So this kid comes up to me...and I said..."Why don't you get lost – stop bugging me! I want to look at these girls." So it turns out it was Miles and I'd forgotten.'

Sometime later, when Miles was only fifteen and still at high school, he joined the musicians' union. This enabled him to work

4

professionally with a St Louis band, Eddie Randall's Blue Devils, a rhythm and blues outfit. It was while they were working at the Elks Club, a place where all musicians used to go for after-hours jam sessions, that Miles finally became close friends with Clark Terry. The latter dropped by to do some after-hours blowing, and on his way upstairs heard a trumpet player he couldn't identify, though he 'knew every horn in town'. The club was on the third floor, and Terry ran all the way upstairs: 'And I see this little cat sitting there with his legs crossed and he's smoking his ass off. So I walk up to him and I say, "Hey man, aren't you the guy...?" and he says, "Yeah, I'm the kid you fluffed off down in Carbondale!" We always had a big laugh about it afterwards.'

After this, the two became firm friends, and Terry became a kind of father figure for the young Miles. Talking of his influences, Miles says: 'The main one must have been Terry. My teacher [Buchanan] played like him...he [Terry] and I used to go out to jam and the place would be crowded in ten minutes. He'd come over to my house and ask my father could I go, you know, and he'd take me to a session. Man! We'd play from six o'clock to six the next morning.'[15]

With Clark Terry as his chaperon and mentor, Miles could rapidly broaden and deepen his experience of the musical activity in the St Louis area. St Louis is the chief city and river port of the state of Missouri and acts as a gateway between South and North. Earlier in the century, it had been a centre for ragtime, and the city was a natural stopping-off point for musicians travelling downstream from Kansas City or Chicago, or upriver from New Orleans. Jam sessions by visiting and local musicians were a prominent feature of musical life around St Louis during the thirties and forties. Miles recalls: 'We always played the blues in St Louis. Bands came up on the boats from New Orleans, guys came from Kansas City and Oklahoma City, all playing the blues... When I was a kid I was fascinated by the musicians, particularly guys who used to come up from New Orleans and jam all night... you listened to everybody and took the parts you liked. You watched how they hold the horn, how they walk... I mean if you're fifteen!'[16]

Miles could hardly have had a better model than Clark Terry. Terry came from a large, poor, ghetto family, and, like the other great contemporary trumpeter, Dizzy Gillespie, whose family were similarly under-privileged, the first music he heard was in the church. Clark Terry is aware that his superb sense of time and feeling for rhythm have their roots in this initial experience: 'The very first thing I heard in the form of pulsating beats was at the Sanctified Church on the corner. They all played tambourines and there was a certain beat that was instilled in you right from a kid. Even the kids who weren't interested in the religious calling, they would congregate on the outside and dance with tremendous respect for this rhythm...

great rapport with the rhythm... It was just around you; you couldn't miss it, y'know, and I get mad at myself even today if I ever miss a beat.' It is unlikely that Miles's early church-going included such unselfconscious and enjoyable rhythmic and musical experiences. His family were at the opposite end of the social scale from the Terry family, and it is almost certain that the more vital African elements were expunged from the music of their middle class church.

The older jazz musicians tended to be secretive about their knowledge, because they feared that the rising young players would be competitors for their jobs. Miles Davis was doubly lucky because his family were able to afford an instrument and lessons, and because the newly established trumpeters such as Terry and (later) Dizzy Gillespie were generous with their help and encouragement – most probably as a direct result of their own struggle to learn.

The approach to trumpet playing and the style that emerged in that area is so individual that it is known as 'The St Louis Sound'. Its main characteristics are a beautifully clear, round and singing brass sound which really projects and hangs on the air, and an epigrammatic and witty melodic flair. In the early forties the most famous example was probably Harold (Shorty) Baker who had played with Don Redman, Duke Ellington and Teddy Wilson, and was with Andy Kirk from 1941-2. Baker was one of Buchanan's favourites, but the whole area was full of other unsung trumpeters who had these same qualities highly developed. Miles's bandleader with the Blue Devils, Eddie Randall, was another of the St Louis trumpet men. Clark Terry says: 'Just as Miles was inspired by me, I was definitely inspired by trumpet players who were older than I ...Levi Maddison was reputedly the most beautiful sound in the area. He went completely stone crazy, but you'd go to his home, those of us who knew him, and he'd just laugh all the time. All he did was laugh, and then we'd say, "Play something", and he'd take out his horn and play in his room and it was just like the angels singing. It was just a pure sound with all the jazz flavourings and colorations you know.'

Levi Maddison used a Heim mouthpiece which was recommended by a trumpet teacher called Gustav who played first trumpet with the St Louis Symphony Orchestra. Clark Terry could not afford to have lessons from Gustav, but he used to get second-hand lessons from musicians who did study with him. Gustav prescribed the Heim mouthpiece for all his students, and many trumpeters in the area used it – including Terry himself, and Shorty Baker. Miles Davis began using a Heim mouthpiece at that time and, according to Terry, has been playing one ever since. Terry believes that this mouthpiece was partially at least responsible for the trumpet sound which was prominent in the St Louis area. It was made of very thin metal, with a flat rim and a very deep cup. A mouthpiece with a deep cup tends to help in the production of a full sound, but also

6

makes it more difficult to play high notes. This may have been one of the reasons why Miles, in his early life, had difficulty with the upper register of the instrument. But his perseverance with the Heim mouthpiece was to result in perhaps the most burnished and singing trumpet sound in jazz.

By the time he was fifteen, Miles was getting the best of both worlds: regular trumpet lessons from Elwood Buchanan and a wide experience of the thriving musical life in St Louis. He was doubly fortunate in that he was learning to read music and to improvise at the same time. The possibility of a choice of career still lay open to him: so far as his family were concerned, he might yet be eligible for symphonic work, but at the same time he was preparing himself for small group or big band jazz playing. He was developing at a time when the romantic idea (mostly held by whites) of the non-reading, improvising genius was dying, while the practical idea that it was really essential to be able to read music was taking a firm hold among Negro musicians. Before this, many Negroes hadn't bothered to learn to read music simply because they believed there was no point in it – they'd never get a job with a symphony orchestra or any similar organization. Such jobs were the exclusive domain of white musicians, and the only outlets for Negroes were in either entertainment or sport – or in jazz which has always been a kind of fusion of aesthetics and athletics. Clark Terry was typical in that he was not only deeply involved in jazz, but was also an excellent boxer, and a close friend of Archie Moore, another St Louis man and one of the greatest fighters of all time. Miles also shared this interest in boxing both as a spectator and as a participator.

On 7 December 1941, the Japanese destroyed most of the American fleet at Pearl Harbor. The following day Congress declared war on Japan and, three days later, Germany and Italy declared war on the USA. America had entered the Second World War. In 1942, most jazz musicians who were the right age were called up into the forces – including Clark Terry. Miles Davis was sixteen, still at school, too young for military service, and became a larger fish in a smaller pool. By now he was the musical director of the Eddie Randall band and wrote arrangements for it. Apart from straight band sessions in clubs, the Blue Devils were also playing floor shows. Miles's reputation began to grow rapidly among local musicians, and visiting musicians began to make a point of going to listen to him.

The young pianist, Gil Coggins, who was to record with Miles a decade later, first heard the trumpeter in St Louis in 1943. Coggins was drafted into the army and posted to the area. He recalled:

There was…a big club with big bands and a bowling alley…In the same building was a cocktail bar, and Miles was playing there

7

with a piano player called St Clare Brooks. He was called Duke Brooks because he knew all Duke's [Ellington] tunes, and there was a drummer... I used to go absent without leave sometimes just to listen to Miles... It was just a trio – no bass. They were playing Duke Ellington tunes and stuff like that...kind of swing music ...So I used to go A.W.O.L. to listen to Miles. And then there was another club where he was playing with a band...about a ten-piece band.

The band was most probably Eddie Randall's Blue Devils.

Emmanuel 'Duke' St Clare Brooks was one of the first local musicians of whom Miles had become aware. In the late thirties, Brooks used to play with the bass player, Jimmy Blanton, in a place called the Red Inn which was across the street from Miles senior's dental surgery. Miles used to go there to hear Brooks and Blanton both of whom were associates of Clark Terry. Like many of the musicians in St Louis, Duke Brooks had a daytime job and did his playing in the evenings and at weekends. According to Gil Coggins, Brooks was a 'natural', and Miles learned a great deal from him. Miles confirms this: 'Duke couldn't read or write any music. We used to have a trio together in St Louis. We played like the Benny Goodman Sextet. He was always showing me things Charlie Christian played. He made a record with Red Calendar, and then he died.'[17] Like all other aspiring musicians, Duke Brooks wanted to get to New York – the Big Apple – to show off his talents and try his luck. And also, like most other young musicians, he had very little money and so had to hitch-hike. He was knocked down and killed by a train en route.

While the Eddie Randall band was playing for the floor shows at the Rhumboogie Club in St Louis, saxophonist Sonny Stitt came into town on tour with Tiny Bradshaw's band. After listening to Miles play, Stitt said: 'You look like a man named Charlie Parker, and you play like him too. C'mon with us.' Stitt was serious and persuaded Bradshaw to offer Miles a job. It was an exciting moment for the young trumpeter: 'The fellows in his band had their hair slicked down, they wore tuxedos, and they offered me sixty whole dollars a week to play with them. I went home and asked my mother if I could go with them. She said no, I had to finish my last year of high school. I didn't talk to her for two weeks. And I didn't go with the band either.'[18] Silent reproaches seem to have been common between Miles and his mother, and the undercurrents of unspoken feeling in the Davis household must have played a large part in creating his exceptional awareness and sensitivity to atmosphere. The growing disharmony of his parents was, no doubt, a strong contributing factor.

Miles and his family often found themselves in conflict. Although

8

he was still a minor and a schoolboy, he was financially fairly independent, earning around $85 a week from music. The $60 offer from Tiny Bradshaw would have meant a drop in earnings but an elevation in musical status. Miles's emphasis of the salary he was offered – 'sixty *whole* dollars a week' – was probably ironic. He had to accept the authority of his parents, and yet, had also to be involved in the breakup of their marriage and even to make some financial contribution to family concerns. Recalling this period he said: 'I was already making $85 a week when I was fifteen. My parents got a divorce when I was young and I helped my sister through college.'[19]

Miles was intellectually precocious and had an almost photographic memory: 'I taught my sister mathematics. See, if I had a book, I could look at it and remember the whole page. It came to me like that. I can remember anything – telephone numbers, addresses...I can just glance at them and remember. That's the reason I used to take care of band payrolls; I could remember all the tabs and shit.'[20] This ability, too, resulted in another paradox: although he was usually the youngest member of the groups with which he worked, he was often the guiding light, the director and the organizer. He was becoming extremely independent and self-sufficient, yet in one sense at least, he was still tied to his mother's apronstrings: 'They used to come scouting for me [bandleaders such as Bradshaw, Earl Hines, Jimmy Lunceford], but I couldn't go with them because I was too young and my mother was having a fit.'[21] And yet, although his parents could prevent him from going off with various bands, they were powerless to stop him from taking a much more serious step at the age of sixteen, when he married a local girl called Irene. Perhaps it was a 'shotgun wedding' which his parents with their middle class sense of honour condoned. A daughter, Cheryl, was born in 1943, and the marriage lasted into the early fifties and produced two more children. In 1943, however, it underlined the contradictions: Miles was a husband, a father and a breadwinner, but still a minor, at high school, and subject to parental authority.

Meanwhile, Miles's musical awareness was expanding. Any good musician, white or black, was grist to his mill. He had a great admiration for Buddy Rich, the swing and big band drummer. A local East St Louis drummer called Larry Jackson, who played with Miles, has said that the trumpeter was always telling him to 'play like Buddy'[22] and that Miles always wanted *any* drummer to play like Rich. Miles also loved Duke Ellington's work and respected Count Basie, and was very much aware of Benny Goodman's small group work. He was versed in rhythm and blues, and at the same time, he'd had regular lessons in 'legitimate' trumpet playing. By now, he'd also heard Charlie Parker's early recordings with Jay McShann, and he'd heard a little of Dizzy Gillespie on record.

9

Parker and Gillespie were just beginning to spearhead the revolutionary music bebop, but Miles has always insisted that parallel developments were going on simultaneously in the mid-west, and that Charlie Christian, the guitarist with the Benny Goodman sextet, was the main influence in this area: 'I think bop branched off from Charlie Christian. There was a trumpet player named Buddy Anderson from Kansas City. He was with Billy Eckstine, and he used to play like Charlie ...There was another boy who played with us who played Kansas City Blues and that kind of thing ...and he sounded like Charlie Parker. His name was Charlie Young. We all used to work together.'[23]

As his involvement with jazz grew, so the pressures to leave East St Louis became more intense. New York had emerged during the thirties as the most important music centre in America, and however good a musician might seem in a provincial city, he could never feel that he had explored the ultimate reaches of his ability unless he had gone to New York and 'made the scene' there. Gil Coggins emphasized these different standards: 'Miles was very experienced before he hit New York... not in the New York way, of course, but so far as playing with bands was concerned.'

During his last two years at high school, Miles had to turn down other offers to leave home and join bands. Among others, he was offered jobs by Illinois Jacquet, and by A.J. Suliman, the trumpet-playing manager of McKinney's Cotton Pickers. But even after he'd graduated from high school in June 1944, pressure was still on Miles to take up formal studies. However, at the beginning of the summer vacation he took a job with a small band from New Orleans, called Adam Lambert's Six Brown Cats. It had just finished a residency at the Club Silhouette in Chicago, and was booked for a date at the Club Belvedere in Springfield, Illinois. The band was looking for a replacement for their trumpet player, Thomas Jefferson, who had returned to New Orleans. Miles got the job and received $100 a week – for two weeks, which was the length of the residency. Although brief, it was a good start for Miles: his was the only horn in the band, which was a modern swing outfit.

Back at home, Miles heard that the Billy Eckstine Band was scheduled to play at the Club Riviera in St Louis. Charlie Parker and Dizzy Gillespie, the two most talked-about musicians in jazz at the time, were with Eckstine, and Miles went along to hear them. He'd just been to a rehearsal with a local group and, with his trumpet under his arm, he was the first person in the hall. For him, every young musician's dream came true – he was asked to sit in with the band ...'This guy runs up to me and says, "Kid, do you have a union card?" It was Dizzy. I didn't even know him. I said, "Sure." "We need a trumpet player. Come on." I wanted to hear him; I could always read, so I got on the bandstand and started playing. I

10

couldn't read a thing from listening to Diz and Bird.'[24] Not for the first time, nor for the last time in his life, Miles was exactly the right man in exactly the right place at the right time.

In fact, he was taking the place of the third trumpet, his old friend Buddy Anderson who had become ill with tuberculosis. Anderson never played trumpet again, and Miles filled in for him around the St Louis area for about two weeks. The band's music was already known to Miles and he recalled: 'I loved the music so much, I knew the third trumpet part by heart.'[25] But the bandleader, Billy Eckstine, remembers the experience differently: 'When I first heard Miles, I let him sit in so as not to hurt his feelings, but he sounded terrible; he couldn't play at all.'[26] In the Eckstine context, with his two idols, Parker and Gillespie, in the band, Miles may well have been over-awed. In such a situation, for a young player accidentally falling into the big-time, two weeks is not long enough to breed confidence. The probability is that he played the written parts reasonably well, but didn't shine if, and when, he got any solos.

When the Eckstine band left St Louis to go to Chicago for a date at the Regal Theatre there, Miles had to stay behind because his parents were still anxious for him to take up some formal studies. His experience with the band, however, had made his mind up: he knew that he had to go to New York. It is also possible that Bird had mentioned to Miles that he, Parker, intended to leave the band when it got back to New York in order to concentrate on small-group playing. Miles's taste of the big-time and the new concepts of Parker and Gillespie had whetted his appetite; and he was finding St Louis stultifying and frustrating. He had learned all he could from the music scene there, and even the book he had been studying so assiduously – *Georgia Gibbs Chord Analyis* – seemed inadequate and sterile in the light of the fresh musical language Bird and Diz were creating. Miles had experienced something which, years later, Gil Evans was to put into words: 'Every form, even though it becomes traditional and finally becomes academic, originally came from someone's spirit who created the form. Then it was picked up and taught in schools after that. But all form originated from spirit.'[27] In Parker and Gillespie, Miles had found that spirit, and he knew that no schools could give him the knowledge and the experience he wanted. He would have to go to the source. Music was in the melting pot, and the crucible was New York.

2
Bird Land

'I spent my first week in New York and my first month's
allowance looking for Charlie Parker.'[1]
Miles Davis

Miles's mother wanted him to go to Fisk University which had a
very good music department, but he managed to get his father's
permission to enroll at the Juilliard School of Music in New York.
His father paid his tuition fees and gave him an allowance. From the
moment he arrived in New York in September 1944, Miles Davis
found himself living a 'Jekyll and Hyde' existence. Officially, he was
enrolled at Juilliard, an institution which taught established western
musical forms and techniques. But his unofficial interests – which
were his real reason for being in the city – lay in the dives and seedy
clubs of 52nd Street where the revolutionary music, bebop, was
being created. He had access to two very different worlds: at
Juilliard he was a protected student with a private income of fifty
dollars a week from his family; on 52nd Street, he was merely
another competitor in the disreputable and *laissez-faire* world of
jazz – a music with no real status. His attempts to reconcile these
two musical worlds were to become a dominant theme in his life and
music. He had arrived in New York in the middle of perhaps the
most turbulent decade in the history of American music, when jazz
itself was undergoing a radical transformation.

Jazz is often described as a music which reconciles and blends two
musical traditions – the non-western (African) and the western
(European) – but this is a distortion of the truth. From its earliest
beginnings, the history of jazz has been dominated by the constant
conflict of both traditions, and by compromises which are
precarious and which finally disintegrate. Broadly speaking, in each
of its phases the music has been created by black musicians and then
taken up by white musicians and the music industry and turned into
'easy-listening' music. During the uneasy international peace of the
1930s, the jazz impulse had been diluted in big-band swing,
culminating in the polished sterility of Glenn Miller. With World
War II came a renewed interest in the blues, a growing racial pride

12

(America needed black support for the war effort), and a resurgence of the virtuoso improviser. All these factors, plus the discoveries and experiments of some remarkable musicians, resulted in the creation of a new music – bebop. There were tendencies in this musical direction in many cities throughout the United States – particularly in St Louis and Kansas City – but the main spearhead of the movement was a handful of musicians centred on New York. In the early 1940s, at a club called Minton's Playhouse in Harlem, new ideas were pioneered by the pianist Thelonious Monk, drummer Kenny Clarke, and trumpeter Dizzy Gillespie. And in 1944, the new music hit 52nd Street when, first Dizzy, and later Charlie Parker, began working there with small groups.

In bebop, several non-western concepts of music were brilliantly reasserted. Its most striking characteristic was an intense, polyrhythmic drive to which even the melodies were subservient. In other words, the dynamic rhythms of the melodies were organically and intricately interwoven with the pulse and multiple accents of the rhythm section, which is typical of an African way of making music. In fast performances, the written or improvised melodies, with their streams of notes, wide interval leaps, displaced accents, and asymmetrical phrases, presented a rhythmic vitality which was so foreign to American listeners that it drew frightened and hostile comments from all sides. Even established musicians – no doubt because they felt threatened – attacked it. But it is interesting to note that, with the exception of Louis Armstrong who called it 'this modern malice', the most gifted members of the jazz establishment such as Duke Ellington, Count Basie, and some others, never attacked the new music or its practitioners, but instead welcomed and encouraged them. As well as revitalizing melody and re-establishing polyrhythms, bebop also offered a contemporary restatement of the basic blues impulse. At all tempos – fast, medium and slow – the blues with its tonal expressiveness, its deeply personal statements, and its roots in the history of black America, was once more made central to jazz. On 52nd Street, every night of the week it was possible to hear this new music which was splitting musicians and public into two factions – the 'hip' people who understood it (or at least claimed to), and the 'squares' who reviled and abused it.

This was the explosive musical climate when Miles Davis arrived in New York and spent his first week and his first month's allowance looking for Charlie Parker...initially without success. After some time, he read that Parker would be appearing at a jam session at a club in Harlem called the Heatwave. Miles turned up at the session and renewed the friendship. Typically, and no doubt to Miles's great joy, Parker 'didn't have a place to stay at the time', so he ended up rooming with Davis. It is unlikely that he and Bird shared the same room – or apartment – for that whole year. Miles was joined by his family after some time, and according to trumpet player Red Rodney, by mid-1945 Davis and Parker had different apartments in the same block. However, Miles was extremely fortunate in being able to spend his most formative period in the close company of the fountainhead of the new music.

Miles flung himself into a regime of study which was exhausting and schizophrenic. By day, he would be at Juilliard and at night, hanging around Minton's Playhouse or the clubs on 52nd Street. Parker gave him a great deal of encouragement: '"Don't be afraid", he used to tell me, "go ahead and play". Every night on matchbox covers I'd write down those chords I heard. Everybody helped me. Next day I'd play those chords all day in the practice room at Juilliard, instead of going to classes.'[2] Other key musicians helped him too. Thelonious Monk wrote out chords for him, as did the pianist Tadd Dameron who had been with Billy Eckstine as an arranger when Miles played with the band in St Louis. Dizzy Gillespie advised Miles to study piano and use the keyboard for working out melodic shapes.

Miles was in perfect condition for learning fast. He was in control of himself – neither smoking nor drinking – and he knew exactly which people could help him most. He had a very high regard for his mentors, but the mild-mannered and industrious young trumpeter was also beginning to develop a healthy self-respect. Coming from the South West, he expected to be upstaged and outclassed by every musician in New York: 'When I got to New York, I thought everybody knew as much as I did, and I was surprised. Wasn't nobody playing but Dizzy and Roy [Eldridge] and Joe [Guy] – long haired Joe. The guys who *were* playing, you didn't even know or hear of.'[3]

At Juilliard, he attended classes to find out if there was anything worth learning there. As far as general theory was concerned, he felt they had nothing to teach him: 'All that shit I had already learned in St Louis.'[4] He also found the pace of lessons too slow...'I did all the homework for summer school in one day.' But he did follow Dizzy Gillespie's advice and take some piano lessons at Juilliard. He also took trumpet lessons from symphonic players, which meant that even as he steeped himself in the new jazz, he was still subject to strong western instrumental concepts. But in 1945 Miles found another trumpet player who was to have a powerful influence, the late Freddy Webster who frequently showed up at the sessions at Minton's in Harlem. Webster had all the qualities of the St Louis school of trumpeters – the big, singing sound and the marmoreally sculpted phrases. He did not play a lot of notes, nor did he play at very fast tempos; he was at his best on medium tempo pieces and on ballads. Given his qualities, it is not surprising that

14

Miles and he became very close, and that Webster had a lasting influence on Davis. Miles says of him: 'I used to love what he did to a note. He didn't play a lot of notes; he didn't waste any. I used to try to get his sound. He had a great big tone, like Billy Butterfield, but without vibrato. Freddie was my best friend. I wanted to play like him. I used to teach him chords, whatever I learned at Juilliard. He didn't have any money to go. And in return, I'd try to get his tone.'[5] Over one point, Miles's memory may have been playing him tricks: Webster played with a fairly wide vibrato.

52nd Street was a block of brownstone buildings between Fifth and Sixth Avenues. Earlier in the century each one had housed one affluent family, but by the end of Prohibition, they were already split up into small businesses and basement clubs. By the mid-forties the Street had reached a peak with such clubs as the Three Deuces, the Downbeat, the Famous Door, the Spotlite, Kelly's Stables, the Yacht Club and the Onyx. The warren-like basements were too small for big bands and so small combos flourished every-where. Apart from the new generation of musicians, some of the older and more established stars worked there regularly. It was to this shabby area with its fast-living pimps, hipsters, drug-pushers and small-time operators that the reticent Miles Davis came to listen and learn at the end of 1944 and the beginning of 1945. It was the other end of the spectrum from Juilliard with its elegant building, unhurried atmosphere and reverence for the past, a world in which the composer was god.

The two worlds proceeded on parallel lines, but when Miles played his first-ever recording session (4 May 1945), the bandleader, saxophonist Herbie Fields, was an ex-Juilliard student. The group was a quintet which accompanied vocalist, Rubberlegs Williams, whose singing was reminiscent of Fats Waller. Indeed, the loose treatment of the four pieces they recorded was similar to the method of the 'Fats Waller and his Rhythm' series. Miles has said of this occasion: 'I was too nervous to play, and I only performed in the ensembles – no solos.'[6] But, in fact, his muted horn is strongly in evidence improvising fleet and pungent obbligati behind the voice.

Later in May, Coleman Hawkins started a residency at the Downbeat Club, with Joe Guy on trumpet. Billie Holiday was the featured attraction of the evening and she and Guy had just been married. In the first flush of marital bliss, Guy often missed some of the sets with Hawkins, and Miles would sit in on those occasions. It was a golden opportunity and Miles made the most of it, checking the Downbeat every night to see if he was needed. If Guy did appear, then Miles would go over to the Spotlite and sit in with Lockjaw Davis and alto saxophonist Rudy Williams. Lockjaw must have been impressed by Miles because shortly after this he hired the young trumpeter for a month at the Spotlite. Miles Davis had got his first real employment as a trumpet player in New York.

After this, he began to get regular work on the Street, and by the early autumn of 1945 he had joined Charlie Parker's group at the Three Deuces. The rest of the quintet comprised pianist Al Haig, bassist Curly Russell and drummer Stan Levey. Miles was still nervous, but Parker showed great kindness in coaxing him along: 'Bird used to make me play. He used to lead me up on the bandstand. I used to quit every night. The tempos were so fast, the challenge so great. I used to ask, "What do you need me for?"...I used to play under Bird all the time. When Bird would play a melody, I'd play just under him and let him lead the note, swing the note. The only thing that I'd add would be a larger sound.'[7]

It was around this time that Miles finally left Juilliard. He'd been spending less time there and more on the Street, and his acceptance by leading musicians gave him enough confidence to burn his boats. As Miles puts it: 'Originally I went there (Juilliard) to see what was happening but when I found out nothing was happening, I told my father to save his money...I realized I wasn't going to get in any symphony orchestra. And I had to go down the Street at night to play with Bird or Coleman Hawkins, so I decided to go that way – all the way.'[8] His decision was final, and with it he irrevocably turned his back on the life his mother wanted for him.

After his stint at the Three Deuces, Parker went into the Spotlite, again taking Miles with him. The rest of the group included Dexter Gordon on tenor saxophone, Bud Powell or Sir Charles Thompson alternating at the piano, bassist Curly Russell, Max Roach (or sometimes Stan Levey) on drums, and tap dancer Baby Lawrence. Dexter Gordon recalls: 'Baby was the floor show, taking fours and eights with the band. Bird would leave Miles and me with our mouths open every night.'[9] The residency was cut short, however, when members of the narcotics squad and vice detectives raided the Street, rounding up 'vicious' elements and closing several clubs, including the Spotlite. Miles then went into Minton's with Sir Charles Thompson and a drummer for a while, after which he was hired by Coleman Hawkins for a brief residency.

Parker was booked for a recording session for Savoy on 26 November, and he asked Miles to do the date. The rhythm section comprised Curly Russell, Max Roach and pianist Argonne Thornton. (It was to have been Thelonious Monk who failed, at the last moment, to turn up.) The session became a social occasion with several other musicians, including Dizzy Gillespie, turning up for the event, and the usual hipsters and hangers-on drifting in and out of the studio. There were long breaks for refreshments, and in the middle of the proceedings, Miles Davis took a thirty-minute nap on the studio floor. Despite all this chaos, the results were such that the record company, Savoy, later referred to the occasion as 'the

16

greatest recording session in modern jazz history'.

Savoy's claims may have been rather extravagant, but nevertheless, the session did produce the first definitive recordings of bebop. Parker and Gillespie had twice recorded together earlier in the year with swing drummers Cozy Cole and Big Sid Catlett, but the November session for Savoy had, at last, the right drummer for the music: Max Roach. Only a year older than Miles, he had grown up with the new music and understood exactly the kind of rhythms that were needed – the shimmering top-cymbal pulse, the snare-drum accents, and the use of the bass drum only for emphasis and punctuation. Another reason for the success of the occasion was, paradoxically, that instead of five confident and fully rehearsed virtuosi, the basic group was a nucleus of three musicians: Parker, then at the full height of his magnificent powers, Curly Russell and Roach. For most of the pieces, Dizzy Gillespie, the leading trumpeter of that time, played piano, and the trumpet player was the nineteen-year-old and still immature Miles Davis.

The material ultimately released from the session comprised two incomplete fragments with beautiful solos by Parker ('Warming up a Riff' and 'Meandering'); two blues in F ('Billie's Bounce' and 'Now's the Time'); one complete performance based on the chord structure of Gershwin's 'I Got Rhythm' ('Thriving on a Riff'); and 'Koko', a fast performance based on the chord sequence of Ray Noble's 'Cherokee'. Dizzy Gillespie knew enough of the keyboard to be able to 'comp' – to play the right chords in the right rhythmic manner – but he was not enough of a pianist to be able to play a solo. At that time, he and Parker were very close, and Bird obviously knew he would get the kind of accompaniment he wanted on the medium and slow pieces from Dizzy rather than from Argonne Thornton. The latter, however, played on 'Thriving on a Riff' and revealed himself to be an inventive and original stylist. With Dizzy on piano, in a purely supportive role, Parker would have to play longer solos, and Miles, as the only other solo voice, would have to shoulder more responsibility. Lack of virtuosity at the piano and on the trumpet became a key factor in the quality, the poise, the sheer depth of feeling of the performances. Every note, every phrase of Parker's was made to tell, given its full weight, and even at fast tempos he seemed unhurried. Miles, too, could not afford to waste a note.

The ensemble passages at the beginning and end of 'Koko' were simply too difficult at that time for Miles, and they were played on trumpet by Gillespie. Either because of contractual difficulties, or because the Savoy did not want to pay a sixth musician on the quintet date, Dizzy's contribution to the whole session – which was considerable – had to be anonymous. On the original 78RPM issues, the pianist is listed as one Hen Gates. Miles has solos only on the

17

two blues and 'Thriving on a Riff'. On the latter, the tempo is brisk and there is no theme statement at the beginning. After Thornton's piano introduction, the first chorus is a solo by Miles with a cup mute, and it is astonishingly fluent and assured. There's no great individuality in his phrasing – indeed he sounds rather like Dizzy – but the long melodic lines and the way he rounds off his phrases are very impressive. After Parker's two choruses, and Thornton's solo, the difficult 'Anthropology' theme is played to conclude the piece, and this is a perfect example of how Miles used to 'play under' Parker at that time. The theme is played by the alto and the edge of its magnificent sound is just tinged by the muted trumpet, so that when Miles fails to make the convoluted phrases at the end of the second and the last eight bars, the omission is barely noticeable.

'Billie's Bounce' is taken at an easy tempo, with Miles playing open horn on equal terms with Parker, and the ensemble has a relaxed, funky edge. Parker's solo stretches for four choruses, and Miles takes two, playing some beautifully poised wide intervals with oblique notes to the chords, and getting a lyrical, singing quality in some of his longer notes. After his solo he goes straight into the theme which is played twice – strongly the first time, and very quietly for the last time. During the final chorus Miles plays a 'clinker' – not a fluff, but an actual wrong note which is clearly audible, and this probably resulted simply from a failure of nerve. In the middle 1940s, recordings couldn't be edited and had to be done in complete 'takes'. If the first theme statement was good and the solos were acceptable, the worst ordeal for a nervous musician was always the final theme statement...would he or would he not ruin the whole take by botching it?

Apart from 'Koko', on which Miles didn't play, the other master-piece from that day's recording was the fourth take of 'Now's the Time'. Dizzy's piano introduction with its relaxed but insistent dissonances sets up an eerie, contemplative mood which is sustained throughout the performance. The theme, one of Parker's many blues compositions, builds tension by the repetition of a rhythmic phrase (riff) in the middle register, punctuated by stabs from the piano and drums. In the last four bars, the tension is brilliantly released when the trumpet rises an octave and a minor 3rd to play a phrase which paraphrases and answers the initial riff. This theme has exactly the same structure and essence as the earliest and most fundamental vocal blues in which a line is sung twice, with perhaps minor variations the second time, over eight bars, and then the punchline is sung over the last four bars. Parker's innovations did not negate the past or invalidate it; instead, they contained it, reshaped it and revitalized it. This example of progressing without losing contact with the roots of the music, was not to be wasted on Miles.

18

The overall shape of 'Now's the Time' follows the classic structure of small-group jazz performances. The theme is played at the beginning and end, and the solos take place in the middle. This again harks back to the roots of jazz: the theme is like the 'call' of the preacher or chain-gang leader, and the solos are the 'response' to that call – replies to it and variations on it. It is an extrapolation from non-western rituals and habits of communal music-making.

After the initial theme statement, Parker plays three choruses, creating and releasing tension by the masterful way he varies the attack and the length of his phrases and by his dramatic use of pauses. The whole solo is shot through with blues feeling – all the expressive inflexions, the vocalized tone, the fluid use of grace notes as a prelude to long melodic statements. Imaginatively and technically it is a virtuoso performance, and yet it never loses contact with the Negro folk tradition – the direct cry from the heart is always evident. There are several striking qualities in Miles's solo which covers two choruses – twenty-four bars. First, its overall structure exactly mirrors the structure of the written twelve bar theme, in that the tension is steadily built up until it reaches a peak with the phrase he plays over the seventeenth and eighteenth bars culminating in his high B flat (concert A flat). After two beats rest in the nineteenth bar, the tension is marvellously released when he hits his top D (concert C) and descends with the most flowing and unbroken line of the solo over the following five bars. In the earlier part of the solo the tension is built by playing short phrases in the middle register and alternating them with long, singing notes which project rich tonal quality. He also stresses weak notes such as the second step of the scale (G over an F chord) and the flattened 5ths, all of which further increases the tension by implying bitonality and tugging the ear away from the tonic. All this tension is resolved with the final descent from the high register which is rhythmically symmetrical and diatonic – going, in fact, straight down the F major scale.

The emotional climate his solo generates is very akin to that of Parker; a buoyant feel with an intensely melancholy edge. And yet, unlike Parker's, Miles's phrases have very little of the blues in them at this stage in his career. The long periods of formal instruction in western instrumental techniques seem to have drained the tonal inflexions of the blues from his playing. However, his sound in this solo is by no means a 'straight' one, because his phrases hang together very well rhythmically – in short, he swings, albeit ponderously. It is an extremely full trumpet sound, almost a massive one. In the early 1950s he was to cite this particular solo as one of his favourites because he 'sounded like Freddy Webster', and other musicians have made the same comment. As with Webster, the solo is economical; every note tells and there are none of the idiomatic grace notes with which Parker often began his phrases. Finally, the

19

powerful inner logic of his improvisation comes out of his intense feeling and is an expression of it. But the most important point of all is that this solo revealed an original conception of trumpet playing. Trumpeter Red Rodney said later: 'The first time we really ever heard Miles was on that...'Now's The Time'...it was a new sound...it was a young guy that didn't play the trumpet very well, but had discovered a whole new way of treating it and playing it.'

Once a musician starts playing and recording he becomes, of course, a public figure whose work will be talked about and evaluated by sages and idiots alike. Miles got his first taste of critics and their wisdom when the 78RPM record, with 'Billie's Bounce' on one side and 'Now's the Time' on the other, was released. It was universally condemned. The *Down Beat* reviewer wrote:

> These two sides are excellent examples of the other side of the Gillespie craze – the bad taste and ill-advised fanaticism of Dizzy's uninhibited style. Only Charlie Parker, who is a better musician and who deserves more credit than Dizzy for the style anyway, saves these from a bad fate. At that he's far off form – a bad reed and inexcusable fluffs do not add up to good jazz. The trumpet man, whoever the misled kid is, plays Gillespie in the same manner as a majority of kids who copy their idol do – with most of the faults, lack of order and meaning, the complete adherence to technical acrobatics.[10]

This critique is typical of the kind of abuse bebop was accorded in the middle 1940s, and Miles's lifelong mistrust and dislike of critics (with a few exceptions) may well date from this period.

In that whole recording session on 26 November 1945, both Parker and Miles revealed their essential difference from everyone else in jazz. Although still embryonic, Miles's musical identity was clearly evident. Parker, on the other hand, was fully mature and gloriously expressed the two opposite poles of his artistic nature: the furious brilliance and aggression of 'Koko', and the contemplative brooding of the nocturnal and bluesy 'Now's the Time'...a prophetic title. Both pieces are small masterpieces – perfect expressions of the duality which is found in all Parker's subsequent work. Miles, in his mature work, was to bring both aspects to greater peaks of expression, and on a much larger scale. The introspective and contemplative side would be sustained for whole long-playing records, reaching its fullest realization in the albums *Kind of Blue*(1959) and *In A Silent Way*(1969). The furiously aggressive side was to reach one peak in the 'live' albums of the early 1960s and another of almost frightening power in 1969 and the early 1970s when Miles was using electronics and multiple rhythm sections.

Another aspect of Charlie Parker's character also revealed itself at this recording session. He had been a heroin addict for some

20

years by then, and was always short of money. In the studio, needing ready cash, he sold the rights to his composition, 'Now's The Time', for a mere $50 dollars. In later years, Miles would guard his own compositions jealously, but before the 1940s were over he was to make many of Parker's mistakes.

The November raids on 52nd Street by detectives and members of the vice squad had been instigated by the military authorities. The war was coming to an end, but there was still concern for the numbers of servicemen who were rendered unfit for duty after a night or two on the Street. Several clubs were closed, and others declared out-of-bounds for military personnel. Parker and Gillespie found themselves out of work in New York, and left early in December for an eight week engagement in California. Shortly after they'd gone, Miles returned to East St Louis. Although he never seemed to mention his wife and daughter (Cheryl) at this time, they had been with him in New York and almost certainly travelled back to East St Louis with him. His wife, Irene, was pregnant with their second child, Gregory, who was born in 1946. But having decided to 'go all the way' and identify totally with the new musical revolutionaries, Miles certainly didn't want to stay in East St Louis. It may have been pleasant to revisit old friends, to sit in with local groups, and perhaps to enjoy the 'local-boy-makes-good' reputation, but this was no longer enough. By a stroke of good fortune, Benny Carter's band was working locally at the Riviera, and they were about to go to the West Coast. This was too good an opportunity to miss; Miles joined the trumpet section of the band and informed Parker that he would be coming to Los Angeles.

At the beginning of February 1946, the Parker/Gillespie quintet finished its residency and, a few days later, the group flew back to New York – all, that is, except for Parker who had cashed in his plane ticket. By this time Ross Russell had started his record label, Dial, which was concentrating on bebop, and sometime in mid-February Parker went along to talk to him. According to Russell, Bird didn't want to record with Gillespie any more: 'It was time for new modes. The trumpet player of his choice would not be a virtuoso capable of fireworks, but a different sort of musician, someone who played a relaxed legato style, with a warm tone, in the lower and middle registers, someone like Miles Davis who would be arriving in Los Angeles within a week or two.'[11]

The Benny Carter band arrived to play at the Orpheum Theatre in Los Angeles, and Miles was already unhappy with the job. It was a big band playing mostly old-fashioned arrangements. Parker was appearing at the Finale club in the black quarter of the city, and Miles was soon doubling up jobs by slipping down there every night when the Carter gig was over. Having two paid jobs was against the tenets of the musicians' union, and when the authorities caught up with him, Miles was fined, after which he left the Carter band and appeared with Bird until the Finale closed because of poor business. Although most of the best local musicians came along to hear Parker and the group, there was, as yet, no audience for the new music on the West Coast.

The rhythm section with Parker and Miles at the Finale comprised pianist Joe Albany, bassist Addison Farmer and drummer Chuck Thompson, and in late February and early March some of the club sessions were recorded. They showed Miles to be much more confident, but to have lost much of his individuality. The influence of Gillespie is evident in his phrases and in his use of the higher registers of the trumpet. His technique seems much improved, but he still fails to make the same phrases on the 'Anthropology' theme. These were, of course, public performances in front of an audience, and there was only one take of each piece.

Parker's first studio recording session for Ross Russell's Dial label took place at Radio Recorders on Santa Monica Boulevard in Hollywood, on 28 March 1946. This was Miles's second time in the studios with Parker, and the occasion uncannily resembled the 'Now's The Time' session in its lack of preparation. On the present occasion, four months later, there had been almost no rehearsal at all, and Bird had reshuffled his personnel the night before the recording was due to take place. He went into the studio with a septet which included Miles, tenor saxophonist Lucky Thompson, pianist Dodo Marmarosa, guitarist Arvin Garrison, bassist Vic McMillan and Roy Porter on drums. Everything – melodies, harmonies, formats and solo lengths – had to be worked out in the studio in recording time. Nothing was written down: Parker simply played the melodies on his alto, taught them to the other horns, demonstrated harmonies – occasionally actually naming a chord – and talked out various routines. His whole approach was thus spontaneous, instinctual, and non–western. It was diametrically opposed to the entire western conception of written musical symbols, of music that can be seen even when not heard. Parker preferred this approach to recording, and, once again, the lesson was not lost on Miles Davis. In his later career, often the most brilliant and lasting of his small-group recordings would be done in the studio, on the day, with no prior rehearsal.

Miles used his cup mute throughout the session, and still sounds like Dizzy. In fact, his approach is antithetical to the persona he revealed on the 1945 session, and on various takes he is often prodigal with notes, and frequently sounds ill at ease. Furthermore, as all four of the tunes recorded that day were either medium-fast or fast, we have no opportunity of hearing Miles at the tempos he favoured then – slow to medium. Uncertain though his contribution was, later in the year he won an award as *Down Beat*'s New Star on

22

Trumpet for 1946. Dodo Marmarosa and Lucky Thompson got similar awards in their respective instrumental categories. Recording with Parker was the sure way of getting noticed fast, and the critics began to be more favourable to Miles.

The Finale Club closed suddenly without any warning. The musicians turned up for work one night only to find the club in darkness, the doors locked, and themselves out of a job. Parker disappeared and could not be found, even by his closest associates, for several days. This was Miles's first real taste of the insecurity and unpredictability of the music profession. Work for modern jazz musicians was now very hard to come by in California. Things were getting desperate for Bird who had no money to live on and who couldn't afford the fare back to New York, but Miles still had an allowance from his father.

The trumpeter, Howard McGhee, and his wife, who were living in Los Angeles, took care of Parker and reopened the defunct Finale Club in May. It was a co-operative venture, and the door takings were simply divided between the house band which comprised Bird, McGhee, Marmarosa, bassist Red Callender, and Roy Porter. Under these circumstances, there was no place for Miles Davis in Parker's group, and perhaps Miles was content to be out of the way because it was becoming increasingly clear that the saxophonist was physically and emotionally very ill. Parker's complete breakdown occurred in late July and, suspected of being insane, he was committed to Camarillo State Hospital for a minimum period of six months.

During his time on the West Coast, Miles had become friendly with bassist Charlie Mingus who was another Bird devotee, and who lived in Los Angeles. In the late spring, Miles had played third trumpet on a record session under Mingus' leadership, but the two tracks they made were never released. In August, both Miles and Mingus played in a group led by Lucky Thompson three nights a week at Elk's Ballroom on Central Avenue in Los Angeles. An announcement in the music press stated that the key member of Thompson's small group would be 'the brilliant young trumpet player, Miles Davis, last heard here with Benny Carter'.[12] But this group soon broke up because Thompson accepted an offer to join the Boyd Raeburn orchestra. By now, Miles was anxious to leave the West Coast, and a way out presented itself when the Billy Eckstine band arrived in Los Angeles during September. Eighteen months previously, the trumpeter Fats Navarro had joined the band, replacing Dizzy Gillespie, but when Eckstine went out to California, Navarro wanted to stay in New York. Miles was hired and spent five months with the band, going east with it in late autumn. After the Eckstine band broke up in the spring of 1947, Miles spent some time in Chicago, appearing on the south side at Jumptown with saxophonists Sonny Stitt and Gene Ammons for the

23

jam session nights. Then he returned to New York, and after a short stint with the saxophonist Illinois Jacquet, he rejoined Charlie Parker.

When Parker returned to New York in April 1947, he was probably healthier than he'd been at any other time of his adult life. The long stay in the Camarillo State Hospital had at last broken the drug habit. He was 'clean' although he was consuming large quantities of alcohol. In New York he found that the new music had at last made a big impact on the general public, that Dizzy Gillespie was already famous, and that it was now possible not only to work regularly, but also to earn reasonable money. Bird was immediately offered a contract for four weeks with a quintet at the Three Deuces. The fee for the group was $800 a week. This meant that Parker could afford to recruit the musicians he wanted and employ them on a steady basis. He chose Miles Davis and Max Roach; the bassist was Tommy Potter who had played with the Eckstine band, and the pianist was a comparative unknown called Duke Jordan. This quintet was to stay together as a unit for over eighteen months, and with it Parker reached the zenith of his career. His sidemen could have worked for better wages elsewhere, but they wanted to be with Bird. According to Ross Russell, Jordan and Potter, the two newcomers, were paid $125 a week, and Bird's old associates, Max and Miles, received $135. Parker had the difference – the best wage he had received in his entire career to date – $280 clear. The quintet opened at the Three Deuces in April, opposite the Lennie Tristano Trio, and the club was so well attended that Parker's residency was extended indefinitely.

Parker was physically and psychologically buoyant, and at the height of his creative powers. Night after night, he pushed his great ability to the limits, never playing anything the same way twice. The inexhaustible wealth of ideas and the powerful feeling with which he invested them kept the rest of the group on their mettle. Miles Davis recalls:

> Bird used to play forty different styles. He was never content to remain the same. I remember how at times he used to turn the rhythm section around. Like we'd be playing the blues, and Bird would start on the eleventh bar, and as the rhythm section stayed where they were and Bird played where he was it sounded as if the rhythm section was on one and three instead of two and four. Every time that would happen, Max Roach used to scream at Duke Jordan not to follow Bird, but to stay where he was. Then, eventually it came round as Bird had planned and we were together again.[13]

Parker's continual extending of boundaries, his invasion of unexplored territory, and the element of creative surprise which he

24

generated, made a deep impression on Miles. Over twenty years later, Davis was to say: 'That's what I tell my musicians; I tell them to be ready to play what you know and above what you know. Anything might happen above what you've been used to playing – you're ready to get into that, and above that, and take that out.'[14]

Parker also continued to inspire and direct his group by example rather than by explicit verbal instructions. However, someone had to verbalize, and one of the chores Miles had to take on, because of Bird's default, was that of musical director. His experiences with he Eddie Randall band in St Louis had, of course, prepared him for this to some extent: 'I was nervous...but I had to get out of being nervous fast because he [Bird] was never there and I had to rehearse the band[15]...He never did talk about music. I always even had to show Duke Jordan, the pianist in the band, the chords.'[16] Miles also recalls: 'The only time I ever heard Bird talk about music was an argument he had with a classical musician friend of mine about the naming of chords. That was the night Bird said you could do anything with chords. And I disagreed. "You can't play D natural in the fifth bar of a B flat blues." "Yes you can," said Bird. Well one night in Birdland, I heard Lester Young do it, and it sounded good. But he bent it.'[17]

On 8 May 1947, the quintet, with Bud Powell replacing Duke Jordan at the piano, recorded for the Savoy label, and the results show a major change in Miles's thinking. The Gillespie influence and the forays into the upper register are gone; the sound is smaller than on the 'Now's The Time' recording, but it is broad, rounded and beginning to project a greater lyricism. Although not yet twenty one, he has achieved some wisdom, some self-knowledge: 'I asked Dizzy, "Why can't I play high like you?" "Because you can't hear up there," he said. "You hear in the middle register." And that's true. There are times when I can't even tell what chords Dizzy is working on when he's up high; and yet he told me what he's playing is just an octave above what I do.'[18]

Although Miles's solos on this session are often much shorter than Parker's we can detect the germs of a highly individual style. The sense of strain is gone, though he does occasionally sound a little unsteady rhythmically, and his middle register work is already showing a good grasp of harmony, original melodic lines, and unusual intervals. This growing identity was to become an integral part of the group idea Parker had conceived a year previously on the West Coast. Instead of sparks being created by the competition of two virtuoso horns, as had been the case when Dizzy was with the band, Parker was looking for the dynamism of contrast. His own gargantuan abilities would be offset against the understatement and lyricism of Miles's horn. The music of the quintet was to become subtly dramatic and, perhaps paradoxically, more potent. This

25

concept was to be a major factor in Miles's own definitive quintet recordings of the middle 1950s.

The 8 May recording session produced two blues ('Cheryl' and 'Buzzy'), a variation on the 'I Got Rhythm' sequence ('Chasin' the Bird'), and 'Donna Lee' which was based on the harmonies of the standard, 'Indiana'. The first three were composed by Parker, but although 'Donna Lee' was attributed to him, it was in fact written by Miles. This was the trumpeter's debut on record as a composer, and it was an impressive one. The piece is fast, difficult, and typical bebop in its rhythmic drive and the way the melodic line flows through the chord changes. Only the symmetry of the phrases suggests that Miles, and not Bird, was the composer.

It was probably the chaos of Parker's own affairs which gave Miles his next big chance. Bird was still under contract to record for Dial, and after the May session for Savoy there was much in-fighting behind the scenes. It was discovered that Parker was also under contract to Savoy, having signed with them at the 'Now's the Time' session. Savoy offered him another recording date on 14 August, and in order to avoid further complications, Miles was made the leader for that event. Either for further camouflage, or at Miles's instigation, Parker abandoned his alto and played tenor saxophone for the occasion. The rest of the group comprised pianist John Lewis, bassist Nelson Boyd, and Max Roach. The four tunes they recorded ('Milestones', 'Little Willie Leaps', 'Half Nelson' and 'Sippin' at Bell's') were all composed by Miles but, although they show marked originality, these themes are rather over-written. The melodic lines are long, convoluted and full of surprises, but they are so lacking in space that they sometimes create a breathless feeling. Also, the underlying harmonies are much denser than those of Parker's usual material. 'Sippin' at Bell's', for example, is a twelve bar blues, but there are eighteen chords in each chorus.

The most striking feature of this session is the way Miles has imposed his own personality on it. The music is unlike Parker's own recordings in that the themes and the way they are played are much more relaxed and 'laid back'. The use of the tenor sax may have something to do with the smoother sound of the ensemble, but the essence of the music goes deeper than that. The liquid spirit of Lester Young hangs over the music. The solos too – and for the first time, Miles shares the honours on equal terms with Parker – echo the smooth fluency of the themes. Miles is poised and assured, tending to understate and imply melodic ideas. The self-editing process is already functioning, and there is a subtle tension between the apparent simplicity of his improvised lines and the complexity of the harmonic structures. All in all, the session is not as powerful as the rest of Parker's recordings in the period, but it offers a new and refreshing dimension – a cooler urbanity – and it gives intimations of

26

Miles's future development.

1947 proved to be a marvellous year for Miles. He was beginning to find a solid musical identity, he was working steadily, and his progress was well documented on record. There were three further recording sessions with Parker for Dial that year, each one showing increasing musicianship and greater maturity in Miles's work, and on 21 December, there was another date for Savoy. On this final one, Miles is in magnificent form, playing with perfect rhythmic poise, using space with drama and delicacy, and revealing an abundance of new ideas. He plays confidently at breakneck speed on 'Bird Gets The Worm'. But even in this piece his group role, as a foil for Parker, is important. Wilfrid Mellers points out: 'Parker's reedy, anguished tone is highlighted in contrast with Miles Davis's muted trumpet, which mutes the anger as well as the sonority.'[19]

It was also in 1947 that Miles, looking for further musical outlets, began to show some independence of Parker. He became established as one of the four trumpet players who dominated 52nd Street. Another of these was Red Rodney who remembers: 'I worked on 52nd Street all the time...I went from one club to the other...Miles did also...We were sort of rivals in a way, I guess. There was Miles, and there was Fats Navarro, myself, Kenny Dorham, and the four of us were all friendly, and, well, we were competitive towards each other because we were the ones who were working, and I was the only white trumpeter. But you know, back then there was no problem of being white or black – among us anyway...In as much as we liked each other, we didn't consider colour.'

Rodney also worked with the Claude Thornhill band in 1947 when Gerry Mulligan and Lee Konitz were with it, and Gil Evans was writing the arrangements. Miles's lifelong friendship with Evans dates from that year. Gil had heard the Parker recording of 'Donna Lee' and he approached Miles: 'He was asking for a release on my tune 'Donna Lee'. He wanted to make an arrangement for a government electrical transcription of it. I told him he could have it and asked him to teach me some chords and let me study some of the scores he was doing for Claude Thornhill...I used to write and send Gil my scores for evaluation. Gil used to say they were good, but cluttered up with too many notes. I used to think you had to use a lot of notes and stuff to be writing.'[20] The improvising and the writing were developing on parallel lines. The excesses and the inessentials were being pared away.

By the beginning of 1948, Charlie Parker and his group had gained international fame and recognition. Parker had won his first poll in *Metronome*, and Miles and Max Roach had gained places in their respective instrumental categories. Miles had won the 1947 critics' poll in *Esquire*, and had tied first with Dizzy in the critics' *Down Beat* poll. But although things looked good, the quintet was

27

not going to stay together. Throughout the year there was growing alienation between Parker and his two strongest sidemen – Miles and Max Roach. Back in the autumn of 1947, Bird had started taking drugs again, and as the addiction progressed, the old instability reappeared. He became unpredictable and unreliable. This was aggravated by the fact that he was now in great demand as a soloist, and would go off on his own to record or to tour. The rest of Parker's group, who had all made sacrifices in order to stay with him, were bitterly resentful when they found themselves out of work. The quintet's morale sank very low and when, in late 1948, Parker deliberately behaved childishly during an engagement (doing such things as expelling the air from a balloon into the microphone and firing a cap pistol at the pianist), and seemed to be trying to humiliate his musicians, it was the last straw for Miles. He walked out of the club saying, 'Bird makes you feel one foot high.'[21] Max Roach also left the group that same night. Although Bird and Miles were to play together once or twice afterwards, and record together again in the early fifties, that evening marked the end of their close association.

Charlie Parker's influence on Miles Davis is incalculable. Even Bird's behaviour on the bandstand seems to have made a deep impression. Parker, for example, hardly ever made announcements. According to one regular witness of the evenings on 52nd Street, the communications between Parker and his musicians seemed to be on a telepathic level. Time after time, he would count-in and begin playing without apparently having even told the group what piece they were going to play. At the end of a set, he occasionally back-announced some of the themes, but usually he announced only the names of the musicians. When he'd finished playing his solos, he didn't look round at the band, or offer any directions, but simply walked off the stand. During the fifties and sixties, Miles's own behaviour was to magnify this pattern. During performances with his groups, he would make no announcements at all, and would not only walk off the stand after his solos, but would actually disappear for several minutes.

Parker was rejecting the idea of the Negro as entertainer, and wanted his music to be taken on its own merits, to speak for itself. His behaviour, always unpredictable, often acted as a short-circuit which burned out the fuses of normal thought patterns; he was re-creating the whole relationship of performing artist and audience. The listeners, onlookers, witnesses were privileged eavesdroppers on the act of creation. His music, his behaviour, his gargantuan appetites for food, drugs, sex, jolted audiences, musicians, and himself into reappraisals of values. His determination to inhabit the frontiers of experience was both magnificently heroic and magnificently foolhardy.

28

Charlie Parker was a supremely tragic figure in that the creative and destructive sides of his nature were interdependent. His great genius was for improvisation in both music and in life. In his quest for self-renewal, he had to be unpredictable and perpetually surprising. He had to flout the tenets of white society which dominated American life, because it demanded that, to be accepted, a person had to be a known quantity. Because of his defiance, and the way he revitalized Negro music, Parker was a genuine culture hero for urban black people of his generation. Artistically, he embodied an apparently massive contradiction: he was the most advanced musician of his generation, yet he never lost touch with the people – with his folk roots. He had the admiration of his peers, and he had the power of communication with the audiences. Dizzy Gillespie described one occasion when this power of Parker's was revealed in a live performance: 'I saw something remarkable one time. He didn't show up for a dance he was supposed to play in Detroit. I was in the town, and they asked me to play instead. I went up there, and we started playing. Then I heard this big roar, and Charlie Parker had come in and started playing. He'd play a phrase, and people might never have heard it before. But he'd start it, and the people would finish it with him, humming. It would be so lyrical and simple that it just seemed the most natural thing to play.'[22]

When bookers, agents, managements, entrepreneurs at last realized that they could expect only the unexpected from Parker, they were reluctant to take on the responsibility of finding him work. He was doomed to despair and drugs, and to scuffling around for small-time gigs in obscure clubs. In 1946 he had described his vision of an ordered life to Ross Russell. It included a settled home with a library, paintings, a piano and a superb record collection. It was a vision of stability and permanence which implied a withdrawal from the transient world of improvisation and jazz. He wanted to listen to the works of twentieth-century European composers, and to compose 'seriously' himself. But that dream was to become more and more remote.

Even in his most creative act – playing music – Parker seemed to be destroying himself, because he always pushed his abilities to the limits. During long engagements, he would become physically and emotionally exhausted, and then he would rely heavily on heroin and alcohol. Sometimes survival would depend on simply not turning up to play; but this physical and psychological self-preservation was also a kind of economic suicide. A jazz musician was once quoted as saying: 'People wonder why we get paid relatively well. Man, we take people's chances for them.'[23] Parker lived always with what Ross Russell has described as the 'sense of peril'. He took people's chances for them – musical chances for the new generation of musicians, lifestyle chances for the hipsters, racial chances for the

blacks – he took them all, and paid the price for being larger than life, premature death.

Throughout his association with Bird, Miles Davis was a quiet, polite, abstemious young man. He was also exceptionally intelligent and sensitive, and could see clearly how Parker was destroying himself. It was obvious that there was a direct relationship between the risks taken and the power of the music produced. Playing safe led to creative death. To survive, Miles would have to look for some sort of balance. But first, like Bird, he would have to experience excess – he would have to go over the edge.

3
The Birth of the Cool

'I always had a curiosity about trying new things in music.
A new sound, another way to do something.'[1]

Miles Davis

Throughout 1947, Miles had gradually expunged most of the clichés of bebop from his trumpet style, and had begun to reveal an approach which owed a debt to Lester Young. During the 1930s, Young's tenor sax style had introduced a new element into jazz – a smaller, lighter sound, and a more delicate, introspective quality. He brought to artistic fruition qualities which he had found in two white musicians of the 1920s – cornettist Bix Beiderbecke, and saxophonist Frank Trumbauer. When Beiderbecke came on the scene, the trumpet was the dominant instrument of jazz, and Louis Armstrong was its prime exponent – a man who phrased with classic grandeur. Bix's palette was much smaller; he confined himself to the middle register of the instrument, but compensated for this by his burnished, singing tone, and the intensity of his lyricism. There can be no doubt that when Miles Davis abandoned the Gillespie approach to the trumpet and began confining himself to the middle register and showing a more delicate melodic flair, he was being influenced – albeit indirectly through Lester Young – by Bix Beiderbecke.

By 1948, there was a growing audience for bebop and in New York the revolution became the new establishment, and imitators abounded everywhere. Miles and other musicians at the centre of the movement were beginning to look round for some new areas to explore. At the same time, the focal point of the jazz scene was moving away from 52nd Street which was becoming an area of strip-joints and restaurants. Instead, the music was now being heard in the more reputable area of Broadway, and in larger clubs such as the Royal Roost where patrons were not browbeaten into drinking alcohol at high prices, but, for the price of admission, could simply sit and listen to the music. It was at the Roost that Miles first led his own groups after leaving Parker.

Meanwhile, he had been branching out restlessly, playing on his own as a soloist and with other musicians around New York. He worked with saxophonist Sonny Rollins on several occasions, becoming firm friends with him. Miles also gigged with bassist Oscar Pettiford, and may well have played with John Coltrane around this time. But the most important event that year was his renewed association with the composer/arranger Gil Evans. This relationship between the black, academy-trained, improvising musician, and the white, self-taught composer, ripened into a friendship that was to endure for decades, and which produced in the later 1950s, some of the finest orchestral music in jazz.

In 1948, Miles was still only twenty-two and unsure of himself, even though he'd achieved a certain amount of success and recognition. On the other hand, Evans was thirty-six and full of knowledge and musical wisdom which he had acquired empirically over the years. He was the perfect father-figure for Miles at the time, because he knew and understood 'straight' music, but he also had a profound understanding and appreciation of the great jazz improvisers. The apparently irreconcilable worlds of formal composition and of improvisation were united naturally and easily in Gil Evans's concept of music. Miles has said of him: 'He is as well versed in classical music in general as Leonard Bernstein. And what the classical guys *don't* know is what Gil knows.'[2]

Gil Evans was born in Canada of Australian parentage, and had no formal musical training at all. When he was fourteen, he heard some Louis Armstrong records which inspired him to begin playing the piano and teaching himself music. In 1941, he became the principal arranger of the Claude Thornhill Orchestra, which was a white 'society' band. Thornhill, himself an arranger, had known and worked with Evans during the 1930s, and both men had been staff arrangers for Bob Hope's radio programme. Thornhill was the first dance band leader to use French horns and to use the tuba as part of the ensemble colour rather than as a rhythm instrument, and his orchestra's sound was, for the most part, soft, dense and static. Gil Evans described the problems it presented: 'The sound hung like a cloud. But once this stationary effect, this sound, was created, it was ready to have other things added to it. The sound itself can only hold interest for a certain length of time. Then you have to make certain changes within that sound; you have to make personal use of harmonies, rather than work with traditional ones; there has to be more movement in the melody; more dynamics, more syncopation; speeding up of the rhythms. For me, I had to make those changes...I did not create the sound; Claude did.'[3]

Evans plays down his own part in all this with typical modesty. Such honesty and generosity are rare enough anywhere, and it was probably Evans's own qualities, (musical and moral) as much as anything else, which drew so many of the most gifted young white musicians towards Thornhill's band. It was Gil who persuaded

32

baritone saxophonist Gerry Mulligan to join it and to write arrangements for it. Other notable members were trumpeters Red Rodney
and John Carisi (who also arranged), and the brilliant young alto
saxophonist Lee Konitz. Gerry Mulligan, who, like Konitz, was a
year younger than Miles, recalls: 'Lee joined Claude's band in
Chicago and knocked us all out (including Bird) with his originality.'[4] Konitz had an exceptionally soft and fluid approach to the
alto, with a smooth, clear, almost diaphanous sound. It was a
saxophone style without vibrato and with no blues inflexions at
all...a white sound which suited the non-vibrato sound of the
Thornhill band. Konitz's style was in every way the antithesis of
Parker's. The pair of them had perhaps only two things in common –
the instrument they played and the great originality of their improvisations. Miles liked them both: 'Thornhill had the greatest band,
the one with Lee Konitz, during these modern times. The one
exception was the Billy Eckstine band with Bird.'[5]

During this period, Parker was actually sharing Gil Evans's room,
and dropping in for a quick nap between his club sessions. Evans
had arranged two Parker compositions ('Anthropology' and
'Yardbird Suite') and one of Miles's tunes ('Donna Lee') for
Thornhill's band, and he became the focal point for aspiring young
musicians who were interested in adapting Parker's ideas to more
formal musical settings. There was something spare and ascetic
about Evans's lifestyle at the time, which gave the impression that
everything – all intellectual and sensuous experience – was subordi-
nated to the experience of music. He was living in a one-room
basement apartment on West 55th Street, behind a Chinese laundry,
and pianist-composer George Russell has described the scene and
the informal seminars which took place there:

> A very big bed took up a lot of the place; there was one big lamp,
> and a cat named Becky. The linoleum was battered, and there
> was a little court outside. Inside, it was always very dark. The
> feeling of the room was timelessness. Whenever you got there,
> you wouldn't care about conditions outside. You couldn't tell
> whether it was day or night, summer or winter, and it didn't
> matter. At all hours, the place was loaded with people who came
> in and out. Mulligan, though, was there all the time...Gil, who
> loved musical companionship, was the mother hen – the haven in
> the storm. He was gentle, wise, profound, and extremely percep-
> tive, and he always seemed to have a comforting answer for any
> kind of problem. He appeared to have no bitterness...Gil was,
> and is, one of the strong personalities in written jazz, and I'm sure
> he influenced all of us.[6]

By the middle and later 1940s, several big bands had already adapted
and used the ideas of bebop. Perhaps the most famous were Dizzy

Gillespie's big band and those of Woody Herman and Stan Kenton. For the most part, however, these had concentrated on one side of Parker's duality – the furiously rhythmic and aggressive aspect. Gil Evans and Gerry Mulligan, in their discussions during the winter of 1947, seemed more interested in exploring Parker's other side which had links with Lester Young – a gentler and more contemplative form of expression. They were also looking for a much more organic relationship between the orchestral score and the role of the various soloists. Evans and Mulligan worked out what they thought was the smallest number of instruments which could express the harmonic and tonal range of the Thornhill band, and wanted to get together a good little rehearsal band. Like so many musical happenings in America, this one was modest in its aims, was born from the enthusiasm of a few little-known individuals, and moved out of the obscure rehearsal rooms to influence the thinking of musicians all over the world.

Miles Davis had been thinking along parallel lines. He too was ready for change after the frenetic excesses of bebop, and drew a characteristic analogy: 'It's just like clothes. All of a sudden you decide you don't have to wear spats *and* a flower up here, you know? You wear the flower and leave off the spats, and then pretty soon you leave off both of them...'[7] Just as Evans and Mulligan were paring down instrumentation to the minimum, so Miles was purging his own trumpet style of excess. This quality of economy he recognized and admired in Gil Evans: 'Gil can use four instruments where other arrangers need eight.' So Miles began going round to Evans's place, taking part in the discussions and meeting new faces: 'I always wanted to play with a light sound, because I could think better when I played that way...I wanted Sonny Stitt with those nine pieces, but Sonny was working someplace, and Gerry [Mulligan] said get Lee [Konitz] because he has a light sound too. And Gerry was playing his baritone – in fact, I didn't expect him to play. I didn't know Gerry until I went down to Gil's house and he was there. We wanted John Simmons because he wanted everything to be light, but Gil said Joe Shulman could play real light...But that whole thing started out as an experiment.'[8]

Miles also wrote to the pianist and composer, John Lewis, who was in Paris at the time, and asked him to write something for the line-up. Lewis was at home with both musical worlds. He had spent fifteen of his first twenty-two years in extensive music studies, and was deeply interested in the possibilities of integrating elements of classical music into jazz.

By mid-1948, external events hastened the genesis of this nine-piece band (trumpet, trombone, French horn, tuba, alto sax, baritone sax, piano, bass and drums). The second recording ban of the 1940s had begun on 30 December 1947 – hence Parker's spate of recording

34

sessions done that autumn and winter to beat the ban. The first recording ban of the decade had lasted from August 1942 until sometime in 1944 – depending on when the various record companies signed the agreement with the American Federation of Musicians. The second ban, which ran throughout 1948, ending on 15 December, had powerful short and long term effects on jazz. It gave the *coup de grâce* to big bands (even Count Basie had to use a small group after the end of 1949) and because the ban did not extend to singers, it greatly increased the public's taste for vocal music. This dealt a very hard blow to jazz and it was not until the late 1950s that the situation improved much. Meanwhile, a few small recording companies had defied the ban which enabled Miles to record twice with Parker during the year. Miles also recorded with a septet led by Coleman Hawkins sometime in 1948. Apart from these isolated exceptions, recording was not possible during the whole of that year. Claude Thornhill's band was also hit by the slump, and when it disbanded for a while, Gil Evans took the opportunity to leave it for good. This meant that by the middle of 1948, Evans and all the gifted young musicians from Thornhill's band were spoiling for something to absorb their energies.

During the summer, Miles had a fairly long residency at the Royal Roost, leading a band that included at various times Parker, trombonist Kai Winding, and tenor saxophonist Allan Eager. The promoter, Monte Kay, who along with disc jockey, Symphony Sid Torin, booked groups into the Roost, offered Miles a two-week engagement there with the nine-piece in September. With this prospect, rehearsals began in earnest.

It was both natural and logical that Miles should be the leader of the band even though it had been born out of collective discussions. Miles had a 'name' and was a musician with outstanding potential; also, his organizing abilities were vital to the whole project. Mulligan comments: 'He took the initiative and put the theories to work. He called the rehearsals, hired the halls, called the players, and generally cracked the whip...Miles dominated the band completely; the whole nature of the interpretation was his...'[9] This was generous of Mulligan, but not totally accurate. During the rehearsals, which took place over a period of several weeks in the late summer of 1948, the wisdom and knowledge of Gil Evans, and his musical conceptions, were very important to Miles. Mike Zwerin, who played trombone with the band during the live engagements, points out that at rehearsals, 'Miles was pleasant and relaxed but seemed unsure of how to be boss. It was his first time as leader. He relied quite a bit on Evans to give musical instructions to the players.'[10] By the time the band was playing in public, however, Mulligan's description of Miles's musical dominance was probably correct.

In September, the band appeared for two weeks at the Royal

35

Roost as a relief unit during a Count Basie engagement. Miles created a precedent by billing the arrangers' names as well as his own in front of the club. His part of the evening was billed as: 'Miles Davis Band, Arrangements by Gerry Mulligan, Gil Evans, and John Lewis'. It was the first time any experimental (and virtually unknown) arrangers in jazz, with the exception perhaps of Duke Ellington, had ever received this kind of credit.

The personnel of the group for this residency was Miles, plus Mike Zwerin (trombone), John 'Bill' Barber (tuba), Junior Collins (French horn), Gerry Mulligan (baritone sax), Lee Konitz (alto sax), John Lewis (piano), Al McKibbon (bass), Max Roach (drums), and Kenneth Hagood (vocals). The last named had formerly sung with Dizzy Gillespie and was probably hired as a sop to the public's penchant for vocals. During its stay at the Roost, the band made at least two radio broadcasts, and nine tracks from these have been issued on record. However, the band failed utterly to interest audiences, and its stay at the Roost was not extended. The only other time it worked live occurred the following year when Miles took it into the Clique Club for a short stint. At the Roost in 1948, one or two critics and a few musicians were impressed with the band's new music. Count Basie, with his typical enthusiasm for the work of good young musicians, was full of praises and was quoted as saying: 'Those slow things sounded strange and good. I didn't always know what they were doing, but I listened and liked it.'[11]

The live recordings taken from air-shots (broadcasts) are less tightly integrated performances than the studio recordings which took place a few months later, because the solo space – particularly that of Miles – is much longer in relationship to the written passages. In a live performance it is, of course, natural for soloists to stretch out more. Although the ensemble sound is fluid and relaxed even on the faster and more boppish pieces, the rhythm section, fired by Max Roach, and with some very muscular chord work from John Lewis, really drives along in the polyrhythmic bebop manner. The relationship of horns to rhythm section is a kind of 'ice and fire' situation which creates some marvellous tension. In his solos, Miles veers towards the fire, producing some fast, rhythmically aggressive phrases. Lee Konitz stays cool in all his solos.

These air-shots give the first real indication of just how tough musically and mentally Miles was becoming, and of how complete a musician he was even at that time. For the most part, his trumpet dominates the ensemble sound, dictating the phrasing of passages which are subtle and complex. The trumpet is also exposed because only the alto is anywhere near it in pitch. In such conditions of delicate balance, the lead player must have nerves of steel for the slightest fluff or wrong note would be clearly audible and mar the whole ensemble sound. Miles is also the main soloist, often having to play the demanding written passages and then go straight into his solo. Even then, he often gets no respite because he has to go straight from the end of his solo into some ensemble passage or bridge to the next soloist. The fact that he does all this in a live session in September 1948, with hardly a falter, is quite remarkable. These air-shots also show how completely the band was ignored at the Royal Roost. There is an audible hubbub of conversation throughout the slower arrangements, and the audience doesn't even seem to notice when a piece has ended.

With the financial failure of his nine-piece band, Miles was forced once more to work as a soloist and with occasional 'pick-up' small groups. Late in the year, he worked at a club called Soldier Meyers' in Brooklyn, and then led a group which included Sonny Stitt, Wardell Gray, Bud Powell, Nelson Boyd (bass) and Roy Haynes (drums), at the Orchid Room (the old Onyx) on 52nd Street. Over the Christmas period he appeared at the Clique – which later became Birdland – with Fats Navarro, Lucky Thompson, Dexter Gordon, Kai Winding, Milt Jackson, Bud Powell, Oscar Pettiford and Kenny Clarke, in opposition to a similarly illustrious bill at the Royal Roost. In January 1949, he worked at the Audubon, a small New York jazz room, with Art Blakey and Sonny Rollins.

The recording ban ended in December, and early in 1949, Miles was once more in the studios as a sideman, recording a couple of tracks with the Metronome All Stars. He had made third place in the current *Metronome* poll which Dizzy had won, with Howard McGhee coming second. Miles also played on a couple of tunes recorded by Tadd Dameron's band in April. He had been working on and off with Dameron's band ever since he'd left Parker. But the most important event was the securing of his own personal recording contract for the first time. When the ban ended, two major recording companies, RCA Victor and Capitol, decided to go all out with bebop (or 'modern') recording programmes. Capitol signed Miles, Tadd Dameron, singers Babs Gonzales and Dave Lambert, pianist Lennie Tristano and clarinettist Buddy DeFranco. The last two had also won places in the *Metronome* poll. Miles had a contract for twelve sides at 78 RPM. The long-playing record had not yet been introduced, and there was much controversy between record companies over the relative merits of the 33⅓ RPM and the 45 RPM disc.

Controversy continued to rage about bebop, but it was still a music with a minority audience, and had no obvious commercial potential. The really popular music in 1949 was traditional jazz – the old styles of New Orleans/Dixieland/Chicago. There had been a revival of interest in this at the beginning of the decade and by the end it was sweeping America and Europe. It was played by old, and often resuscitated, blacks, and by young, romantically minded whites in search of some (totally imaginary) lost purity. The other commercially viable music of the time was largely vocal – crooners such as Bing Crosby and Frank Sinatra, and vocal groups such as the Andrews Sisters and the Inkspots. Given this climate, Capitol showed courage – even recklessness – in the people they signed. Miles Davis was a young trumpeter whose virtues were not at all easy to spot. He was not a virtuoso like Dizzy, and he had only recently been leading a nine-piece band which was a total financial flop. His performance in the January 1949 *Metronome* poll may have established him in Capitol's eyes as a rapidly rising star – he had come only tenth in the previous year's poll – but the reason he was ultimately signed was due to the chance enthusiasm of an individual who happened to have the ear of the record company. The arranger, Pete Rugolo, suggested that Capitol should sign Miles in order to record the library of the nine-piece band. The company agreed, and Rugolo supervised the three sessions which took place on 21 January, 21 April 1949, and on 9 March 1950. As the band didn't exist except in the recording studio, the personnel differs on each of the sessions. Only Miles, Konitz, Mulligan, and the tuba player, John 'Bill' Barber, are present on all three dates.

The discipline of the 78 RPM record, with its three-minute time span, had a salutary effect on the nonet's music. Although many of the finest solos in jazz may have been played live, the finest examples of total performances – the integration of soloists with ensembles – have usually been done in the studio. The reasons for this are simple; to impose a time limit is to impose a form, and to make the most effective use of that form, a balanced sequence of events must take place. From the time of his earliest recordings with Parker, Miles Davis seems to have been aware of this, and there is often a great difference between his live performances and his studio recordings in any one period. In the studio recordings of the nonet, the solos are shorter and the rhythm section is much more restrained. The general atmosphere and 'feel' of the band has, therefore, a greater cohesion and relaxation...what Miles calls a 'soft sound...not penetrating too much. To play soft you have to relax...you don't delay the beat, but you might play a quarter triplet against four beats, and that sounds delayed. If you do it right, it won't bother the rhythm section.'[12]

Eight of the tracks were originally issued in pairings on 78s, and there was a ten-inch LP in the early 1950s, but it wasn't until 1957 that all the tracks (except for the vocal 'Darn That Dream') were reissued on one twelve-inch LP, and entitled *The Birth of the Cool*. These performances received a great deal of critical acclaim which hindsight has shown to have been well justified because they have stood the test of time, and still sound fresh and full of sparkle. They offer an extraordinary variety of ideas and concepts. Mulligan's composition and arrangement, 'Jeru', presents an asymmetry – odd numbers of bars and beats – which was new to jazz at the time. John Carisi's piece, 'Israel', contains some brilliant passages of counterpoint and polyphony, and also plays off the lower instruments against the higher ones in an intensely dramatic way. Gil Evans's arrangement of 'Moon Dreams', apart from a few bars of baritone solo, is an entirely composed (pre-composed may be a more accurate expression) piece which turns from mellow-textured 'mood' music into dissonance and jagged movement, producing a disturbing musical vision with dark undertones. 'Boplicity', composed by Miles himself under the pseudonym Cleo Henry (his mother's name), and arranged by Gil Evans, is notable for the marvellous relaxation of the whole ensemble, the written variations on the initial melody, and the fluid way the ensemble passages are interwoven with the two soloists (baritone and trumpet). In 1951, Miles cited this as his own favourite...'That's because of the arrangement. Gil Evans did it.'[13]

Even in these more compact performances, Miles still dominates the band. His clear, non-brassy sound gives the written passages a particular flavour, and he gets – and deserves – more solo space than anyone else. He sounds more at ease and poised on these studio recordings than he did on the Roost air-shots, and his flow of ideas is excellent. He alternates long melodic lines with lovely pauses, broken rhythms and longer notes with just a hint of *vibrato* which enhances their swing and their emotional power. His solo on 'Godchild' (Appendix A, Fig. 1) demonstrates all these qualities.

The nonet recordings spawned the cool 'West Coast Jazz' school of the 1950s. This was a largely white movement which received an enormous amount of radio play, and made records which were promoted vigorously by the record companies. The fact that most of the music was sterile and ephemeral did not seem to matter. It had a surface palatability which disc jockeys found easy to accept. From Miles's own seminal band, John Lewis went off to form the Modern Jazz Quartet, Gerry Mulligan formed his pianoless quartet with trumpeter Chet Baker (who was influenced by Davis), and Lee Konitz worked with Lennie Tristano and formed groups of his own. These musicians were all at the centre of the movement and had the essential talent and vision to create something really valid. As had been the case with bebop, it was the second-raters who absorbed the mannerisms and missed the substance. But Miles's nonet recordings had at least one deep and lasting influence. They raised the whole question of the relationship of the soloist to the ensemble, and Miles and a few other leading musicians would spend the following decades finding various answers and solutions to this problem.

While *The Birth of the Cool* recordings did not win a great audience for Miles, they established him as someone separate from

Charlie Parker. Before that he had been regarded more or less as an interesting and talented acolyte. But now he began to gain more undivided critical attention, and the reviews in *Down Beat*, for example, were all appreciative. These recordings also raised Miles's stock with other musicians; he was seen to be a leader with a flair for new sounds. Tadd Dameron, who only four years previously had been teaching Miles chords, said in 1949: 'Davis is the furthest advanced musician of his day, and 'Boplicity' is one of the best small-group sounds I've heard.'[14] And musicians who were more in the mainstream of American music were also favourably impressed. The bandleader, Elliot Lawrence, for example, referred to 'those great Miles Davis sides on Capitol'. Even the Chicago-style traditionalist, Eddie Condon, murmured approval. The band and its music were a critical success, but it existed only on record. From the point of view of *living* music, which has a voluntary, paying public, the nonet was a non-starter.

It was to take Miles another five or six years before he could achieve enough know-how and financial backing to lead bands that functioned regularly both in the studio and in clubs and concert halls.

4
Cold Turkey

'I got hooked after I got back from the Paris Jazz Festival.
I got bored and was around cats that were hung. So I
wound up with a habit that took me four years to break.'
Miles Davis

Early in 1949, Miles worked for a few weeks in Chicago, and then
returned to New York to spend some time with a group led by Tadd
Dameron. In May, he went to Paris with Dameron to play at the
Salle Pleyel opposite Parker's quintet. The French had acquired a
vigorous interest in bebop since Dizzy Gillespie's big band and
Howard McGhee's quintet had played there the previous year.
There were two big annual jazz events in France in the late forties –
the Paris Jazz Fair in the spring, and the Nice Festival in the
summer. The two main stars of the 1949 Paris Fair were Charlie
Parker and Sidney Bechet, each of whom represented very different
eras of jazz. Miles and Tadd Dameron were to play with a pick-up
group which included James Moody on tenor sax, Kenny Clarke on
drums, and the French bassist Pierre Michelot. During the week,
soloists and performers from other areas of the music were also
featured; Hot Lips Page, the swing-era trumpeter was there, and on
one night, the old blues singer, Leadbelly, gave a recital to a tiny
audience at the Cité Université.

Bird and Miles were lionized in Paris, fêted everywhere, admired,
bombarded with questions, and seemed to be always surrounded by
adoring fans and musicians. Miles was asked the usual questions –
what mouthpiece he used, how much he practised and so on. For
both Parker and Davis, it was their first real experience of the
enormous dichotomy between their acceptance in America and
their following abroad. In New York, they were members of a small
clique of musicians who had a tiny cult following. In Paris, they were
international celebrities whose every word and note carried weight.
The media covered their visit thoroughly, and there were broadcasts of the music and recorded interviews with the musicians.
Denis Preston recorded an interview with Miles for BBC Radio,
and found the trumpeter more co-operative than Sidney Bechet. At
least thirteen numbers from Miles's Paris concerts were recorded

41

for radio, and they give a vivid impression of the excitement of the occasion. Unlike the nonet air-shots, the French air-shots reveal a totally partisan audience which applauds wildly – solos, performances, anything and everything. As Miles remarked a few years later: 'In Europe, they like everything you do. The mistakes and everything. That's a little bit too much.' [2]

Three of the pieces played by Miles and the quintet are 'Crazy Rhythm', 'Embraceable You' (which Miles *announces* in a crisp and pleasant voice), and 'All The Things You Are'. It is difficult to believe that the trumpeter here is the same man who, only two or three weeks previously, had recorded 'Boplicity'. In Paris, Miles plays with a broad tone and powerful aggression. He makes frequent forays into the upper register, and even ends 'Crazy Rhythm' with a sustained F sharp (E concert) above his top C – a very high note indeed. He plays a lyrical and deeply-felt solo on the ballad 'Embraceable You', and then with 'All The Things You Are', goes back to wild athleticism. He takes all kinds of risks, some of which don't come off and so there are a few fluffs. This is really the result of the occasion; it is a live performance and the improviser is intent on pushing his own physical and creative resources to their limits. Although he is always supposed to be unaware of audiences, it is highly significant that during his earlier career, the orgiastic side of Miles's trumpet playing showed itself only in live performances. Not until the sixties and seventies does it appear in the clinical surroundings of the recording studio.

If Miles walked on air in Paris, he came back to earth with a painful thump when he returned to New York. The acclaimed international star was reduced to an out-of-work and scuffling musician. Apart from an occasional gig, he was unemployed for the rest of the year. In August, he and Tadd Dameron rehearsed an eighteen-piece band, but because of the effects of the recording ban, the time was not ripe for such a unit, and the project did not get beyond the rehearsal stage. Like his nine-piece venture, this was another bitter setback for Miles; it seemed his luck had run out.

He was just twenty-three, yet he'd already made musical history with Parker, and on his own with the nonet recordings. He was becoming the new influence on trumpet players, and was regarded by musicians as one of the leaders of the scene. His life had been notable for iron self-discipline, and he had remained abstemious in his habits. He had gained international recognition at the Paris Jazz Fair. In terms of American ideals and aspirations, he was a total success. He had every right to expect the natural rewards – regular work, a financial situation viable enough to enable him to lead a regular group, and certainly more recognition in his own country. Instead, he found no work at all, and no real prospects of any in the foreseeable future. It is hardly surprising that despair and boredom

42

made him turn to drugs.

His addiction was a total surprise to people who thought they knew him well, because he seemed the most self-controlled, cleanest-living musician of the bop generation. The pianist, Gil Coggins, comments: 'He was the type of man...with that bourgeois shit. He never wants you to catch him nodding...he had that control...he keeps people at a distance because he don't want to get hurt.' As Miles said, boredom was probably a major factor. It was several months since he'd left Parker and, on his own at last, facing an apparently bleak future, he must have craved for the 'sense of peril' he had, up to this point, experienced only vicariously through Bird. Miles may have begun taking heroin for kicks, but he soon became completely addicted to it and slid rapidly into chaos and degradation. The clean-cut, self-disciplined, bourgeois young man underwent a rapid and horrible transformation into an uncontrolled, unreliable, amoral person. For four years he worked only fitfully, his health deteriorated, and he touched rock-bottom, sometimes living off any women who liked him or took pity on him ('When I was using dope...I used to take bitches' money.'³), and often prepared to do anything to get enough cash for a fix.

After the last nonet studio sessions in March 1950, Miles had no immediate prospects of any further recordings. His contract with Capitol had been fulfilled and the company, discouraged by the very moderate sales of the nonet tracks, was not interested in renewing it. In May, he appeared as a sideman on six tracks recorded with the vocalist, Sarah Vaughan, and said of them later: 'I like the things with Sarah...I like the sound I got, especially on 'It Might As Well Be Spring'.'⁴ In June, Miles led a septet which included J.J. Johnson, Tadd Dameron and Art Blakey, opposite Parker's group at Birdland. In the late summer, Miles worked as a sideman in a small group which Billy Eckstine took on tour. It was while he was on this concert tour that he was arrested on suspicion of being a heroin addict. The charge was subsequently dismissed, but the resulting publicity had a bad effect on his career. The critic, Leonard Feather, wrote: 'News of the arrest has shocked American music circles, for Miles has frequently expressed his disapproval of the habits of so many of his fellow-boppers.'⁵ After this incident, Miles simply disappeared from the New York scene, taking himself and his habit to Chicago. He also had his family there with him at least some of the time, and this year saw the birth of his third child, a son whom he named Miles (IV).

In Chicago, Miles lived in hotels and was apparently still getting some financial assistance from his father. Gil Coggins saw him there and recalled: 'He was in a marvellous hotel then. I think it cost $28 a week, and *then*...$28!...that was a pretty nice hotel! And that time he was messing around with everybody. His old man was sending him $75...his old man would pay for his phone bills – $35... that's a lot of calling...Shit [heroin] was cheap – you could get a capsule for a dollar...it was pure, you know, potent.' But with an increasing drug habit and very little work, Miles was often in desperate financial straits. His brother Vernon spent some time with him in Chicago, and Babs Gonzales tells a pitiful story about the pair of them being so hard-up that they tried to make off with the money ($300) of a would-be drug-buyer, but were themselves tricked by one of their associates who disappeared with the ill-gotten gains.[6]

Meanwhile, new opportunities to record were about to present themselves to Miles. Immediately after the second recording ban had ended, a new, small, independent label called New Jazz was started by Bob Weinstock, an enthusiast whose early love for traditional jazz and the blues had expanded to include contemporary developments. Weinstock was regularly in the audience at the Royal Roost, or 'Metropolitan Bopera House' as it was dubbed, and he had been deeply impressed by Miles's nine-piece band. Weinstock had started the New Jazz label for 'kicks with a very limited distribution planned'. After his first recording in January 1949 with Lee Konitz, the initial sales were so promising that Weinstock took his own label seriously and spent the next two years personally riding buses from city to city, building his distribution. By 1950, he'd also introduced the Prestige label, and wanted Miles to record for it. He was convinced that Miles had found his true identity with the nonet recordings, and no doubt Weinstock was hoping for some kind of continuity with them. The first problem was finding Miles. Weinstock knew that the trumpeter's family lived in St Louis, and when he was on a business trip there he went through the Davises in the phone book and eventually got through to Miles's home:

> They told me he was in Chicago. I said, 'Please, if you should hear from Miles, ask him to call me in New York. I want to record him.' Finally he got in touch with me, and he came back East. Miles, at that time, although he still dug the cool music of Mulligan and Evans, some of the primitiveness in him started to come out. I say primitiveness, because to me the music of the bop masters is primitive music, like the original New Orleans music of King Oliver and Louis. He sort of drifted back into that element, and he liked Sonny Rollins, as crude as Sonny was at that time, and John Lewis. On his first date, you can hear a very different Miles Davis than on the Capitols.[7]

Weinstock was perceptive in recognizing the connection between bebop and the New Orleans music of Oliver and Armstrong. He was more perceptive, for example, than Louis himself who would have been outraged at the comparison. But Weinstock's analysis

44

and terminology are wrong. In both bebop and the music of Oliver and Armstrong in the 1920s, the non-western elements are very potent, and it is this aspect which Weinstock calls 'primitive'. The music of Charlie Parker is not at all primitive; it is extremely subtle and sophisticated. According to the criteria Weinstock seems to be using, Duke Ellington would have to be regarded as more primitive than Glenn Miller...an obvious absurdity.

Despite his inactivity, Miles was voted into first place in the 1951 *Metronome* poll, and continued to win this category in 1952 and 1953. This must have been due to his performances on record because, according to Leonard Feather, it was doubtful if he worked more than six or seven weeks during the whole of 1951. Financially, the situation was becoming desperate, and Miles was often reduced to earning small sums of money by transcribing music from records for lead sheets. He recalled: 'I'd take the $30 for the transcribing, go uptown, and get high.'[8] But this lowly chore was one of the lesser indignities he had to suffer during the period of his addiction. According to Babs Gonzales, Miles was exploited pitilessly by club owners and entrepreneurs, and made to play for very little money; in fact, the hoods who ran one club in New York used to beat up Miles and Bud Powell and other musicians who were addicts and in debt to them. The only other way Miles could make any money, was by recording, but as he was playing very little, his embouchure or 'chops' were often in poor shape. Furthermore, as a result of his drug habit he was often in very poor health, which also affected his trumpet playing. The trumpet is a most demanding instrument physically, and the player needs to be very fit. But the desperate need for cash occasionally made him accept a recording session when he was in no real condition to do it. In later years, he came to regard much of his output over this period as inferior, and commented: 'When I had a habit, I didn't care.'[9]

With the knowledge that Weinstock wanted to record him, Miles went back to New York at the beginning of 1951. It was about seven months since he'd been in the studios, and he broke that long silence on 17 January with a double date, recording first as a sideman with Charlie Parker's quintet, and then as a leader with his own sextet. It was a demanding experience after such a long lay-off, but the recordings were all for 78 or 45 RPM singles, and so the tracks were very short. The brief reunion with Parker was a happy occasion, with Bird in tremendous form and Miles playing some sparse, delicately poised solos which presaged his later style.

Miles's own session on 17 January was, in fact, his very first one as leader of a small group. The earlier nine-piece was not only half way towards being a big band, but it was also a unit which bore collectively much of the responsibility for the music, and there was always the father-figure of Gil Evans in the background. With his sextet, the onus was entirely on Miles; he had to choose the musicians and decide on the kind of music he wanted to produce. He did not choose any of the young white musicians who had been associated with the nonet, but instead used the twenty-one-year-old tenor saxophonist, Sonny Rollins, trombonist Benny Green, John Lewis (the only link with the nonet), bassist Percy Heath (who'd worked with Gillespie and Howard McGhee), and drummer Roy Haynes. It was a group of young black musicians whose musical experience had been shaped by the bebop masters.

So far as personnel was concerned, Miles had made a clear choice; but the music he chose to record showed indecision. Of the four pieces recorded, two of them ('Morpheus' composed by John Lewis, and 'Down' written by Miles) hover uneasily between the cool style and the hotter, funkier approach. 'Morpheus' is very odd. The theme, with its dissonant chords and passages of percussion, veers towards western abstract music, but then it suddenly turns into a fast blues with altered chord changes. 'Down' starts off as a funky blues played over a deeply grooving half-feel, but after four bars it reverts to straight 4/4 with a smoother feel, and the final bars of the theme are pure 'cool' school in the tonal quality of the voicings and the legato phrasing.

The other two pieces recorded that day were the standard tune, 'Whispering', and the Rodgers and Hart ballad, 'Blue Room'. The rhythm section is really excellent throughout all four tracks, and Benny Green improvises some impeccably conceived and executed melodic lines; but the real power of these performances lies in the contribution of the two people who make the most mistakes – Sonny Rollins and Miles. Rollins squeaks now and then, and sometimes either fails to round off his phrases or just manages to scramble through them, but his sound, the urgency of his attack and the efforts of an obviously original mind to express itself, make his contribution a telling one. Miles too, even though he fumbles a double-tempo run on 'Whispering', and falters on both takes of 'Blue Room', nevertheless makes his impact by virtue of his huge, non-brassy trumpet sound and the depth of feeling he expresses. Of his early recordings, his playing on 'Blue Room' is technically perhaps the poorest, and yet this is one of the most moving and memorable tracks of that period.

About a week after this session, Miles recorded a track with the Metronome All Stars. Of the eleven musicians in this pollwinners' band, only two – Miles and Max Roach – were black. In the early 1950s there was an outcry in the American musical press because polls which were conducted in Europe were dominated by black musicians. The easy association of black and white musicians that had prevailed in the 1940s, was now beginning to dissipate in strain and mistrust. But on 8 March, Miles was back in the studios, this

46

time as a sideman with Lee Konitz. Whether Miles was ill that day, whether he was just bored, or whether it was simply that Lee Konitz wanted to take most of the solo space, may never be known. The material and the treatment are cool, rather abstract and very western, and apart from one chorus on the chord sequence of 'Pennies From Heaven', Miles hardly plays at all. His sound and poise on that one chorus are good, but he seems very ill at ease in the fragments he plays on the other three pieces. Not surprisingly, the reviews were mediocre.

For his next Prestige recording session, which took place on 5 October 1951, Miles was not only in better physical and mental shape, but also revealed a surer sense of identity. He had been playing at Birdland just before this record date, which must have helped to improve his performance. Also, this was his first recording for a *long-playing* record, which meant that, for the first time in the studio, he was not forced to compress his performances into three-minute units. His unit, from now on, was to be the duration of a long-playing record, which meant about twenty-five minutes a side. He could fill this with long or short pieces according to his inclinations. This increased freedom was perfect for Miles, because his reflective approach to improvisation blossomed when it could stretch out. On five of the seven tracks recorded that day, Miles takes double solo space, playing the first solo, and then a second one when the others have had their say. He again took a sextet into the studio with Rollins, alto saxophonist Jackie McLean, pianist Walter Bishop junior, bassist Tommy Potter, and Art Blakey.

For the first time on record, Miles plays really long solos, and gives us a glimpse of the extent of his improvising power, revealing a great variety of rhythmic and melodic ideas. His sound is now so pure, so clear, that it is almost not a trumpet sound at all, but a disembodied sound emanating directly from him. That gloriously lyrical sound is given all the inflexions from the Negro vocal tradition – slurs, smears, half-valve choked effects, and superbly expressive bent notes. His sound has strong feminine overtones because it is so smooth and singing, but his rhythms are often aggressively masculine – though they are always subtle. Miles seems to have made some progress in reconciling the warring elements of his nature, and is beginning to achieve some internal unity at last.

The results were by no means flawless, however. The ensembles are sometimes a little ragged, and in Miles's own solos there are one or two passages – particularly those attempting to use the upper register – which sound very uneasy. But several things come off superbly: a beautiful version of the song, 'It's Only A Paper Moon', a long, self-communing trumpet solo on 'My Old Flame' and Miles's second solo on 'Blueing' is a gem. At that time recording engineers had still not learned how to record rhythm sections properly, and so the piano, drums, and particularly the bass, didn't quite match up to the sound of the horns. After 'Blueing' has petered out raggedly, Miles is heard saying in injured tones to Art Blakey: 'Play the ending, man. You know the arrangement!' Considering that the main soloists were so young – Miles was twenty-five, Bishop twenty-four, Rollins twenty-two, and McLean a mere nineteen – it is remarkable that the quality of the music is so sustained. Charlie Parker was present in the studio while the tracks were being recorded, and no doubt he gave some courage to his young protégés.

After this happy session, the old problems reasserted themselves; lack of work, lack of money, and an increasing need for drugs. Miles hardly worked at all for the rest of the year, and his health fluctuated wildly. At times he became a near derelict. His old friend and mentor, Clark Terry, came across him one day on Broadway. Miles was actually sitting on the kerb in a daze. Terry asked him what was wrong, and Miles replied, 'I don't feel well.' Clark Terry took him to a restaurant and bought him some ham and eggs. Even after eating, Miles looked so ill and worn out, that Terry, who was staying at the Hotel America on West 47th Street, took him back there and put him to bed. Then, Terry recalls: 'I went out and purposely stayed out so that he could get some rest...and of course, people who are strung out on narcotics are not responsible for things they do, and when I came back...to see how he was doing and bring him a cup of tea...and I come back with the tea and my door was open and Miles was gone and all my belongings! But I don't hold it against him because he wasn't responsible. I just love him the more because he overcame that y'know.' However, Clark was so worried about Miles that he phoned his wife in St Louis and asked her to tell Davis senior about his son's condition. But when she told Miles's father the news he simply said 'The only thing that's wrong with Miles now is because of those damn musicians like your husband that he's hanging around with.'[10]

Nevertheless, once Miles's father became fully aware of the situation, he did everything he could to help, and tried to persuade Miles to go for a cure. Red Rodney, who had joined Parker in 1949, had also become a junkie, and despite several attempts, didn't manage to kick the habit until the end of the fifties. During one of his attempts at rehabilitation, Rodney was a patient in an institution in Kentucky, and one day got a message that Miles was in reception, having been brought there by his father. Rodney recalls: 'I ran down the hall, and by the time I got there he was gone...he didn't stay. They wanted him to check in and stay for four months, and he refused. He said he wouldn't stay that long, and he and his father left.' Miles was obviously not fully ready to quit the habit. Some years later he said from the wisdom of experience: 'You can't *talk* a man out of a habit until he really *wants* to stop.'[11]

48

During 1952, Miles spent some periods of time at home in East St Louis, and on one of these visits he played locally with tenor saxophonist, Jimmy Forest's band for a few weeks. This, apart from a tour with a package called Jazz Inc, headed by disc jockey Symphony Sid, and including Milt Jackson (vibraphone), Zoot Sims and Jimmy Heath (tenors), seems to have been the only extended public appearance he made that year. Also, he had only one recording date. This was a session for the Blue Note label, and for it he used a sextet which included J.J. Johnson, Jackie McLean, pianist Gil Coggins, bassist Oscar Pettiford, and Kenny Clarke on drums. But apart from these isolated events, 1952 was an empty and miserable year for Miles Davis. Early in the year, Leonard Feather wrote an article for *Melody Maker*, heading it: 'Poll-topper Miles has been at a standstill since back in 1950', and in a long piece reviewing Miles's whole career to date, he said: 'One of the most influential of modern jazzmen, through his trumpet work and through the school of orchestral bop started by his Capitol records, Miles in the past year has seen his career slip away from him while his imitators have been progressing.'[12]

During both 1952 and 1953, Miles's development was static because of his poor health and the infrequency of his work, but he did set about reviewing his musical experience to date and reinterpreting some of the music of his immediate past. In the first few months of 1953, he did three recording sessions which were wildly different in emotional climate and artistic achievement. In January he recorded two of his own compositions ('Compulsion' and 'The Serpent's Tooth') and Monk's ballad, 'Round Midnight', with a sextet which included Charlie Parker and Sonny Rollins on tenors, Walter Bishop (piano), Percy Heath (bass), and Philly Joe Jones (drums). This session was a very uneasy one and the music is full of flaws. In the themes, the three horns seem to suffer from sour intonation and they don't blend at all. Miles has some problems with articulation as well as intonation, though both he and Bird produce moments of powerfully emotive music. But the renewal of the old relationship with Parker did not seem to bear fruit. The two men had words on the date, because Bird had rather incapacitated himself by drinking too much gin. Miles was angry, and pointed out that he (Miles) had never failed Bird on a record date. Parker, who must always have been conscious of Miles's bourgeois origins, replied with irony: 'All right Lily Pons...To produce beauty, we must suffer pain – from the oyster comes the pearl!'[13]

In February, Miles was in the studios again, this time with a septet comprising the two white saxophonists Al Cohn and Zoot Sims, trombonist Sonny Truitt, and a rhythm section of John Lewis, Kenny Clarke and bassist Leonard Gaskin. The four pieces they recorded were all written by Al Cohn, and the resulting music could

49

hardly be more different from that of the earlier session. This septet sounds oddly like a pit orchestra in a Broadway musical; the arrangements are light, reminiscent of showbiz music, and impeccably played. The solos are all swinging and accomplished. Cohn and Sims come out of the Lester Young school, and this music is a reversion almost to a pre-1940 swing style. Considerable craftsmanship is involved, but little substance.

Then in April, craftsmanship and content came beautifully together on a second session for Blue Note, when Miles recorded some tracks which, in later years, he admitted to liking. The material consisted largely of a couple of themes associated with Dizzy Gillespie's big band, and some compositions by Jimmy Heath and J.J. Johnson, both of whom played on the date, along with Gil Coggins, Percy Heath and Art Blakey. The horns blend superbly, the themes are executed cleanly, and Blakey's powerful polyrhythms inspire some very muscular trumpet solos. These Blue Note tracks were nearly all very short – around the three- or four-minute mark – despite the advent of the LP. Whereas the February recording date had seemed like a musical aberration for Miles, this April session with his close associates sounds right and natural. With the three record dates in the early months of 1953, and the sextet session in May of the previous year, Miles had reviewed his own immediate past. There was one further quartet session – just Miles and a rhythm section – in May, and after that the survey was complete.

Outside of the ordered world of the recording studios, however, things were going badly and Miles was reduced to appearing as a soloist in various towns with local musicians. His great companion during this period was drummer and fellow-junkie, Philly Joe Jones, whose musical relationship with the trumpeter was to form the basic nucleus of the first great Miles Davis Quintet in the middle fifties. Miles and Philly Joe had worked together off and on since 1952 and established an almost telepathic rapport. Because it was economically impossible to run a permanent group, the two of them worked as a unit to which they added local musicians for each gig in each new town. Philly Joe recalls:

Miles and I had been barnstorming around the country. When we got to a city where we had a gig, I'd get there first and find another horn player, a piano player and a bass player. In those days we were really putting the music together. We'd get on the plane and he'd hum the arrangements we'd play. When I got the musicians together, he never had much to say to them except 'Hi'. He'd have me talk to them...It got to be a drag, because every town we'd play, I'd try to find the musicians that were the cream of the crop, but they wouldn't be worth shit. We finally had to sit down and hash over the musicians that we both knew who could really play. We had it all in our minds what we were going to do .[14]

50

The ordeal of having to rely on often very inferior local musicians was beginning to wear Miles down. At the same time, other trumpet players with regular groups were beginning to gain reputations which were eclipsing Miles's own fame. The young trumpeter with Gerry Mulligan's quartet was Chet Baker, and he, though strongly in debt stylistically to Miles, was rapidly overtaking Davis in terms of exposure and popularity – largely because the quartet had both identity and stability as a unit and was building up an international audience. Also, the early fifties saw the rise of the phenomenal young trumpet star (and one of Red Rodney's pupils), Clifford Brown, who, with Art Farmer (another emerging talent) was featured soloist with Lionel Hampton's band. Miles was becoming a forgotten man, and the reality of his situation was brought home to him brutally when he spent several months off the scene in the backwater of Detroit, where he was eking out his existence with a local rhythm section at a club called the Bluebird Inn.

Clearly, addiction was rapidly destroying Miles; it was imperative to free himself of drugs. He tried psychoanalysis without success, and then in desperation kicked his habit 'cold turkey'. He told *Ebony* magazine: 'I made up my mind I was getting off dope. I was sick and tired of it. You know you can get tired of anything. You can even get tired of being scared. I laid down and stared at the ceiling for twelve days and I cursed everybody I didn't like. I was kicking it the hard way. It was like having a bad case of flu only worse. I lay in a cold sweat. My nose and eyes ran. I threw up everything I tried to eat. My pores opened up and I smelled like chicken soup. Then it was over.'[15]

Miles Davis was one of the very few who broke the habit by themselves, without help or treatment. Many of the others – Fats Navarro and Sonny Berman among them – died prematurely. A few others, like Gerry Mulligan, managed to kick the habit with the aid of psychoanalysis. But to do it 'cold turkey', as Miles had done, was remarkable. Years later, he was to say that two of his heroes – boxers Sugar Ray Robinson and Jack Johnson – had given him moral strength by their example: 'Sugar Ray inspired me and made me kick the habit...when he started training – he wouldn't make it with chicks. He disciplined himself and all that...and Jack Johnson too!'[16]

The four years of addiction had left terrible scars, and the effect of this experience on Miles's subsequent life and work cannot be over-estimated. Up to 1949, he had shown iron self-discipline, and then as a junkie, had revealed great weaknesses. Without the protection and insulation of his privileged family background, he was plunged into a life-style exactly like that of the black ghettos in big cities. Miles Davis has always been a very proud man, and he has said little about the kinds of degradation he suffered during this

51

period, but the knowledge of his own ignominies and of the indignities he was forced to suffer, must have filled him with horror. No doubt, the strength he found to break the habit was inspired as much by self-loathing as by the examples of his heroes. After this whole experience, nothing would ever be the same for him again, and his vision was immeasurably deepened. His father commented: 'It had to put a hard crust on Miles. There was always somebody trying to get him back on dope again. He had an iron will that broke it and that will power applied to everything he did as a result. I'm proud of him.'[17]

Miles had travelled to the limits both physically and psychologically during the four years of addiction, and now that he had come out of the experience intact, he had greater strength, greater identity and greater profundity – all of which were to reveal themselves in his life and art. Some years later, he said: 'I don't think nothing about death. I should have been dead a long time ago. But it missed me when I was on dope. That's why I don't have any fear in my eyes. Some people accuse me of being mean and racist because I don't bow and scrape. When they look in my eyes and don't see fear they know it's a draw.'[18]

5
The First Great Quintet

'The thing to judge in any jazz artist is does the man
project, and does he have ideas.'[1]
Miles Davis

Miles had kicked the drug habit by the beginning of 1954, but the
four years of addiction had taken their toll and although he was
careful about what he ate, and obsessive about exercise, he was
dogged by ill-health. It seemed that his fanatical fitness campaign
was not so much to promote magnificent health as to keep sickness
at bay and ensure merely that his body was functioning normally.
But from this point onwards, he was blessed with all kinds of
musical insights, and the seven years up to 1960 were a period of
extraordinarily varied and sustained development. It is a period in
which he produced one small group and orchestral masterpiece
after another. A hint of the riches to come occurred in 1954 when he
revealed, at the comparatively late age of twenty-seven, rising
twenty-eight, a fully mature and totally original approach to the
trumpet. In a sense, this year resembles 1947 when Miles was
recording with Parker and made tremendous strides towards finding
his own distinctive voice on trumpet. At that time, of course, he was
working (and recording) regularly with Bird's group, which enabled
him to sustain his progress. In 1954, although he was still working
irregularly and had no permanent group, he managed to achieve an
important continuity of personnel in his recording sessions. There
were six that year, and on all of them the bass player is Percy Heath.
On the first two sessions, the drummer is Art Blakey, and on the last
four sessions, Kenny Clarke. On the first five sessions, the pianist is
Horace Silver. This continuity must have promoted the kind of
rapport with a rhythm section which Miles needs to allow him to
create most freely. Two or three of his studio performances, from
April onwards, rank with the greatest small group recordings in
jazz. During this year there emerges on record, for the first time,
the intangible, indefinable capacity he has for welding together
disparate personalities so that by some strange alchemy the whole
ensemble becomes greater than the sum of its parts. But this extra

53

touch of magic did not appear on the first three studio sessions of 1954.

The first two dates took place on 6 and 15 March, with a quartet (Silver, Heath and Blakey). This was Miles's first time in the studio for ten months and, as is often the case after a long lay-off, the result was a profusion of ideas and a stronger sense of identity. A sure sign of an intensely creative period in a jazz musician's career is a wealth of new written themes, or new ways of treating older material. On these March sessions, Miles recorded four new compositions of his own, and an original blues ('Blue Haze') which started a fashion for beginning blues performances with a bass solo. Also, his treatment of one standard ('Old Devil Moon') was so fresh that it brought the tune to the attention of other people, and within seven months of Miles's version, it was recorded by Sarah Vaughan, J.J. Johnson, and Carmen McRae.

The music throughout these two sessions shows a general movement away from bebop and towards a much sparer style in which there are no empty mannerisms. For the most part, each note of Miles's improvisations is organically related to the notes before and after it. Only in the faster pieces such as 'Take-Off' and 'The Leap', is he at all prodigal with notes, but even here there are innovations which point to his future development. Both these compositions use pedal points – moments when the harmonic sequence is arrested and the soloist plays over one chord for a few bars. The interest at these points becomes not so much linear and harmonic as rhythmic and spatial, and they are used in these performances to create tension which is released when the chord changes are played again. This enhances the drama of the music, and the most dramatic use of the device occurs in 'The Leap' where the pedal points last a full sixteen bars, the final two bars being an instrumental break which launches the soloist into the next section of harmonic changes. As might be expected after such a long lay-off, there are occasional failures of lip and judgment in Miles's solos, but the tonal beauty of his sound had definitely increased, and on the ballad, 'It Never Entered My Mind', his sound with the cup mute is the best of his whole career up to that time – superbly rounded and glowing. On 'Blue Haze' he treats the blues as blues, and not merely as a springboard for flights of harmonic and melodic fantasy, and his five choruses are eloquent with all the bent notes, slurs and smears which Miles uses to 'put his own substance, his own flesh on a note',[2] to quote Gil Evans. Horace Silver vividly remembers the recording of 'Blue Haze':'We'd tried it and it didn't seem to work at all. Then Miles told Bob Weinstock to put out all the lights in the studio – so the only light we had was from the window of the control booth. Miles sat in a chair and pulled his cap right over his face – and he also took his shoes off. Then he beat it in at just the right tempo…and

54

the whole thing happened perfectly.'

On his next recording session (3 April), Miles played all four pieces using a cup mute, and the full sound he gets obviously inspires him because he produces consistently incisive phrases. However, the cup mute sound has only a limited expressivity because it is bland and has only a narrow range of tonal inflexions. The group was a quintet with Kenny Clarke on drums, the alto saxophonist Dave Schildkraut, and Silver and Heath, and although the rhythm section is excellent, and Miles in good form, the music is not totally satisfactory because Schildkraut lacked authority as a soloist, because Horace Silver had not yet fully grasped his role in Miles's music, and because the cup mute sound is too one-dimensional.

But on his very next session (29 April), Miles produced his first full-scale masterpiece and did it in a most casual, almost accidental way. Bob Weinstock and Prestige would not pay for rehearsals, and so (as had usually been the case with Parker), everything had to be done in the studio. This spontaneous approach usually served to put Miles on his mettle, sparking his creative flow. Horace Silver comments: 'Miles has a genius for head arrangements. In the studio, he'd sit with his head in his hands while we were setting up, and then he'd show a few things – voicings he wanted, and rhythmic things. Then we'd try it over a few times and there we'd have a nice head arrangement.' On this present occasion, however, Miles had made some attempt to prepare for the date. As well as the rhythm section of Silver, Heath and Clarke, he had also booked his old associates, Lucky Thompson (tenor) and J.J. Johnson (trombone), and he'd asked Thompson to bring some arrangements to the session. The latter stayed up half the night writing music, but all to no avail. Horace Silver describes what happened: 'We tried them in the studio, but nothing came off. They didn't seem to work and neither Miles nor the producer Bob Weinstock were happy. Eventually, they were abandoned and we busked a couple of head arrangements which turned out to be classics!' These classics were the medium-paced blues, 'Walkin'', and the fast blues, 'Blue 'n' Boogie'.

Undoubtedly, the frustration caused by the group's failure to make anything of Lucky Thompson's arrangements was a major factor in these superlative performances of familiar material. It served to focus the identity of the individual musicians. Miles had at last refined his trumpet style so that there was no more decoration at all, and the improvised phrases of his solos were totally organic. From the point of view of actually meaning what you play, his example also seems to have inspired both Johnson and Thompson who make all their phrases tell, and who play with great urgency. Throughout the session there is a feeling that whoever is soloing is being listened to with close attention by the horns who are not

55

playing, and that their attention is supporting the soloist, helping him to greater levels of expression. And there is a continuing dialogue of quite remarkable brilliance between the soloing horns and the rhythm section.

The solo order and the overall shape of the two performances are absolutely crucial to their artistic success, and this factor was, of course, Miles's responsibility as leader. After an eight-bar horn introduction over offbeats, the theme of 'Walkin'' is played twice. This theme, with its use of flattened 5ths, and its stark call-and-response pattern, is highly evocative – a distilled essence of the traditional and the post-bop blues. The atmosphere and sense of drama are heightened by the sonorities of trumpet, trombone and tenor all in unison, and their beautifully posed timing...an elastic, laid-back, lazy feel which is on a knife-edge of balance. Kenny Clarke's immensely sensitive and subtle use of the high-hat cymbal which he opens and closes to point up the rhythms of the theme, also intensifies the drama. After the theme is played, the rhythm section moves into a straight 4/4 feel (the bass playing four beats to the bar instead of two), and Miles takes the first solo, playing seven choruses. He is followed by J.J. Johnson who also plays seven, then Lucky Thompson's tenor sax solo is the emotional high-spot of the performance. He plays for a few choruses and then Miles and Johnson play a backing figure which is a further distillation of the main theme, and Thompson's solo increases in intensity and power. When the backing riff stops, he has a couple of choruses to wind down, after which Horace Silver plays, not exactly a solo, but an interlude of two choruses which refer back to the simplest fundamentals of the early blues. His right hand phrases would sound almost like a parody of the blues were it not for the single-note counterline he plays with his left, which imbues his contribution with real feeling. Miles plays a further two choruses and then leads the front line into a convulsive riff which is punctuated by Kenny Clarke, after which the rhythms subside, reverting to the two-in-the-bar feel and the main theme is repeated twice. The introduction over offbeats now becomes the coda, and the whole lengthy performance ends with the peak or apex having occurred in the middle of the saxophone solo, and everything else leading up to, and down from, that.

Miles's first solo (Appendix A, Fig.2) which, as it were, sets the scene and the musical standards for the whole performance, has gone beyond bebop and into the realm of archetypal blues expression. His ideas are so clear, so surprisingly original and yet simple, that they strike the listener with immediate impact and linger in the memory long afterwards. The emotional climate of the solo is potent; it is buoyant and full of energy, but there are melancholy, even tragic, undertones. It is a deeply personal statement, and

56

shows increased rhythmic sophistication when compared with his 'Now's The Time' solo, another blues in F, recorded nine years earlier. One of the most striking features of this solo is the way it swings. Gil Evans has described this combination of apparently contradictory qualities: 'Underneath his lyricism, Miles *swings*. He'll take care of the lyricism, but the rest of the band must complement him with an intense drive. And it's not that they supply a drive he himself lacks. Actually, they have to come up to him...As subtle as he is in his time and phrasing and his courage to wait, to use space, he's very forceful. There is a feeling of unhurriedness in his work and yet there's intensity underneath and through it all.'[3] In his 'Walkin'' solo, Miles makes brilliant use of triplets, and it is this, particularly in his third chorus, which sets his improvision apart from bebop and takes it beyond stylistic pigeon-holes. In fact, it recalls the work of Louis Armstrong at the time of 'West End Blues'. Curiously, Louis was then the same age (twenty-eight) and also made great use of triplets. Because Miles's solo goes right to the roots, to the heart of the jazz mainstream, this gives it a kind of mythic power. The entire performance of 'Walkin'' has this same power, which is why, even now, almost thirty years after it was recorded, it still sounds fresh and still offers new revelations on repeated hearings. And this is also true of the other piece recorded that day, the fast 'Blue 'n' Boogie'.

Miles's next recording in this remarkable year, was with a quintet on 29 June. This time the saxophonist was his old friend, Sonny Rollins, and the rhythm section was the same marvellous unit – Silver, Heath and Clarke. During this whole period, Miles is looking for his repertoire, his library of themes on which he wishes to improvise. He had discovered the 'Walkin'' theme in 1952, and was to continue using it until the middle 1960s. Similarly, on this June date with Rollins, Miles had discovered two themes which he would use for the next six or seven years. They were the Gershwin tune 'But Not For Me', and Rollins's own composition, 'Oleo', which is based on the chords of 'I Got Rhythm'. Two more Rollins compositions were also recorded on this session. One was the fast 'Airegin' (Nigeria spelled backwards), which Miles was to use with his later quintet, and the other was the gospel-flavoured, 'Doxy', a sixteen bar melody with a funky two-in-the-bar feel.

'Oleo' is the outstanding track of a very good day's work. Although it is based on the 'Rhythm' thirty-two bar sequence, Miles's version with its dramatic use of space and timbre is so unusual as to make it a completely fresh composition. It was with this recording that Miles Davis introduced a totally new sound to jazz – the amplified sound of the metallic harmon mute with its stem removed. The mute has to be placed very close to the microphone, and the resulting sound is full and breathy in the lower register and thin and piercing in the upper. The two registers can therefore be played off against each other in a very dramatic way, and this muted sound is much more expressive than, for example, that of the bland cup mute which Miles was using earlier in the year. The harmon mute can be used to express the most delicate nuances of feeling, and because its timbre is round and full and has a clear tongued edge, it is rhythmically very eloquent. With such qualities – the mixture of sweet and sour tonality and the muscularity of rhythms – it was the perfect vehicle for Miles's requirements. Like so many of his innovations, it sounded so right and was so immediately attractive, that it spawned imitators everywhere.

The first sixteen and the last eight bars of the theme of 'Oleo' are played by muted trumpet and tenor sax in unison accompanied only by the bass. The middle eight is played by the piano with the full rhythm section. The solos echo this pattern, each horn being accompanied by bass and drums only, except for the middle eights when the piano joins in. This deployment of instruments points up the drama of the performance, giving it a very satisfying shape. The timbre of the harmon mute is thrown into marvellous relief when accompanied only by bass and drums. The overall impression is stark and compelling, and Miles is clearly inspired by the new combinations of sound. His solo is elegant and exciting, full of buoyant rhythms and beautifully sculpted phrases.

In 1954, Bob Weinstock and Prestige were doing very well. Although it was only a small, independent label, Prestige had some of the most important contemporary musicians under contract. As well as Miles, Thelonious Monk and the Modern Jazz Quartet (John Lewis, Milt Jackson, Percy Heath and Kenny Clarke) were also signed to Prestige. One of the reasons why Heath and Clarke functioned so well together was because they were a regular unit in a working band. Miles's use of them as his studio rhythm section for most of that year suited everybody: musically they were perfect for him at the time, and as they were signed to Prestige the extra exposure was good for them and for Weinstock. The growing success of the label enabled Weinstock, in April 1954, to turn over all recording to Rudy Van Gelder, one of the finest sound engineers. The excellent recorded sound of Miles's sessions from April onwards, was due to the genius of Van Gelder. At last, the rhythm section was properly recorded, which gave added point to the horn solos, increasing the impact of the whole performance. The mid-fifties mono sound of Prestige (and Blue Note and Savoy which Van Gelder also engineered) was so good that even twenty years later it did not seem dated.

Miles's last date in 1954 was on Christmas Eve and was the brainchild of Weinstock who had the idea of using three MJQ members (Jackson, Heath and Clarke), Thelonious Monk and Davis for another 'all-star' session. Ten years previously, Miles had had lessons from Thelonious who taught him harmony and some of his tunes, and now on this session they were reunited as equals...but perhaps not quite equals: Miles's star was rising, while Monk was going through a period of obscurity and unemployment which had begun in 1945 and was to last until 1957. Monk was Weinstock's rather than Miles's choice on piano, and there was some tension in the studio. Charlie Mingus recalled in *Down Beat* some months afterwards: 'He [Miles] cursed, laid out, argued, and threatened Monk and asked Bob Weinstock why he had hired such a non-musician and would Monk lay out on his trumpet solos.'⁴ Some years later, Miles explained to Nat Hentoff: 'I love the way Monk plays and writes, but I can't stand him behind me. He doesn't give you any support.'⁵ There were even rumours after the event of punch-ups in the studio, but when Monk was asked whether Miles had punched him, he simply said, 'What me? He'd better not!' The massive Monk would probably have been more than a match for the diminutive Miles.

The underlying tension in the studio served to put the musicians on their mettle, adding a dimension which made the results, yet again, classic tracks. It also gave the performances more form, because after recording Monk's composition, 'Bemsha Swing', Miles asked the pianist not to play during the trumpet solos. Thus, on the other three pieces recorded that night – Miles's own 'Swing Spring', Milt Jackson's 'Bag's Groove', and Gershwin's 'The Man I Love' – the trumpet solos are accompanied only by bass and drums which makes the atmosphere more spacious and airier. The vibraphone solos are accompanied by the entire rhythm section with Monk's idiosyncratic piano giving a dense, more angular backing.

Monk, like Miles, had converted his technical limitations into assets, creating a sinewy and economical style with no superfluities. Since the early forties, he'd been using the rhythm section rather as an abstract expressionist painter would use a canvas – splashing his keyboard on to it in melodic shapes and colours. His use of space – his pauses and his melodic and rhythmic interpolations – was dramatic in the extreme. Despite the clash of styles and tempera-ments, Miles was fully aware of Monk's virtues and of the originality of his mind:'A main influence he has been through the years has to do with giving musicians more freedom. They feel that if Monk can do what he does, they can. Monk has been using space for a long time.'⁶ Monk's solos are as powerfully emotive as Miles's are. Relief from their intensity is provided by the vibraphone of Milt Jackson who is the only truly virtuoso soloist on the session, and whose fleet improvisations are more symmetrical and less abstract than either Monk's or Miles's.

The strong individuality of the three soloists and the propulsive

59

rhythm section of Heath and Clarke give these performances great dynamism. Even the occasional error and failure has a kind of magnificence. This is true, for example, of Monk's solo on 'The Man I Love', when the pianist gets so carried away with his variation on the theme that he loses its relationship to the chord sequence and stops playing. The bass and drums continue 'strolling' until Miles prompts Monk with a few notes on the trumpet, and the pianist suddenly fills up the yawning space with a flowing melodic line. This heightened sense of drama is echoed in Miles's own solo which follows. He begins with open trumpet, then suddenly jams the harmon mute into the bell and carries on playing; the whole atmosphere is changed violently from the expansive reflections of the open sound, to the claustrophobic brooding of the harmon.

The outstanding track is 'Bag's Groove', a long improvisation on the blues in the key (once more) of F, and this reveals just how far Miles Davis had refined his art. From the point of view of sound, of sheer tonal beauty, his two solos eclipse all his earlier work. Now, Chico Hamilton's description does not seem exaggerated: 'Miles Davis is a sound...the whole earth singing!'[7] And to this gloriously pure sound are added the expressive vocal inflexions of the blues. His two solos – a long one at the beginning and a shorter one at the end – are notable for his apparently inexhaustible flow of melodic ideas which seem to grow organically out of each other. His first solo (Appendix A, Fig.3) comes immediately after the theme which means that Miles is once again setting up the whole performance – establishing the standard and the creative atmosphere for the other musicians. This solo is superior to his 'Walkin'' improvisation, though it is, in essence, the same sort of solo. All the qualities of the earlier solo are magnified and brought into sharper focus. The melodic phrases are more finely conceived, the lyricism more intense, and Miles's interpretation of the blues is more personal. The rhythmic definition of his phrases – their poise and the way they relate to the basic pulse – is exquisite. The complete 'Bag's Groove' performance and the other three pieces they recorded on that Christmas Eve were a fitting end to a remarkable year.

1954 was an immensely important landmark in Miles Davis's career. At the beginning of it, he had only recently freed himself from drug-addiction, and though he was a very promising trumpeter with a highly original style, the deficiencies of his self-knowledge were reflected in the uncertainties of some of his solo work. By the end of the year he had become a master soloist, and he had acquired the knowledge and skills he needed to go on to the next stage of his development. First, he had perfected the trumpet sounds he was to use and explore for the next sixteen years or so: the singing open sound, and the muted, inward-looking timbre of the harmon. Gil Evans has said: 'Miles...is aware of his complete surroundings and

60

takes advantage of the wide range of sound possibilities that exist even in one's basic sound. He can, in other words, create a particular sound for the existing context.'[8] As well as perfecting his basic sound, Miles had also begun to collect a repertoire of themes, and had also revealed that he had the vision and the inner strength to lead ensembles and to inspire great performances. The format of the 'all-star-blowing-session' was not going to satisfy him any longer. What he needed now, more than anything else, was to form his own quintet on a regular basis. Having brought his instrumental art to a pitch of perfection, he was now free to examine Parker's legacy – the idea that the soloist is integrally related to the small-group ensemble, and that the combination of the two entities is the key to a rich and dynamic music.

Miles's reputation had risen steeply among musicians, and his records were bought by a tiny, but loyal following. He was also now being noticed for the talents he encouraged and nurtured as well as for his own playing. Both Horace Silver and Sonny Rollins had made their names through recording with Miles. But although Davis had become a cult figure, he had no real financial basis for a regular band. His years of addiction and obscurity had wiped him from the mind of the majority jazz audience. He had received critical acclaim for his nine-piece band and for his trumpet playing; in the early fifties several of his solos had been transcribed and printed in *Down Beat*. But these considerable achievements were not enough to enable him to lead a permanent quintet, because that meant having enough engagements to pay the musicians a living wage.

On 12 March 1955, the universal impression that an era was ending, was clinched by the death of Charlie Parker at the age of thirty-four. He had spent his last few months as a virtual derelict, wandering around homeless, dossing down in people's apartments, taking aimless trips on the subway, and even begging on the Bowery. Red Rodney commented: 'I do suspect that he died at the right time. I don't think that he had anything more to say. I don't think he could have improved upon anything, because he was sick. He no longer had the fire...he was ill...physically ill.' Bird's worsening health must have been partially responsible for his failing powers, but he also felt that he had come to a creative impasse. He admitted to Lennie Tristano that he had taken the blues and the ballad as far as he could. He seemed to have no way left to go musically, which is probably why, like Bix Beiderbecke, he cast longing and ineffectual glances at the world of 'straight' music. During the last two years or so of his life, he had been travelling the same musical territory which he had opened up and pioneered in the early forties, and he had been going round in ever diminishing circles. His actual death was caused by all, or any one, of four ailments: stomach ulcers (perforated), pneumonia, advanced cirrhosis of the liver, and a heart attack.

61

Parker's death shocked his old associates. It was hard to believe that the unpredictable genius, the gargantuan appetites, the huge energy and force were all snuffed out, gone forever. It forced everyone to reassess Parker's achievements and to take new stock of their own. Bird was less than six years older than Miles...the trumpeter would be twenty-nine on 25 May that year. It was time he started doing something; he had already wasted four of his best years, and a jazz musician was considered old at forty. On the other hand, he was now experiencing a kind of rebirth and was brimming with ideas – new things to say and new ways of saying them. His contract with Prestige gave him a modest form of patronage; for a small advance and scale payment for each studio session, recordings of his recent work were available to the public. This, however, was not enough to enable him to launch a new band. What he needed was some kind of promotion, publicity, investment, to create an audience which was aware of his existence and interested in paying to listen to his music.

His luck, which seemed to have deserted him since 1949, suddenly returned, and Miles found himself once again to be the right man in the right place at the right time. The place was the second Newport Jazz Festival and the time was July 1955. Miles was added to the bill almost as an afterthought, and presented as a soloist with a pick-up group assembled for the occasion. The other musicians (Gerry Mulligan, Zoot Sims, Thelonious Monk, Percy Heath, and drummer Connie Kay) had all, except Kay, recorded with Miles and so were well aware of the values he emphasised in his music. This group played two pieces by Monk ('Hackensack' and 'Round Midnight'), and finished their appearance with a version of Parker's 'Now's The Time'. Miles's solos made a great impact on audience and critics, and the reviews were all excellent, extolling the power and vitality of his contribution, and talking about his 'resurgence'. Miles commented scornfully: 'What are they talking about? I just played the way I always play.'⁹ By the end of the year, the readers of *Down Beat* had voted him into first place on trumpet. The publicity from his Newport appearance had also created so much general interest that by the late summer he was able to form a quintet on a regular basis for the first time in his life.

Up to this point in time, Miles had had a personal manager, but no booking agent to find work for a group. His manager was a personal friend called Harold Lovett, a black lawyer with such an interest in jazz that he was called 'counsellor' by many musicians. Lovett was extremely fond of Miles and their relationship seems to have been based more on mutual liking and respect than on financial considerations. The admiration and affection Lovett felt for Miles made him defend the trumpeter's interests with fanaticism, and his

62

loyalty had stood the harsh test of Miles's years as a junkie. However, it was very difficult at that time for black musicians to advance their careers without the help of the white musical establishment. Virtually all the leading booking agencies were white, and Lovett was quick to take advantage of Miles's Newport success and get him signed with the Shaw Agency, which had represented both Charlie Parker and Dizzy Gillespie. At the agency, Jack Whittemore was the man personally responsible for booking Miles's group.

Though he had not worked in public very much during the first six months of 1955, three recording sessions in June, July and August, show that Miles was trying out different group sounds and contexts. The first date, on 7 June, was with a quartet – just Miles with a rhythm section. The pianist was Red Garland, the drummer Philly Joe Jones, and the bassist, Oscar Pettiford, was the only man on the session who would not become a member of the Miles Davis Quintet. Six tracks were recorded and the results were not very propitious. The actual recorded sound is very poor – one of the worst group sounds Miles ever produced on record, and it's difficult to believe that Van Gelder engineered the session. The bass is thin and barely audible, the piano is thin and tinny, and Miles's trumpet sound is rather pinched. He also seems distinctly uneasy, as if the old muscular troubles (dodgy lip) and identity doubts had returned. He plays on the whole without fire or conviction, and he also drops several 'clinkers'. To complete the dismal picture, he sounds out of tune on almost every track, and this, added to the bad recording quality, prevents piano and trumpet from blending at all comfortably. It could be that irregular work in the first six months of the year had set Miles back a little. But it could also be the fact that he was starting a new group with new people. The whole aesthetic balance of the rhythm section is the reverse of the one with which he had been recording for the last year or so. Now, instead of forceful piano and light drums, his context was giving him light piano and heavy drums. This factor may have caused him to lose his touch momentarily.

As if the June session had made him lose his nerve, the following month Miles recorded with a totally different group which included his old associate, Charles Mingus, who played bass and wrote the arrangements. Unlike the quartet date, this was not a freewheeling blowing session, but a tightly controlled and highly organized event. As well as Miles and Mingus, the line-up included trombonist Britt Woodman, vibist Teddy Charles, and Elvin Jones on drums. This time the recorded sound is much better and Miles makes incisive use of the harmon mute, producing a rich, bell-like sonority. His playing on 'Nature Boy' and the ballad, 'Easy Living', is exquisite and deeply affecting.

On 5 August, he was in the studio with yet another group: a sextet this time with Jackie McLean, Milt Jackson, Percy Heath, pianist Ray Bryant and drummer Art Taylor. Four tunes were recorded, and this was a very good session indeed. The rhythm section is excellent and Miles himself is in magnificent form. His muted and open sounds are superlative and his long solos show an extraordinary fecundity and completeness of imagination. Once again, his use of triplets during his muted solo on the blues, 'Changes', recalls the work of young Louis Armstrong.

In September, Miles did his first *Down Beat* blindfold test with Leonard Feather. These tests consist of playing tracks from records to a musician without giving him any information about them. He then comments on the music and tries to identify the musicians involved. Feather himself devised this fascinating series which involved musicians in the difficulties of aesthetic judgment. Miles not only identifies eight tracks out of nine, but also names many of the supporting musicians. While being generous in his praise of individuals, he is also highly critical of how they play, their relationship to the ensemble, the way the pieces are arranged and interpreted. Again and again, he says things like: 'I think they played it too fast, though. They missed the content of the tune', or, 'You can't play that kind of song like that, with those chords. There's another way to swing on that.'[10] He gives unreserved praise to Louis Armstrong and Bobby Hackett, awarding them five stars – the *Down Beat* maximum rating. But when Feather plays him Duke Ellington's version of 'Stormy Weather', Miles exclaims: 'I think all the musicians should get together one certain day and get down on their knees and thank Duke...Yes, everybody should bow to Duke and Strayhorn – and Charlie Parker and Diz...Give this all the stars you can.'[11] Miles's confident judgments are based on a knowledge and understanding of the whole jazz spectrum from traditional jazz to the contemporary music of the day, and from small group to big band. He was, in every way now, ready to start his own group.

On drums, he naturally chose Philly Joe Jones who had shared his dreams of a regular group. Jones had built up tremendous stamina and drive by working with rhythm and blues groups, while still absorbing the influence of new stylists such as Max Roach. Philly Joe had 'that thing', and admiration for his playing occasioned one of Miles's most quoted remarks: 'Look, I wouldn't care if he came up on the band-stand in his BVDs [underwear] and with one arm, just so long as he was there. He's got the fire I want.'[12] The bass player was Paul Chambers, a brilliant, twenty-year-old musician from Detroit who had recently arrived in New York. In September, he had worked with pianist George Wallington in the Café Bohemia, which is where Miles probably heard him. In the recording studios, Miles's pianists had ranged from the powerfully rhythmic Horace Silver, to the flowing delicacy of Ray Bryant whose keyboard work

64

resembled that of the Swede, Bengt Hallberg. Both Bryant and Hallberg were, in fact, precursors of the Bill Evans style of piano playing which Miles would favour three years later. In the early autumn of 1955, Davis plumped for Red Garland who was more rhythmic than Bryant and more delicate than Silver.

At first, Miles wanted Sonny Rollins to join the group, and was actually quoted as saying: 'I want this group to sound the way Sonny plays, the way all of the men in it play – different from anybody else in jazz today.'[13] But Rollins, who was another heroin addict, had disappeared to Chicago in one of his attempts to kick the habit. Miles consulted the rest of his band, and they all recommended the tenor saxophonist, John Coltrane, who was living in Philadelphia, Philly Joe's hometown. The drummer had worked with Coltrane there, and recommended him strongly. Miles had met Trane a few years previously and knew something of his qualities. Coltrane joined the group but continued to live in Philadelphia.

Like Philly Joe, Coltrane had worked a great deal with rhythm and blues bands. During the forties, he'd played first with Eddie 'Cleanhead' Vinson, and then with Gillespie's big band, and when that broke up, with Dizzy's small group. After a period with Earl Bostic, he had joined Johnny Hodges, but had been fired for being a heroin addict. Back home in Philadelphia, he earned a living working with rhythm and blues bands such as Bull Moose Jackson, King Kolax, and Daisy Mae and the Hepcats. Coltrane was deeply frustrated and miserable. He and Rollins were close friends, and it was rumoured that Sonny deliberately stayed off the scene in order to give Coltrane a chance to get an outlet, some exposure, and some recognition. Trane was, at that time, almost completely unknown, whereas Rollins was already a cult figure with some LPs of his own, and the prospect of making more when he was ready.

So Miles Davis had formed a brand new quintet of virtually unknown musicians, and it was difficult to see how this unit was going to develop into anything extra-special. Coltrane, although the same age as Miles, was still an immature stylist; Red Garland, on the evidence of the quartet recording in June, seemed to be all surface and no depth; Philly Joe seemed to overpower everyone with his volcanic energy. The band did not fit the prevailing ideas of what a group should be, and complaints and criticism came from musicians who failed to see the potential of the group. Just as, ten years previously, musicians had failed to appreciate Thelonious Monk's qualities and had advised Coleman Hawkins to get rid of him when the pianist was with his group, so people asked Miles to get rid of Coltrane and Philly Joe. Miles commented: 'People used to tell me Trane couldn't play and Philly Joe played too loud. But I know what I want, and if I didn't think they knew what they were doing, they wouldn't be there.'[14]

Miles himself was artistically strong enough to impose his own identity on the band. Also, he was news after his success at Newport, so the quintet got bookings; it worked and drew audiences. At the beginning of October, Miles signed a contract guaranteeing him twenty weeks a year at Birdland. The first three engagements, of two weeks each, were 13 October, 24 November, and 19 January (1956). The new group also had engagements at the Sutherland Hotel, Chicago, in the autumn, and at the Café Bohemia late in the year. On 27 October, Miles recorded a couple of tracks ('Budo' and 'Ah-Leu-Cha') with the group for Columbia, and then on 16 November they went into the studio to make their first album for Prestige.

This first album, called simply *The New Miles Davis Quintet*, was a clear statement of Miles's basic musical intentions at the time. Of the six pieces recorded, four were standard song tunes, and two were original compositions – 'Miles' Theme' which is based on the 'I Got rhythm' sequence, and 'Stablemates', a theme written by saxophonist Benny Golson, who was a friend of Coltrane's. The only time trumpet and tenor state a theme together in unison and harmony is on 'Stablemates'. On 'Miles' Theme', they are in loosely improvised canon, and on the four standards Miles states the themes by himself, using the harmon mute and phrasing in his own inimitable way. In other words, on the four standards, the group is essentially a quartet but features saxophone solos by a fifth member. The format is therefore very loose. It is the other end of the spectrum entirely from his 1949 nine-piece band. With the quintet, the basic material is the tempo, the chord sequence, and the melody – if there is one. Now, with a regularly working group, the ensemble techniques and different approaches could be developed by the musicians.

Clark Terry, who spent several years with Duke Ellington's orchestra, has said that Ellington always wanted his music to be in a 'state of becoming', and this is a good description of Miles Davis's attitude to music. Something Sidney Bechet once said is also pertinent: 'Those Dixieland musicianers...they tried to write the music down and kind of freeze it...that's why they lost it. You can't keep the music unless you move with it.'[15] This looseness and movement were very evident in the quintet's first album, which served notice on the jazz world that there was a new bandleader and band in existence with a fresh sound and a fresh concept. The harmon mute – a totally new sound – dominated the album, ranging from the voluptuous tenderness of 'There Is No Greater Love', to the almost claustrophobic aggression of 'How Am I To Know' and 'S' posin''. Coltrane, too, immature though he may have been, produced some tumbling, impassioned solos which revealed a new tenor sound and the embryo of a new rhythmic feel. The rhythm section, driven along by Philly Joe, pivoting on the magnificently solid bass

66

of the young virtuoso, Paul Chambers, and filled out by the crisp chords of Red Garland, had already been drawn into focus by Miles's own playing. To quote Cecil Taylor on Miles's relation to his rhythm sections: 'His conception of time has led to greater rhythmic freedom for other players. His feeling, for another thing, is so intense that he catapults the drummer, bassist and pianist together, forcing them to play at the top of their technical ability and forcing them with his own emotional strength to be as emotional as possible.'[16]

Bird was gone, but Miles had arrived. The king was dead; long live the king.

6
Miles Ahead

'You add to playing your instrument the running of a
band and you got plenty problems.'[1]
Miles Davis

1956 was a year of prodigious activity for Miles Davis. During its
course, he recorded enough material for five and a half quintet
albums and was also featured soloist with a nineteen-piece brass
ensemble under the direction of Gunther Schuller. The reputation
of the quintet also grew steadily throughout the year, and there
were so many engagements that Coltrane found it impractical to
continue to live in Philadelphia and in June he and his family moved
to New York. Early in the year, the quintet played on the West
Coast, and from spring to late autumn appeared for much of the
time at the Café Bohemia in New York. In November, Miles spent a
few days on his own in Paris as soloist with a package show.

As Miles's popularity and fame increased with audiences and the
record-buying public, evidence of critical appreciation also began to
appear during the year. Two books were published, both of which
were written by Europeans, and both of which devoted long chapters
to Miles and his nine-piece band. *Modern Jazz* was by Alun Morgan
and Raymond Horricks, two Britishers; Morgan in particular had
shown himself to be an extremely sensitive and perceptive critic of
Miles's earlier work. The other book was by the French composer
and critic, André Hodeir, and was called, *Jazz: Its Evolution and
Essence*. Hodeir's book was universally acclaimed when it first
appeared, and has since become established as a classic of jazz
criticism. This sudden elevation in critical status, coming as it did,
hard on the heels of Miles's success at Newport and in the *Down
Beat* poll, was another piece of good fortune.

An aura of glamour was now beginning to surround Miles. His
first marriage had not weathered the strains of his drug addiction,
and although he kept in touch with his three children, he was
separated from his wife and would soon be divorced from her. He
was now enjoying a second lease of life as the young, good-looking
trumpeter-about-town with an eye for pretty girls. He kept himself

68

in peak physical shape by working out regularly in the gymnasium, and he was also mentally buoyant. All the other members of his quintet, however, were junkies at that time. Although he'd kicked the habit, Miles didn't develop a 'holier-than-thou' attitude, but was totally realistic about addiction. He told Nat Hentoff: 'I just tell them if they work for me to regulate their habit. When they're tired of the trouble it takes to support a habit, they'll stop if they have the strength.'[2] Despite all his work and the problems of running a band, Miles had energy for leisure and entertainment, and spent plenty of time at Maddison Square Garden or St Nick's in New York, watching boxing matches. He also found time during the year to change his record company.

The Prestige office was situated on Eighth Avenue, near Maddison Square Garden, and musicians would often call in at the office after going to a boxing match, and talk business. The relationship between the small, independent label and musicians was easy-going and informal. Weinstock was definitely performing an invaluable act of patronage in recording some of the most creative musicians at a time when no one else seemed interested in doing so. Some musicians called Prestige the 'junkies' jazz label, because addicted musicians who needed money for a fix could often walk in without making prior arrangements, record some tunes and get ready cash as soon as the session was over. It was probably this kind of happening which gave the 'blowing sessions' such currency, and made Prestige reluctant to pay for rehearsal time. Before the end of 1955, Miles was feeling thwarted and frustrated by the low-key, low-budget policy of Prestige. Weinstock valued Miles and the new quintet very highly, calling them 'the Louis Armstrong Hot Five of the modern era', and although he knew they were about to become economically very valuable, he still either would not or could not increase his financial investment in Miles. There were meetings between the two men, at this time, during which Miles would stare expressionlessly at Weinstock and Weinstock would sweetly stare back at Miles, and neither would exchange a word for a solid twenty minutes. It was for self-preservation and self-protection that the famous Miles Davis persona began to appear – the inscrutability, the unpredictability, the refusal to be pinned down, the sudden juxtapositions of gentleness and violence. Even his favourite musicians, like John Coltrane, would never know what he was thinking or what he was going to do next. Coltrane once said: 'After I joined Miles in 1955, I found that he doesn't talk much and will rarely discuss his music. He's completely unpredictable; sometimes he'd walk off stage after just playing a few notes, not even completing one chorus. If I asked him something about his music, I never knew how he was going to take it.'[3]

George Avakian, the producer in charge of jazz and pop albums for Columbia Records, had been at the Newport Festival, and had been greatly impressed by Miles's playing and by the reaction of audience and critics. After hearing the first Prestige album by the new quintet, Avakian was convinced that Columbia ought to sign Miles, and persuaded his superiors of this. He was authorized to approach Davis and offer him an advance of $4,000. This immediately eclipsed Miles's financial dealings with Prestige, and he was anxious to accept Columbia's offer, but his contract with Weinstock still had a year to run and he owed four more LPs. It was a very awkward situation which had to be handled carefully and subtly.

Miles was also keen to record for Columbia because they were not, like Prestige, a small independent label, but a wealthy international company who could afford massive promotion for their records and their artists. They had already signed Dave Brubeck, and his first album for them, *Jazz Goes to College*, had become the biggest selling LP in jazz history. Miles and Harold Lovett carried out delicate negotiations with Weinstock and Columbia, and it was ultimately agreed that the trumpeter could leave Prestige as soon as he had fulfilled his commitment for four more LPs. In addition, it was agreed that he could record for Columbia while the Prestige contract was still in force as long as the results were not released until the expiration date of that contract. This was a highly satisfactory outcome because no enemies were made, and while honouring his agreement with Weinstock, Miles could still pick up his advance from Columbia.

Once again, luck was on Miles's side, because the pressure to record enough material for five more albums that year came at exactly the right time. His new quintet was equal to the challenge, and far from there being a falling-off as the recording sessions proceed during the year, there is a notable rise in the creative power of the individuals and in the collective dynamism of the group. In March, Miles recorded three tracks – two blues and Brubeck's ballad 'In Your Own Sweet Way' – with a pick-up group comprising Sonny Rollins, pianist Tommy Flanagan, Paul Chambers, and drummer Art Taylor. After that event, all the other small group sessions were done with *the* quintet. To fulfil his Prestige contract, Miles simply took two days – 11 May and 26 October – and on each occasion, functioning as if the quintet were doing a session in a club, he recorded enough material for two LPs.

One of the basic truths of recording improvised music, Miles had learned from Parker, was that the most creative and dynamic solos usually occurred on the first takes, and so he always tried to capture that initial magic in the studio. J.J. Johnson has said: 'I've recorded with Miles and I know how he operates. Most of the time he goes into the studio and one take is it! Goofs or not, there's no second or third take. That's his philosophy on the recording bit.'[4] That was

70

certainly the philosophy behind the marathon sessions for Prestige which resulted in four classic LPs: *Cookin', Relaxin', Workin',* and *Steamin'.* The first two were from the October session, and the last two were made up mostly of tracks from the first session in May, so the four albums, containing some three hours of music, document marvellously the essence of the quintet in the earlier and later parts of that fateful year. They also showed that Miles Davis could achieve a miraculous duality: popularity with the general public and great critical acclaim.

One of the main reasons why the quintet's music reached a wider audience was that its repertoire consisted largely of the superior songs and ballads of the day, and their themes were usually played by Miles using the distinctive harmon mute. His muted sound was, by then, brilliantly evocative and expressive, which brought the quintet's performance very close to actual vocal music. The rest of the group's repertoire included one or two of Miles's tunes, the occasional theme by Parker or Gillespie, and a couple of Sonny Rollins compositions. For a person with Miles Davis's background and credentials, the introduction of the more popular material, and the way it was treated, was both surprising and exciting. But some of his fans were shocked at first by this development.

Gil Evans has pointed out: 'Miles is a leader in jazz because he has definite confidence in what he likes and he is not *afraid* of what he likes. A lot of other musicians are constantly looking around to hear what the next person is doing and worry about whether they themselves are in style. Miles has confidence in his own taste, and he goes his own way.'⁵ So just as Louis Armstrong had done, Miles chose to feature a high proportion of popular songs in his repertoire; and also like Louis, his interpretation of the themes, his sound and his phrasing were highly distinctive so that his own identity was always imposed on the material he used. Of all the trumpet players in jazz, Louis and Miles (the Miles of this period) are the most instantly recognizable. The way they played was very different, but their emotional power and the architectural beauty of their phrases had much in common. Miles was very aware of Louis's work and told Nat Hentoff: 'Louis has been through all kinds of styles...You know you can't play anything on a horn that Louis hasn't played – I mean even modern. I love his approach to the trumpet; he never sounds bad. He plays on the beat and you can't miss when you play on the beat – with feeling.'⁶

But the biggest single influence on the music of Miles's quintet was the pianist Ahmad Jamal, who was four years younger than Davis. Jamal was born in Pittsburgh in 1930, and in the late forties and early fifties worked with his trio at the Pershing Hotel in Chicago where he had a big reputation and was very popular locally. It was during this period that Miles frequently visited Chicago, often staying there for weeks or even months, and he liked Ahmad Jamal's trio so much that he took every available opportunity to hear them. Pittsburgh was also the birthplace of that other trio pianist, Erroll Garner, whose style fused the rhythmic directness of the older jazz tradition with the melodic and harmonic developments of modern jazz. Garner drew most of his material from popular songs and hits from musical shows, and was almost certainly an influence on Jamal. Count Basie's piano style was the other great influence on Jamal. Basie's understatement and his dramatic use of space are mirrored in Jamal's music, and it was these qualities, allied to the impeccable swing and varied pulse of the rhythm section of the latter's group, which attracted Miles. In a *Jazz Review* interview in the autumn of 1958, Davis stated: 'Listen to the way Jamal uses space. He lets it go so that you can feel the rhythm section and the rhythm section can feel you. It's not crowded ...Ahmad is one of my favourites. I live until he makes another record.'[7] Although Miles Davis's music has changed in later years, his regard for Ahmad Jamal seems to have remained constant. Even in the early 1970s, he was still taking people to listen to the Jamal trio.

Many of the tunes in Miles's book were songs which had been recorded by Frank Sinatra (Appendix B), and many others came straight out of Jamal's repertoire. Often only a month or two after Jamal had recorded a song, it would appear on a Miles Davis album. (See Appendix B for list of titles and comparative recording dates.) Almost all the jaunty, medium to fast standard tunes came from Jamal's book – 'But Not For Me', 'Gal in Calico', 'Surrey With The Fringe On Top', 'All Of You', 'Billy Boy', 'Squeeze Me', 'Will You Still Be Mine' – to name a few; and also the way his trio played them, his concept of performance, influenced Miles. The themes were played over a two-in-the-bar feel from the rhythm section. This means that while the bass plays two notes (minims) per bar, the drums play four beats but emphasize the second and fourth. This creates a deep, swaying pulse and tends to make the performance feel unhurried and spacious. Drama occurs when the bass switches to four notes to the bar, making the pulse shallower and more urgent. This two-beat feel has been called 'a kind of upside-down Dixieland', and it does hark back to the immediacy of earlier jazz forms. It is a 'catchy' rhythm. From Jamal also, Miles took the 'tag' endings to performances; after the theme had been played through for the final time, the rhythm section would repeat the last four bars of the harmonies over and over again until Miles, or whoever else was soloing, gave the cue for the ending. This minimized the harmonic interest and put the emphasis on rhythmic interplay.

The LP which Miles recorded with his quintet for Columbia during his Prestige period, was drawn from material done in three sessions;

one in October 1955, and the other two in June and September 1956. This album was given the title *Round About Midnight*. With this and the five Prestige LPS – all six albums being recorded in the twelve-month period running from October 1955 to October 1956 – the music of this magnificent quintet was fully documented. It is extremely unlikely that any other jazz artist has made so many albums of such high quality in so short a period of time. The rapport within the group was almost telepathic. Philly Joe Jones and Red Garland had played together a great deal in Philadelphia and had known Coltrane there. Miles's association with Philly Joe had also bred a deep mutual understanding. Ralph Gleason recounts: 'Philly Joe Jones...once remarked that his and Miles's minds were so attuned that he could go 'way out beyond easily countable time in a drum solo and come right back in with Miles, because each *knew* where the other was.'[8] Bassist, Paul Chambers, not only laid down a solid beat, but often simultaneously created counter melodies to the lines played by the soloist.

The personalities of the three main soloists were brilliantly complementary. Miles often left audacious gaps in his spare melodic lines. Coltrane was urgent, compulsive, blowing floods of notes as if he hadn't enough time to get in everything he had to say. Red Garland, with his smooth rhythms and sprightly single-line melodies or his suave block chords, brought a welcome relief from the intensity of the two horns. And for each of these three, the rhythmic section changed its character. Behind Miles, the drums were often compact and understated, the piano chords sparse, resulting in an unhurried, spacious atmosphere. When Coltrane soloed, the drums would broaden and intensify the beat – usually using the ride cymbal – the piano would intensify the rhythmic strength of the chords, and the bass would underpin the whole band with an even, flowing, unstoppable four crotchets to the bar. There would be disturbing polyrhythms under Coltrane's solo, and often a feeling of strife, as if his phrases were beating themselves into existence against the rhythm section. When Garland began his solo, suddenly the agitation would disappear and the tension would be released by the whole rhythm section playing as one man with an effortless impetus which reassured the listener and enabled him to bask in the normal joyous rhythm of jazz – except that, with this group it is supra-normal...a groove that bordered on ecstasy.

A perfect example of this whole process occurs in the performance of the standard, 'If I Were A Bell', on *Relaxin'*, which was recorded on 26 October 1956. Miles, using the harmon mute, plays the melody over a two-beat feel from the rhythm section, after which there is a driving four-in-the-bar feel and Davis solos with great power. The harmon sound intensifies the impact of the solos because the wild feeling seems bottled-in, which produces a claustrophobic, furiously contained effect. The tight rhythm section also contributes to this. Then, Coltrane enters and the whole climate changes; we are suddenly out in the open with his broad and bubbling sound and a looser feel from the rhythm section with plenty of polyrhythms. Trane's solo grips and disturbs with its pell-mell phrases and the very vocal 'cry' in his sound. Then, abruptly, it stops and after a piano break, Red Garland plays his solo over a smoothly riding pulse, with Philly Joe ticking off each bar with a snare drum rimshot on the fourth beat. Garland plays single note lines first, with flow and invention, and then his solo ends with some block chords. The very stylized nature of many of Garland's solos helps to provide the reassurance which makes these group perform-ances so satisfying and memorable.

Like Louis Armstrong's classic small-group recordings of the later 1920s, these performances of the Miles Davis Quintet are full of moments of genuine inspiration, full of surprises, full of collective and individual magic. The basic strength of the group comes from the dialogue between the powerfully active and extrovert rhythm section and the violent introversion of the two horns, which results in a profusion of ways of creating and releasing tension. From this latter point of view, the quintet's music vastly enriched the jazz vocabulary. The emotional range of the group is also extremely wide – wider than that of probably any other small-group in jazz before or since – ranging, as it does, from the unbounded joy of Red Garland's contributions (and some of Miles's on the up-tempo popular songs) to the complex sorrow of the trumpeter's ballad interpretations with the harmon mute. This aspect of Davis's work introduced a totally new element into jazz: the quality of profound, and sometimes almost painful, introspection.

These ballad performances were usually done by Miles with the rhythm section working as a quartet, and a perfect example of this is the October 1956 version of Richard Rodgers's ballad, 'My Funny Valentine' on *Cookin'*. After Garland's four-bar piano introduction, Miles plays one chorus, referring only briefly to the original melody, and creating tremendous tension by his tonal inflexions and his use of space – the pauses he leaves, the way he varies the length of his phrases, his use of long notes and his juxtaposition of upper and lower registers. Throughout, the bass improvises a brilliant coun-terline to the trumpet, though perhaps it would be more accurate to call this part of the performance a dialogue between trumpet and bass. The piano lays down the chords, and Philly Joe, using brushes, creates an unobtrusive background rhythm. The trumpet and bass dialogue builds to such intensity over the thirty-six bar chorus that Miles's solo spills over into the first two bars of the next chorus as the rhythm section, apparently responding to internal pressure, gathers itself and moves into a double-tempo feel. This time-change

74

dramatically releases the almost unbearable tension, and Red Garland's piano solo which follows is bright and jaunty all the way. Beneath it all, Paul Chambers' bass plays two beats to the bar thus preserving the slow ballad pulse, while occasionally varying his line superbly to imply the double tempo. At the end of the piano solo the performance reverts to its slower, darker atmosphere and Miles plays out the last twenty-four bars with taut phrases, cliff-hanging pauses, and an impassioned coda. Once again, Garland's piano solo is essential to the shape and meaning of the piece as a whole. It not only eases the tension, but also throws into even greater relief the starkly brooding quality of Miles's muted trumpet (Appendix A, Fig.4).

Although the five quintet albums on Prestige were to have a huge, world-wide influence on jazz, inspiring musicians of all nationalities, Miles's own fame was then much greater than that of his group. It was as a star soloist, and not as a bandleader, that he went to Europe one week after that last Prestige session. He was reluctant to leave his group behind, but had to accept the work that his burgeoning international reputation was bringing in. At the same time, the package tour reunited him with several friends and associates: The Modern Jazz Quartet (MJQ), Bud Powell, and Lester Young. The tour was a short one, comprising a couple of nights at the Salle Pleyel in Paris and one or two concerts in Amsterdam and Stockholm. In Paris, the MJQ played its own set, and then Miles, Lester Young and Bud Powell appeared with a French rhythm section. Accompanying Miles were pianist, Rene Urtreger, bassist Pierre Michelot, and drummer Christian Garros. Musicians on package tours rarely listen to one another's sets, but some observers in Paris noted that Miles stood in the wings listening attentively to Bud Powell and Lester Young.

After the first Paris concert, all the musicians went to the Club St Germain to relax, and there, one or two English writers and critics, including Alun Morgan, managed to talk to Miles Davis. He was affable and ready to talk about his past, his own music and that of other people, but he was abrupt, tending to finish a sentence and, having decided that that was the end of the conversation, to disappear without saying goodbye. He talked enthusiastically about the October session for Prestige and said that the band had behaved in the studio exactly as if it was in a club with an audience, and that all the tracks were first takes. When he was pressed to extend his stay in Europe and visit England, he told Alun Morgan: 'I've got to get home after this tour. I've got four guys depending on me back there. I've got the best rhythm section in the world right now. Philly Joe Jones is just great and you know that Coltrane is the best since Bird.'[9]

And yet, back in New York later that month, Miles had both Coltrane *and* Sonny Rollins with his group at the Café Bohemia, and before the end of November Coltrane had left the band. The exact reasons for this sudden departure are not known, but one Michael Harper has speculated: 'Miles is more paradoxical than any musician I ever knew, even Coltrane. I heard he gave Trane an ultimatum to stop drinking and taking drugs or get out of the band. I think that for some unknown reason, Coltrane was really bored with the music and in effect engineered his own discharge. I also think Miles let him go in the hope that Trane would straighten himself out and come back after he was clean.'[10] By the time he left the Miles Davis quintet in 1956, Coltrane's addictions were so far advanced that he was tending to fall asleep when he was not actually playing, and he was also becoming inefficient and unreliable. Miles may have tried to jolt the saxophonist from time to time to sting him into revolting against the inexorable progress of his destructive habit. Thelonious Monk, who went backstage at the Bohemia to say hello to the group, witnessed Miles slap Coltrane's face and punch him in the stomach. The saxophonist was so meek and humble that there was no glimmer of revolt or anger. Monk is reported to have said to Trane: 'As much saxophone as you play, you don't have to take that. Why don't you come to work for me?'[11] So Coltrane went back to his mother's home in Philadelphia where, in the spring of 1957 he too managed to kick the habit cold turkey. He was out of Miles's band for almost exactly one year, rejoining it in late 1957 on a rather more equal basis with the trumpeter.

After Coltrane left the group, Miles continued working for some time with Sonny Rollins on saxophone, but in the spring of 1957, the quintet disbanded altogether. Miles's recorded output had been prolific, and the development of his group from its shaky origins in the quartet recordings of June 1955 to the classic quintet albums of 1956 had been meteoric. It was time to step back and put some kind of perspective on the situation. In March 1957, Leonard Feather wrote in the *Melody Maker:*

> Miles Davis said in Chicago that he will pack away his horn as an active performer in the jazz world at the end of his current engagement in the Windy City's Modern Jazz Room. Now thirty years old, Miles started playing professionally when he was thirteen for $3 a week, and his combo now earns $700 a night. 'I've had it', he told reporters. 'This is no sudden decision. I've been thinking about it for a long time, and after I close here I'm calling it quits.' He said he had no immediate plans but revealed that he had a record company offer for $200 a week as musical director, and another offer of a teaching post.[12]

The intense pace of the previous eighteen months had exhausted Miles, making him yearn for repose, change, and fresh musical areas to explore. Also, one event in the previous year had made a deep impression on him; the October recording sessions with the nineteen-piece Brass Ensemble of the Jazz and Classical Music Society. Gunther Schuller, who had played French horn on *The Birth of the Cool*, was the director of this ensemble which recorded pieces composed and arranged by J.J. Johnson, John Lewis, and the reed player Jimmy Guiffre. The album, which Schuller had conducted, was done for Columbia, Miles's new record company. Playing the flugelhorn solos with this brass ensemble had revived Miles's interest in working with orchestral scores, and his thoughts turned once more to his old friend, Gil Evans. Prestige could not have borne the financial burden of such an ambitious project, but Columbia could afford such things. It was time to establish the kind of relationship he wanted with his new company, and history was about to repeat, and improve, itself in a way that was almost uncanny.

During the forties, after spending about eighteen months with Parker's quintet playing regularly in clubs and recording frequently, Miles had signed with Capitol, a major record company, and produced the formally composed nonet performances. Now, after about eighteen months of intense recording and gigging with his own quintet, he had signed with Columbia, another major company, and was about to produce more formally conceived and composed music. Miles's quintet, of course, functioned in a largely intuitive way, and like Parker, Davis was reluctant to verbalize or talk about his music with the members of his group. A jazz musician's most precious gift is his intuition, and however conscious and verbalized his ideas become, the essential non-verbal faculty must be preserved.

The aspirations of the western intellectual have rarely been expressed more succinctly than in André Malraux's phrase: 'Converting as wide a range of experience as possible...into conscious thought.'[13] In music this would mean, of course, to write it down, to 'kind of freeze it', to quote Bechet again, and that is why in western music the composer rather than the player or the improvising composer, is regarded so highly. This process of analysis and committal to paper of ideas has become so entrenched, that sometimes the score or blueprint of contemporary 'straight' works seems to be valued more highly than the music it represents. The instincts of most jazz musicians are opposed to this trend and, for example, John Lewis, who understands both cultures, has said: 'We have to keep going back to the goldmine. I mean the folk music, the blues and things that are related to it. Even things that may not have been folk to start with but have become kind of folk-like...Like some of Gershwin's music and James P. Johnson's.'[14] And Miles Davis, who was also aware of this, but who felt the need for some more formal musical setting than that of his freely improvising quintet, had found his ideal associate in Gil Evans. Talking of their relationship

77

Miles said, some years later: 'Now I've learned enough about writing *not* to write. I just let Gil write. I give him an outline of what I want and he finishes it. I can even call him on the phone and just tell him what I've got in mind, and when I see the score, it's exactly what I wanted. Nobody but Gil could think for me in that way...Gil is always listening to gypsy, South American and African things. Every time he comes to my house he's got some new record for me.'[15]

Miles Davis and Gil Evans could, therefore, talk about and analyse music on an intellectual level without in any way destroying their intuitive faculties, which is one reason why their collaboration has resulted in such powerful and lasting music. During the seven years which lay between *The Birth of the Cool* recordings, and his 1957 collaboration with Miles Davis on *Miles Ahead,* Evans had worked fitfully as a freelance arranger in New York, but he had also spent much time reading musical history, biographies of composers and music criticism. He had also listened to a great deal of recorded music. He was filling in 'the gaps in my musical development',[16] as he termed it, because as an auto-didact he had missed out on certain things. Like Miles, he was also a late developer, and at that time, in his middle forties, was at last arriving at his first real maturity. His relationship with Miles, renewed in early 1957, was to become symbiotic. He was to give Miles context, structures, new sounds; Miles provided Evans with the motive, the incentive he needed to emerge from his state of almost mystical contemplation which was leavened now and then with journeyman musical writing. In Miles, also, Evans had a soloist of great stature and with a mind which complemented his own. He also had the support of Columbia Records who were rich enough to finance the recording of a large ensemble.

Miles Ahead was in every way a total collaboration between Miles Davis and Gil Evans, and its sustained quality is a direct result of this. The soloist not only understood the score, but had helped to arrive at its shape and atmosphere; the composer not only understood the soloist, but knew intuitively how to create contexts which enhanced the elements of his style. For this recording, Miles used the flugelhorn which increased the lyrical, singing characteristics of his playing, but expunged the bite and attack which gave his trumpet solos an extra dimension. His approach on *Miles Ahead* is softer and more delicate, and the album is pervaded by Miles's intimate self-communing which generates an atmosphere of urbane melancholy. Even the perky lines he improvises on Ahmad Jamal's tune, 'New Rhumba', and the cheeky humour of his playing on 'I Don't Wanna Be Kissed', have a wistful edge.

The orchestra, scored for and conducted by Evans, was an expanded version of the earlier nonet. Apart from Miles's flugelhorn,

78

the instrumentation included five trumpets, three tenor trombones, bass trombone, three French horns, tuba, alto saxophone, bass clarinet, three flutes doubling clarinets, bass and drums. The way Evans doubled up and strengthened highly mobile bass lines was to have a deep influence on Miles's later small-group work. On 'Blues for Pablo', there is a marvellous integration of lower and higher instruments, and the bass line is doubled up in some passages by bass clarinet and bass trombone, while the performance alternates fluidly between the slow pulse and the double-tempo feel. The whole context, with its incessant movement and shifting textures, inspires Miles to play with an intensity which matches his small-group work. Evans's superb recomposition of the Delibes piece, 'Maids of Cadiz', also results in a Davis solo of exceptional quality. Miles's great sensitivity is very noticeable in the different ways he responds to the various contexts Evans creates for him. Gil Evans's extra studies in the early fifties had brought spectacular results, and Max Harrison, the extremely perceptive British critic, pointed out that Evans could now handle the orchestra with a freedom and plasticity that have been surpassed only in a very few works such as Stockhausen's 'Gruppen fur drei Orchester'. Other critics, too, noted the variety and originality of the instrumental combinations Evans discovered. Max Harrison also pointed out that Evans's 'endless mixtures of sound...are new not only to jazz writing but to all orchestral music'.[17] One of the reasons for this is that Evans was using and balancing in the studio instrumental combinations which were not self-balancing acoustically.

Miles Ahead received a flood of enthusiastic reviews. Even the *New York Times* critic, John S. Wilson, who had been so impervious to Miles's small-group work ('the limp whimpering and fumbling uncertainty that have marked much of his work with small groups have smacked more of inarticulateness than of art'[18]), was pleasantly surprised: 'a promising but hitherto diffused talent suddenly takes a turn that brings it sharply into focus...There are times when Mr Evans seems to move out of the proper realm of jazz but, in or out, he has created an album that bubbles with fresh imaginative music'.[19] Even Max Harrison did not seem to grasp the fact that, so far as Miles's small-group work was concerned, a very different aesthetic was involved. He wrote: 'The bulk of the Prestige solos are but faulty images of the thing perfectly realised in collaboration with Gil Evans, yet so much praise was given to them that when Davis did make a great record there was nothing new left to be said...his unprecedented work on *Miles Ahead*, an expression of everything towards which he had been working for so long'.[20] But the mainspring of the small-group performances is the improvisation and interplay between the musicians. The form is created as a by-product of the very different character of the three main soloists, and the

79

performances are not inferior to, nor better than, *Miles Ahead*. They are simply different.

Since Miles Davis had begun his 'comeback' in 1954, his albums had astonished musicians and enthusiasts alike with their fresh sound and the new aesthetic criteria they posited. Each new release often came as a shock, and to date, *Miles Ahead* had certainly produced the biggest ripple of interest. Dizzy Gillespie was so taken with it that he wore out his copy in two weeks and then went round to Miles and asked for another one. Columbia got so excited about it that they released 'Blues For Pablo' and 'The Maids of Cadiz' as a single on 45RPM. But it was the album as a whole which provided the sort of revelatory shock which people began to expect from new Miles Davis releases. It was conceived as a unity, and the ten performances were linked together by organic bridge passages so that they seemed to be umbilically connected. These passages were also edited skilfully to create continuity between tracks from different recording dates. And on *Miles Ahead* the technique of splicing from different takes of the same piece was used for the first time in Miles Davis's recording career. Apart from these technical and structural innovations, the whole concept of a concerto setting for one improvising soloist, sustained and developed throughout a long-playing record, was a completely fresh one. It was also the first time that the flugelhorn had been played with this kind of expressivity and gentle lyricism. Once again, Miles had introduced a new instrumental sound to jazz, and once again, a host of imitators began playing the flugelhorn; from the relative obscurity of brass bands, it suddenly became one of the most fashionable instruments in studios, in concert halls, and in jazz groups. While it was the perfect instrument for *Miles Ahead*, its smooth urbanity was not entirely satisfying to Miles, and he was never again to use it exclusively on an LP. He needed that other dimension: the unbridled bite of his open trumpet, and the intense timbre of the harmon mute.

Miles Ahead was recorded in May 1957, and released the following autumn. It established Miles's talent and position in jazz; his small group was the pace-setter with a rapidly growing world audience, and his orchestral collaboration with Gil Evans had taken him (and Gil) literally 'miles ahead' of everyone. New standards of excellence had been established in both categories. The question was, where to go after that? Meanwhile the Miles Davis legend was growing. Everything he touched seemed to turn to musical gold. He was living in a West-side apartment in New York which seemed to be always buzzing with visitors – friends and sidemen – with a TV set which was perpetually on. He was pursuing his non-musical interests: sparring in the gym, photography, and fast cars. He was buying more clothes, dressing more sharply, and acquiring expensive furniture for his apartment. He was, at thirty-one, perhaps one of the most eligible men in New York.

With the orchestral album under his belt and the small group disbanded, Miles took the opportunity in the summer of 1957, to undergo
minor surgery. The previous year, he had started to suffer from nodes
(a benign corn or polyp) on the vocal chords. This made his voice very
hoarse, and his eerie, husky whisper can be heard between some of the
tracks on the Prestige albums. It was quite unlike the ringing Ivy
League tones in which he had introduced 'Embraceable You' at the
Paris Jazz Fair in 1949, and this present Armstrong-like 'gravel' voice
was an embarrassment to Miles. The operation to remove the nodes
from his vocal chords resulted in one of the most often-quoted
anecdotes about him. He was told not to raise his voice for at least
ten days after the operation, but the second day after he'd left
hospital, he met an entrepreneur who 'tried to convince me to go
into a deal that I didn't want', to quote Miles's own words. The fiery
Miles Davis temperament showed itself and he shouted in exasper-
ation, permanently damaging his vocal chords – or so it seemed.
The hoarseness has remained ever since. Whether this story is true,
or whether the nodes simply returned, may never be known, but in
April 1975, according to Clark Terry, Miles had thirteen more
nodes removed from his vocal chords.

7
The First Great Sextet

'I don't buy polish…Polished Negroes are acting the way
they think white people want them to act, so they can be
accepted.'[1]
Miles Davis

From the autumn of 1957, there began for Miles Davis a period of
popularity in America and Europe which was accompanied by
universal critical acclaim and even greater artistic achievements.
After winning the *Down Beat* readers' poll in 1955, Miles had come
second to Dizzy Gillespie in 1956. But in 1957, he was back in first
place, and in the following two or three years he also captured every
coveted award in the USA and Europe: in America, the *Metronome*
and *Playboy* polls; and in Europe, polls in Holland's *Muziek Espress*,
Hamburg's *Jazz Echo*, Paris's *Jazz Hot*, and London's *Melody
Maker*. Also, *Miles Ahead* was awarded France's 'L'Oscar du Disque
de l'Academie du Jazz', which was the equivalent of the American
Grammy award. Although all this recognition must have been very
gratifying for Miles, he kept a fairly clear perspective, commenting
drily: 'I love wood. That's why I hang up those *Down Beat* plaques I
win. Otherwise, winning a poll doesn't mean anything to me. Look
at who some of the other poll winners are.'[2] It became impossible to
ignore Miles Davis. Up to this point he had been written about
mostly in jazz magazines, with occasional reviews in the music
columns of one or two dailies. In January 1958, however, he emerged
from the underground cult level when there was a photograph and a
feature on him in *Time* magazine. This gave a potted history of his
career, contained the usual romantic ideas about artists ('often lies
awake nights rehearsing new arrangements in his head'), and let
everyone know about his international reputation ('In Europe he is
perhaps the most widely imitated modern US jazzman'.)[3]

Equally suddenly, Miles was elevated from being merely a great
trumpet player and jazz musician, to being a representative of the
black race. Seven months after the *Time* article, he was listed in *Life
International* as one of the fourteen black people who 'have contributed significantly to the fields of science, law, business, sports,
entertainment, art, literature and the preservation of peace among

82

men',[4] including Miles Davis in this group of people whom they termed: 'Outstanding men of the Negro race [who] have in many areas of human achievement reached a stature that can only be defined as greatness'. Miles's typically truculent comment was: 'Why didn't they put me in the domestic edition if they believed it?' And it does seem that it was his prestige abroad which lay behind this recognition in his mother-country. *Life International* included a photograph of Miles with the caption: 'The man of the moment in US jazz is a "cool" trumpet player, Miles Davis, who has been foremost in creating the craze for the small band and more melodic "chamber" jazz. Although trained in the "bop" tradition, Davis moved musically to a muted horn style that has made him widely imitated at home and abroad.'

Miles's popularity and prestige coincided with, and of course, contributed to, a general increased awareness of jazz on the national and international level. By 1957, there were glimmerings of academic recognition for jazz in the USA, and Brandeis University inaugurated a programme of commissioning jazz and jazz-oriented compositions. The first commissions, each of $350, were awarded to Jimmy Giuffre, Charlie Mingus, George Russell, Milton Babbitt, Gunther Schuller and Harold Shapero. Also, Schuller and John Lewis collaborated to promote the idea of Third-stream music which purported to fuse European compositional techniques with jazz elements. But Miles Davis's experiences with the Brass Ensemble, run by Lewis and Schuller, had merely prompted him to look for other solutions to the problem of musical development and to work with Gil Evans. Sometime later he commented: 'Somebody came to me... and asked me to play with that orchestra that Gunther and John have been working with. What do they call it? Orchestra USA? Anyway, I just told him, "Get outa here!"'[5] And at the other end of the spectrum from Third-stream, was the 'funk' trend in which non-western elements were exploited, often very uncreatively, by musicians who reduced vocalized tone sometimes to the level of caricature, and concentrated on a kind of ethnic cliché and the indiscriminate use of blues 'licks'. The really creative exponents of this approach were Miles's old associates Horace Silver and the drummer, Art Blakey. Miles himself, whose 1954 recording of 'Walkin'', had triggered off the renewed interest in ethnic roots which resulted in funky jazz, was always too vital to be identified with the mere mannerisms of any trend. And finally, by 1957, while most jazz musicians were still eking out a very precarious existence, for a few there were rich rewards: Brubeck and Garner could earn $3,000 per week in clubs, and up to $2,500 for a concert, and even a sideman could earn up to $20,000 a year. While the average jazz album sold fewer than 5,000 copies, the best sellers sold from 30,000 to 50,000. Jazz had become big business in America for the first time since the 1930s.

In this burgeoning economic climate, when Miles Davis was able to command the highest fees of his career to date, he chose not to work for over three months in the summer of 1957. This hiatus seems to have happened because he was artistically in limbo. When he disbanded his quintet in March, it was certainly in order to concentrate on preparing *Miles Ahead*. He and Gil Evans finished the recording sessions (but not the mixing and editing) for it by the end of May, and Miles then had a fallow period lasting until September. During this time he had throat surgery, and took stock of his general situation. There can be no doubt that he was somehow unsure of what to do next. When he did decide that he wanted to form a quintet again in the autumn of 1957, none of the original members was available.

At first, Miles used the drummer Art Taylor, who had played on *Miles Ahead*, pianist Tommy Flanagan, and the Belgian tenor saxophonist, Bobby Jasper, who had immigrated to the States the previous year. Jasper soon left, and Miles, who was looking once again for the kind of group balance he'd had with Parker and Coltrane – powerful, multi-noted saxophone and understated trumpet – managed to persuade alto saxophonist, Julian 'Cannonball' Adderley to join him. Adderley had been leading a quintet with his brother Nat on trumpet, but had found the economics of running a group very daunting. He said:

> Nobody was really making it except for Miles, Chico [Hamilton] and Brubeck. I had gotten an offer from Dizzy to go with his small band. I was opposite Miles at the Bohemia, told him I was going to join Dizzy, and Miles asked me why I didn't join him. I told him he'd never asked me...Well, Miles kept talking to me for two or three months to come with him, and when I finally decided to cut loose in October 1957, I joined Miles. I figured I could learn more than with Dizzy. Not that Dizzy isn't a good teacher, but he played more commercially than Miles. Thank goodness I made the move I did.[6]

Cannonball was to stay with Miles until September 1959, and also helped with the organization of the group, collecting money and paying the musicians. The saxophonist had iron self-control and a genial disposition. He never, for example, touched drugs, and his reliability gave Miles a solid moral (as well as musical) support. The relationship blossomed into a friendship which ended only with Cannonball's untimely death in 1975.

Miles's visits to Paris in 1949, and in 1956 with the package tour, had brought him a fairly big following in France. In 1957, he was still much more famous than the other members of his group, and so when he got an offer to go on his own to Paris towards the end of

November, he accepted it. The plan was for him to work with a group comprising Kenny Clarke who was now resident in Paris, and the French musicians Pierre Michelot (bass), Rene Urtreger (piano) and Barney Wilen (tenor sax). They were booked to play a concert at the Olympia Theatre followed by three weeks at the Club St Germain. At this time, the trombonist and ex-associate of Miles's, Mike Zwerin, was staying in Paris, and he describes the atmosphere of that first theatre concert:

> It was 1957, and Miles was the big man – his clothes, his girls, his new loose rhythm section, his fresh open playing. So all of us who hung out at the Old Navy (café) were excited about Miles's arrival in Paris...The Olympia Theatre was sold out that night, but by curtain time Miles's whereabouts were still a mystery. Finally, the curtain went up, revealing Barney Wilen, Rene Urtreger, Pierre Michelot, and Kenny Clarke all set up. They started playing 'Walkin'' and sounded fine. But no Miles Davis. Barney took a tenor solo, and as he was finishing, backing away from the micro-phone, Miles appeared from the wings and arrived at the mike without breaking his stride, just in time to start playing – strong. It was an entrance worthy of Nijinsky. If his choreography was good, his playing was perfect that night. He had recently made his 'comeback' and was really putting the pots on. He was serious, and he was trying hard instead of just catting...For the first week of his stay at the Club, as we called the St Germain, I was down there almost every night.[7]

Miles Davis's only other recording that year took place in Paris and was the opposite in every way of *Miles Ahead*. The latter was scored, premeditated, exquisitely realized. But his background music for Louis Malle's film *L'Ascenseur pour L'Echafaud*, recorded in December 1957, happened almost by accident, and was totally improvised by a small group. The results, far from being a finished masterpiece, were in fact like sketches and notes for some bigger work. And in a sense, that is exactly what they were, because they pointed to a completely new direction, opening up avenues of exploration which seemed to offer inexhaustible possibilities for improvisation.

Louis Malle was an avid Miles Davis fan, and when he heard Miles was coming to Paris to play at the Club St Germain, he met the trumpeter at the airport and asked him to play the background music for the film. Miles agreed to try. *Lift to the Scaffold* (American title: *Elevator to the Gallows*) was a thriller with Jeanne Moreau as the main star, and although the story line was fairly banal – a murder is committed and the killer gets stuck in a lift on the way out of the building where he committed the crime – the atmosphere is height-ened by the brilliant use of contemporary locations: buildings, motels, lifts, limousines, powerful mechanisms created by man but which end up suffocating him.

Using the group which was working with him at the Club St Germain, Miles improvised the music in a studio, watching shots from the film and conferring with Malle. The entire music was realized one December night between midnight and morning, and although the resulting ten short pieces are really no more than fragments, they afford several insights into Miles's development. For perhaps the first time, it became clear to him that it was possible to create absorbing music with neither formally written themes nor any real harmonic movement. The tracks were at first released in France on a ten-inch LP, and later in America on one side of a twelve- inch LP, and this was the first time that Miles's own composing had filled up so much space on an album. The music had grown out of minimal predetermined material, each track having a tempo, a tonal centre, and perhaps one or two other factors, and yet it had a complete identity; it was very much Miles's music, and quite different from anyone else's. Several of the tracks have a strong modal flavour, hovering ambiguously around D minor and F. Miles probably felt free to experiment so audaciously because he was producing applied music intended to point the action and atmosphere of a film.

The music also threw into new relief the two polarities which were noticed first in Charlie Parker, and which gradually became more obvious in Miles's work: the quiet, brooding aspect on the one hand, and the furious aggression on the other. The only two fast pieces ('Sur L'Autoroute' and 'Dîner au Motel'), feature his aggressive playing, and for both he uses the harmon mute which buzzes furiously up and down like a fly on a window pane, producing the claustrophobic, bottled-in rage which mirrors brilliantly the action of the film. On the medium and slow tracks, the tonal beauty of the open horn and the extreme spareness of the phrases give an unearthly beauty to this reflective music. On the final piece, 'Chez Le Photographe du Motel', Miles plays the first half with open horn, and then towards the end puts in the harmon mute and the music concludes with a magnificent repeated and sustained high A (G concert) with the legato phrases leading to it also being repeated, until the legato figures at last descend and the sustained note is played down the octave. (Appendix A, Fig. 5b) Louis Malle commented: 'I must say that in the last sequence of *Scaffold* Miles's commentary – which is of extreme simplicity – gives a really extraordinary dimension to the visual image.'[8] And Jean-Louis Ginibre, writing in *Jazz Magazine*, commented:

Ascenseur pour L'Echafaud would have remained a relatively minor film without the music of Miles Davis...[he] knew how to give tragic dimensions to this banal enough drama, and I think

86

that Miles, in helping Louis Malle's film also raised himself to greater heights, and became aware of the tragic character of his music which, until then, had been only dimly expressed. In this sense, *Scaffold*...marks a decisive turning point in the work of Miles Davis.[9]

A year or two later, Miles told Louis Malle that the experience of making the music for the film had enriched him.

Back in New York at the end of the year, Miles found himself once more without a band, but with some new musical ideas, and he began trying to coax back Coltrane, Red Garland and Philly Joe Jones. If the year had been crucial for Miles, it had been even more important for Coltrane. During it, he had freed himself from drug addiction, and finished his musical apprenticeship by spending several months with Thelonious Monk at the Five Spot, and learning and playing Monk's pieces. Coltrane describes this process:

> I'd go by his house and get him out of bed. He'd get up and go over to the piano and start playing. He'd play one of his tunes and he'd look at me. So I'd get my horn out and start trying to find what he was playing. We'd go over and over the thing until we had most of it worked out. If there were any parts that I had a lot of difficulty with he'd get his portfolio out and show me the thing written out. He would rather a guy would learn without reading because you feel it better and quicker that way. Sometimes we'd get just one tune a day.[10]

Twelve years previously, Monk had used the same methods when he was giving lessons to the nineteen-year-old Miles Davis.

The quartet which Monk led at the Five Spot throughout the summer of 1957 became a legendary unit, and among the many visitors was Miles Davis who could witness everything he'd suspected about Trane coming true – 'the best since Bird' – so he asked Coltrane to rejoin him, and the saxophonist accepted immediately. By this time, Miles's groups were the most prestigious in jazz, and Coltrane could be sure of wide exposure and good money. He would also have plenty of freedom to develop his ideas. From his short-lived group of the previous autumn, Miles kept on Cannonball Adderley, and from the original quintet, he succeeded in persuading Paul Chambers, Red Garland and Philly Joe Jones to rejoin him. The group was now a sextet, and with the bigger line-up came a very different musical climate. Coltrane has said:

> On returning...I found Miles in the midst of another stage of his musical development. There was one time in his past that he devoted to multi-chorded structures. He was interested in chords for their own sake. But now it seemed that he was moving in the opposite direction to the use of fewer and fewer chord changes in

87

songs. He used tunes with free-flowing lines and chordal directions. This approach allowed the soloist the choice of playing chordally [vertically] or melodically [horizontally]. In fact, due to the direct and free-flowing lines in his music, I found it easy to apply the harmonic ideas that I had. I could stack up chords – say, on a C 7, I sometimes superimposed an E flat 7, up to an F sharp 7, down to an F. That way I could play three chords on one. Miles's music gave me plenty of freedom. It's a beautiful approach.[11]

Cannonball Adderley's alto saxophone sound was very full, his technique – his speed – was brilliant, and his phrases were shot through with the inflexions of the blues. Like Coltrane, he learned a great deal from observing and listening to Miles:

> I was with Miles from October 1957 to September 1959. Musically, I learned a lot while with him. About spacing, for one thing, when playing solos. Also, he's a master of understatement. And he taught me more about the chords, as Coltrane did too. Coltrane knows more about chords than anyone...From a leader's viewpoint, I learned by watching Miles, how to bring new material into a band without changing the style of the band. And when it was necessary at times to change the style somewhat, Miles did it so subtly so that no one knew it. As for rehearsals, we had maybe five in the two years I was there, two of them when I first joined the band. And the rehearsals were quite direct, like, 'Coltrane, show Cannonball how you do this. All right, now let's do it.' Occasionally, Miles would tell us something on the stand. 'Cannonball, you don't have to play *all* those notes. Just stay close to the sound of the melody. Those substitute chords sound funny'...I certainly picked up much advantage as a potential leader from the exposure of being with Miles...He *would* tell us to leave the stand if we had nothing to do up there.[12]

Musically, and in human terms, this period with the sextet seems to have been an exceptionally happy one for Miles Davis. He obviously loved the two saxophonists both as musicians and as people. In March 1958, he paid Cannonball a great compliment by agreeing to appear as a sideman on the saxophonist's own album, *Somethin' Else*. Not surprisingly, Miles dominates the album musically, soloing with more aggression and power than was usual at that time. Also, the general method of Adderley's quintet, which included Hank Jones (piano), Sam Jones (bass) and Art Blakey (drums), was exactly like that of Miles's middle-fifties quintet. And in June that same year, Miles appeared for the last time as a sideman on someone else's album. *Legrand Jazz* was made by a ten-piece group which included Miles and Trane, and featured arrangements by the French composer Michel Legrand. Miles soloed on Fats Waller's 'Jitterbug

88

Waltz', 'Wild Man Blues' (composed by Louis Armstrong and Jelly Roll Morton), 'Round Midnight' (Monk) and John Lewis's 'Django'. Coltrane, despite the acclaim he was getting from musicians, had still not acquired the same kind of confidence as Miles, and when his turn came to play a solo, he asked Legrand how he wanted the solo played. He was told, naturally, to play it the way he felt it. It was this lack of confidence which kept Coltrane a sideman in Miles's band, and it would take him another eighteen months to build up enough self-assurance to leave and form his own groups.

After *Legrand Jazz*, Miles's days as a sideman were over. People were begining to realize that his attitude to music was unlike that of anyone else in jazz. He told Nat Hentoff: 'I never work steady. I work enough to do what I want to do. I play music more for pleasure than for work.'[13] This method of working, with frequent rest periods, served two main purposes. Firstly, the music was always fresh and rarely suffered from the staleness which is induced by uninterrupted strings of dates; and secondly, it enabled him to avoid the over-exposure that may well have accompanied the group's popularity. He was well aware of the importance of scarcity-value.

As he became more successful both artistically and financially, Miles was concerned to maintain control over his own affairs. In particular, he wanted to be free of the usual pressures of the music business. Hentoff tells one typical story:

> When a poweful entrepreneur once asked Miles to let a protégé sit in with his combo while Miles was working at his club, Miles refused. The potentate, paternalistically amiable only so long as his demands were being met, threatened Davis: 'You want to work here?' Miles said with literally obscene gusto that he didn't care and told the man he was going home. The club owner tried to smooth over the hassle, and asked Miles to return to the stand. Later that night, however, the protégé nonetheless was sent up to the band. Miles and his men walked off.[14]

By now, however, Miles Davis had surrounded himself with a team of people whom he coached to look after his interests. There was his personal manager, Harold Lovett, there was Jack Whittemore of the Shaw Artists Corporation who booked his work, and there was Columbia Records. Whittemore tried to arrange a work schedule that gave Miles long periods at home to recharge his batteries. He also tried to get the maximum fees for Miles's dates, and the trumpeter took a hand in the negotiations if things were difficult. At this time, Miles was doing one-show concerts for $1,000, and he was offered a Town Hall contract for two performances on the same night. Whittemore told Davis that he might be able to get the price up to $1,500 for the two shows. Miles then said: 'I'll take $1,000 for the first show and $500 for the second, but you tell the promoter to rope off half the house for the second show and sell tickets for just the half that's left.'[15] Miles received $2,000 for the two performances.

On some occasions, Miles even had to resort to fisticuffs to protect himself. One night during a package tour run by jazz promoter, Don Friedman, Davis arrived late for a concert in Chicago – although still long before he was scheduled to perform. Friedman came up to him announcing that he was going to fine Miles $100 for being late. It was at that point that Friedman, to coin Sinatra's phrase, 'became punched'. When a reporter asked Davis why he'd done it, Miles said only, 'I should have hit him in Detroit yet.'[16] Don Friedman tells a slightly different story: 'I once went two rounds with Miles Davis in 1959. We fought, and it was about even, then Cannonball Adderley pulled us apart. I turned away and Miles hit me – knocked me out. I couldn't go home for a week because I didn't want my wife to see what my face looked like. But Miles couldn't play for a week either!'

The novelist James Baldwin's description of Miles as a 'miraculously tough and tender man' begins to make sense when examined in the light of his survival in this artistic, social and economic climate. Miles Davis was well aware that his reputation for fireworks, his unpredictable behaviour, allied to the trappings of success – flashy cars, expensive clothes, etc. – made him seem a mysterious and glamorous figure. In the late fifties, he once remarked innocently: 'They say people come to see me just because they've heard I'm so bad. Ain't that a bitch!'[17] He had never forgotten that many people went to see Charlie Parker for the same reason. This is not to say that the whole of Miles Davis's behaviour was a calculated pose culled from Parker; it was a much deeper phenomenon than that. Harold Lovett, for example, who must have been closer to Miles than most people were, was totally fascinated by him even to the extent of aping his dress and mannerisms. The bonds that made Lovett a fanatical protector of Miles's interests were far deeper than those between a mere manager and his star. Lovett was playing John the Baptist to Miles's Jesus. He expounded, preached, cajoled and fought for Miles and his music. He even attempted to describe the Davis charisma: 'Miles is just a brand new Negro in his thinking. He knows what he wants and is getting it. He has prepared himself for it. He can direct his group from off-stage with his presence. He can go to the dressing-room and they know he's listening. He's as much a composer as he is a bandleader and he doesn't write anything down. His group rehearses on the date and musically it's as well organized as the Modern Jazz Quartet. It isn't luck with Miles, it's training.'[18]

As if to prove the potency of his presence even in absentia, on the first album with the new sextet, Miles didn't play at all on one track, and on a second track, he played no solo. The album was called

Milestones, and it showed several changes in Miles's thinking. It was recorded on two consecutive days in April 1958, and this was the first small-group album he'd made for some sixteen months. The first striking change is that there are no standard tunes on it. In fact, the nearest thing to a standard is the old folk song, 'Billy Boy', which is a feature for the rhythm section only. It had been recorded by Ahmad Jamal a few years previously, and Red Garland's version faithfully follows Jamal's. The other pieces on the album are all composed by Miles or by friends of his. There are *three* blues in the key of F: a fast one, 'Dr Jekyll', composed by altoist Jackie McLean, and first recorded by Miles in 1955; a slow one, 'Sid's Ahead', which is a variation on Miles's own early blues, 'Weirdo'; and the medium-paced 'Straight No Chaser', by Monk. The two other tunes on the album are 'Two Bass Hit', by John Lewis, and a new piece by Davis called 'Miles' on the album label, but 'Milestones' everywhere else.

Milestones takes the art of small-group jazz to a very high level indeed. In the context of Miles's career, it is very much a transitional album. With three horns in the front-line, the old loose Davis quintet method, as exemplified on Cannonball's *Somethin' Else* the previous month, had to be modified. All the themes on *Milestones* (except, of course, for the trio track) are played by all three, or by two of the horns in unison and harmony. Miles is particularly concerned to show off and contrast his two saxophonists, and so there are only two piano solos on the whole album; one on 'Straight No Chaser', and the one on the trio track. In fact, on the second day of recording, Red Garland arrived too late to play on 'Sid's Ahead', the longest track on the album. The pianist playing the rich, harmonically ambiguous chords behind Coltrane and Adderley, is Miles Davis himself. The theme is stated by the three horns in harmony over a rhythm section of bass and drums, and Miles plays his own solo with just those two instruments backing him.

Three of Miles's solos on this album are classics, and each is totally different in character. They occur on 'Sid's Ahead', 'Straight No Chaser' and 'Milestones'. They are all open horn solos because on this album, as on *Miles Ahead*, Davis does not use the harmon mute at all. His open sound is particularly sonorous, and its glowing, luminous quality is accompanied by an apparently effortless plasticity of inflexion which imbues every phrase, every idea with intense life. So soft and full is his sound on the title track, 'Milestones', that it suggests he may be playing flugelhorn rather than trumpet. These three horn solos are the expressions of a powerfully original mind, and Miles's self-editing process functions relentlessly.

His solo on the slow blues, 'Sid's Ahead', has an emotional depth which is almost unbearable. Here, Miles develops and expands ideas which had their germ in the *Scaffold* music. The solo (Appendix A, Fig.6) is seven choruses long, and apart from its sparseness and severity, there are also quite specific references back to the film music. For example, the skeletal repetitions of some of that music are echoed in the last eight bars of his third chorus and culminate in a phrase in the last bar which closely mirrors the leap from F (concert) to D above the stave and down to A flat, which Miles played at the beginning of 'Florence Sur Les Champs-Elysées' (Appendix A, Fig. 5a). And the solo rises remorselessly to the repetitions, for the first seven bars of the final chorus, of high A flat (concert) which is, of course, the flattened 3rd of the blues scale, and the descent in bar eight leading to the stoic conclusion. This also harks back to the final section of the film music, 'Chez le Photographe du Motel' (Appendix A, Fig. 5b) where Miles repeats high G (concert) for several bars before descending. This was the passage which drew ecstatic murmurs from Louis Malle: 'A really extraordinary dimension to the visual image.' On 'Sid's Ahead', the music is not applied, but pure, and the extraordinary dimension is given, not to a visual image, but to the emotional power of the solo. After the initial theme statement, Coltrane plays the first solo, accompanied by bass, drums, and Miles's moody piano chords. Trane's solo has a similar emotional depth and he sustains the atmosphere of brooding set up by the elemental blues theme. Miles then follows, supported only by bass and drums, so that even the instrumentation is pared down to the three basics: drums, bass and horn.

Canonball Adderley, magnificent saxophonist though he was, seems to have realized that he couldn't hope to match the power of the two solos he had to follow. He simply could not sustain the mood set up by Coltrane and Miles, and he meanders aimlessly, quoting phrases from standard tunes and producing a few bluesy licks. This particular area was just not his bag, but the medium-paced blues, 'Straight No Chaser', was, and on this Cannonball solos first. At this bright and bouncy tempo he is in his element, and plays an excellent solo, bubbling along joyfully. He is followed by Miles who plays a very different blues solo. This time, although the underlying sadness is always present, his phrases dance and sing along with a kind of impish delight. As is usual with Miles Davis, the past is ever-present, and in one chorus he actually quotes the first phrase of the old traditional tune, 'When The Saints Go Marching In', repeating it and then putting it in a minor key to fit the chord changes. But this quote is organic to his racy reinterpretation of the past, and is brilliantly woven into the fabric of the solo. After Miles, Coltrane roars in with wild verbosity. Under his onslaught it seems that the blues/jazz tradition is creaking at the seams. He piles chord on chord, plays across, through, against, alongside the pulse. Then suddenly he finishes and the rhythm section creams out in a simple groove with Red Garland's piano solo. Philly Joe ticks off the bars with a rimshot on every fourth beat – 1-2-3-tick – reassuring everyone, and Garland plays the first half of his solo with single-note lines, and the second half with block-chords, but with this tremendous surprise in store: the melody which he underpins with the block chords is none other than the trumpet solo Miles played in November 1945 on Parker's historic recording of 'Now's The Time'. Garland had paid a similar tribute to Miles in November 1957 when he recorded with his own quintet, but his own album was not issued until two years later.

The piece which most obviously opens up new territory and points to future developments, is the title track, 'Milestones'. Once more, this explores areas touched on in the *Scaffold* film music. The structure, which is forty bars long, is based on only two scales and they are closely related. The first sixteen bars are based on the G minor 7th chord which implies the scale (once again) of F major, or the Dorian mode; the second sixteen bars are based on the chord of A minor 7th and the implied scale is that of C major (Aeolian mode). The final eight bars go back to the first scale. The whole piece is thus built on only two separate scales, with harmony now becoming decorative rather than functional. In other words, when each scale is used, different chords can be picked out from the notes of that scale; the chords may thus change while the scale (and key) remains constant. This is similar to the harmonic ambiguity which was a strong feature of one or two of the film music tracks. The second sixteen bars of 'Milestones', for example, has E and A roots played by the bass, but they sound like suspensions on D minor.

But even more important than this reduction of harmonic move-ment, are the rhythms of the piece and the way the structure builds and releases tension. The written theme and its structure (which is rigorously preserved for each soloist) are a brilliant refashioning of the old call-and-response idea. The first sixteen bars are the 'call', and they set up a superbly springy rhythmic pulse. Here Miles the composer, by using extremely simple devices with immense subtlety, has created an entirely fresh feel, a new rhythmic dynamism and springboard. The three horns play, in simple triads, a three note riff which moves up and down the scale. The notes are short, played with great precision, and don't fall on the fourth beat of any bar. The rhythm section plays a bright 4/4 and Philly Joe once more ticks off the last beat of every bar with a rimshot, thus providing a kind of punctuation for the horn riff. During the second sixteen bars, this buoyant pulse is interrupted and held back with great artistry, thus producing a feeling of slowing up, though the actual tempo remains the same. This impression is created because the bass, instead of 'walking' purposefully up and down the scale playing crotchets, simply repeats pedal notes E and A, while Philly Joe's rimshot falls on different beats in the bar, thus stopping the regularity of rhythm.

93

The two saxophonists continue playing up and down the scale in harmony, but this time with longer notes (minims), while Miles plays the same kind of thing slightly out of phase with the saxes; his rising and falling notes are played *against* theirs, dragging the phrases back. The tension rises as all these factors pull against the memory of that first springy rhythm, and then suddenly the last eight bars arrive, the original beat is back, and the tension is released magnificently. Miles is, once again, using very simple devices to say extremely complex things. This composition has deservedly become a standard tune in the repertoire of jazz musicians all over the world. The structure – the way the piece 'breathes' – is preserved for the three horn solos, and they match the quality of the conception of the composition. Wilfrid Mellers comments on Miles's own solo: 'Bird was a composing improviser, and Miles is an improvising composer…When the trumpet [flugelhorn?] emerges from the beat of Time…the soft, suave tone veils tremendous passion: which gradually breaks through until the line swirls with almost Parker-like agitation. The effect of the piece depends on the contrast between the passion the line generates and the immensely ancient, modal quietude of its first statement.'[19]

I have dwelt on the album *Milestones* because it is one of the great classics of jazz and occurs at a key point in Miles Davis's career. The music on it glows in the memory. It is profound, delightful, full of confidence and immense optimism. Throughout, there is the feeling that the past is rich, the present enjoyable, and the future full of promise.

8
Porgy and Bess

'*Porgy and Bess* was the hardest record I ever made.'[1]

Miles Davis

By 1958, Miles Davis's fame, coupled with his method of working were beginning to cause some problems. The long rest periods he liked were not appreciated by the rest of the group who were not paid when they were not working. Also, being with Miles meant sharing some of his fame and the aura of glamour which surrounded him, so the musicians in his group invariably got offered other jobs. Sometimes their engagements would clash with Miles's own concerts and he would have to employ a deputy drummer or pianist for the evening. For a time, Miles tried paying his musicians a 'retainer', but it was not enough to stop them from working with other bands, and when the desired object was not achieved he stopped this expensive practice. Philly Joe Jones was very much in demand, and by 1958 was often missing Miles's jobs. Because of this it became imperative to find another drummer. Cannonball recommended Jimmy Cobb, who had worked in Adderley's quintet, and as there was even doubt as to whether Philly Joe would turn up for the recording sessions of *Milestones*, Cobb was asked to stand by in the studio. Jimmy Cobb was, naturally, overjoyed at the prospect of joining Miles's group. He recalled:

> That was the best job you could have…it was the best paying jazz gig at the time that black people could have…that was about as high as you could get playing jazz music, so I was feeling pretty good about it. So I sat through the record date, and right soon after that he (Cannonball) told me that Joe had gone, and come down and play. Most of the things they played, I knew them, because of course they were very popular things, and I heard Joe play them, so it really wasn't that hard.

There were factors other than conflicting bookings which had made Philly Joe and Red Garland miss some of Miles's gigs. Both of them, and bassist Paul Chambers, were still drug addicts, and their condition made them unreliable. Jimmy Cobb said: 'We went to Washington once with the band and we opened on a Friday, and I think Red got there Saturday midnight. Miles liked the way he played so he put up with that sort of thing a long time.' Very soon after Philly Joe left, Red Garland did so too. To replace him, Miles hired the young white pianist, Bill Evans. Jimmy Cobb was to stay with the group for five years, but Evans was with it for a few months only; from spring to autumn in 1958. In this short time, however, he made a great impact on the music and on Miles himself. Also, the following year Evans was temporarily reassociated with Miles Davis when the sextet made the historic album, *Kind of Blue*.

By mid-1958, Miles Davis was becoming recognized as a discoverer of major talents, or at least as a catalyst which enabled major talents to realize themselves. At the beginning of that year, each member of his group was the leading exponent, the *influence*, on his particular instrument: Miles on trumpet, Coltrane on tenor sax, Cannonball on alto, Paul Chambers on the bass, Philly Joe on drums, and, perhaps to a slightly lesser extent, Red Garland on piano. Bill Evans was, even at this early stage of his career, an original, a major keyboard stylist, and his exposure with Miles was probably a key factor in his winning the *Down Beat* critics' New Star award in late 1958, which, perhaps ironically, was partially responsible for the brevity of his stay with Miles Davis. The sensitive Evans did not feel entirely comfortable with Miles's sextet. He said later: 'I felt the group to be composed of superhumans.' Also, he was the only white man in the group and Miles would tease him about that. Jimmy Cobb said:

> They were close, but Miles used to bug him, you know. He would just fool with him. It was good hearted...Like, we'd be talking and Bill would say something and Miles would tell him, 'Man, cool it. We don't want no white opinions.' That kind of shook him because he didn't know how to take that, and Miles would be giggling behind him...and piano players, when they first got with the band they were always confused because he would tell them when to play and when not to play, so they got so they wouldn't know *when* to play.

Bill Evans had studied the piano music of the French impressionist composers, and he brought Debussian chord voicings to support his supple and flowing melodic lines. His work has quite remarkable sensitivity and depth, and in the late fifties his sound was startlingly fresh. Miles commented: 'Another reason I like Red Garland and Bill Evans is that when they play a chord, they play a *sound* more than a chord.'[2] This sound in Evans's case is created by the inner voicings of his chords and this quality made him the perfect man for Miles's musical needs at the time. Evans's creative ability with inner voicings was the exact requirement necessary for exploring the decorative, as opposed to the functional, aspect of harmony.

By May 1958, both Jimmy Cobb and Bill Evans were with the sextet, and there were subtle changes in the approach and emphasis of the music. Cannonball Adderley noted some of them:

> Especially when he started to use Bill Evans, Miles changed his style from very hard to a softer approach. Bill was brilliant in other areas, but he couldn't make the real hard things come off. Then Miles started writing new things...Miles at first thought Jimmy Cobb wasn't as exciting [as Philly Joe] on fast tempos, and so we did less of those. And although he loves Bill's work, Miles felt Bill didn't swing enough on things that weren't subdued. When Bill left, Miles hired Red again and got used to swinging so much that he later found Wynton Kelly, who does both the subdued things and the swingers very well.[3]

Later that year, Miles told Nat Hentoff: 'Boy I've sure learned a lot from Bill Evans. He plays the piano the way it should be played. He plays all kind of scales; can play 5/4 and all kinds of fantastic things. There's such a difference between him and Red Garland whom I also like a lot. Red carries the rhythm, but Bill underplays, and I like that better.'[4]

In Bill Evans, Miles had with his group a pianist with the same inward-looking and self-examining approach as himself. A remark Wilfrid Mellers made about Evans, is also an accurate description of Miles: 'Evans's ability to make melodic lines "speak" is of extraordinary subtlety; and always the sensuousness leads not to passivity but to growth.'[5] But it was to take about a year before Miles found the perfect fusion of his own talents and those of Bill Evans. This occurred on the album *Kind of Blue* which was recorded in early 1959, several months after Evans had officially left the band. But the first intimations of the exquisite music Miles would produce in this new setting occurred when he took the group into the studios in late May 1958, to record a couple of movie theme tunes, 'On Green Dolphin Street', from the 1946 film of that name, and 'Stella by Starlight', from a film called *The Uninvited* (1943), and a piece he had written himself, 'Fran Dance' (Put Your Little Foot Right Out).

From Bill Evans's solo piano at the beginning of 'Green Dolphin Street', when he plays the melody *colla voce*, to the coda with the sad, descending harmonies of the two saxes over which Miles's trumpet with harmon mute improvises, the whole performance is flawless. It has an atmosphere of sumptuous brooding, a kind of sadness of the ages allied to a rather more western European sensibility. The rhythm section, with Jimmy Cobb sounding relaxed and confident on drums, alternates pedal points and freewheeling time with chord changes in the usual Davis manner of building and releasing tension. The four solos – Miles, Coltrane, Adderley and Evans – are superb, and their order brilliantly devised: the two masters of understatement, Miles and Evans, playing before and after the two prolific soloists. It is a long performance, lasting almost ten minutes, and it is totally absorbing.

'Stella by Starlight', is half that length, and Cannonball does not play on this track. Although it does not quite have the power of 'Dolphin Street', it is a hauntingly beautiful performance with one magnificent dramatic moment. This occurs after Miles has interpreted the theme, using the harmon once more, and with Jimmy Cobb using brushes to create a gentle pulse. Then, instead of playing a solo, Davis projects a strident sustained high note while Cobb changes to sticks, and the rhythm section drives along massively as Coltrane enters. This suddenly raises the intensity, and Trane sustains this atmosphere of sobriety and swing by also, like Miles, simply playing the melody and embellishing it. This is another surprise, and a delightful one, because Coltrane's beautiful sound with its expressive long notes gives new dimensions to the tune.

There may have been very personal reasons for the romantic eloquence of these performances, because it seems that Miles had fallen deeply in love again. He had met Frances Taylor, a dancer who had spent eight months in Leonard Bernstein's *West Side Story* when it opened at the Wintergarden Theatre on 26 September 1957. Miles had seen the show when Frances (and Chita Rivera) were still with it. His enormously tender composition, 'Fran Dance', which was subtitled 'Put Your Little Foot Right Out', was inspired by Frances Taylor. Frances and Miles were ultimately married in 1960 after what she described as 'four years of rehearsal'. However, not all the musicians on this session were entirely happy about the exquisite restraint of the music. According to Bill Evans, Paul Chambers and Jimmy Cobb were 'getting edgy having to hold back and wanted to cook on something. Miles just turned and said " Love for Sale" and kicked it off.'[6] The result was a classic performance of great drive. This track was not released for many years probably because during the late fifties it did not fit in with Miles's prevailing ideas, and during the sixties it seems to have been simply overlooked.

Despite the fact that it has often been suggested (usually by whites) that Miles Davis is prejudiced against whites, many of his deepest friendships and closest associations have been with white people. His attitude has probably always been something like that of Jonathan Swift who said: 'I love Tom, Dick and Harry, but I hate that animal Man.' Miles's association with whites at key points in his career, has often resulted in greater insights which led to fresh musical ideas. Gil Evans has been a constant friend and colleague since 1947. Other influential and fruitful friendships were with Lee

98

Konitz and Gerry Mulligan in the late forties and early fifties; with Bill Evans in the late fifties; and in the late sixties and the seventies, with Joe Zawinul, Dave Holland, John McLaughlin and Dave Liebman. Certainly, Miles has always been scrupulously fair in recognizing genuine talent when he sees it whether in blacks or whites, and once when asked if he thought the ability to swing was exclusive to black musicians, he is alleged to have said: 'I once nearly gave myself a hernia trying to get two black cats to swing!'

To survive, Miles Davis had to be extremely tough and he demanded a certain toughness from the musicians who worked with him. Black or white, he kept them alert by his unpredictable and often mystifying behaviour. Not only did he tease Bill Evans about being the only white man in the group, but he also frequently had the other musicians guessing what he would do next. During club engagements which usually lasted a few days or a week, he would sometimes, in the middle of someone's solo, disappear from the scene for the rest of the evening. Jimmy Cobb described how confusing this was: 'From time to time he would start a tune...and he would play on it, and then while the band was playing on it, he would leave...but most of the time it would be pretty close to the end of the night where I guess he figured the proprietor wouldn't be mad any more and wouldn't dock him, or something like that. But he used to do that quite often.' Miles also tended to needle new sidemen by comparing them with their predecessors. Lena Horne once said: 'Miles is a potentate. He's also a puritan, and the combination can be pretty sadistic.'[7] When Jimmy Cobb replaced Philly Joe, Miles said to his new sideman: 'My favourite drummer is Philly Joe.' For some time after Cobb joined, Miles would stand behind him counting the bars or beats, as if calling in question Jimmy Cobb's time-playing – the most sacrosanct part of a drummer's craft. Some years later, when Coltrane had left the band and Hank Mobley was the saxophonist, Miles is alleged to have said quite audibly while Mobley was playing: 'Any time Sonny Rollins shows up with his horn, he's got the job.' And sometimes, when someone fell below his own standards, Miles could be rude and unkind, as he was to Barney Wilen in 1956. The French saxophonist was playing with Miles at the Club St Germain, and during an intermission he told Mike Zwerin: 'You wouldn't believe what Miles said to me in the middle of my solo on the last tune. He said, "Man, why don't you stop playing those awful notes".'[8] Despite this sometimes cruel behaviour, Miles Davis had a great affection and respect for his musicians, and usually treated them with thoughtfulness and generosity. When Bill Evans left the sextet in the autumn of 1958 in order to try his luck with his own trio, Miles went out of his way to help him by phoning agents and talking to them about the pianist.

When Bill Evans was in the band, the western European elements in the music had intensified, but at the same time Miles was also going more deeply into his own ethnic roots. Paradoxically, he did so by collaborating once more with his friend Gil Evans. Their next project was to record excerpts from Gershwin's opera, *Porgy and Bess*, with the aim of transferring the full flavour of the vocal score into music for orchestra only. Miles, on flugelhorn and muted (harmon) trumpet, was to be the 'singer'. At this period, Davis was still living in his mid-town apartment, a relatively new building on Tenth Avenue, near 57th Street. In it he had a good piano and an adequate mono record player, and during the first six months of the year, whenever Miles was at home 'resting', Gil Evans went there to talk about the project, and to try out the various musical ideas.

Their version of *Porgy and Bess* was recorded in four three-hour sessions which took place in July and August 1958, and the orchestra was similar to the *Miles Ahead* unit: four trumpets, four trombones, two saxophones, three French horns, two flutes, tuba, bass and drums. But the way this ensemble is used, and its relationship with Miles's flugelhorn and trumpet, differ very subtly from *Miles Ahead*. There is much more of Miles on *Porgy*, and he assumes very much the role of preacher, while the orchestra plays that of congregation. It is a wonderful reinterpretation of the call-and-response pattern, with sections of the orchestra responding to one another, and all of them responding to Miles. Two pieces, 'Summertime' and 'It Ain't Necessarily So', are simply solos by Davis, and the ensemble plays the same role as a gospel choir backing a singer – replying to his phrases with hypnotically repetitive riffs. Gil Evans and Miles devised this kind of mutual incitement: Miles responding to the written orchestral responses. A perfect example is the deeply moving, 'Gone, Gone, Gone', which is an instrumental version of the old, antiphonal Negro funeral service.

This communication between Miles Davis and the orchestra under Evans's direction, attains an ominous, terrifying grandeur on 'Prayer'. This remarkable piece literally makes the hair rise on the back of one's neck. It has no real harmonic movement at all, staying in B flat minor throughout, without any modulations. The first part is out of tempo, with a brass tremulo over which Miles does some magnificent calls, using all the tonal inflexions of which he is now master – slurs, bent notes, stabs, long singing notes which cry out powerfully. In his pauses, the orchestra screams out ragged responses, which are the more affecting because of their very raggedness. Evans's writing for brass instruments is superb on *Porgy* – far more dynamic than on *Miles Ahead* – and it is this which helps to give the dialogue between Miles and the orchestra such potency. Eventually, 'Prayer' changes from the out-of-time tremulo to a repeated figure *(ostinato)* played by the lower instruments in slow 12/8 time – the most typical church rhythm. This starts very quietly, repeating its dark incantations with gradually increasing insistence. Over this ritualistic, hypnotic figure, Miles continues his calls, at first plaintively, but, as the other instruments take up the *ostinato,* Davis's calls climb to the upper registers of the trumpet, becoming more insistent, more passionate, until it seems that the total ensemble has ignited. At that point he sustains a blazing E flat concert above his top C, and descends with a long swooping phrase. This is a magnificent climax, and the cumulative grandeur of the gradually increasing choir of instruments is heightened simply because, even under the pressure of the dynamic incitement of the orchestra, Miles keeps his grip on the prayerful aspect of the occasion; he plays no fast or glib phrases, but picks his notes at eloquent intervals, with a nobility of phrasing that is extraordinary. After this peak, there is a slow dispersal of voices from the *ostinato*, which subsides to the lower instruments and stops on a long note. In this performance, Miles seems to have cut his way back through layers of experience, through bebop, through early jazz, through western orchestral music, through and beyond the whole western tradition, to the archetypal expression of the black race where the 'field holler' began, and where the spokesman (soloist) is expressing the aspirations of a complete and homogeneous society.

The level of inspiration throughout *Porgy and Bess* is exceptionally high: Miles plays as one possessed and Evans writes with the same intensity. They do more than justice to Gershwin's great opera, transforming it, deepening it, and uncovering roots of which even Gershwin was probably unaware. The album is full of musical felicities because the music conforms with Gil Evans's own basic criteria: it is *alive* – the 'form originates from the spirit'. It also encompasses a wide range of expression, from the gentle lyricism of 'Bess, You Is My Woman Now' and 'Bess, Oh Where's My Bess', to the ominous grandeur of 'The Buzzard Song' and 'Prayer'. There are two wonderful resting points, one either side of the album, in the long solos by Miles on 'Summertime' and 'It Ain't Necessarily So'. Once again, his playing – muted on the first and open horn on the second – reveals a deeper level of artistry because on each track he plays the entire solo from *within* the tune, developing the inner logic of each of the pieces.

Miles handles the responsibility of the whole album quite brilliantly, playing the written parts, in which he is often leading the whole ensemble, with great feeling and accuracy, and playing solos which are more than equal to their context. He said afterwards that it was 'the hardest record I ever made'. The strains of the previous decade or so had made him suffer occasionally from ulcerous pains, and he said later that when he was recording *Porgy*, 'I felt like I'd been eating nails.'[9] But he was very pleased with the results and said, 'I like this record. I'd buy this record myself.'[10] Also, talking of their version of the cries of the vendors on Catfish Row, Miles said: 'You listen, and you *know* what's going on. You *hear* that old strawberry-seller yellin' out strawberries...*straw*-berries.'[11]

The whole Davis/Evans version of *Porgy and Bess* was, as *Miles Ahead* had been the previous year, recorded in only four three-hour sessions, which was not enough time for an album of such complex music. On one track at least, 'Gone', there are clearly audible errors from some of the instruments, and some scrappy ensemble playing in general. Years later, Gil Evans said: 'On most of those records, one more session would have cleared up most of the clinkers. Looking back on it, I'm outraged at myself for not sticking up for my rights.'[12] However, despite the inadequate recording time, *Porgy and Bess* is a major contribution to twentieth-century music. It is outstanding in the way that a sustained dialogue is created between a great improvising soloist and a great orchestrator.

Columbia were now doing everything in their power to promote Miles Davis and his music. They had, the previous year, distributed an excellent potted biography which consisted mainly of Miles talking about himself, and which starts in his typically offhand way: 'You want me to tell you where I was born – that old story? It was in good old Alton, Illinois. In 1926. And I had to call my mother a week before my last birthday and ask her how old I would be.' This biography was published in its entirety in *Down Beat* in the spring of 1958, and provided a basis for articles in several other publications including the feature in *Time* magazine mentioned at the beginning of this chapter.

Since 1956, Columbia had also signed Duke Ellington and Billie Holiday, and the company were feeling so enthusiastic about their jazz stars in the summer of 1958 that they threw a party in the Edwardian Room of the Plaza in New York. At this party, Miles's sextet and Duke's orchestra played, and Billie Holiday and Jimmy Rushing sang. Columbia also began some systematic image-building, projecting Miles Davis as the Byronic black man, the 'mean, moody, and magnificent' jazz musician. The cover of the first CBS album, *Round Midnight*, showed a brooding Miles in sepia tints, his eyes masked with dark glasses, his downturned head in his hands and his trumpet slung across his chest. The cover of *Milestones* was to have a magnificent portrait of him in open-necked shirt, sitting down and staring impassively straight at the camera. The two albums with Gil Evans, on the other hand, heightened the enigmatic, mysterious aspect of his image by having no picture of him on the front covers at all. *Porgy* was particularly enigmatic in that the front cover picture showed a man and woman from the waist down only. The two half-bodies are sitting and the woman's hand is reaching out to touch a trumpet which is lying across the man's lap. The symbolism must have been obvious even in the naïve 1950s.

The rest of this year was spent in concerts and tours and, in his rest periods, preparing for the next recording project which was to take place the following year. As 1958 ended, it must have seemed that his career was on a never-ending upward spiral. He had reached another pinnacle of artistic and financial success, he was in love again, he was a national and international celebrity, and he was acknowledged as a leading representative of his race. The following year was to bring yet further musical masterpieces, but it would also bring some rude shocks which were to have a profound effect on him.

9
Is It Jazz?

'An artist's first responsibility is to himself.'[1]
Miles Davis

For some years now, every new record release by Miles Davis had astonished musicians and fans alike with the freshness of its sound, and by 1958, his music had established itself as, in critic Whitney Balliett's phrase, the 'sound of surprise'. And now, at the beginning of 1959, after the brilliant small-group album, *Milestones*, and the magnificent orchestral album, *Porgy and Bess*, most people thought that Miles's music had reached its peak of expression. Early that year, however, he recorded an album which brought to even greater heights the brooding, meditative side of his music which had revealed itself for the first time on Parker's 'Now's The Time' session in November 1945. This was called *Kind of Blue*, and it was to be perhaps the most influential single album in jazz history.

Miles Davis's aesthetic ideas were clearly formulated by this time, which accounts for the confidence and potency of his musical vision. He was steadily expanding his knowledge of earlier jazz forms and performances and the interview he did with Nat Hentoff in *Jazz Review* (December 1958), shows just how perceptive and clearly thought-out were his criticisms of other musicians. He talks lovingly of Billie Holiday, the old blues singer Leadbelly, Bessie Smith and Louis Armstrong. Hentoff plays him Louis' 'Potato Head Blues', and Miles comments: 'There's form there, and you take some of those early forms, play it today, and they'd sound good. I also like all those little stops in his solo. We stop, but we often let the drums lay out altogether. If I had this record, I'd play it.'[2] At the same time, Miles was expanding his interests in other areas of music. He told Hentoff: 'I've been listening to Khatchaturian carefully for six months now and the thing that intrigues me are all those different scales he uses...they're different from the usual western scales.'[3] By now, too, very few of Miles's contemporaries held any interest for him. Of the leading pianist, Oscar Peterson, who was popular with musicians as well as with the general public,

104

Miles said: 'Nearly everything he plays, he plays with the same degree of force. He leaves no holes for the rhythm section.'[4] And talking of music in general and his own group in particular, Davis comments: 'I usually don't buy jazz records. They make me tired and depressed. I'll buy Ahmad Jamal, John Lewis, Sonny Rollins. Coltrane I hear every night…He's been working on those arpeggios and playing chords that lead into chords, playing them fifty different ways and playing them all at once. He's beginning to leave more space except when he gets nervous…I never have anybody write up anything too difficult for us, because the musicians tighten up.'[5]

After an incubation period of some ten months, Miles Davis went into the recording studios again on 2 March 1959. Bill Evans had left the group the previous autumn and the pianist was now Wynton Kelly, but when he got to the studios, Kelly was perturbed and mystified to find Bill Evans there. Nothing had been said to Wynton Kelly about the occasion, and as he'd only recently joined the sextet, he was still unsure as to whether he was or wasn't the regular pianist. Jimmy Cobb explained: 'That's what Miles used to do sometimes. He used to bring two players down for certain ideas he had…He had that thing for the blues and he knew how Wynton played, and he had that thing for the pretty things, and he knew how Bill played…' In fact, on that first day, three pieces were recorded and although Kelly played on only one of them, he was paid for the whole day's work. The album was finished on another session which took place in late April, during which two more pieces were recorded.

The opening track, 'So What', immediately established the mood and atmosphere of the album *Kind of Blue*. Bill Evans plays a quiet introduction with impressionist chord voicings, and then a melodic riff is played by the bass, while the rest of the sextet reply to each of his repeated phrases with a mournful two-note riff in three-part harmony. It is yet another variation on the call-and-response technique, with the bass calling (preaching) and the horns and piano saying 'amen' (or 'so what') to each of his statements. The bass riff and the 'amens' of the ensemble go on for sixteen bars, and are then raised a semitone for eight bars before going back to the original tonality for the final eight bars. Thus, in this thirty-two bar structure, Miles has reduced the harmonic movement to two broad areas; the first sixteen bars are based on the scale of C major but harmonized with the chord of D minor 7th (the Dorian mode); the middle eight is based on the scale of D flat major, but harmonized with the chord of E flat minor (also Dorian); and the final eight goes back to the first tonality. Here, Miles was following up lines of thought first hinted at in the *Scaffold* film music, and first brought to fruition in his composition 'Milestones', which is also based on just two scales. Working with Gil Evans on *Porgy and Bess* had also helped to define these harmonic ideas. Miles said:

> When Gil wrote the arrangement of 'I Loves You, Porgy', he only wrote a scale for me to play. No chords...And in 'Summertime', there is a long space where we don't change the chord at all. It just doesn't have to be cluttered up...All chords, after all, are relative to scales and certain chords make certain scales...You go this way, you can go on for ever. You don't have to worry about [chord] changes and you can do more with the [melodic] line...I think a movement in jazz is beginning away from the conventional string of chords, and a return to emphasis on melodic rather than harmonic variations. There will be fewer chords but infinite possibilities as to what to do with them.[6]

The tensions set up by the theme of 'So What' – the unusual role of the bass, the mournful 'amens' which are really sardonic 'so whats', the decorative function of harmony with its sudden organic use when the theme shifts up a semitone – combine to inspire the soloists. Miles plays two superbly austere choruses and is followed by Coltrane. With the latter, Bill Evans's accompaniment changes from the graceful ebb and flow he used for Miles, to more insistent and ominous chords. With Cannonball there is a more cheerful and relaxed feeling, and finally, Evans himself plays a solo with riff backing from the horns which is a subtle variation on the original 'amen' response, and which gives the performance tremendous lift.

The second track, 'Freddie Freeloader', has Wynton Kelly on piano and is a blues in B flat. Like 'So What', it is taken at a medium, strolling tempo, and this traditional form too, Miles has reduced to its starkest, most elemental basis. It is built on the three traditional chords of the blues – the tonic, sub-dominant and dominant – with only one tiny variation when a different harmony is used for the last two bars. This time, a harmonized, two-note 'amen' is the main thematic motif; a falling phrase like a gentle sigh, creating an atmosphere of sophisticated melancholia. It is quite remarkable how the blues has been reduced to its simplest form while the feeling which infuses it has becomes more subtle, more refined, more evocative. Once again, the solo order is brilliantly organized. Wynton Kelly plays first, and suddenly, after the introversion of 'So What', and the melancholy theme of this blues, Kelly's solo sparkles with unrestrained joy. He plays single note triplets and some block chords which swing mightily, and the muscularity of his phrases, his pulse, his effervescent ideas, throw the whole of the album into relief, enhancing the impact of all the rest of the music. He is followed by Miles who builds to a magnificent climax in his sixth and final chorus, when he is followed by Coltrane, and then by Adderley whose irrepressible spirits burst out in fluid, bluesy phrases.

Bill Evans, who wrote the original sleeve note for *Kind of Blue*, commented: 'Miles conceived these settings only hours before the recording date, and arrived with sketches which indicated to the group what was to be played. Therefore you will hear something close to spontaneity in these performances. The group had never played these pieces before the recordings.'[7] Also, according to Evans, each piece was done in just one take. But one piece on the album was definitely worked on consciously over a period of six months. This was 'All Blues' which opened side two. Miles worked at it on his piano at home, and took his ideas round to Gil Evans for his opinions and suggestions, but even then the piece found its ultimate form only in the studio on the actual day of the recording. Miles told Ralph Gleason: 'I wrote it in 4/4, but when we got to the studio, it hit me that it should be in 3/4. I hadn't thought of it like that before, but it was exactly right.'[8]

The striking feature of 'All Blues' is a plaintive, repeated three-note riff played in harmony by the two saxophones throughout the beginning and ending of the piece, and intermittently by the piano during the solos. This riff is yet another variation on the three-note theme of 'Milestones', and there is something of the same way in which the tension ebbs amd flows according to whether the notes are played short or long. Miles knew exactly what he was doing here, and said of this riff: 'You can get a lot of tension by repetition...I didn't write anything for me to play; I just play what I feel like at the time.'[9] Over this hypnotic riff, Miles plays a series of haunting calls using his harmon mute. The unhurried nature of the piece gives him time to remove his mute (while the saxes are playing the riff) and play the first solo. His use of the open trumpet sound here gives an added textural richness. Indeed, the whole piece is remarkable for the original and subtle way Davis creates the textures he wants. 'All Blues' is built up of layers of sound: the drums play straight, unobtrusive 3/4; the bass states the pulse by playing, for the most part, a dotted minim (i.e. one note per bar); over this Bill Evans plays a long, sustained trill in the middle register of the piano; to this is added the hypnotic saxophone riff. Over this rich texture, Miles calls with the astringent sound of the harmon mute. Just as he plays his solo with open trumpet so the other textures change and loosen up as the musicians start reacting to the soloists. As is usual with Miles, the formal elements of 'All Blues' are deceptively simple, and the whole is infinitely greater than the sum of its parts.

There are no fast pieces on *Kind of Blue*: 'So What', 'Freddy Freeloader' and 'All Blues' are medium tempo performances, and 'Blue in Green' and 'Flamenco Sketches' are skeletal ballads. Miles Davis's titles are usually just methods of identifying particular pieces; they are rarely descriptive of the music. Often, he names compositions after things, people or phrases from his everyday environment. 'So What' is one of the expressions he has used a great deal, particularly to people who come up and tell him how much they like his music. And 'Freddy Freeloader' was the nickname of an ex-bartender in Philadelphia, a hipster who just hung around the jazz spots and ran errands for musicians.

The homogeneity of mood on *Kind of Blue*, and the superlative response of the musicians to the contexts Miles devised, combined to make this one of the seminal albums, and one of the most enduring classics, of jazz. It has been bought, loved and learned by non-musicians as well as by musicians, and it has influenced world famous musicians as well as obscure performers. The more it is listened to, the more it reveals new delights and fresh depths. Typically, at the time, the musicians in the studio didn't realize that they had just made a historic recording. Jimmy Cobb recalled the playback in the studio:

> After it was over and we heard it, we went through the things…and it sounded so nice in the studio…and it came out so good on the record…I said 'Damn! – it sounded good!' But since then it got to be something special in the music…a lot of people started listening to the music with that record, and a lot of guys started to play jazz from behind that record…and I had a few people tell me that they had worn out three to four copies of that record.

However, the restrained elegance of *Kind of Blue* could be achieved only in the cloister-like atmosphere of the recording studio working with unfamiliar material. In live performances, Miles's groups were too irrepressibly dynamic to function in so restrained a way. With this album, Miles had taken the western aspects of his music to their limits. 'Blue in Green', for example, takes civilized melancholia, and the introverted, self-regarding sensibilities which are European in origin, about as far as they will go without turning into mawkishness. The piece is so sad and nostalgic that it is almost painful. The qualities of Bill Evans are of crucial importance to the music of *Kind of Blue*, and it is significant that on this piece, Evans's contribution was more organic than on the other pieces. All the compositions on the album were written by Miles Davis, except for 'Blue in Green', though that too is attributed to Miles on the LP sleeve. However, some years later, Bill Evans said: 'Actually it's my tune, even though Miles is credited as co-writer for reasons only he understands. One day at Miles's apartment, he wrote on some manuscript paper the symbols for G minor and A augmented, and he said, "What would you do with that?" I didn't really know, but I went home and wrote "Blue in Green".'[10] This begs the question of what, precisely, the act of composition in jazz consists. The cause of Evans's writing 'Blue in Green', as he points out, was Miles Davis's defining the area of interest: the relationship of two particular chords. In a Zen pupil-and-master sense, by pointing Evans in a particular direction,

108

Miles was certainly 'composing' himself.

This vexed problem of composition had begun with the early confusion about the composer of 'Donna Lee' (was it Miles or Bird?), and would continue to be a recurrent theme throughout the rest of Miles's career. There is, of course, money in composing: the composer gets a royalty every time his music is played, and if it is recorded, he can expect a steady income so long as his records either sell or get played in public on radio or television. Because of the financial advantages, some bandleaders throughout the history of jazz have exercised what might be called a sort of *droit du seigneur* so far as their sidemen's compositions were concerned, either taking over the rights completely or at least sharing them. In some cases, the problem was far simpler and less abstract than the question of the authorship of 'Blue in Green'. For example, two of Miles's most famous tunes of the early fifties, 'Four' and 'Tune Up', have been claimed by the saxophonist and blues singer, Eddie 'Cleanhead' Vinson, who said: 'He [Miles] was in Kansas City and he needed some tunes. He said, "Well, man, can I take these?" I said, "Yeah, just put my name on it." I hadn't bothered to copyright it at the time...I've seen him since, we're still friends! Oh, he's tried to pay me, but I just enjoy his playing anyway.'[11] There is an authentic note in this claim, because of the lack of rancour. Miles himself has made the following remarks about the relationship of improvising and composing: 'Do I like composing better than playing? I can't answer that. There's a certain feeling you get from playing that you can't get from composing. And when you play, it's like a composition anyway. You make the outline.'[12] The irony and the difficulty lie in the fact that themes and structures are accepted as compositions and can be registered as such, but the improvisations on them, which is often where the most potent music is created, cannot usually be registered as compositions.

In 1959 Miles Davis's reputation was blossoming and the scope of his activities widening. Although the specialist magazines still wrote about all aspects of his music, he was featuring more often in the non-specialist, national press. By now his fans were often people who were, not jazz enthusiasts, but Miles Davis fans. In March, a long feature written by Nat Hentoff was published in the sophisticated, up-market magazine, *Esquire*. In April, between the two recording sessions which produced *Kind of Blue*, Miles was recorded and filmed for a major TV programme, a thirty-minute show in a prestige series produced for CBS by a Welshman called Robert Herridge. The show was called 'The Sound of Miles Davis', and it immediately broke all the rules. Cannonball Adderley was ill and couldn't make the programme, so the first item was a nine-minute quintet version of 'So What', which took the show right up to the middle commercial – the show was sponsored though CBS didn't network it. The second half featured Miles with Gil Evans and the orchestra (which had already played some riffs behind the solos on 'So What') playing three pieces from *Miles Ahead*: 'The Duke', 'Blues for Pablo', and 'New Rhumba'. The programme was not shown until July 1960, when it caused quite a stir because of its uncompromising emphasis on the music, and the casual, relaxed appearance of the musicians. Instead of the usual formal black suits, for example, Miles wore a tweed jacket and a sports shirt with a silk, Ascot-knotted kerchief, and Gil Evans wore a 'sloppy' sweater, though one reviewer hastened to mention that 'the effect wasn't pretentiously messy, beatnik-slobbism; only comfortable.'[13] Between the recording and the transmission, Davis watched the film at least five times.

Shortly after the TV recording, Coltrane also fell ill, and although Miles had signed a contract to play a Milwaukee night club, he cancelled the booking, thus risking legal proceedings and a fine. This gives some indication of how highly he rated his two saxophonists; if either of them had been fit, he would certainly have fulfilled his part of the contract and played at the club. But there were already signs that Adderley and Coltrane might not stay with the sextet much longer. Miles's growing fame was reflecting on all his musicians, and Adderley with his direct, blues-based style, and Coltrane with his passionate innovations, were both building up a substantial following. Cannonball was already getting inquiries from club owners about when he would start his own band, because they noticed the tremendous audience response when Cannonball's name was announced. But for the moment, there were strong inducements to stay with Miles. Adderley stated clearly why he wanted to stay: 'Jazz has no place for stagnation. I know one thing for sure. You can't repeat yourself night after night when you're working with Miles Davis. Miles and Coltrane are creating all the time and the challenge is tremendous...Miles's group is as it should be. It's a laboratory. New and exciting music is played each night...I learn so much being around him.'[14]

But despite all the critical acclaim, the recognition, the prestige both in the USA and abroad, Miles Davis was still experiencing racial discrimination. In the early summer of 1959, for example, he drove to Chicago for an engagement, and rolled his imported Ferrari (a sure badge of money and status) into a motel on the shores of Lake Michigan, only to be told that there had been a mix-up with the reservations. But back in New York in August, Miles was to suffer an indignity so gross that it made the Chicago incident seem negligible.

One hot night, when the Davis sextet was working at Birdland on Broadway, Miles escorted a girl out of the club and hailed a cab for her. Afterwards, he speculated that it may have been this which

110

sparked off the whole incident, because the girl was white. After her cab drove off, Miles took a breather on the pavement outside the club. As he stood there, a police patrolman came up and told him to move along. Miles replied, 'I work here', and added that he just wanted a breath of fresh air and would soon be returning to the club. The patrolman asked Miles if he was a 'wise guy', and said: 'If you don't move, I'll have to lock you up.' Miles replied, 'Go ahead, lock me up.'

The reports of what happened next are conflicting, but it seems that as Miles's attention was fixed on the first patrolman, a second one came up behind him and beat him savagely on the head with a blackjack. Covered in blood from his head wounds, Miles was taken to jail and his temporary cabaret card confiscated. A musician could not work in New York unless he had such a card. During the fracas, an angry crowd of onlookers jammed the sidewalks blocking the traffic, and later a crowd gathered outside the 54th Precinct where Miles was being held. He was kept in jail overnight and released on $1,000 bail the following day. He needed five stitches in his scalp, and said later, 'They beat me on the head like a tom-tom.' One eye-witness commented: 'It was the most horrible, brutal thing I'd ever seen. People were crying out to the man not to kill Miles.'[15]

The incident was given a great deal of publicity in the New York press, with indignant headlines everywhere and strong sympathy for Miles. The Negro paper, *Amsterdam News*, gave Miles's story prominence, and said that he had suffered from a 'Georgia head-whipping'. And press around the world covered the story, the London *Melody Maker*, for example, printing a photograph of the blood-spattered Miles standing with Frances in the police precinct. Ironically, it was Miles Davis who was charged with disorderly conduct and assault. The two policemen claimed that Miles had made the first violent move: 'Davis grabbed the stick and was going to hit the officer,' claimed the second patrolman, 'So I hit him with a billy on the head'. Miles's contention was that he was trying to protect his mouth from being battered, or his lip damaged, which is why he may have seemed to be trying to 'grab the stick'. The day after the affair, the Local 802 of the American Federation of Musicians sent the Police Commissioner a telegram requesting a complete investigation because of the conflicting accounts, and a few days later, the police said Miles could have his cabaret card back any time he wanted to collect it.

Repercussions from the affair rumbled on for months, finally stopping in the spring of 1960. In October, Miles was cleared of the charges of disorderly conduct, which still left the simple assault charge. His manager, Harold Lovett, threatened to file a million-dollar damage suit against the city of New York. But after Miles was also cleared of the other charge (the judge commented: 'It would be

111

a travesty of justice to adjudge the victim of an illegal arrest guilty of the crime of assaulting the one who made the arrest ')[16] he was not anxious for Lovett to proceed with the filing of his suit for false arrest, assault and battery, and malicious prosecution. Jack Whittemore, his booking agent, explained: 'Miles feels that if he pushes the City too far, even though he might win his damage suit, he would then be the target for the police who would be looking to nail him on any little charge they could think of. He feels he has proved his point if he is found innocent on all charges.'[17]

As the decade drew to an end, there was a feeling of change in the air. In the early autumn, Cannonball Adderley finally left the sextet even though Miles offered to guarantee him an annual salary of $20,000. Also, the new technique of stereo recording had just been introduced, and *Porgy and Bess* had been Miles's first album in stereo. When Gil Evans was editing and mixing the tapes for that LP, he was assisted by a Columbia employee called Teo Macero who, in 1959, was officially made the CBS A and R (Artist and Repertoire) man for Miles Davis. He became the key man in Miles Davis's recording career, and has retained that role ever since. This was a significant change for Miles because, from the late fifties onward, actual recording techniques were to play an increasing role in music generally, and in Miles's music in particular. His orchestral albums, especially, needed great technical expertise for their realization, because the ensemble led by Gil Evans was not self-balancing like a symphony orchestra.

Teo Macero was a master craftsman of recording techniques, and one of the pioneers of stereo recording, but he was also much more than this. He had a Master's degree from Juilliard, and had also played tenor saxophone with Charlie Mingus's Composers' Workshop. Between 1953 and 1955, Macero had played on several of Mingus's albums, and had also appeared in 1956 at the Newport Festival with him. It was Teo Macero who produced Mingus's album *Mingus Ah Um*, which had such a seminal influence on jazz (and rock) thinking in the 1960s. His experiences with Mingus must have stood Teo Macero in good stead when he began working with Miles. His expertise was not only technical and electronic; he also knew the problems of playing an instrument, and was still composing music himself – something he continued to do all the years he was with Columbia. In the middle 1950s he'd had a Guggenheim award to write a composition. Columbia, in their laudable efforts to promote understanding of jazz, assigned Macero to work with Leonard Bernstein on an album called *What is Jazz?* Teo recalls: 'I wrote a lot of the little examples for that album. Then I wrote an arrangement of "Sweet Sue"... which never came out. According to Lenny, it was too lugubrious...Lenny said he wanted something to swing, and I said, "Then don't ask me, get somebody like Miles."

112

He said, "That's a good idea," so we got Miles…Miles wrote the chords himself.'

The Miles Davis Quintet version of 'Sweet Sue' on *What is Jazz?* is still a most lugubrious rendering of a normally bright tune. But that marked the first time that Macero and Miles worked together in the studio. After assisting Gil Evans with *Porgy*, Teo was the producer, the man in the studio control booth, for *Kind of Blue* (where he had little to do) and for all subsequent albums, except for a brief period in the early sixties when he and Miles fell out and were not on speaking terms. George Avakian, the man who had signed Miles for Columbia, and who had produced the first orchestral album, *Miles Ahead*, had left CBS, and it was his role in the company that Teo Macero was assuming. So far as Miles Davis was concerned, Teo was going to expand this role: he was not there merely to help the artist realize his music and record it, but also to become an intermediary between Miles and the CBS bosses. This became clear on the very first major project he did with Miles and Gil Evans: the recording of *Sketches of Spain*, the album with which Davis closed the old decade and opened up the new one.

It was while he was on the West Coast with his sextet early in 1959, that a friend played Miles a recording of 'Concierto de Aranjuez' for guitar and orchestra by the contemporary Spanish composer, Joaquin Rodrigo. 'After listening to it for a couple of weeks,' Miles said later, 'I couldn't get it out of my mind. Then when Gil and I decided to do this album, I played him the record and he liked it. As we usually do, we planned the programme first by ourselves for about two months.'[18] For the album, Evans rewrote and extended the middle section of the Concierto, which takes up most of side one, and for the rest of the music he went to the library and did some detailed research into Spanish music, flamenco, and the life of the Spanish gypsy. The other piece on side one is a version of an excerpt from Manuel de Falla's 1915 ballet, 'El Amor Brujo', and the second side of the album has three compositions ('The Pan Piper', 'Saeta', 'Solea') which are credited to Gil Evans himself.

More time was spent on recording and editing *Sketches of Spain* than was spent on any of the other orchestral albums, and it was Teo Macero's proselytizing on behalf of Miles and Gil which won the extra time. It was unheard of then to do ten or fifteen sessions in the studio with a big orchestra for one album, particularly with a jazz artist, but the first four studio sessions for *Sketches* were completely unproductive because Miles had flu. The president of CBS, Goddard Lieberson, expressed some concern to Macero who said: 'Miles is sick… We've had four sessions where we've received absolutely nothing from him – they were like giant rehearsals, and we were over time with the sessions too. It doesn't look like we'll finish it in five or six sessions.'

Lieberson said, 'Well, do you think it will be worth it?'

Macero replied, 'Absolutely. When we're finished we're going to have something of gigantic proportions!'

Lieberson said simply, 'Stay there until you finish it.'

It took fifteen three-hour sessions with the orchestra to record the album. But Macero's enthusiasm and Columbia's faith and daring were fully justified and amply repaid. The finished results were ultimately hailed as a masterpiece, and the album has sold steadily over the years since it was first released. In 1976, for example, sixteen years after its release, it sold 463 copies in Great Britain, and three years later, in Germany, 4,000 were sold. By 1980 it had 'gone gold'.

Apart from the forty-five hours of recording, just to get the basic tracks on tape, Teo Macero also spent about six months editing the tapes and putting the album together. Here, for the first time, stereo recording techniques were fully exploited. Teo says: 'There were a lot of new tricks which we tried at the time. We had the bands going off the side and one band going in the middle and then coming back and splitting it and going to the sides again. Then the whole band going out – there's a little march [on 'Saeta']...if you listen carefully, you'll hear all these things – movement...'

Sketches of Spain reveals yet a further step away from the western concept of orchestral function which insists that the ensemble has to play together with machine-like precision, and that individual musicians should merge anonymously into the ensemble which exists to express the will of a composer. *Sketches* moves even further away from this idea than *Porgy* had done, inclining more towards the non-western idea that the individuality of the musicians should be a clearly evident part of the whole, and that the music's power is heightened by a slight raggedness. What had been perhaps a deeply subconscious idea on the two previous orchestral albums, now became formulated as a conscious thought. Miles said: 'It was hard to get the musicians to *realize that they didn't have to play perfect.* [my italics] It was the *feeling that counted.*'[19] He was referring specifically to 'Saeta', but the remark stands in its general application to his whole approach. The great gap between the two musical cultures was becoming more and more apparent. The composer, Bill Russo, once said: 'The melodic curve, the organic structure, and the continuity of a Miles Davis solo...cannot be perceived very easily by a classically trained musician.'[20] And at this stage of his career, Miles Davis seemed to be turning his back on much of the western musical tradition, and concentrating more on ethnic elements. With *Sketches of Spain,* he knew exactly what he was doing, and stated at a press conference in 1960: 'Flamenco is the Spanish counterpart of our blues.'[21] When asked what he and Gil Evans were going to do next, he replied: 'Gil and I are interested in

114

doing an African ballet album. I think that will be the next direction.'[22] But something he put into words in 1964 clarifies his thinking on this whole matter of the two cultural standpoints: 'As for Gunther Schuller, I can see why [Leonard] Bernstein would get along with him. It's like the difference between talking to a Spanish nobleman and talking to a gypsy. Bernstein can talk to Schuller, who's a classical musician and doesn't really play jazz; but he can't talk to Tony Williams, my drummer – they'd have nothing in common.'[23] Miles Davis is plumping for the values of the gypsy.

Although the three great orchestral albums are always discussed as if they are virtually the same sort of thing, each one has a very distinct and separate identity. *Sketches* in particular differs strongly from the first two in several important ways. Here, for the first time, there is an extensive use of percussion (tambourines, maracas, castanets etc.) for colour and texture as well as for rythmic purposes. Throughout the album there are frequent long periods based on a single scale where the interest is textural and spatial rather than harmonic, and where Miles solos over this mobile (but harmonically static) backcloth. There is also a frequent use of *ostinati* – repeated rhythmic figures – several of which often go on simultaneously and are sustained for long periods, thus creating a hypnotic, 'possessed' effect. There are passages where Miles solos – 'calls' – out-of-time against a rich tapestry of sounds.

The trumpeter's inward-looking self is exquisitely expressed on the 'Concierto', but a wilder, more primeval meditation is given voice on 'Saeta' and 'Solea'. Here his vocalized tone is developed and expressed to its fullest extent. On 'Saeta', which occupies the same sort of role on *Sketches* as 'Prayer' did on *Porgy,* the passionate muezzin calls which Miles utters over a droning tremulo, again make the flesh crawl. 'Solea' is a tour de force. It is a long piece presenting a continuous dialogue between Miles and the ensemble which lasts for ten minutes, and yet the interest, the movement, the efficacy of Miles's phrases which are often very 'eastern' in their intervals, are all sustained throughout.

All the conceptual implications of *Sketches of Spain* were not to be more fully explored until Miles recorded *Bitches Brew* in 1969. Meanwhile, when *Sketches* was released in 1960, it was so different that many critics simply didn't know what to make of it. At the same 1960 press conference, Miles was asked: 'Mr Davis, do you feel this new work of yours is jazz?' Miles replied: 'It's music, and I like it. I'll play anything I take a fancy to, if I feel it's possible for me to do it.'[24] Asked the same question in Great Britain, Miles replied: 'I think so...what do you think?'[25] John S. Wilson, the *New York Times* reviewer, failed to see anything of merit in the album at all, and wrote:

115

This is the third album that Mr. Evans has written and conducted for and with Mr. Davis, and one is struck by the continued exploitation of a similarity of sound on all three as Mr. Evans creates a rich, exotic, hanging background through which emerges the languid, pained sound that Mr. Davis squeezes from his trumpet...For the listener in search of jazz, there is mighty little of that commodity evident in any of these selections except for a portion of the 'Concierto'.[26]

Sketches of Spain brought to a fitting climax the period of intense creativity which had begun in 1954. These six productive years seem to divide naturally into two parts: the classic small-group recordings of 1954-56 plus the *Scaffold* film music and the orchestral album, *Miles Ahead* of 1957, are all like preparations for the tremendous achievements in the years 1958-60: *Milestones, Porgy and Bess, Kind of Blue* and *Sketches of Spain*. And there is an almost uncanny parallel with Miles Davis's second great creative period: 1964-67 when he is once more producing conceptually fresh small-group music which is a preparation for the huge achievements of the years 1968-70: *Miles in the Sky, Filles de Kilimanjaro, In a Silent Way, Bitches Brew, Live-Evil, Jack Johnson*.

By the beginning of the 1960s. Miles had won both the *Down Beat* international critics' poll and the readers' poll. As a kind of bonus, the *Down Beat* readers also voted him jazz personality of 1959. As one club-owner remarked: 'The trouble with you is that everybody *likes* you, you little son of a bitch!'[27] With his popularity and prestige at their highest points, and with controversy about his work raging more violently than ever, Miles Davis was about to start a period of intense travel abroad where interest in his music and his mystique had mushroomed from Europe to Japan.

10
After Coltrane

'I pay my sidemen the highest prices because they're
worth it and I've got the best rhythm section in jazz. I'm retired now because
I don't do nothing unless I want to.'[1]

Miles Davis in 1960

By the beginning of 1960, the London *Melody Maker* readers' poll
had voted Miles Davis top on trumpet. For the first time in the
history of that poll, Louis Armstrong had lost his title as the 'World's
Top Trumpeter'. The honour now belonged to the thirty-three-
year-old Miles, whose whole view of himself and his function was
totally opposite to that of Armstrong. Miles said: 'I ain't no entertainer, and ain't trying to be one... My troubles started when I
learned to play the trumpet and hadn't learned to dance...they want
you to not only play your instrument, but to entertain them too,
with grinning and dancing.'[2] In the same *Melody Maker* poll, Gil
Evans had ousted Duke Ellington for first place in the big band
composer/arranger category.

By this time, Miles's super-stardom had reached such a pitch that
very often when he was announced on stage or in clubs in America,
there would be moans and screams from girls in the audience, rather
like the reception by teenagers of a popular singer such as Sinatra.
At this point in his career he was, in fact, well-served by critics.
Three of the most professional and most perceptive critics in the
USA – Leonard Feather, Nat Hentoff and Ralph J. Gleason –
analysed, assessed, expounded and explained Miles brilliantly.
Hentoff published a long and graphic account (*Hi Fi Review*,
February 1960), of one of the recording sessions for *Sketches of
Spain*. This had a kind of documentary realism and included dialogue
as it was spoken in the studio, giving a vivid impression of the
occasion. Later in the year, Feather was to intercede on Miles's
behalf with the British public, and at regular intervals, Gleason
peppered local papers from coast to coast in the USA, with articles
and explanations about Davis.

It was at this time that people were beginning to notice Miles's
apparent oblivion of audiences: his never making announcements
either of tunes or of the names of his musicians, and his persistent

refusal to acknowledge applause. He had been behaving this way for years, of course, but now that so many people were aware of him, many of whom had only recently discovered his music, his stage demeanour was the subject of comment. Ralph Gleason tried to make sense of this:

> He eschews the spotlight; never smiles, makes no announcements. Many people are annoyed when, at the close of his solo, Davis walks off the stage. The Davis syndrome in performance is free individual creation, always a major part of jazz, carried to the ultimate...Davis's music is as uncompromising as any in history. Sociologically, he has become a symbol of the contemporary Negro as well, winning his success solely on his merits with no bending to public taste, no concession to entertainment and absolutely no cultivation of 'contacts' or of anyone likely to do him any good. In other words, no 'Uncle Tomming'.[3]

There were also in-depth articles in French jazz magazines in that same year, and one of them, in a long piece entitled, 'Why so Mean, Miles?', commented: 'The behaviour of Miles Davis is not that of an ordinary star. It is that of a strong man who has decided to live without hypocrisy.'[4]

Where the bebop movement had failed to get the status of the musician elevated to that of artist rather than entertainer, Miles Davis was succeeding. Gleason's analysis, though illuminating and perceptive, nevertheless errs on the side of romanticism. Gleason (more so than Leonard Feather who has probed very deeply into the Davis psyche over the years) was fascinated by the trumpeter almost to the point of adulation. Quite clearly, Miles knew how to 'impose himself', to make his presence felt and to shape events as he wanted them, because he was aware of all the salient factors in any situation.

In February 1960, the winter weather was so bad that, instead of flying to Chicago where they had an engagement at the Sutherland Lounge, the quintet had to go by train. Despite sub-zero temperatures, when the musicians arrived at the hotel, there were queues of people standing in the snow – which was six feet deep in places – waiting to get into the place. The audience was not deterred by the threat of fire either. Jimmy Cobb recalls:

> And then another peculiar thing happened while we were working there...on the first floor of the hotel there was the reception desk, and right across from the reception desk was a little travel agency. Some time that day they had a short in the wires in the ceiling and it started smoking...it caught fire. The room where we were working was right on the first floor – you could walk directly from the reception desk into the club. And the club was packed! And the firemen were outside the door putting out this fire, and

118

nobody left! Smoke was all in the joint and nobody left...and the place was packed...Yeah, Miles was very popular.

The previous autumn, the jazz world had been shaken by the appearance at the Five Spot in New York of the alto-saxophonist, Ornette Coleman. He had dispensed with chord sequences and traditional scales altogether and was playing 'free' jazz. But Coleman had not, like Miles, Mingus and Coltrane, got to his present position by working through and mastering all the known techniques of jazz: he had got there by rejecting everything except the old format of theme-solos-reprise of theme, and by expressing a kind of naked emotion – the blues and roots of the music. For those who remembered Bird and bebop, it seemed like a second coming, and many musicians not in Miles Davis's impregnable position, feared they would be made stylistically redundant overnight. Coleman was hailed by Leonard Bernstein, John Lewis, Gunther Schuller and others, as the new Messiah. He was lionized, given a huge amount of press and publicity, and found it relatively easy to get well-paid work. By September 1960, his two albums for Atlantic were selling 25,000 at a time when six thousand was a good average sale for a jazz record. Miles Davis believed that many of Coleman's detractors were simply jealous, and commented: 'I like Ornette, because he doesn't play clichés.'[5] And Jimmy Cobb said later: 'At the time I don't think anybody was really worried about being dated with what Miles was playing.' But it must have seemed ironical to Coltrane that he was getting so little recognition, whereas Ornette, who was five years younger, was getting so much. One of Trane's disadvantages was that he was always in the shadow of Miles Davis's fame and prestige. His liking and admiration for Miles were very great indeed, and the two of them had been through much together. Teo Macero said of Trane: 'He'd smile like a little boy when Miles would play something he liked.'[6]

Everywhere Miles's group went, there was controversy – some-times very bitter controversy – about Coltrane, and his impact was intensified by his stamina (both physical and mental) which was formidable and, in fact, without precedent in jazz. He was taking the whole art of improvisation into another realm of values entirely. No longer was it simply a pretty variation on an easily digested melodic theme; now, with Coltrane, it was becoming a vast and incessant flow of original ideas all conceived and expressed at white heat and with what Ralph Gleason called 'the urgency of his almost primeval cry'.[7] So it must have become clear to Coltrane, at the beginning of 1960 that, in order to realize his own potential and to get the kind of recognition he needed, he would have to leave Miles and go out on his own. Jimmy Cobb describes the situation in those last hectic months Coltrane spent with Miles's quintet: 'Coltrane

119

would play all night, and come off in the intermission and go somewhere and play...stand in a corner or something...You know, Miles had to make him stop, because he would play an hour solo himself, and we were only supposed to be on the stand for forty minutes or something. He had incredible chops – he couldn't stop. Miles used to say, "Man, look, why don't you play twenty-seven choruses instead of twenty-eight?"...Coltrane would say, "I get involved in this thing and I don't know how to stop."' On one occasion when Coltrane said he didn't know how to stop, Miles said: 'Try taking the saxophone out of your mouth!'⁸

In March and April, the Miles Davis Quintet became part of a JATP (Jazz At The Philharmonic) package tour organized by Norman Granz. The itinerary was a tour of Scandinavia, France and Germany, and this was the first time Miles had been abroad with his full group. Although Coltrane wanted to leave, Miles managed to persuade him to do the tour. Jimmy Cobb recalled: 'All he had with him were his horns, an airline bag, and a toilet kit. He didn't really want to make the gig, but Miles talked him into it. He sat next to me on the bus, looking like he was ready to split any time.'⁹ There was savage controversy over Coltrane in Germany and France. It was rumoured that at one major concert in Germany, when Coltrane was booed, Miles had angrily stopped the music and taken his group offstage. In France, apart from bewilderment at Miles's stage behaviour, there was considerable dismay about Coltrane, and many members of audiences walked out. The furore reverberated in the French jazz papers for months afterwards. But Coltrane and Miles were a new breed of musicians whom even the experienced Norman Granz failed to understand. He was mystified and furiously angry when he tried to set up a jam session involving Coltrane and Stan Getz for a television programme, and Trane had the audacity to refuse to do it. But given the direction and development of Coltrane and Miles since 1955, it should have been obvious that neither of them would want to indulge in this kind of activity. Their battle was not an external one with other instrumentalists, but an internal affair against old, received ideas and old habits of thought.

Back in the USA, after a few more engagements with Miles, Coltrane left the quintet in order to start his own group. His departure was a severe blow to Miles who almost broke down and wept during their last gig together, which was in Philadelphia. So strongly did he feel that he even went to the microphone and made a brief announcement about the saxophonist's imminent departure from the group. And, as Jimmy Cobb commented: 'He never talks with nobody about nothing, so you know, he really must have felt something for Coltrane.' The saxophonist's departure left a gap which, in some ways, Miles was never able to fill again. Trane had been interested in artistic growth, and his incessant exploration of

120

the unknown had sparked off ideas in Miles and had given the trumpeter the kind of challenge he needed. Also, Coltrane's 'sheets of sound' had been a superb contrast with Miles's own spare phrasing. From now on, Miles was going to have to produce the contrasts – spare brooding and multi-noted aggression – himself. There was simply no other saxophonist of Coltrane's calibre in jazz at that time. The only other one who might have matched his power was Sonny Rollins, and he was in semi-retirement. When Trane left, Miles must have felt quite naked and insecure, and to fill the saxophone vacancy he turned to an old friend and an established star, Sonny Stitt, the man he had first met in St Louis around 1943. But despite the personnel change, the popularity of Miles Davis and his group continued to grow. During the year, Miles himself was chosen favourite jazz instrumentalist by a poll of America's leading disc jockeys in *Billboard* (trade paper of the music industry). And in *Down Beat*'s first disc jockey poll in May, six of Miles's albums were placed, *Porgy and Bess* being voted first, and *Kind of Blue* third. In August, the quintet with Sonny Stitt had a residency at the Village Vanguard in New York, playing to packed houses and ecstatic audiences. One critic wrote: 'The room was literally jammed...Many of the audience were obviously in protoplasmic harmony with the proceedings; that is, their neurons were jumping.'[10] And after this engagement, the group went off again to Europe for a British tour followed by dates in Paris and Stockholm. This time the French gave Miles and the group a tremendously warm reception, cheering them at the end of the first piece, 'Walkin'', and never ceasing to acclaim them for the rest of the night. Both houses at L'Olympia were packed – 2,000 people at each performance.

Charlie Parker had never played in Britain, and this tour was to be Miles Davis's first visit. A build-up in the musical press started some weeks before he arrived and was an attempt to make up for some fifteen years of ignorance on the part of the British public. This publicity campaign culminated in a long feature article in *Melody Maker* by Leonard Feather who emphasized the glamour surrounding Miles and attempted to reconcile the apparently para-doxical qualities of the trumpeter. Feather insisted that Miles was not anti-white, pointed out that 'the more sensitive an artist is, the more difficult he may find it to deal with insensitive people', and tabulated Miles's trappings of success:

Miles has found out the hard way, that money is power, even in race relations. He may tend to work a gig for less money if the promoter is a Negro. His fee for a single job nowadays ranges from $2,500 to $4,000 out of which his four sidemen only cost him a total of two or three hundred a night. Miles today is a wealthy man, owning some $50,000 worth of stock. He just bought an

121

entire building in a good section of Manhattan, where he lives on the first two floors renting out the rest of the building as apartments. He drives a Ferrari that cost $12,500 and he likes to drive fast. He has a substantial five-figure annual income from Columbia Records. Miles's apparent aloofness on the stand has a devastating effect on women, who often find his good looks more irresistible than his most lyrical solo. Recently he was married to a lovely, petite girl named Frances Taylor, who teaches dancing. He has remained close to his daughter and two sons (seventeen, fourteen and ten) by an early marriage.[11]

Despite all the column inches and the comforting presence of Sonny Stitt who was already known to the British public via JATP, there were terrific outcries from critics, who should have known better, about Miles Davis's stage behaviour. However, one or two writers rose to the occasion, and that most perceptive of critics, Max Harrison, wrote:

The concerts revealed – again as no record has – the force with which high notes were attacked and sustained, and the controlled vehemence of some of the up-tempo phrasing showed that Davis's music has expanded its scope to the point where his mode of expression can now be as violent as it is intense...in his best moments...he extemporised solos of sometimes fierce, often acutely concentrated lyricism that were so moving as to be almost disquieting. One can analyse such improvisations in terms of their unusual melodic style, tone, personal dynamics and nuance, but the mystery of their strange power to move us remains unexplained.[12]

A few other British critics made intelligent and honourable attempts to say something pertinent about the music, but for the most part, the Miles Davis tour of Britain revealed a sadly parochial press. The *New York Post* commented acidly: 'Miles Davis packed his trumpet and took off for Paris, Stockholm and home, where the citizenry is less likely to be fuddled by his sophisticated approach to jazz...Londoners were bothered by the fact that he seldom acknowledged applause. Jazz in this city is back in the New Orleans era. Boisterous Dixieland is the favourite. Davis dropped into this wasteland late in September'.[13]

For economic reasons, these foreign tours had to consist of concerts in big halls, but Miles did not feel really comfortable under such circumstances. He explained: 'Nobody can relax at concerts, the musicians or the people, either. You can't do nothing but sit down, you can't move around, you can't have a drink. A musician has to be able to let loose everything in him to reach the people. If the musician can't relax, how's he going to make the people feel what he feels? The whole scene of jazz is feeling.'[14] Miles certainly preferred the intimate atmosphere of a club for making his music, and of

122

course, under such conditions, when the audience are almost touching the star of the evening, the fact that he is not announcing titles or acknowledging applause becomes insignificant.

After the European trip, Miles returned to New York and in November 1960 took a two-week residency at the Village Vanguard, a tiny club (capacity perhaps two hundred) situated in Greenwich Village. The evenings were shared with the Bill Evans trio with legendary bassist, Scott La Faro, and drummer Paul Motian. It was after hearing the Evans version of 'Some Day My Prince Will Come', during this engagement, that Miles began playing that unlikely song himself. At the Vanguard, Miles and the group were in their element, and reviews mentioned the very active responses of audiences to the music. It was also noted that Miles went about his business in an amiable way, chatting with members of the group and nodding politely when applauded.

In January 1961, a long feature article entitled 'Miles Davis: Evil Genius of Jazz', was published in the American Negro magazine, *Ebony*. The writer, Marc Crawford, was black and the piece which took up seven pages of the magazine and was liberally illustrated with photographs, presented a detailed account of Miles as a successful and independent member of his race. There were photos of Miles playing, of Miles and his wife, his mother, his father, on the farm, in restaurants, and finally a whole sequence of pictures of him working out in the gym. But even in the heat of resentment at racial prejudice, Miles retained his balance and fairness:

> I don't like to stress race because I have friends of all colours. But everything I see around me stresses it. People say 'Would you want your sister to marry a Negro?' That's jive even to ask the question. I might not want to marry your sister. It makes me sick. It makes me prejudiced. All I want for my kids is a simple thing. To be free. To not have to think about colour or anything. Just think about what it is they want to do and do it. And Negroes who try to act the way they think other people want them to act bug me worse than Uncle Toms.

Later in the year, Marc Crawford also looked Miles up in Chicago where the trumpeter was staying at his in-laws' home. Crawford wanted to write another feature, this time on Miles's relationship with Gil Evans. He found Davis in a relaxed and expansive mood, clad in a dressing-gown and slippers, sipping Dutch beer and listening to Ravel's piano concerto in G major. Miles had just cooked himself a late breakfast of eggs, hamburger and tomatoes, garnished with salts of garlic and celery. Perhaps it was the pleasant change of actually having a *black* writer who wanted to interview him which made the trumpeter so co-operative. Eventually, in the middle of the proceedings, Miles phoned Evans who flew from New York to

123

'hang out' with Davis for a few days. Evans said that he worked only for Miles and himself, that he could not do anything he did not want to do, and that he considered himself a 'commercial arranger', but only in the sense that 'what I write is popular'. And he rejected Miles's contention that he (Evans) was just beginning to receive the acclaim his talents had long deserved. Evans said: 'I haven't been around music for twenty years just waiting to be discovered. Nor am I a recent discovery. I am just now able to do the things I couldn't do before. My product just wasn't ready.'[15]

Shortly after this, Miles was back in New York and he allowed his house to be used for a confrontation between musicians of his own generation and various jazz writers. For this event, Miles laid on a bar with a barman and a plentiful supply of food. He and Frances acted as hosts, but did not take a leading part in the discussions. The man in charge of operations was Cannonball Adderley, and the other main participants were musicians Gerry Mulligan, J.J. Johnson, Horace Silver, Billy Taylor, Gil Evans and Philly Joe Jones. The critics and writers present were Nat Hentoff, Ira Gitler, John S. Wilson, Dave Solomon, Martin Williams and Stanley Dance, and they were grilled about why they labelled everything – 'East Coast', 'West Coast', 'Hard Bop' etc. – after which they were asked to define the qualities that made a real critic, and to say who fell into this category. As is usual in this kind of confrontation, the replies and the arguments were inconclusive, but once everyone had let off steam the evening subsided into chat and more drinking until all took their leave, saying goodnight to their pleasant host and charming hostess.

After the engagement at the Village Vanguard in November 1960, Sonny Stitt had left the quintet, and there were two candidates for the saxophone vacancy: Jimmy Heath and Hank Mobley. Heath would have been a very good choice; he had already recorded with Miles, and his style would have suited the quintet. Unfortunately, however, he had had some trouble with the authorities and was on parole. Although he played a few engagements with Miles, he ultimately lost the job because his parole board refused to allow him to travel beyond a ninety-mile radius of Philadelphia. Hank Mobley, although four years younger than Miles and Jimmy Heath, was basically from the same generation. He had worked with Max Roach, Dizzy Gillespie, Horace Silver, Art Blakey, and Thelonious Monk among others, and had established himself as one of the most important of the younger tenor players of the fifties. When Jimmy Heath became ineligible for the job, Mobley joined the Davis quintet but stayed with the group for barely a year, because his style was so unsuited to Miles's music. Mobley's laid-back way of playing – a kind of legato approach which phrases *over* the rhythm section and almost never cuts into it – was antithetical to the whole approach

124

of Miles and Coltrane.

In March 1961, when Miles Davis went into the studios to make another album, John Coltrane was working with his quartet at the Apollo Theatre, and Miles asked him to come to the studio in the intervals between the sessions at the Apollo, and play on some of the album tracks. The group was in the middle of recording the title track, 'Some Day My Prince Will Come', when Trane walked in with his horn. Hank Mobley had the chords written on a sheet of manuscript, and Coltrane, who had never played this tune before, simply looked at the chord symbols and played a solo which is alive with expression and tonal beauty. Coltrane played on one other track, a modal piece in 3/4 called 'Teo'. It was based on four scales played for unspecified duration by each soloist (cf. 'Flamenco Sketches'), and had a Spanish feel. On this track, Trane's playing is superlative, with a magnificent entry and a flow of ideas which bubbles into a climax of 'sheets of sound' – phrases which double back on one another and are both continuous and circular. Miles was clearly inspired by this, and played a second solo on the piece, achieving greater intensity than he had in his first one. For Hank Mobley, it must have been depressing to hear such a contrast to his own playing on the album. *Some Day My Prince Will Come*, although it has two gems by Coltrane, some fine playing by Miles, and some excellent work from Wynton Kelly, is nevertheless very patchy. It is uneven in quality, and it is lacking in that group identity which always characterizes the best Miles Davis albums. Not surprisingly at this stage in his career, the trumpeter's musical vision was faltering.

There had always been a difference between Miles's live performances and his studio recordings. In the studio, the duration of the music is circumscribed and therefore form becomes important. Also, in the studio, every nuance, every tiny inflexion is captured, and in a very real sense, many of Miles's studio recordings were exquisite. But in live performance the idea of form became less important; the pieces began, offered a string of solos, and then ended. The interest lay in how much each player could say in his solo, how inventive his musical language was, and how much he could communicate his feeling to the audience. So in live performance, one would expect a soloist to take tremendous risks revealing not only superb phrases and ideas, but also muffed lines, occasional mistakes and failures. As Miles's quintet was producing only uncertain results in the studio, it was an obvious step to try to capture on shellac the dynamism of the group's live performances. In April 1961, the quintet had a booking at the Black Hawk, a club in San Francisco, and two of the nights there were recorded for a live album.

The Black Hawk was a small and shabby jazz club of which its owner, Guido Caccienti, once said, 'I've worked and slaved for years to keep this place a sewer.'[16] But it had good acoustics, and was renowned for the quality of the music to be heard there. Most of the leading jazz musicians, including Charlie Parker, had played there and had found the relaxed atmosphere conducive to good music. The very shabbiness of the place deterred the expense-account type of (white) businessmen of whom Miles once said: 'They ain't come to hear good music...They drink too much, they get loud...I can't stand dumb-ass people not respecting the other customers that have come to hear the music. Sometimes one table like that has bugged me so that when I get home or to my hotel, I walk the floor because I can't sleep.'[17] Guido Caccienti had a rare respect for music and musicians. He said, 'You gotta dig music, you come in here.'[18] And he never complained when Miles didn't bother to play the last set of the evening – which happened most nights.

The Black Hawk sessions were Miles's first premeditated attempt to make a live album. Two nights (the Friday and Saturday) were recorded, and Miles and Teo Macero later edited the tapes down to make two albums out of enough material for perhaps four. This is why the tempos of various pieces go up and down: different versions of the same piece were spliced together. Jimmy Cobb commented with some feeling, because drummers are always blamed for fluctuating tempos: 'They'd take the same tunes and Miles would find solos he liked better on one version than another, and if it was close enough he'd just...splice...They spliced that album to pieces...But it was close because Teo was doing it and he's a musician, and Miles was probably telling him where to do it...But you can hear the splices.'

The Black Hawk sessions are notable for the exceptionally dynamic playing of the rhythm section and their interplay with Miles. It is not just a dialogue of trumpet and drums, but a three-way affair with Wynton Kelly's piano incessantly responding to and interacting with the trumpeter's phrases. Kelly shows exceptional imagination in all his performances with Miles from this point on. In contrast to the previous month's studio session, at the Black Hawk the group feeling is phenomenal, and Kelly's inspired piano accompaniment makes Miles push his abilities to the limits. His playing is now shot through and through with the funky phrases of the old blues tradition, and his sustained use of the highest registers is really thrilling. Wynton Kelly has attempted to describe something of his relationship with Miles Davis: 'He's a pretty cat. If you really knew him, you couldn't knock him. He's more like a sideman than a leader. And he's always creating, playing outside the chords and me and the rhythm section finding him. When he gasses himself you can feel it all over the bandstand and sometimes I'll look up and catch that little smirk on his face and then I know for sure.'[19]

A few weeks later, Miles was 'Fashion Personality For The Month

126

of May' in the *Gentleman's Quarterly*, and on the nineteenth of that same month, he allowed himself to be persuaded to play a concert at New York's Carnegie Hall. This was to be a benefit concert for an organization called the African Research Foundation, and the proceeds were to go to buy a mobile medical unit to be sent to Tanganyika (now Tanzania). Before this, no one had ever been able to persuade Davis to appear on a New York concert stage, and on this occasion it was his interest in the African Research Foundation which prompted him to agree to do so. Miles was to appear with his own quintet, and also with the orchestra led by Gil Evans – the first time Davis had ever appeared in public with the Evans unit.

The concert was a sell-out, and Miles, showing devastating form, dominated the whole evening. It was almost as if he was demonstrating to himself and to the world that he was self-sufficient, that he could carry any event of any magnitude by himself – without the aid of John Coltrane. It was an evening of inspired music, and it was also recorded by CBS. All the critics wrote ecstatic reviews, and even the old sceptic, John S. Wilson, was captivated, admitting:

> The evening was a triumph for Mr Davis. He played brilliantly... And although he has often been charged with treating his audiences disdainfully, he not only smiled on a couple of occasions but acknowledged applause with a quick glance over the footlights and a slight nod of the head...Last night [he] seemed intent on proving his all-round capabilities on the trumpet. He played with tremendous fire and spirit, soaring off into high-note runs with confidence and precision, building lines bristling with searing emotion and yet retaining all the warmest, singing elements of his gentler side. He was in the spotlight almost throughout the evening, yet he never faltered, never seemed to tire and poured out a stunning series of magnificent trumpet solos.[20]

All the other reviews were equally superlative, and justifiably so, because the existing LP, *Miles Davis at Carnegie Hall – The Legendary Performance of May 19, 1961*, which preserves only about half of that evening's music, shows that, in the words of another reviewer, 'Few jazz performances have touched the heights of that evening. It was jazz at its finest.'[21] With the Evans orchestra, Miles performed the 'Concierto de Aranjuez', 'Saeta' and 'Solea', but these were not issued on the live album because *Sketches of Spain* had only just been released.

This hugely successful concert was almost spoiled and cut short by a political incident. When Miles was in the middle of 'Some Day My Prince Will Come', Max Roach, dressed in a white jacket and carrying a placard on which was painted: AFRICA FOR THE AFRICANS! FREEDOM NOW!, walked up and sat down on the stage apron, while Davis and the crowd looked on in amazement. A moment later Roach was joined by another demonstrator. Miles waved his trumpet at Roach in dismay and then stopped the music and walked off-stage. Security guards carried off Max Roach and his companion, and backstage people talked Miles into going back on, which he eventually did to prolonged applause. The anger Davis felt expressed itself in the even greater intensity of the music. One critic noted: 'He returned to the stage...a different musician, swinging with what Gerry Mulligan has termed "controlled violence".'[22]

Later, Miles said, 'I don't know what Max was doing. Ask him.'[23] Roach said: 'I was told some things about the Foundation that I thought Miles should know. Some people tried to contact him, but they couldn't get to him. I went on stage because I wanted Miles to be aware of these things.'[24] Roach was referring to accusations by a group of African nationalists who picketed outside the hall before the concert, that the Foundation was in league with South African diamond interests seeking to 'enslave' Africans instead of helping them. But these reasons seem lame and unconvincing. After the concert Roach shouted through the stage door: 'Tell Miles I'm sorry. Tell him he was so great I was crying during the first half. Tell Miles I love him.'[25] However, inadvertently, by riling Miles, Max Roach had made some contribution to one of the great performances in jazz history, and 1961 had seen the emergence of a new Miles, a player who was now going to explore the resources of the trumpet and of himself, to their utmost limits.

11

In and Out of the Doldrums

'When it comes to human rights, these prejudiced white
people keep on acting like they own the damn franchise!'[1]

Miles Davis

Throughout the rest of 1961 and the following year, and well into
1963, although Miles Davis seemed to be at the pinnacle of his
career and in a virtually impregnable economic and artistic position,
he was nevertheless beset with anxieties and problems. These were
to do with the personnel of his group, with the race question, with
his own position in American society, and with his artistic direction.
But to an outsider, it must have seemed hardly conceivable that
Miles Davis could have any doubts about his direction, or that he
might feel, from time to time, rather insecure. His track record, his
achievements, the number of classic albums he had produced, were
already legendary. From the end of the 1950s onwards, each new
record release was often accompanied by the issue or reissue of his
early recordings. In 1959, his previous record company, Prestige,
had reissued one album and promoted six others, and taken a full
page advertisement for them in *Down Beat*. In the summer of 1961,
Prestige also released for the very first time the last of the famous
1956 quintet sessions: *Steamin' With The Miles Davis Quintet*. By
cleverly timing the release dates of the stockpile of albums Miles
had done for them in order to terminate his contract, Prestige had
cashed in on every increase in Miles's popularity.

To an outsider also, Miles Davis seemed to have all the trappings
of security and success: his expensive cars, and his brownstone
house in Manhattan with its marble-tile floors, leopard-skin rugs,
white brick walls, abstract paintings and electronic gadgets. Apart
from Miles and Frances there were four children, three of them
deriving from Miles's first marriage: Cheryl Anne in her late teens,
Gregory a year younger, and Miles junior who was born in 1950.
The fourth and youngest child, Jean-Pierre, belonged to Frances
from a former marriage. There were also pets around the house: an
Italian greyhound named Milo, and some turtles. None of the
children was particularly musical, although Cheryl Anne enjoyed
singing, and Gregory had played drums.

129

However, certain things were disquieting for Miles Davis, and one bugbear in particular was that he'd never been approached to do a tour sponsored by the US State Department. During the 1950s, America had begun sponsoring tours abroad by jazz groups. Dizzy Gillespie's big band tour of the Middle East had taken place in the late fifties, and with its personnel of twelve black and four white musicians had shown the world, as the State Department intended it to, that racial harmony was possible in America. By 1961, these tours were frequent occurrences, and yet Miles Davis had still not been asked to do one. Travelling abroad with a group was such an expensive operation that it made government subsidy very important. There was also prestige attached to being a representative of the USA in foreign parts. Miles's brief campaign to get himself noticed by the State Department began with a typically oblique move. He made an announcement to the press that he would *not* do any overseas tours for the State Department until conditions improved for Negroes in the USA. Miles said: 'Why should I go, the way they treat Negroes in this country? I don't want to go as a second-class citizen.'² But nobody paid much attention to his remarks, and by mid-summer he felt so slighted that he complained bitterly to Leonard Feather:

> I'd rather have somebody curse me out than ignore me. Anyhow, I don't want them to send me over just because I'm a Negro and they want to woo Africa...If I ever went on one of those tours, they'd have to give me a badge to wear over there. A platinum badge. It would have to say on it that this man did such and such a thing for his country and government...If Charlie Parker had been French, they'd have had a monument built for him over there, but millions of people in this country never heard of him, or just read about him when he died and then forgot him... Come to think about it, I hope the State Department does ask me to make one of those tours – just so I can have the pleasure of saying no.³

But later in 1961, he managed to make a racial breakthrough in an area which had defeated both Ray Charles and Nat Cole. The National Association for the Advancement of Coloured People (NAACP) asked Miles to play a benefit for them at San Francisco's Masonic Temple in October. The manager of the 3,200 capacity hall at first refused to allow it to be used for this purpose, giving the same reasons as he had done in the cases of Charles and Cole: 'Not because of race or colour, but because we had been advised the kind of audiences these artists draw could be destructive to our $7,000,000 auditorium.'⁴ But in Miles's case, the decision was reversed and the concert went ahead.

In September 1962, *Playboy* published a long interview with

Miles dealing exclusively with the question of racial prejudice. This two-day interview at Miles's home was by the black journalist, Marc Crawford, who had written the article in *Ebony* the previous year. On this present occasion, Crawford set the scene as follows:

...his rather unusual five-storey home, a converted Russian Orthodox church on West 77th Street near the Hudson River in New York City. Miles was between gigs at the time and we accompanied him on his restless daily home routine, asking questions at propitious moments while he worked out in his basement gymnasium, made veal chops Italian style for his family, took telephone calls from fellow musicians, his lawyer and stock-broker, gave boxing lessons to his three sons, watched TV, plucked out beginner's chords on a guitar and, of course, blew one of his two Martin trumpets.

This was Miles's most comprehensive discourse on race, and it showed that the sense of injury was both deep and far-ranging. There was still the feeling that his music was not at all valued by the American cultural establishment, and that jazz musicians were regarded as inferior to their classical counterparts: 'The average jazz musician today, if he's making it, is just as trained as classical musicians. You ever see anybody go up bugging classical musicians when they are on the job and trying to work?'

Similarly, the general social humiliations were distressing. Miles gave several devastating examples, of which two are as follows:

I sent for an electrician to fix something in the house. When he rang the bell, I answered and he looked at me like I was dirt, and said, 'I want to see the owner, Mr. Davis.' When I said, 'You looking at him,' the cat turned beet red. He had me figured as the porter. Now he's mad and embarrassed. What had I done but called to give him work? That same week I had seen a lot of them West Point cadets, and in a bar I asked why there was so many of them in town. Man, I just asked the cat a question and he moved up the bar and didn't speak! But then somebody recognized me and he got red as that electrician. He came trying to apologise and saying he had my records. I told him I had just paid enough taxes to cover his free ride at West Point, and walked out. I guess he's somewhere now with the others saying I'm such a bastard. It bugged me so, man, I wasn't worth a damn for two or three days. It wasn't just him ignoring me I was thinking about, but in two or three years, Gregory, my oldest boy, may be doing some Army time. How am I supposed to feel about him maybe serving under this cat?

In 1962, Miles's group, which was now a sextet with J.J. Johnson on trombone, won first place in the *Down Beat* critics' poll, unseating the Modern Jazz Quartet (MJQ) which had held the position ever since 1954. This must have seemed ironic to Miles; good though his current sextet was, it could not be compared with the great quintet and sextet with Coltrane and Adderley. During 1962, Miles and the group worked off and on at the Village Vanguard, and had a nine-day engagement, supported by black satirist and comic, Oscar Brown, at the Music Box Theatre, Los Angeles. But the run of consecutive great recordings, each one a masterpiece, was over for the time being. Indeed, Miles seemed reluctant to go into the recording studios at all at this time, largely because he felt he had nothing to say. So far as recording was concerned, 1962 was his poorest year for a decade. It was rumoured he planned an album of Tadd Dameron tunes, but nothing materialized. In fact, all that was produced during the year was three undistinguished studio tracks with a septet which included bongos and vocalist, Bob Dorough, and one or two South American, bossa nova style pieces with Gil Evans and the orchestra. There was not enough material for even one album. But the backlog of albums still poured steadily on to the market, and Miles's financial situation was very good. By the early 1960s, when a jazz musician 'made it', he could earn as much money as the leading conductors and soloists on the 'serious' music scene. But of the few really high earners in jazz, Miles Davis was the only one still playing small clubs.

Miles's sextet carried within it the seeds of its own disintegration. There had been fluctuations in the rhythm sections as early as autumn 1961, when Philly Joe Jones briefly replaced Jimmy Cobb at Birdhouse Club, Chicago. Red Garland had also replaced Wynton Kelly for a while, and early in 1962, when Cobb and Kelly were back, Sonny Rollins had joined for a time. J.J. Johnson, who had a strong musical life of his own, left the group permanently at the beginning of 1963 in order to fulfil some writing/composing assignments. By this time, Hank Mobley had also gone, and the rhythm section of Kelly, Chambers and Cobb were thinking of striking out on their own as a trio. External events precipitated a complete change of personnel.

At the very beginning of 1963, Miles and the group simply failed to appear for a two-night engagement at a theatre in Philadelphia. The promoter, a disc jockey called Woods, sued Miles for $25,000 which he claimed the cancellation had cost him, and the matter was eventually settled by Miles's paying $8,000 in instalments. Shortly after this, Miles had to cancel a gig in Detroit in order to protect bassist Paul Chambers from possible arrest in connection with a marital legal action. This cancellation resulted in another legal action against Miles for compensation. Finally, a few weeks later, neither Paul Chambers nor Wynton Kelly turned up for an engagement in St Louis, so Miles had to cancel yet again. This brought yet

132

another lawsuit against him. This final disaster was too much for Miles, and when he was booked for a three-week residency at the Black Hawk, he decided not to take Chambers and Kelly with him. He commented: 'They both wanted to come out to San Francisco with me, but even though they're both excellent musicians, I had to say "No".'⁵ Either events caught Miles napping, or he couldn't find the musicians he wanted, because he telephoned the Black Hawk a few nights before his scheduled opening and obtained a week's delay. He said that the left side of his face was still swollen from a root canal operation on a lower molar; but the real problem seems to have been personnel, because he ultimately arrived without a pianist, and British-born Victor Feldman who was living in Los Angeles, had to take over the piano stool for a few days. The group for the booking turned out to be a sextet with Frank Strozier on alto sax, George Coleman on tenor, Harold Mabern – piano, Ron Carter – bass, and Jimmy Cobb still on drums. As usual, when Miles was not sure he could rely on his new and unproven group, he played even more powerfully himself.

During the engagement at the Black Hawk, Jimmy Cobb left to join Chambers and Kelly, and the drum chair was filled temporarily by another Los Angeles musician, Frank Butler. While he was on the West Coast, Miles went into the studio and recorded some tracks with the Feldman-Carter-Butler rhythm section, but must have been dissatisfied with the up-tempo performances, because he went back to New York and re-recorded them with different musicians. The resulting album, *Seven Steps to Heaven*, is schizo-phrenic (half from the West Coast and half from the East Coast sessions) and shows graphically the difference between Miles at his most mannered and self-indulgent and Miles at his most vital.

The West Coast sessions featured a quartet – Miles with harmon mute and the rhythm section – playing three very slow pieces: the ballad, 'I Fall In Love Too Easily', and two lugubrious re-interpre-tations of material from the traditional jazz of the 1920s, 'Basin Street Blues', and 'Baby Won't You Please Come Home'. The choice of these two old tunes astonished the jazz world at the time and no doubt helped to take everyone's mind off the shortcomings of their treatment. It is difficult to pinpoint exactly why these two performances are so unsatisfactory. There is an almost imperceptible slackness, a kind of self-indulgence; it is Miles doing his ballad formula to death, and without the necessary interplay between himself and the group. The muted trumpet is too far forward in the mix, and the piano and rhythm section very distant. Victor Feldman was, and is, a marvellous musician, but in this case his accompan-iment seems ordinary, and the overall atmosphere is one of bland, easy-listening music. In fact, a similar atmosphere had pervaded some tracks Miles had recorded the previous year with Gil Evans.

133

They were ultimately issued on a very unsatisfactory album (which neither Miles nor Gil wanted released) called *Quiet Nights*, and the meagre big-band material which made up the bulk of the album was eked out with another small-group track from the West Coast session, 'Summer Night'.

However, a return to Miles's customary creative standards occurs on the three New York performances on *Seven Steps To Heaven*. In recruiting his new rhythm section Davis had, for the first time in his career, chosen musicians from the younger generation. His new drummer, Tony Williams, was just seventeen, bassist Ron Carter was twenty-six, and pianist Herbie Hancock was twenty-three. So far as saxophonists were concerned, Strozier had left the group after the Black Hawk residency, and George Coleman was to stay with Miles for just over a year. For Herbie Hancock, being asked to join the Miles Davis quintet was something of which he'd hardly dared dream. Later, he recalled the experience:

> I got a call from Tony Williams, and he told me that Miles was going to call and ask me to come over to his house to play...Miles called me up. He asked me if I was busy, if I was working. I was at the time, but I told him no; so he asked me if I would come over to his house the next day...Next day I went over. Tony was there with Ron and George Coleman. We ran over some things while Miles walked around and listened. Philly Joe Jones stopped by too. Then Miles called up Gil Evans. He said, 'Hey, Gil, I want you to hear my new drummer.' Because Tony really knocked him out. After we rehearsed the next day, he told us we were going to do a record in two days. I was wondering what was going on; he hadn't even told me whether I was in the group or not. So I didn't say anything, and we did the record – *Seven Steps*. Then we had another rehearsal, and he mentioned a job at Bowdoin College. I said, 'Wait a minute, Miles. You haven't told me if I'm in the group or what.' and he said, 'You made the record didn't you?' so I said, 'Yeah, okay.' That was fine. I was jumping through hoops.°

In the studio, the new young rhythm section immediately proved itself; the brash, unstoppable pulse of Tony Williams' drums, and the broad foundation of Ron Carter's 'singing' bass notes, spurred Miles into pushing himself, yet again, to the limits. On the title track, 'Seven Steps' and on 'Joshua', his use of chromaticism, which had begun to appear on the Black Hawk and Carnegie Hall live albums, was now substantially in evidence. On *Kind of Blue* with such modal pieces as 'So What' and 'All Blues', Miles had stuck to the basic scale or mode for his notes. But with the live albums, it was noticeable that on the same pieces he tended to alternate funky rhythmic phrases with more abstract ones which used any of the

134

twelve notes in any octave – also, of course, using the microtones in his inflexions. There is a kind of paradox here: on the live albums there is a tendency towards greater 'concrete' phasing in his use of bluesy and funky phrases, which is accompanied by an opposite tendency towards more abstract chromaticism. It is often the tension between these two approaches which creates the drama of the solos. After 1960, the focal point of his solo work becomes less harmonic and gradually more rhythmic and linear. In the three New York tracks of *Seven Steps*, this abstract chromaticism is already much more prominent.

Although the young rhythm section showed tremendous confidence and panache on their first recording with the great trumpeter, the difficulties of trying to live with a legend were keenly felt by all of them. At first, on live gigs Hancock tried to adopt a sort of Wynton Kelly approach, and Tony Williams played some Jimmy Cobb patterns which often derived from Philly Joe Jones. But when George Coleman took his saxophone solo, the rhythm section would abandon its self-imposed roles and open up, playing around with the pulse much more freely. Again, a kind of schizophrenia resulted, and Hancock recalled:

And then one day Miles said, 'Why don't you play like that behind me?' I remember when that happened, we were in Detroit …some club there, and we were playing all kinds of crazy things behind George. and behind Miles we played really straight. Anyway, that's when Tony and I started playing our little musical games behind Miles in a way, because we were developing this thing…After *four days* it turned around and *he* was leading *it*. Not only was he in it, but he really established that thing. And his playing was different after that. It was a most uncannily rapid adaptation to this other sound that I could ever imagine…That's what Miles does. He feeds off everybody else and kind of puts it together.

If Miles Davis's previous rhythm sections had been superb – the best in jazz at their time with Garland, Chambers and Philly Joe in the middle fifties, and Kelly, Chambers and Jimmy Cobb in the later fifties and early sixties – his rhythm section in 1963 was yet again superior. So far as straight 4/4 time-playing was concerned, it was to prove itself to be possibly the greatest rhythm section of all time, and Hancock, Carter and Williams seemed to have an inexhaustible variety of ways of creating and releasing tension, expanding and contracting space. This interaction between the rhythm section was also a continual dialogue with whoever was soloing. In fact, there was no longer the idea of a soloist and rhythm section. When a horn was playing, it was a quartet which was functioning on equal terms. Only the bass spent most of its time in a supportive role. Piano and

135

drums commented, spurred and generally conversed with the leading voice.

The new group was formed in May 1963, and appeared at the Antibes Festival in France on 27 July. To the followers of Miles's music, the new approach was once more shocking and exhilarating. With a completely new band to introduce to the public at large, Davis very wisely stuck to his old repertoire of a sprinkling of ballads and songs, some blues and some modal pieces. The performance at Antibes was recorded, and live albums were also issued of the group's performances the following year at the New York Philharmonic Hall (February), in Tokyo (July), and at the Berlin Festival (September). So five live albums (the New York Philharmonic Hall concert yielded two) documented the way Miles's new band dealt with the old material. He was not to make a studio album with the band until the beginning of 1965.

There had always been interaction in the way Miles's previous groups functioned, but there had never been anything as fundamentally wild and extreme as the performance at Antibes. Even the more conventional songs for which he used the harmon mute ('Autumn Leaves' and 'All of You') were full of internal movement. Miles's own playing now encompassed an awesome range of expression veering from tenderness to ferocity and from sparseness to prodigality. The whole group's use of space was now intensely dramatic; pauses and almost empty bars being juxtaposed against bars crammed with multiple activity. On these songs, however, Miles's solos were generally more diatonic and funky/lyrical; but the fast and more modal pieces were now taken at breakneck speed, and his open horn work was extremely abstract and chromatic. His dialogue with the drums is wild as the rhythm section boils along. The concentration and inspiration of Davis and the whole group is at white heat in these performances, and the self-indulgence of some of his recent performances in the studio has been completely banished; the enervating, self-regarding sadness obliterated by an outgoing and blistering creative onslaught. Miles had done it again – found the key musicians of the next generation, found new ways of expressing himself, and fresh avenues of exploration. According to Ralph J. Gleason, Miles was so delighted by the test pressings of the Antibes concert that he played them until they were almost worn out. Gleason commented: 'It was not a happy time for him in many ways, but these test pressings made it better.'[7]

During the autumn, Miles and Gil Evans collaborated on the music for a play called 'The Time of the Barracuda', which starred Laurence Harvey, and had a brief run in California. The music was recorded in Hollywood, and the tape recording was used for the play. Evans conducted and Miles played on the tape. The play was supposed to open on Broadway in New York in November, but for

136

some reason it never did. The collaborations between Miles and Gil seemed doomed at this point in time. Columbia despaired of getting the two of them back in the recording studio, and at the end of the year issued *Quiet Nights* which contained only twenty minutes of the orchestra and Miles, and a further six minutes of the small-group performance. Gil Evans said, 'They never should have released it; it was just half an album. But I guess they had to.'' Miles himself was furious that the album was issued, and blamed Teo Macero for the whole affair. His relationship with Macero has been a stormy one, and this was one of their first real rows. Teo recalled:

> He didn't talk to me for two-and-a-half to three years!...when we released *Quiet Nights*. He thought I was an insane person...I was crazy. But I said, 'Look, call me what you want. I don't care. It doesn't make any difference. But one thing you must remember – for three years you've had records spilling out, and all that period I always put together the records and they always came out.' He was, I think, in a very bad period of creativity. I think that that might have been one of the things that upset him.

Seven Steps to Heaven was released in the late summer, receiving mixed reviews, and at the end of the year, *Miles Davis in Europe* (the Antibes concert) came out to universal acclaim. In January 1964, it won the *Jazz* magazine Jazz Album of the Year award, thus giving a good start to what was going to be a crucial year for Miles and the band. It had become obvious that the renewed vitality of the trumpeter and his group, the fresh treatment of old thematic material, was merely a reprieve from the real problem: the need to find new musical concepts which expressed the identity of this young band which was so totally different from Miles's earlier groups. With the spate of live concert recordings, it was noticeable that the music was getting rather repetitious. In an effort to keep things exciting for musicians and audiences, the old modal pieces ('So What' and 'Milestones') and the blues 'Walkin'' were played at ever increasing tempos until they were sometimes simply too fast for comfort or coherence. By late 1964, there were several versions of live performances of these pieces, as well as of Miles's favourite songs and ballads – 'All of You', 'Autumn Leaves', 'My Funny Valentine'. They all, of course, have some wonderful moments and produced some excellent music, but two of them stand out as something more than that: classic performances. The Antibes concert is the most sustained in terms of quality of inspiration in all areas – fast, medium, or slow pieces – and this is probably because the concept and the material were completely fresh to the young band at the time.

The other classic album from this period comes from the concert the group played at the New York Philharmonic Hall on 12 February, 1964. During this performance, nearly all the up-tempo pieces were

137

taken too fast and played rather scrappily, whereas the slow and medium tempo tunes were played with more depth and brilliance than Miles had achieved before. The fast performances were issued on an album called *Four and More*, and the magnificent slower pieces were released under the title *My Funny Valentine*. It may have been the very importance of the occasion at the Philharmonic Hall which caused both the greatness of the slower things and the scrappiness of the fast ones. For Miles, the concerts were a benefit for voter registration in Mississippi and Louisiana, and the co-sponsors were NAACP (National Association for the Advancement of Coloured People), the Congress of Racial Equality and the Student Non-Violent Co-ordinating Committee. However, Miles also told *Melody Maker* that one of the concerts was to be in memory of President Kennedy. The latter had been assassinated the previous year, and his death crushed a lot of hopes for the more speedy attainment of racial equality. Miles had expressed a certain confidence in Kennedy in 1962: 'I like them Kennedy brothers – they're swinging people.'' So, for Miles Davis, the concerts were for his own people and also in memory of a president he had admired.

For his young rhythm section, the occasion was oppressively important, which may have accounted for the slight desperation of some of the fast pieces. Herbie Hancock described the psychological pressure:

That was my first time playing at the Philharmonic Hall and that was, like, a big deal, because the new Carnegie Hall was the Philharmonic Hall. Just from the prestige standpoint I really wanted to play good – the whole band really wanted to play good because that was the whole band's first time playing there... although Miles had played at Carnegie Hall before...but it was really a special concert. Only the New York Philharmonic plays there...and I tell you something...it was really funny...When we walked away from that concert, we were all dejected and disappointed. We thought we had really bombed...but then we listened to the record – it sounded fantastic!

The *My Funny Valentine* album from that concert is one of the very greatest recordings of a live concert. The rapport between the large audience and the quintet is as close and immediate as if the event were taking place in a small club, and the charged atmosphere enhances the inspired creative act. There is here a kind of complicity between audience and musicians, a unity which is quite rare. In the first chorus of 'Stella by Starlight', for example, when Miles plays a particularly incisive phrase, there is a clearly audible yell of ecstasy, and other good moments are greeted with immediate delighted applause. Even the *theme* of 'All Blues' draws an instant response.

The playing throughout the album is inspired, and Miles in par-

138

ticular reaches tremendous heights. Anyone who wanted to get a vivid idea of the trumpeter's development over the previous eight years or so, should compare the October 1956 version of 'Funny Valentine' and the 1958 version of 'Stella by Starlight' with the versions on this 1964 live recording. The earlier performances are romantic, melancholic and their emotional range is narrow though deep. On the later versions, there is a strong movement away from romanticism and towards abstraction, and the emotional range is very much greater.

In the later 'Funny Valentine', for example, Miles probes much more deeply into both the song's structure and his own emotional and technical resources. Despite the very occasional and oblique references to the original melody, and the very free harmonic approach (Miles once said: 'We play "Funny Valentine" like with a scale all the way through'), the thirty-six bar structure of the song is always there. Miles plays open trumpet on this version (he used harmon mute on the earlier one), and even in the extreme upper register, where most trumpeters sound strained and brash, he is still able to project his unique, lyrical sound and to bend his notes expressively. He plays the first eight bars *colla voce* with Hancock's piano accompaniment, then the bass and drums pick up the pulse. The whole ensuing trumpet solo is a dialogue with the piano and rhythm section, and the internal movement is realized with great subtlety. Alternations between the slow pulse and the double-tempo feel enhance the dramatic inner logic of Miles's solo which moves to a blistering climax in his second chorus when he suddenly rises on the last quaver of the twenty-ninth bar, ascends for three more bars above trumpet top C to F, G, G sharp and A, and then descends, bending his high F superbly on the way down.(Appendix A, Fig.7). After the dazzling power of this solo, the listener needs the relief, the simple romanticism of George Coleman's tenor solo which follows. The rhythm section also reassures us by playing a steady double-tempo feel. This familiarity and continuity, this everyday grooving done supremely well, is necessary after the disquieting areas into which Miles's solo took us. In the performances on this album, Miles Davis had taken the technical and emotional exploration of standard song structures as far as was possible before they disintegrated completely and metamorphosed into something else.

In the late spring, George Coleman left the quintet. He gave his reasons in a *Down Beat* interview in March 1980: 'Miles was ill during that time – a lot of times he wouldn't make the gigs and it was frustrating...His hip was bothering him – and so there was a lot of pressure on me, and sometimes the money would be late and I'd get it in a cheque and have to try and get it cashed, so I really got tired of it; so I just decided to leave.' In his stead, tenor saxophonist Sam

Rivers joined Miles for a couple of months, during which time the group played in Tokyo at Japan's World Jazz Festival. Miles Davis was the star of this six-day festival, and was paid well over $20,000 for his six concerts. Leonard Feather reported Miles's popularity in Japan:

> It was Davis who drew the crowds; his photo adorned the cover of the current *Swing Journal*; he got the full VIP treatment, with first-class air transportation, a private air-conditioned limousine from hotel to concert hall, the right to refuse to be photographed during his set (even without flashbulbs), and the privilege of being the first American group on the show, so he could get out fast instead of having to wait around backstage...His status as the cynosure and chief attraction of the festival was the source of discomfort and obvious envy on the part of a couple of the older musicians...Miles Davis achieved an immediate rapport. The opening bass figure of 'So What', the first cadenza of 'Stella by Starlight' brought immediate applause, the result of strong record association.[10]

When Sam Rivers left the band, Miles managed to persuade tenor saxophonist, Wayne Shorter to join. The latter had been playing with Art Blakey's Jazz Messengers, and was strongly influenced by John Coltrane. Shorter also wrote excellent small-group compositions. Miles had been trying for some time to get Shorter to join his band, and had even gone as far as telephoning Art Blakey's backstage dressing areas to speak to the saxophonist. More pressure had been put on by Harold Lovett who also phoned Shorter and said; 'What's the matter with you man, don't you dig Miles?'[11] During all these communications, Blakey is said to have walked around angrily muttering, 'He's trying to steal my tenor player.'[12] At last, after Sam Rivers had gone, both Tony Williams and Herbie Hancock phoned Wayne Shorter and talked him into joining Miles's group. Shorter had no reason to regret the move: 'It wasn't the bish-bash, sock-em-dead routine we had with Blakey, with every solo a climax. With Miles, I felt like a cello, I felt viola, I felt liquid, dot-dash...and colours started really coming. And then a lot of people started calling me – "Can you be on my record date?" It was six years of that.'[13] Shorter was with Miles when he played the Berlin Festival in September, and the occasion revealed that this was the best saxophonist Miles had so far found for the band. Tonally, there were definite resemblances to Coltrane, and Shorter also showed great variation in the length of his phrases and in his attack. At last, after some four years of trial and error, Miles had achieved a stable personnel.

But things were in a state of flux on the jazz scene in general. By 1964, the avant-garde movement spearheaded by Ornette Coleman and John Coltrane had gathered many more adherents, and there was much controversy about it in the specialist jazz press. The second wave of New Wavers included saxophonists Archie Shepp and Albert Ayler, and many white musicians such as Roswell Rudd, Mike Mantler and Paul Bley. The phrase 'free music' was bandied about a great deal and it seemed to denote a music 'freed' from the 'restrictions' of set structures and harmonies. Miles Davis must have observed this movement with some interest and even concern. Earlier in the year, he had used almost the same terms to describe some of his own aspirations: 'I intend recording some 'freedom' music...I get away from the normal bar structure. You know, away from the straight thirty-two bars. For example, we'll have maybe eleven bars written, and then I'll play. Then maybe twelve bars written, and then I'll play again. We did something like this on the 'Time of the Barracudas' score.'[14]

Miles's concern with high standards in all kinds of jazz was boldly expressed for all to see in the third blindfold test he did for Leonard Feather. This took place in June 1964, and the only record he liked out of the eight he listened to, was 'Desafinado' by Stan Getz and Joao Gilberto. For the rest of the test, he severely castigates old friends like Clark Terry, his idol – Duke Ellington – and a couple of representatives of the avant-garde. In the case of Terry and Duke, Miles blames the record companies for the ill-conceived tracks. Feather plays him a piece by Eric Dolphy and Miles explodes: 'That's got to be Eric Dolphy – nobody else could sound that bad!...You have to *think* when you play; you have to help each other – you can't just play for yourself.'[15] And finally, when Feather plays him a Cecil Taylor piece, Davis says: 'Is that what the critics are digging? Them critics better stop having coffee. If there ain't nothing to listen to, they might as well admit it.'[16] Miles is generally disgusted with his contemporaries, and also totally disaffected by the avant-garde. At the same time, there is no doubt that during this period, he was equally dissatisfied with himself. The re-examination of his own immediate past, and the glance even further back at old tunes like 'Basin Street Blues' and 'Baby, Won't You Please Come Home' had not yet resulted in any new vision. Meanwhile, retrospective views of him were starting to classify him as a man of the 1950s. 1964 saw the thirtieth anniversary of *Down Beat*, and in their birthday issue (2 July 1964) there was a very long feature on Miles by Leonard Feather, reviewing his whole career and bringing it up to date with recent interviews. It was entitled 'Miles and the Fifties', and it was extremely comprehensive. In it, Miles reveals that he is still irritated by the gulf between the western musical establishment and the jazz world, and still upset about the unequal status of musicians. He concludes with a prediction which seems more rooted in wishful thinking than in actuality: 'Nowadays some of the

141

teachers don't teach the way they used to, with that same old dry legit tone, because in the first place you can't get a job with it. The old symphonic repertorial music is going to go out. They're going to concentrate on the guys that write more or less modern music. Pretty soon all the schools of music will be together and understand one another and learn from each other's approaches, and you won't hear Beethoven's Fifth any more as a standard on a concert.'

Of the future of jazz all he could say was: 'There is no next trend. If there's another trend, then we're going backwards; because, look, you had Duke, and you had Charlie Parker and Dizzy, and you had Lenny Tristano, right? And they're all just levelling off. There's not going to be another trend unless it's the walking-off-the-stage trend.' But nevertheless, it was becoming essential for Miles to find a fresh concept to suit his brand new regular band, and in January 1965 he recorded his best studio album since *Kind of Blue*. This new one was called (perhaps ironically, because it was the name of the record label on which most of the avant-garde music was being released) *ESP*. Probably because of Miles's estrangement from Teo Macero over the release of *Quiet Nights*, the live albums of 1963-4 had been put out without the usual Davis-Macero consultation. And now, Miles chose to do his first studio album for eighteen months in Los Angeles, not New York, and the man who supervised the whole project was not Macero, but Columbia's West Coast A and R man, Irving Townsend.

The freshness and absence of cliché on *ESP* came as a revelation. The germ of the idea could be seen in the greater abstraction and chromaticism of the live albums. Although Miles did not discuss music much with his group, one day he stated to Herbie Hancock that he wanted to abandon completely formal chord constructions in his solos:

> By the time we got to *ESP*, Miles said, 'I don't want to play chords any more'...I guess what he wanted to go for was the core of the music...Here's how I look at it...now I don't know if this is the way Miles looks at it, but a composition is an example of a conception, so Miles, rather than play the composition, he wants to play the conception that the composition came from...That's why you hear melody fragments and you kind of hear the momentum and the sound of the tune somewhere – something that distinguishes that tune from another one...but maybe the chords are not there. Even when we were playing 'Walkin'' or any of those other (familiar) things, he didn't want to play the chords after we played the melody.

ESP comprises three up-tempo pieces in 4/4, three slow pieces in 3/4, and one variation of the blues in F with a rock feel. The fast pieces are characterized by skeletal, angular themes, abstract and

142

chromatic improvisation, considerable group interplay, and a pulse which is sometimes implied rather than actually stated by the drums. The slow 3/4 performances are loose and lilting with a kind of abstract lyricism, and the solos are austere, understated and mournfully reflective. The underlying melancholy, however, also tinges the greater activity of the fast performances.

Standing out from this atmosphere of abstract severity is the blues 'Eighty-One', jointly composed by Miles and Ron Carter. This is the only piece on the album with some funk built into its theme, and its use of rock rhythms jolted the jazz world which, at the time, was very snobbish about anything which smacked of 'popular' music. But there had been hints of spontaneous rock rhythms in the improvisations of his new group the previous year. During the Philharmonic Hall concert, for example, there had been a passage of spontaneous rock during Herbie Hancock's solo on 'All of You'; and a few months later, in Tokyo, the same thing had happened during Miles's solo on 'Funny Valentine'. In the studio, 'Eighty One' was characterized by a lovely bass ostinato, a crisp and even drum rhythm, and a theme which brilliantly juxtaposed legato triplets, long notes and stab notes. The feel and the bass riff were maintained for the first part of each solo, after which the rhythm section played a straight 4/4 feel. All the musicians seemed to respond to the clear disciplines of this piece, and Miles in particular played a magnificent solo. Davis had a hand in the composition of three other pieces on the album, and was the sole composer of 'Agitation', a fast and very abstract performance. *ESP* is also something of a landmark in Miles Davis's recorded work because it was the first album on which he used the 'open bars' technique in which there is no set chorus-length for the solos, and events happen on cue.

Shortly after this recording, Miles Davis went into hospital for surgery and spent most of the rest of the year out of action. Several months previously, he had begun to suffer from severe pain in the left hip, which was eventually diagnosed as being caused by calcium deposits. It seems to have been a kind of severe arthritis. In Japan the previous July, he had been in such pain that a doctor had to be summoned before Miles played the first concert. He had delayed the operation as long as possible, but in April he was in hospital and underwent major surgery on the 14 April, the deposits having to be scraped from the bone. But according to Gil Evans, it was not only a question of arthritis; the hip joint had begun to disintegrate, and the surgery also included taking some bone from Miles's shin and grafting it on to the hip bone. Ten years later, this repair job itself was to start disintegrating, necessitating more surgery and the insertion of an artificial (plastic) hip joint.

The first operation was so serious that Miles Davis was in hospital

143

from April until July (1965), by which time he was so bored that he got hold of a pair of crutches and discharged himself. He had hoped to be well enough to start playing again in July, but that was out of the question, and to keep Tony Williams and Herbie Hancock in work (Carter and Shorter had other outlets), he asked Sonny Rollins to play the dates that had been booked. However, Miles managed to get out and about a little, and visited the Five Spot to hear Roland Kirk whom he applauded rather ghoulishly by banging on the floor with his crutches. He paid for his impatience to leave hospital, because on 4 August he fell down at his home and broke a leg, which considerably delayed his recovery. Meanwhile, rumours went around that he was suffering from sickle-cell anaemia – a kind of cancer of the bone marrow common among blacks.

It was a particulary galling time to be laid up; he had just got his new personnel stabilized, and there was a feeling that Miles's own position in the jazz world might not be so impregnable. By the end of the year, the *Down Beat* readers' poll had voted John Coltrane into first place in the Hall of Fame category, Jazzman of the Year, Record of the Year (*A Love Supreme*) and first on tenor saxophone. Miles Davis was still first on trumpet, his group was second to Dave Brubeck's, and he had three albums placed in the Record of the Year category. But generally, it was Coltrane's year, and many vigorous and vociferous new musicians were coming up in his wake.

It would be foolish to suggest that Miles Davis's health problems have been psychosomatic; they are too serious, too real, for that. Nevertheless, there seems to have been a strong link in each decade of his mature career between, on the one hand, his problems of creativity and the deep inner necessity to change his music and his life-style, and on the other hand, his physical well-being. In the early fifties he was a heroin addict, and managed to kick the habit only by a supreme effort, after which he went on to a period of gloriously creative music. Similarly, in the early sixties, when that first brilliant phase had spent itself, his health declined and he began to suffer from the bone malady, after which he was to have another resurgence of creativity. Perhaps one simple explanation might be that periods of enforced convalescence gave him the breathing space he needed to review his past and consider the future.

It was not until November that Miles began playing again with his quintet; it had been an eight-month lay-off. He opened in mid-November at Philadelphia's Showboat Lounge, then went to Detroit for a one-week stand at the Grand Bar. After that, he went to New York's Village Vanguard for a Thanksgiving Week engagement, followed by a stint at the Bohemian Caverns in Washington D.C. Ron Carter was not available for these engagements, and the bass position was filled in Philadelphia and New York by Gary Peacock, and in Detroit by Reggie Workman. Miles finished off the year with

144

a booking at the Plugged Nickel in Chicago, with Carter back on bass.

Miles Davis's return to the New York scene, in particular, was welcomed by many musicians and friends who turned up at the Vanguard to greet him. Also, his fans arrived in strength and there were long lines of people waiting outside the club. But there was one discordant note during the Vanguard engagement. During one intermission, the saxophonist, Archie Shepp, who was strongly identified with the rising avant-garde movement, went to the dressing room and asked if he could 'sit in' with the band. Outside, in the club, people near the dressing room door could hear an argument. However, the dispute seemed to have been settled, and Miles and the band started their next set by playing the old tune, 'Four'. But when Wayne Shorter finished his solo, Archie Shepp walked out of the shadows playing his tenor and sat in with the band. Miles Davis simply melted away and was not seen again that evening. Accounts of the occasion said that Shepp's playing sparked Miles's group into new vitality, but Miles himself must have had a most unpleasant shock. Up to this point, musicians of most styles and persuasions had always shown the utmost respect for his musical standards and his ability, and the idea of sitting in with the band was unthinkable – especially if the leader had expressly objected to it. Now, it seemed that there was a new generation of musicians who were not in awe of Miles Davis.

There was now an even greater discrepancy between Miles's live performances and his studio recordings. On gigs, he was still playing the old tunes, but in the studio, beginning with *ESP* he was recording much fresh material. During the next two years, he released only three albums: *Miles Smiles* in 1966, and *The Sorcerer* and *Nefertiti* in 1967, and these three albums with *ESP* defined an area of abstraction which many jazz musicians are still using to this day. The essence of this way of playing is as follows: a melodic fragment sets up the theme of the performance; a pulse (usually 4/4 or 3/4), a tempo, and a series of phrases played against that pulse. The improvisations are explorations of these factors posited by the theme, and so the soloist tends to refer back to thematic fragments. Paradoxically, this 'advance' in concept is a return to roots, because it is a movement away from the harmonic improvisations of bebop and post-bop jazz, and towards melodic (and rhythmic) improvisation which was characteristic of the swing era and earlier jazz forms. The approach to improvisation set up by Miles's mid-sixties group came to be referred to as 'time – no changes', because there was a pulse but no set harmonic sequence. In fact, the soloist was free to play any kind of melodic shapes he wished because the bass and piano players were using their ears to follow wherever his inspiration took him.

Miles Smiles carries on the exploration of abstraction, but the music is fleshed by powerfully surging rhythms. Again, there is a harking back to roots with the physical pulse of the multiple rhythms. 'Footprints', a Wayne Shorter compositon, is another reworking of the blues, this time in the tonality of C, and an *ostinato* bass line gives the piece coherence. Another powerful performance is 'Freedom Jazz Dance', a composition by saxophonist Eddie Harris. The theme is a sort of abstraction from the blues in that an angular phrase is played and then echoed with a slight variation (the 'call'), and then the 'response' is a brilliant melodic line which weaves its angular and chromatic way up to a high stab note. For many people, 'Footprints' and 'Freedom Jazz Dance' expressed the musical essence of a period; they created reference points, standards against which other performances were judged.

It is difficult to say exactly why Miles's next two albums, *The Sorcerer* and *Nefertiti*, were not so satisfying. The playing is remarkably fresh and free from cliché, and an extremely high level of invention is sustained by everyone. Most of the themes are written by Wayne Shorter, and his highly original melodic shapes obviously inspired the players. There are also one or two fine themes written by Hancock and Tony Williams, but Miles is credited with no compositions on either album. The causes of dissatisfaction lie in the atmosphere and feeling of the music in general. There's a curious lack of abandon, a kind of self-consciousness, as if the musicians were all outside the music watching themselves playing. There's an almost wilful avoidance of cliché, a kind of 'creativity at all costs' atmosphere, and the music seems to be veering more towards cerebral western concepts. On the fast pieces, tension is continually created and rarely released, because the pulse is perpetually 'creatively' disturbed, and the soloists resolutely avoid repetition or any harmonic resolution of phrases. And on the slower pieces there is sometimes a monotony of mood, an oppressively effete melancholia. The most memorable performances are the ones which experiment with structure: Shorter's 'Nefertiti' and 'Fall', both of which feature the whole quintet throughout, with no solos as such. The former is striking in that Shorter's superb melody is repeated by the horns throughout, and the dynamism of the performance consists in the continual reaction of the rhythm section to the phrases of the tune. Both this piece and 'Fall' are considerably less abstract than the other pieces on the two albums, and feature strong tonalities and repetitions or *ostinati* which enhance the improvised movement.

This whole period was one in which Miles Davis was absorbing the influences and ideas of his sidemen. Shorter's unusually imaginative melodic themes were both evocative and inspiring, and Miles was also feeding off the improvising of his fertile young musicians.

146

This must have been one of the reasons why he wrote nothing for these two albums. Yet, acording to Herbie Hancock, Davis was entirely responsible for the concept of the music. Hancock said:

I don't know why he didn't *write* so much, but on the other hand, his influence on the compositions was as though he'd written them. I didn't know Miles before 1963, but he's a master at being able to conceptualize a composition – someone else's composition – understand the heart of it and reshape it to get the most value out of it – musically and from a musician's standpoint, because we have to play it, so it has to be interesting enough for us to want to play it and be stimulated by it...in a composition there are certain things you can do that reach outwards towards the audience...in the dynamics, in the contrasts...and Miles knows how to do that...how to leave things out...because they're provocative, not only for us, but also for the audience.

But in 1967, Miles Davis was again at a crossroads, and this may explain why the two albums of that year seem somehow incomplete, as if they are preparations for something else. Earlier in the year, Gil Evans had said that Miles was even toying with the idea of leading a big band, but this venture was never to materialize in the way in which Evans imagined. By the end of the year, not only Miles, but the whole American jazz scene was at a kind of crossroads because the USA had been gripped by rock and roll fever. On 16 July 1967, the jazz scene had also lost one of its most vital leaders; John Coltrane, Miles's old friend, died of cancer of the liver when he was at the height of his powers and his fame. This left Miles Davis as the most eligible man to provide some kind of leadership for an ailing, unconfident jazz scene.

12
Miles in the Sky

'I have to change. It's like a curse.'[1]
Miles Davis

In 1966, Miles Davis became forty years old, and his daughter,
Cheryl Anne, made him a grandfather. A year or so later, his
mother died of cancer. Although Miles's prestige was still high, his
popularity had begun to decline. Also, his consistently excellent
music was beginning to be taken for granted, and the press notices
and reviews of albums tended to be more perfunctory. Furthermore,
his record sales were falling off. Clive Davis, president of Columbia
Records at the time, has said that Miles's sales dropped to around
40,000 or 50,000 per album, whereas a few years previously he'd
always sold more than 100,000 and sometimes more than 150,000.
There were also rumours that he was not so well off financially. In
Music Maker, September 1966, one Pat Sanchez wrote: 'For the
past two or three years he has worked so irregularly that much of his
fortune is said to have evaporated. Sometimes the unemployment
has been a matter of choice...At other times illness has been the
genuine cause of his problems.'

   1966 also saw the publication of Leonard Feather's *Encyclopedia
of Jazz in the Sixties*, and in a fairly long entry on Miles, Feather
summed up his present position: 'Davis's major contributions as
soloist and as orchestral innovator were made in the 1950s...
Although his combos in recent years have rarely produced any
significant new group music, the solo contributions of leader and
sideman alike have assured their lasting importance.' This was the
general view of Miles Davis at the time, and musicians were beginning to mutter – as they had done at other stages of his career – that
he was finished, that he'd reached the end of the road and would
have to spend the rest of his life repeating himself and reworking the
ground he had already covered. But Miles had brought a whole new
dimension to the jazz life: the idea of sustained conceptual development. Up to this point, nearly all jazz instrumentalists who
were innovators had developed their enlargement of the language

148

in their youth as the natural outcome of their animal spirits and buoyancy. After ten years, or less, in music, they became prisoners bounded by the walls of their self-made creative compounds. Perhaps the only other musician who had shrugged off this pattern and sought for greater conceptual freedom was John Coltrane. Significantly, he had begun his really creative phase when he had first joined Miles's quintet in 1955. After finally leaving Miles Davis, he had pursued an intense programme of exploration, development and change, which was terminated by his death in 1967. But towards the end of his life he had confessed to a fellow saxophonist, 'I can't find anything new to play,' which echoed the dilemma of Charlie Parker. Coltrane's truly creative life had spanned only about twelve years, whereas Miles already had behind him some twenty-two years of constant change and search.

So by the end of 1967, Coltrane was dead, and Miles was still king – if perhaps a jaded and precarious one – of the jazz world. But that world itself was losing currency, and one of the reasons for this was the momentous rise of rock music. And the leading force in this new movement was none other than Miles Davis's own record company – Columbia. When Clive Davis joined Columbia Records in 1960 as one of the company's two corporate lawyers, Miles was already one of their biggest stars. In particular, three of his albums – *Porgy and Bess*, *Kind of Blue*, and *Sketches of Spain* – had established him as one of the best-selling jazz artists of all time, and therefore one of the company's mainstays. And this was remarkable, because Columbia's general policy at the time, under the guidance of Mitch Miller, was to promote and produce middle-of-the-road (MOR) music. Their steadily large profits came from such things as albums of Broadway musicals by entertainers who were heavily exposed to the general public. Their two biggest artists, for example, were Barbra Streisand and Andy Williams. But this comfortable situation was destroyed in the early 1960s when the Beatles burst on the scene and, with their clean-cut, boys-next-door image, made rock respectable as well as exciting.

Radio play is, of course, the life-blood of record sales, and by 1965, when Clive Davis became administrative vice-president of Columbia, Top Forty air time had given way to the Beatles, to Peter, Paul and Mary, to Joan Baez, and to Bob Dylan. MOR music was getting hardly any exposure at all, and the effect of this was immediately apparent in Columbia's sales. In the early part of the decade, they had had eleven gold discs virtually in succession – each album having earned over $1,000,000. But in the mid-sixties their sales slumped to a mere 75,000 per album. Faced with this crisis, even the most reactionary elements in Columbia were forced to capitulate to rock music.

In 1966, Clive Davis was made vice-president and general manager,

149

and he began systematically signing up rock stars for Columbia. His first acquisition was the British artist, Donovan. A year later, the Monterey Pop Festival gave even more impetus to the rock scene, and Columbia were now signing groups for advances of up to $15,000. Laura Nyro and Janis Joplin also went to Columbia, and the company, by the end of 1968, was clearly established as the leader of the record industry. Record sales were once more being measured in millions and their stars were playing to huge audiences right across the country. Clive Davis had acquired Blood, Sweat and Tears for an advance of $25,000, but in 1969 the financial stakes escalated dramatically when he signed Johnny Winter for an advance of $300,000 for six albums over a three-year period.

The huge sums of money and the general atmosphere of frantic excitement at Columbia, were relegating Miles Davis to the status of fringe artist so far as his record company was concerned. To make matters worse, the relegation was not merely financial. Part of Columbia's excitement was not just monetary; it was the thrill of trail-blazing, of creating and opening up new areas of musical exploitation. Rock music, with its massive amplification, its use of electronics, its thrusting rhythms, and its flamboyant stars with their colourful clothes and rebellious images, had become central to the whole era – the music of the sixties – just as jazz had been the music of the previous decade, though its popularity had never reached the enormous proportions that rock was now enjoying. And at the end of the fifties, Columbia, with its easy-listening music policy, had had only one great trail-blazer with a world-wide influence and audience – Miles Davis.

Miles had been their man with his finger on the pulse of the age, but this was no longer the case, and he was being shunted into the sidings of 'art' music and mentally bracketed with the company's 'serious' catalogue. Columbia were loyal to him, of course; they could not forget his great past, but they didn't seem to think he had much of a future. He was a prized possession, a trophy almost, but not exactly a prime asset. This was probably the reason why Columbia had made an attempt to change their marketing image of Miles. The Byronic and brooding black man was exchanged for *Miles Smiles*, and on the cover of that album there was a photograph of Davis doing exactly that. The cover of *Nefertiti* had an exotic close-up of Miles on the front with bare torso and a kerchief knotted round his neck, and on the back another photo of him in elegant, casual clothes, sitting on his enormous fur-covered bed. The soberly suited successful-American-businessman image had been kicked out along with the Byronic brooding – but only from record sleeves at this time: in public performances Miles was, sartorially speaking, still his old conservative, though sharp, self.

Clive Davis described the Miles/Columbia relationship as he saw it:

150

Paris Jazz Fair, 1949
Left to right: Sidney Bechet, Big Chief Russell Moore, Baroness Pannonica de Koenigswarter, Miles

Paris Jazz Fair, 1949. Left to right: Hot Lips Page, Miles, Tommy Potter.

Miles and John Coltrane in the recording studio, mid 1950s

Miles and Red Garland, mid 1950s

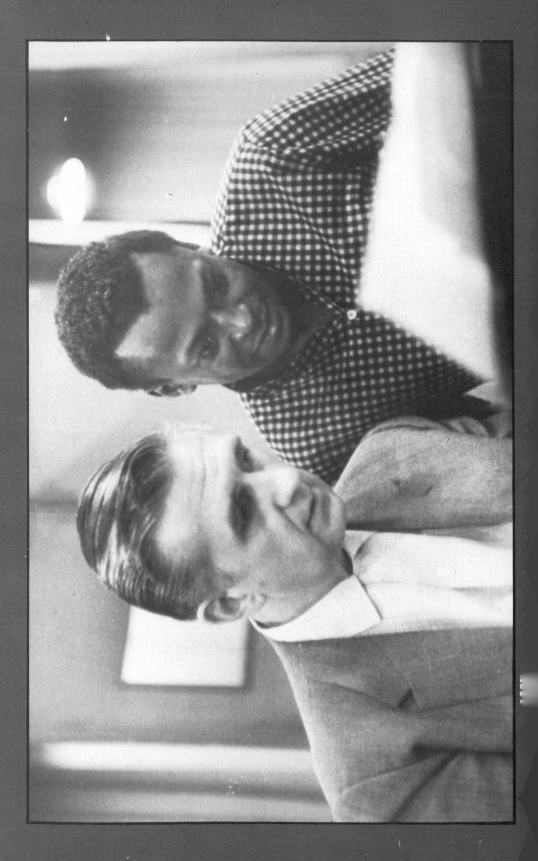

Miles and Gil recording <u>Miles Ahead</u>, 1957.
Lee Konitz can be seen on the extreme right

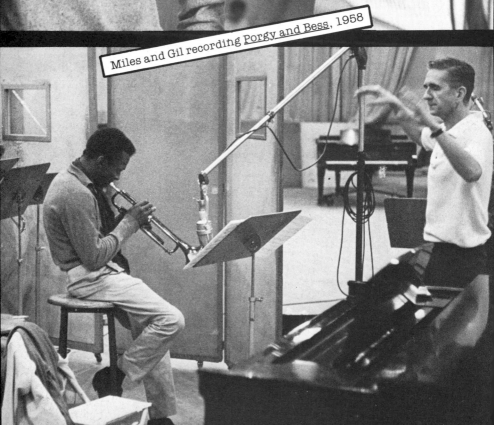

Miles and Gil recording <u>Porgy and Bess</u>, 1958

Miles, 1958

Miles at the piano with Bill Evans looking on, late 1950s

Left to right: John Coltrane, Cannonball Adderley, Miles, Bill Evans, late 1950s

The rhythm section in London, 1961.
Left to right: Jimmy Cobb, Wynton Kelly, Paul Chambers

Miles. Hammersmith Odeon, London, 1967

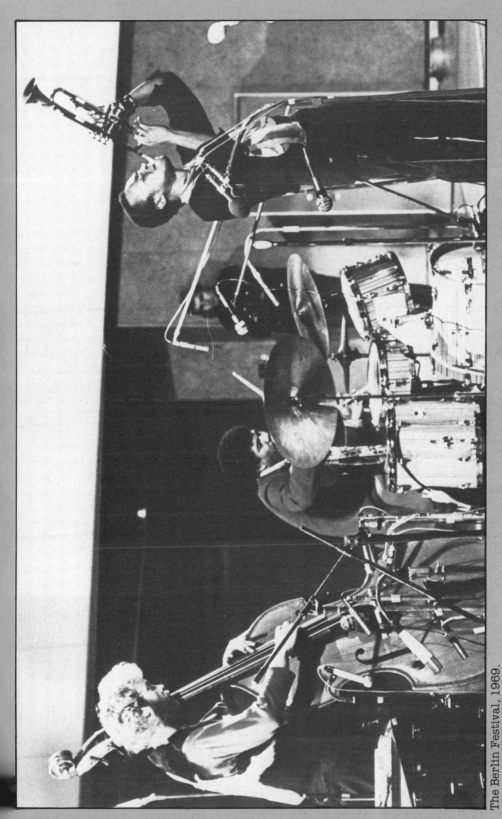

The Berlin Festival, 1969.
Left to right: Dave Holland, Jack DeJohnette, Miles

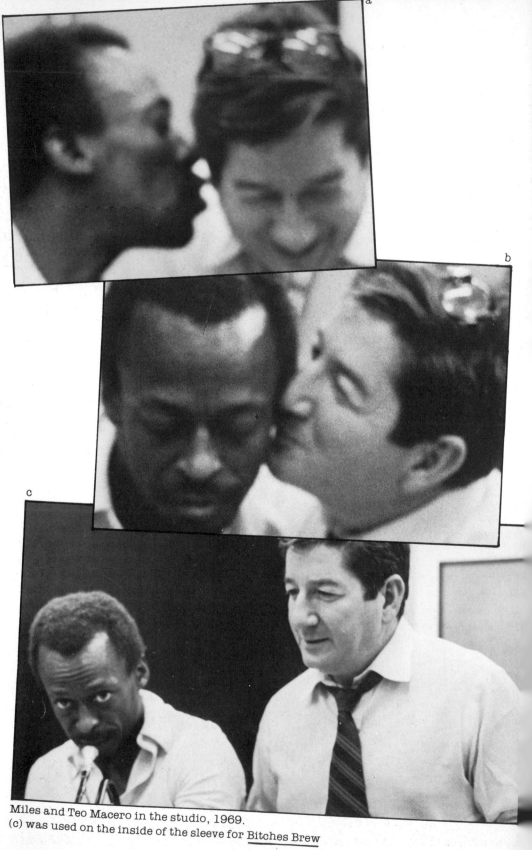

Miles and Teo Macero in the studio, 1969.
(c) was used on the inside of the sleeve for Bitches Brew

Miles with Clive Davis, vice-president of C.B.S. Records

Miles in the early 1970s

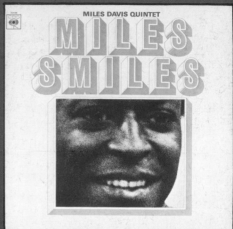

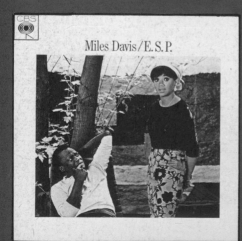

A selection of key album covers

Miles in 1974

Cover of <u>Directions</u>, released March 1981

Miles Davis
Directions

In the process of becoming the star of the jazz world, he'd acquired some expensive habits: exotic cars, beautiful women, high fashion clothes, unusual homes. He'd also gotten in the habit of calling Columbia regularly for advances. I decided to subsidize him. I felt that he contributed to Columbia's jazz and progressive music roster just as Vladimir Horowitz contributed to our classical list. It eventually got to be our problem, however. 50,000 albums barely takes you out of red ink. We began to give Miles additional money each time he recorded an album; we weren't making any money at all.[2]

Elsewhere in the jazz world, a certain disquiet was becoming apparent, and a few more perceptive observers of the scene were beginning to look around for new directions. *Down Beat* was still the leading music magazine in 1966 – *Rolling Stone* began a year later – and in the 15 December issue, Mike Zwerin, the old associate of Miles's who had played on the first *The Birth of the Cool* sessions, wrote: 'Jazz is going to have to make some adjustments, I think, with the electronic world of rock and roll if it is to retain its validity as a reflection of contemporary life...Increasingly sophisticated electronic devices are being introduced by a few groups that sometimes can swing very hard as well as improvise around a free and dissonant form of the blues. They swing and they improvise, and that – according to my definition – is jazz.'

Twelve months later, an article under the headline, 'Death of an American Art?' appeared in the *Louisville Times*. The writer, Jim Morrissey, said of *The Sorcerer*: 'This is the first Miles Davis record that left me cold.' And he comments on the jazz scene in general: 'My complaint is that too many of the jazz greats are producing non-communicating music. They get deeper and deeper in their own bag where fewer and fewer of their fans hang out. There must be some kind of wedding between jazz and some of the solid contemporary sounds that are evolving out of the early rock and roll garbage. Twenty years ago jazz was pop music. Today it has only a small proportion of the public on its side.'[3] This impassioned plea in a regional paper came, shortly after the 1967 Monterey Pop Festival had clinched the arrival of progressive rock on the national scene, and introduced a gawping world to the brand new concepts of Peace and Love, flower-power, and hippiedom.

The jazz scene itself was in disarray, and thus was not facing these potent new developments with a united front. It was split, broadly speaking, into two factions: on the one hand the avant-garde, and on the other, the majority of musicians who were making a living working veins which had been pioneered years previously. The situation was further complicated by a strong racist element. The newer faces in the avant-garde – notably Archie Shepp and Albert

Ayler – in an attempt to expose white exploitation of jazz musicians, and possibly also to dislocate conventional thinking on the matter, were identifying themselves with the oppressed black population. They disassociated themselves from the word 'jazz' and called their music 'black music'.

Miles Davis, as usual, stood alone in this controversy and openly criticized both factions. As Leonard Feather put it, he had taken small-group improvisation to such a peak of brilliance that he had nowhere to look except down. He was disaffected with the more conventional scene because he rarely saw evidence of real direction and imagination in it; and he deeply disliked much of the avant-garde music he heard, for the same reasons. His attitude to both sides is clearly expressed in another blindfold test in 1968. As he had done in the similar test four years earlier, he severely criticised every piece that was played to him, except one; in this case, the pop group Fifth Dimension. His comments are very interesting because they show the kind of criteria he applied to his own work at this time. Of the track 'On the Que-Tee' from Freddy Hubbard's album, *Backlash,* Miles commented:

> No kind of sound, straight sound, no imagination...Freddy's a great trumpet player, but if he had some kind of other direction to go...if you place a guy in a spot where he has to do something else, other than what he can do, so he can do *that*. He's got to have something that challenges his imagination, far above what he thinks he's going to play, and what it might lead into, then above *that*, so he won't be fighting when things change. That's what I tell all my musicians; I tell them to be ready to play what you know and play above what you know. Anything might happen above what you've been used to playing – you're ready to get into that, and above that, and take that out.[4]

In this same blindfold test, Miles also dismissed a track by the Thad Jones/Mel Lewis band, though he did have a few kind words to say about Thad. Two groups, therefore, one small and one a big band, from the younger (Hubbard) and the older generation, both of which were highly regarded by most of the jazz community, held very little interest for Miles Davis. He was disgusted with contemporary/mainstream jazz; but his dislike of the so-called 'avant-garde' was even stronger and his condemnation more vitriolic. Feather played him 'The Funeral' from *Archie Shepp in Europe*, and Miles commented: 'People are so gullible – they go for that – they go for something they don't know about...because they feel it's not hip *not* to go for it. But if something sounds terrible, man, a person should have enough respect for his own mind to say it doesn't sound good. It doesn't to me, and I'm not going to listen to it. No matter how long you listen to it, it doesn't sound any good...and people will go

152

for it – especially white people. They go for anything ridiculous like that.'[5]

In the above diatribe, Miles was making two clear points: first, he didn't see any value in the music; second, he didn't rate it as 'black' music because it seemed to get the bulk of its response from white audiences. Such audiences are, of course, steeped in the western notion of artistic progress which extrapolates its values from industrial technology in which the latest model is not only the best (of engines, machines etc.), but it also makes previous models redundant. Gil Evans, discussing this same problem in 1967, said: 'There's an old saying, I think it was George Bernard Shaw who said it, "I am better than you are, because I was born after you." I see this happening all the time.'[6] But the values of technology simply do not work in art. Shaw's plays did not invalidate Shakespeare's; Miles's great sextet recordings of 1958 and 1959 did not invalidate his quintet albums of 1956; the advent of Dizzy Gillespie in no way diminished the greatness of Louis Armstrong's recordings of the late 1920s. By 1968, the movement started by Ornette Coleman had been in existence for nine years – long enough for anyone, including Miles, to make up his mind about it. Davis had always believed in progress and development, but he had always been aware of his roots. He did not jettison; he added to what he already knew, and each stage of his development contained the essence of his previous stages. He seemed to view truly creative activity as a recurrent three-stage process: first, you start with what you know (and his criticism of many musicians would probably be that they *stay* with what they know); then you get into new and less familiar areas; in the third stage, the new area is absorbed and becomes familiar. Then the process starts all over again. This is the way Miles had proceeded throughout his career to date.

And he had always had wide musical interests ranging from the classics and 'serious' music to ethnic music of various kinds. He was deeply interested in Spanish music and he knew something of pre-jazz American music such as the rural and urban blues, the gospels and worksongs. He had often expressed his distaste for the word 'jazz' and his dislike of the limitations theorists put upon it. His albums had enlarged the whole idea of what an improvising musician could do and of the contexts he could use, and several times, particularly towards the end of the 1950s with *Sketches of Spain*, his music had forced some critics to ask 'Is it jazz?' There can be no doubt that he enjoyed the confusion he caused in inflexible minds. Even in the late sixties, jazz criticism was still largely the preserve of whites, and now Miles was moving yet further away from any white critical standpoint, and into some area of which he seemed to be the sole inhabitant. He was moving away from his old musical associates and away from the younger generation of

153

musicians – except, of course, for those in his own group.

During the 1968 blindfold test, Leonard Feather must have felt quite confused when they came to the only track which Davis liked and which he deemed worthy of a proper critique. This was 'Prologue, The Magic Garden' by the Fifth Dimension. Miles commented:

> That record is planned, you know. It's like when I do things, it's planned and you lead into other things. It makes sense. It has different sounds in the voicing, and they're using the stereo... coming out from different sides and different people making statements...That's the way you should record!...I liked the composition and the arrangement. It's Jim Webb and the Fifth Dimension. It could be a little smoother – they push it too hard for the singers. You don't have to push that hard. When you push, you get a raggedy edge, and the edge gives another vibration. I liked the instrumental introduction too. We did things like that on *Porgy and Bess* - just played parts of things.[7]

During the later sixties, Herbie Hancock was probably closer musically to Miles than was anyone else except Gil Evans. Hancock had already written his popular hit, a rhythm and blues piece called 'Watermelon Man', and his musical interests were very wide, ranging from Stockhausen, Bartok and Stravinsky to pop music. He was, for a jazz musician, remarkably unprejudiced and never made a generic condemnation of music of any kind, preferring to listen to and judge any piece on its own merits. Talking of rock and pop music, he said: 'I think it's become very artful...the Beatles, for example; some of their songs are very artful. And Dionne Warwick, James Brown, Mary Wells, Smoky and the Miracles, the Supremes...I like all kinds of music, and there are certain types that are directly related to me. Rhythm and blues is part of my own personal background, not just from being a teenager during the time rhythm and blues first started, but because I'm a Negro; and so far as pop music is concerned, it is probably basic to everybody's listening.'[8] Rhythm and blues was still providing a link between black musicians of all generations; Miles himself had started out with such a group. This experience and his general musical interests coincided almost exactly with those of Hancock.

But an even greater shock awaited Leonard Feather when he visited Miles Davis in a Hollywood hotel in 1968. He wrote: 'I found strewn around the room records or tape cartridges by James Brown, Dionne Warwick, Tony Bennett, the Byrds, Aretha Franklin, and the Fifth Dimension. Not a single jazz instrumental.'[9] The names all have two things in common; the artists were very popular, and they were all noted for musical quality of one kind or another. James Brown was the king of soul music, Aretha Franklin the queen, and

154

the Fifth Dimension leading exponents of rock music. The Byrds were an extremely musical white group who came out of Los Angeles and made their reputation by 'covering' Bob Dylan hits. Dionne Warwick was a superb singer who showed a Billie Holiday influence, but with strong soul overtones. Her repertoire consisted mainly of songs and arrangements written by Burt Bacharach, probably one of the most gifted songwriters of the century. Tony Bennett sang in the Sinatra vein, and to that extent was the odd man out on the list. The popularity, the musical quality were there, but he was much closer to the night club type of intimate 'torch' singing than the others, and his audience was most probably predominantly white. As Miles had done the previous decade, these artists were all proving that it was possible to make excellent music and still be successful commercially. The difference was that Miles had done it with purely instrumental music, whereas now, in the middle and later sixties, the emphasis was heavily on vocal music. The basic problem facing Miles Davis and all other jazz musicians, was how to reinstate instrumental music as a major force on equal terms with the ubiquitous vocal groups.

Meanwhile, the internal dilemma of jazz – a kind of tribal warfare between reactionary and avant-garde elements – seemed to be taking everyone's mind off this central problem. The split, and the wider problem of the relationship of artist and audience, had been starkly revealed in October 1967, when the Miles Davis quintet and the Archie Shepp quintet shared the same bill at the Jazz Expo' concert in London, England. Miles elected to play first because, so the story went, he said that he didn't want to play to an audience of sick people – the implication being that they would be sick after listening to the Shepp group. The Hammersmith Odeon has a capacity of 3,500, and both houses were packed. The mystique surrounding Miles was still strong, and this was only his second visit to the UK; it was seven years since he had last played there. A large proportion of the audience was there to see the Miles they knew – the Miles of the live albums, and of the famous quintets and sextets of the fifties. At the same time, much space in the musical press had been devoted to the avant-garde movement, and many of the audience had come because they wanted to hear Archie Shepp.

The curtain rose to reveal Miles Davis wearing an impeccably tailored russet coloured suit and a neat collar and tie. The rest of the quintet – Shorter, Hancock, Carter and Williams – were wearing dinner jackets and black bow-ties. This reassured the audience; it was what everyone expected, because the image and presentation had been exactly the same during Miles's previous visit. There was that same statuesque quality about the group, a kind of rapt intensity which created the impression that their external stillness, their apparent oblivion of the audience, were symptomatic of violent

155

internal (imaginative) activity. The audience were expecting a series of fairly short pieces probably including 'So What', 'Walkin'', and some famous ballad such as 'Funny Valentine' or 'Stella by Starlight', all of which would be given the usual jazz formula of 'theme-solos-reprise of theme'. The atmosphere was pregnant with anticipation of the familiar.

But the audience was doomed to a certain disappointment. Miles had moved on musically, and both his subject matter and his method were foreign to the majority of his listeners. He played one long, continuous set lasting about an hour, and during its course, one or two familiar themes appeared and disappeared. There was a wisp of 'Round Midnight' and some themes from *Miles Smiles*; there were obvious tonal centres; there were solos; but the drums boiled and bubbled, keeping up a continuous dialogue with whatever else was happening, and the group played brilliant collective improvisations without ever getting into the really tight rhythmic grooves for which Miles was, and is, justly famous. In other words, there was never any proper release of the immense tension which was generated, and because of this, the audience were denied the satisfaction of complicity in the performance. Instead, they were kept on the outside – respectful, attentive, but not really involved. When the curtain fell, the applause was warm, but somewhat mystified.

The second half of the concert was a very different affair. Every-thing about Archie Shepp's group was the antithesis of Miles's quintet. They wore casual, colourful, flamboyant clothes, and Shepp capped his anarchic regalia with a brightly hued fez. They bobbed, weaved and moved vigorously as they played giving an impression of great physical effort. From the first notes of Shepp's tenor, they plunged into a total, non-tonal freak-out with raving horns and rolling drums, which lasted all of twenty minutes. For the first five minutes it was a tremendously dramatic experience, but soon num-erous sections of the audience became very restless, and many people walked out. It was 'energy' music with a vengeance, and it was totally iconoclastic: a complete rejection of the whole jazz/bourgeois/white/western tradition. The reactions of the audience were extreme. As opposed to the numbers (and they were a minority) who walked out in angry disgust, there were those who stayed either out of curiosity or to cheer. From the first half of the evening, when the audience had been excluded from the performance and given the role of mystified outsiders watching a sacred and barely compre-hensible ritual, the situation had changed radically: the audience were now being forced to commit themselves to either total rejection or to some kind of acceptance of the event.

The one musical element which Archie Shepp's and Miles Davis's concerts had in common, was that they both played continuous sets with much internal movement. In other words, the structure of their performance was organic, arising largely out of group interplay, and the time continuum was non-western in the sense that there were no real beginnings and endings, but a soundstream giving the impression of an eternal ebb and flow. There were, however, several extra-musical elements in Shepp's concert which helped to account for the fact that a substantial section of the audience were able to identify with his group. First of all, his performance was essentially a theatrical event (Shepp was actually a dramatist of some repute) which was heightened by its context – appearing after Miles's group which seemed to be setting up most of the values Shepp was about to knock down. The clothes and mannerisms of Shepp's group were those of the younger generation, and his musicians' physical involvement with the music was nearer to the extrovert atmosphere of the rock scene. Also, the younger generation in the latter half of the sixties worshipped iconoclasm – the smashing of traditional attitudes and old cultural mores. It was a case of *épater les vieux*. Many of Shepp's supporters enjoyed the discomfort of the members of the audience who walked out. The shattering of dreams, illusions and expectations was made concrete by the visual appearance of the group on stage and by the reactions of outraged listeners.

By the end of 1968, rock hysteria had reached a peak in America, and jazz was experiencing an all-time low. In August of that year, Dave Holland, the young English bass player, joined the Miles Davis quintet in place of Ron Carter, and was astonished by what he found:

> When I joined the band, it was on a sort of decline in America. We played a lot of clubs where there were sort of thirty or forty people in the audience in a night. We played gigs out in San Francisco in, I think it was September of that year...and I was amazed that so few people would come. I thought that, working with Miles, it would be a packed house every time. We played Basie's – the first gig I did – well that was full. There were always places that were like that. We played places that were packed. But...I thought that Miles felt it necessary to make another move. There was definitely that period where Miles said to himself, 'I've got to make a change. There's got to be a change in the music.'

The situation was rapidly becoming like that of the 1930s, when big bands dominated the scene and small groups found themselves out of context and without prospects. It was in the thirties, for example, that King Oliver ended his days as janitor of a pool room, and clarinettist Johnny Dodds had to work as a taxi driver and play only in his spare time. In that decade, jazz musicians were faced with the choice of either joining some orchestra, if they were flexible enough and good enough sight-readers, or taking some other kind of employment. But in the later sixties, the problem was much more

157

serious, because the whole financial basis of instrumental music was being undermined. During the thirties, the big names such as Louis Armstrong, Duke Ellington, Benny Goodman and the Dorsey brothers managed to survive and stay in the limelight by leading big bands. But thirty years later, it looked as if even the big names – and Miles's was one of the very biggest – might find themselves scuffling for work. There was, of course, no chance at all of jazz receiving the kind of massive state subsidy which so-called 'serious' music enjoys and without which it would cease to be performed.

Although the outlook was bleak, one jazz group in particular was doing very well: a quartet led by saxophonist Charles Lloyd. Miles Davis was aware of this group and said of it in 1968: 'Charles Lloyd...has a good group.'[10] Both Tony Williams and Ron Carter had recorded with Lloyd during their period with Miles, and Lloyd's current group included pianist Keith Jarrett and drummer Jack DeJohnette, both of whom were to play and record with Davis a few years later. The Charles Lloyd quartet was an acoustic unit, but its performance covered a wide area of expression, ranging from freely improvised passages to wildly swinging jazz pieces reminiscent of the Adderley group, rock-based blues and pieces with a strong soul or gospel tinge. Lloyd and Jarrett wrote most of the themes, but their repertoire also included an occasional rock/pop song such as the Lennon and McCartney tune, 'Here There and Everywhere'. George Avakian, the man who had signed Miles for Columbia in the fifties and produced *Miles Ahead*, signed up Lloyd for Atlantic Records, and made sure that the quartet was promoted as vigorously as if it had been a rock group. He persuaded Atlantic to invest money in buying advertising space, giving press conferences, and making sure that anyone who could or would write reviews was able to attend the concerts. Avakian also ensured that the group appeared at prestige concerts of all kinds, and after a resounding success at the Monterey Jazz Festival in 1966, he engineered an event the following spring which was to win over rock audiences for the quartet. Avakian tells the story:

A friend...suggested to Bill Graham, operator of the Fillmore Auditorium (San Francisco), that the Charles Lloyd Quartet play a set on a Sunday afternoon to see what would happen. Graham put the quartet on with no special announcement about its music; the audience for the most part had no idea that it was listening to jazz. 'There were some kids who started to walk away,' Graham recalled...'but once the group's strong rhythmic sound began to penetrate, the uninitiated audience became fixed. They really dug Lloyd.' A wild ovation at the end of the first number under-lined the quartet's instant success; what was to have been a half-hour fill-in set wound up with forty minutes of encores.[11]

Coming virtually from nowhere, as Lloyd had done, he was a man without a past and with all the future before him. For Miles Davis, with his credentials as one of the leading musicians of the previous twenty years, a precipitate move was out of the question; nor was it his style. Despite his reputation for impulsive, self-willed behaviour, when it came to music, he never moved until he was absolutely sure of his ground. Each step had always to be carefully tested and secured. However, things were becoming pressing because of poor record sales and the dwindling jazz club scene. Clark Terry said of Miles at this time: 'I happen to know that there was a period when in spite of all his many possessions – investments, home, car – there was a period when he needed to bolster these; he really needed to get into a higher financial bracket.'[12] And this was corroborated by Clive Davis when he stated that Columbia began to give Miles additional money each time he recorded an album, and went on to say: 'Miles nonetheless called constantly to ask for more. He has a raspy, low voice – a fiery whisper that conveys heat over the telephone while you are straining to find out how much money he wants. He is spellbinding, and he can talk. After a while, the money business got to be a sort of joke. For Miles called often – sometimes urgently – and I had to figure out each time if he was serious. Walter Dean got some of his calls too...sometimes he spent *hours* on the phone listening to that hoarse, almost demonic voice and dodging its monetary thrusts.'[13]

Miles Davis knew one fundamental truth about the record industry; companies will only promote after they have invested money in their artists. Also, the amount of promotion is proportionate to the amount of investment. The artist's quality means little; it is his price which calls the tune. By demanding more money, Miles was simply raising the stakes. But he did not confine his attack to the internal machinery of his own record company; he began making himself accessible to journalists of all kinds, so that at the end of the 1960s he was talking in print even more than he had done at the beginning of the decade. He attacked and criticized the status quo, the record companies, and the rising white rock groups whose success was diminishing the status of black artists. It was bitterly ironical that rock music, which came from rhythm and blues roots, was beginning to undermine black soul music. *Billboard*, on 6 December 1969, reported:

A few months ago, soul records made up as much as forty per cent or more of the playlists of some top forty stations. Today, George Wilson, a Vice President of Bartell Broadcasting and program director of WOKY in Milwaukee, has only five records in his top thirty-six that are by black artists. A couple of these are the Supremes and the Fifth Dimension, who are considered pop artists rather than soul artists...The college kids a few months ago

159

used to dig soul because they thought it was hip. But I think the growth in popularity of progressive rock on the campuses has hurt soul.

At this time, the civil rights movement was rapidly gaining momentum. The decade had begun with Negroes asking for their rights, with sit-ins, boycotts and marches; it ended with blacks *demanding* their rights, with riots, demonstrations and a series of assassinations. As a leading black citizen, Miles Davis couldn't possibly allow himself to be shunted into a cultural backwater by Columbia. Furthermore, he was now in search of a black audience. Until now, his audience and his record-buying public had been largely white. Only a tiny minority of blacks knew anything about him at all, and he felt this keenly. A few years later, he said: 'I don't care who buys the records as long as they get to the black people, so I will be remembered when I die.'[14] If Columbia regarded him as they did their classical music roster, Miles Davis would never get to the black audience at all.

As early as 1966, Miles was complaining in the Negro magazine, *Jet*: 'I get awards all over the world. What I need now is some rewards.'[15] And a year or two later, he is complaining bitterly to Clive Davis about his treatment at the hands of Columbia:

> Then one day Miles called me to complain about his record sales. He was tired of low sales, and angry about it. Blood, Sweat and Tears and Chicago had borrowed enormously from him – and sold millions. These young *white* artists – he was in a rather militant frame of mind – were cashing in while he was struggling from advance to advance. If you stop calling me a *jazz* man, he said at one point, and just sell me alongside these other people, I'll sell more. In part, I agreed with him.[16]

By the beginning of 1969, Miles had formed a relationship with a black-owned marketing and public relations firm called New Wave Communications, and was ready to launch a full-blooded campaign. Its immediate aim was to suggest that Columbia should set up a special marketing programme with several black promotion and talent agencies. The idea was to promote black Columbia artists in the black community through records, concerts and night clubs. As one of the New Wave officials put it: 'The trouble with a company like Columbia is that when they get a good black artist they don't promote him. And they spend very little money with the black media.'[17]

Miles took these steps because he had only two choices: to be on top, or to be very much the underdog. His position in American society was not static; you do not stand still, you move up or down. In the middle and later sixties he was moving down, and he was doing everything in his power to reverse that movement. The key to that was to increase his white audience and to create for the first time a substantial black audience for his music. Dave Holland put it in the following way: 'He wants to be rich, he wants to be powerful, and the only way to do that is to be on top in the profession. He wasn't prepared to be a memory — somebody to go and see because you used to dig him. He wanted to be somebody who appealed to the generation that's happening now. And he's always done this, I've noticed. He always makes music which goes right to the next generation.'

Two things always seemed to presage as major change in Miles Davis's music: a tendency to write much more of the music himself, and a closer association with Gil Evans. On his last two albums, none of the compositions had been attributed to him, and even if he had reshaped all the pieces written by his sidemen, the fact remains that the germ of all the pieces came from them and not from Miles. But suddenly, with *Miles in the Sky*, he is writing again, Gil Evans is once more involved in, as he called it, 'midwifing' pieces, and Miles's two compositions, 'Stuff' and 'Country Son', take up well over half the playing time of the album. Dave Holland comments on Miles's renewed writing activity, which began with this album and was to increase in intensity over the next two or three years: 'I think he started writing more then, because only he knew what he wanted to do at that point. I don't think anybody else really understood.' And Teo Macero recalled the following pep-talk:

> For a long time he didn't write any music, and I said, 'Look, you're one son-of-a-bitch that I know can write better than anybody else — I don't care who it is — you wanna get off your ass, get a piece of paper and a couple of pencils, and get home and write some goddam music. Why get somebody else to write your music? You've got the talent; you're a very creative artist.' He didn't know quite how to take this. I said, 'You've got more talent than anybody I know. You can create better than anybody I know, but you're too goddam lazy!' Well, I tell you, he went home, and then there was a period when every record that came out was written by Miles Davis.

Throughout his career to date, the instrumentation of Miles's small groups had remained more or less the same. It had usually been the classic post-war line-up of trumpet, tenor or alto sax, piano, double bass, drums, and occasionally an extra saxophone or trombone. But for *Miles in the Sky*, he now began introducing other instrumental sounds. For the first time, he used electric guitar, electric piano, and electric bass guitar — the last instrument hitherto associated only with rock and pop music and rhythm and blues. But this new departure is done with his customary caution; the guitar is used only on 'Paraphernalia', and the electric piano and bass guitar only on 'Stuff'. Miles had been thinking of the electric keyboard for some time, and when Joe Zawinul had started using one with Cannonball's group, Davis had flown all the way to Mexico City to hear the sound of this new instrument in context. Zawinul tells the story: 'We played Mexico City and he wanted to hear that because 'Mercy Mercy' (Adderley's hit record) had just come out on the radio, and he just wanted to hear it. Funny, man, that night the electricity broke down in Mexico City and there was no electric piano! And Miles said, "Hey, man, I come here washed and clean, and then the goddam piano ain't working!"'

Miles in the Sky is a transitional album referring back to the concepts of the previous two, but looking forward in that it set up new criteria and changed the role of the instruments. One piece, 'Black Comedy', composed by Tony Williams, is very much in the manner of the preceding two albums with a scheme so skeletal as to be little more than a fragmentary riff, and a series of highly abstract solos. It is familiar territory to the musicians and they play it with confidence and panache. Miles's solo is especially potent, and Tony Williams keeps up an unfailing dialogue with the rest of the action. But 'Black Comedy' is the only track which looks back in this way. Wayne Shorter's composition, 'Paraphernalia', is in brisk 4/4 with a section in 3/4. During the solos, the 4/4 section is of indeterminate length (open bars), and the 3/4 section, which has a set length, is cued in when the soloist plays certain phrases. On this piece, George Benson's guitar is used to add texture and colouring to the rhythmic feel, and for most of the performance, which is in the tonality of D, Benson simply repeats a rhythmic figure using single strings and working on octaves of the root. To circumscribe the role of an instrument so severely, shows a great change in Miles's thinking. The guitar's role is entirely supportive, and there is a similar change in the role of the drums. For the most part, Tony Williams is confined to a steady *ostinato* on hi-hat and cymbals, and though he does depart from this at intervals, using the rest of the drumkit to create multiple rhythms in reaction to the soloists, it is his straight time-playing which gives the track identity and life.

It was commonly believed, in contemporary jazz circles in the sixties, that if all members of a group were outstanding improvisers, then everyone should be seen and heard to be creating on an equal basis and no one should be 'relegated' to a supportive role. It was this attitude which lay behind Tony Williams' drum dialogues with the rest of the group which was what usually happened in live performances right up until he left Miles in the spring of 1969. In the recording studio, however, from now on things were never going to be quite the same again. Miles Davis seemed to be turning away from the idea that creativity manifests itself in a perpetually inventive

162

way of disturbing (and disguising) the pulse of a piece of music. Instead, he was turning towards the non-western practice of a very clear, unambiguous pulse, and rhythmic repetition which creates a continuum in which all kinds of musical events, including rhythmic variations, can take place. Tension can then be created and released by the superimposition of one rhythm on another, by changes in rhythm, and by moving out of a regular time-feel altogether. Drama would occur when the listener suddenly became more aware of the pulse, or of its absence, or of a new pulse.

With Miles's composition, 'Stuff', this becomes much more obvious because the whole piece is based on a rock beat. This direction had been indicated by the track 'Eighty One' on *ESP*, but Miles had chosen to ignore it while he explored the more abstract areas that album had opened up. 'Stuff' is a long piece — well over half a side of the album — and Tony Williams lays down a funky eight-to-the-bar cymbal beat all the way, spicing it now and then with some rapid fill-ins. Only very occasionally do his convoluted rhythms become oblique to the basic pulse, and when they do, they are made much more dramatic simply because they are juxtaposed against his long stretches of straight time-playing. Hancock's electric piano chording is spare and very funky; he understands this idiom completely. The theme, which is full of melodic fragments, displaced accents, slurs, smears and trills, is some 164 bars long and takes almost six minutes to play. This nicely sets up that hypnotic, repetitive, non-western time-feel, and the continuity of rhythm is superbly contrasted by the dislocated theme. Miles takes the first solo, and his phrases echo the asymmetry of the theme. He does not sound as magnificently confident as he does on 'Black Comedy', but somehow, the very tentativeness of his playing gives it more weight; we can sense his groping for a way into a new musical area. After solos by the saxophone and keyboard, Tony Williams plays a brief drum solo over the rock feel laid down by bass guitar and piano, and the horns play the piece out with a shortened version of the theme. 'Stuff' was the first Miles Davis composition for a very long time, of which the most memorable part was the rhythmic feel and the theme; the solos were important, but the indelible memory was of the piece as a whole.

'Stuff' opens the album, and the final piece on side two is Miles's other composition, 'Country Son'. This has no written theme for the horns at all, and thus presages Davis's future methods. It is a three part structure in D Minor. The first part has a swinging 4/4 feel, the second section is an out-of-time interlude and the third section is a slow rock pulse. The drama arises from the juxtaposition of these three sections. The performance begins with Miles launching into a wild improvisation on the 4/4 section. He's using a straight mute; another departure, and further evidence of his search for

163

fresh sounds. The extremes of his playing are highlighted on this track because he moves from aggression on the swinging section to an exquisite tenderness on the free interludes. After solos by Shorter and Hancock, Miles winds up the album with a solo starting on the free section and moving into the slow rock feel. Here, some of his phrases (Appendix A, Fig. 8) are to be played again and developed a year later on *In a Silent Way*.

The two Miles Davis compositions which point to new directions, open and close *Miles in the Sky*. It is clear that they were put in key positions on the album intentionally. There is change in the air; later in the year there would be changes in his group...and a completely new rhythm section by the spring of 1969. But first, after more musical conferences with Gil Evans, Miles was to go into the studios to try out yet more new ideas on an album which was to be called *Filles de Kilimanjaro*.

13
Play What's *Not* There!

'For me, a group has to be mixed. To get swing, you have
to have some black guys in there.'[1]
Miles Davis

The year 1968 not only saw a crisis point in the American jazz scene;
it was a year of great turbulence and instability in American society
as a whole. The anti-Vietnam war demonstrations were at their
height; Richard Nixon was elected to the office of President for the
first time; Bobby Kennedy and Martin Luther King were both
assassinated. It was a year when radical change was in the atmosphere and, like an epidemic, the feeling spread abroad so that even
in Europe there were repercussions. In the summer of that year,
student riots took place in Paris, disrupting the city and embarrassing
General de Gaulle.

1968 also saw the beginning of another powerfully creative phase
in Miles Davis's career, and one which mirrored in almost uncanny
detail the magnificently productive period which had begun ten
years earlier (1958–61). In the earlier and the later phase, the
personnel of Miles's group was in a state of flux after a period of
relative stability. And in each period, Miles uses some white
musicians; Bill Evans and Gil Evans in the earlier one, and in the
later one, Gil again plus Dave Holland, Joe Zawinul and John
McLaughlin. Also, in both periods, Miles fell in love again and
remarried. Even the nature and the order of the albums produced in
each phase is almost exactly paralleled: *Milestones* in 1958 and *Filles
de Kilimanjaro* in 1968 – both albums with a wide range of expression;
then two exquisite expressions of Miles's reflective side – *Kind of
Blue* in 1959 and *In a Silent Way* in 1969; then a re-assertion of
non-western roots with *Sketches of Spain* in 1959 and *Bitches Brew*
ten years later; and the faltering concept and schizophrenia of *Some
Day My Prince Will Come* (1961) are both mirrored and magnified
in *Black Beauty* and *Live at Fillmore* (1970); and the great live
albums of 1961, *Blackhawk* and *Carnegie Hall*, are echoed in the
swashbuckling power of *Jack Johnson* and *Live/Evil* of 1970.

Throughout his life, personal relationships have meant a very great deal to Miles Davis; that is, relationships in his public life with his musical associates, and also relationships in his private life with his women companions. Dave Holland commented: 'When he goes into something, he really goes all the way; if it's drugs, he goes all the way (as he had in the early fifties); if it's women, he goes all the way; if it's music, he goes all the way. And he's a very inspiring man to be around, because of that.' During the earlier creative phase, Miles had married Frances Taylor, and her face had adorned the covers of some of his albums. Miles explained: 'I got this album, *Some Day My Prince Will Come*, and you know who's on the jacket cover? My wife – Frances. I just got to thinking that as many record albums as Negroes buy, I hadn't ever seen a Negro girl on a major cover unless she was the artist. There wasn't any harm meant – they just automatically thought about a white model and ordered one. It was my album and I'm Frances's prince, so I suggested they use her for a model, and they did.'[2]

Frances also appeared, with Miles, on the covers of the *Blackhawk* and *ESP*. A couple of years later, however, things must have cooled off between Miles and Frances, because he had become very friendly with the actress, Cicely Tyson, and a huge close-up of her right profile fills the whole front cover of *The Sorcerer*. Of this, Miles said: 'I have this thing about helping black women, you know. Because when I was using dope it was costing me a couple of grand a day and I used to take bitches money. So when I stopped to clean up, I got mad at *Playboy* and I wouldn't accept their poll because they didn't have no black women in their magazine, you know. So I started putting them on my covers. So I put Cicely's picture on my record. It went all round the world!'[3] *Nefertiti* had a companion shot of Miles's left profile, so that the two albums, if placed alongside each other, presented a highly romantic picture of Miles and Cicely Tyson quite literally 'tête-à-tête'.

Miles and Cicely drifted apart but remained good friends. Meanwhile, in February 1968, Miles and Frances were divorced, and a few weeks later, Davis had formed a relationship with a beautiful twenty-three-old girl called Betty Mabry. She and Miles were eventually married in Gary, Indiana on the last day of September after Davis had completed an engagement at the Plugged Nickel in Chicago. Observers noted that Miles was in excellent spirits during that engagement, though the wedding was kept a secret from everyone except his most intimate friends. Betty Mabry said: 'He called me from Chicago and said, "Sweetcakes, get your stuff together and come to Chicago, we're getting married"...one of the sexiest men alive is Miles Dewey Davis. We're going to be married for ever, because I'm in love, and Mr Davis can do no wrong as far as I'm concerned.'[4] The photograph on the front of *Filles de Kilimanjaro* looks very like Miles's new wife, and the longest piece, 'Mademoi-

166

selle Mabry', is named after her. But the marriage lasted only for one year, after which time Miles and Betty split up.

By mid-1968, both Herbie Hancock and Tony Williams were thinking of leaving Miles and forming their own groups. They had already made albums under their own names, and the exposure with the Davis quintet had earned them an international reputation. Also Ron Carter was tired of the constant travelling and wanted to be based more in New York. The result was that there were frequent deputies on the bass with Miles and he was looking out for a regular bassist. Early in July, he spent a couple of days on holiday in London and visited the Ronnie Scott Club. There the young British bass player, Dave Holland, was working with singer, Elaine Delmar. Although he was only twenty-one, Holland was already a magnificent musician, but he was still flabbergasted when, just before the last set, Philly Joe Jones who had been in the club with Miles, came over and said, 'Miles wants you to join his band. Talk to him about it after the set.' However, at the end of the evening, Miles had disappeared and gone back to his hotel. The following day, Holland got a message to call Miles at his hotel, but on phoning he was told that Davis had checked out and gone back to America. This was extremely confusing, and Holland asked Philly Joe if he thought it was a genuine offer. The drummer replied in the affirmative and told Holland to write to Miles. But for another two weeks, Holland thought things over and did nothing. Then he was telephoned one Tuesday by Jack Whittemore, Miles's booking agent, who said, 'Miles has been talking about you. He wants you to come over tomorrow. There's a gig starting at Count Basie's on Friday and he wants you in there.'

Dave Holland said, 'Look I haven't had any notice and I've got to get my things together.'

'Can you make it?' Whittemore asked tersely.

'OK. I'll make it.' Holland replied.

He managed to take a plane on the Thursday, arriving in New York that evening. He was staying with drummer Jack DeJohnette, whom he already knew, and on arrival at his place, received a message to go and see Herbie Hancock straight away. Dave Holland has indelible memories of the events of the next twenty-four hours:

So I went over to Herbie's house...It was one of those hot summer nights in August that they get in New York, where humidity is like a hundred per cent, and where you sit and you just sweat, and I remember there was a thunder storm over the Hudson with this incredible lightning...New York hit me with everything it had the first day. So I went over to Herbie's house that night and went over a few pieces, some of them I knew and some I didn't, and the next night I turned up at Basie's for the

167

gig...I was the only white person in the club, which is in the middle of Harlem...So I was sitting there waiting for the musicians to arrive; and one by one, everybody arrived. Miles arrived, and Tony arrived last. And Tony got up on the stand straight away and started getting his drums ready, and then everybody else got up on the stand – so I got up on the stand. One said hello to me, and I'd met Herbie already. I didn't speak to Tony, and Miles just said hello and didn't say anything else. And the next thing I knew, the music was started. Miles did something that said, 'everybody go', and it just started up. And it was like trying to keep up with a tidal wave. There was this great rush of sound and energy and I was on the crest of it, trying to hold on, and I knew that if I fell off it would go on without me. And for four or five months, that's the way it was.

But that week at Count Basie's club was to be the last gig Herbie Hancock did as a regular member of Miles's group, though nobody knew it at the time. After it was over, Hancock got married and went to Brazil for his honeymoon. On the very first night he suffered from food poisoning. A doctor told him his liver was swollen, and throughout his time there, Hancock was under treatment. Meanwhile, Jack Whittemore phoned to say that a gig had come in for the band, and could Herbie get back to do it. The doctor, however, insisted that Hancock should stay in his hotel for a few more days until he was completely better. When he phoned Miles and his agent to tell them this, he felt that they simply did not believe that he was ill, but thought that he wanted to prolong his honeymoon. At the same time, Miles, knowing that both Herbie and Tony wanted to leave the band, and having just got a new bass player, was worried by the possibility of finding himself, as he had done in 1963, with an entirely new rhythm section on his hands. So when Herbie failed to make the engagement, Miles used Chick Corea on piano, and when he found that Corea could do the job very well, he asked him to do it permanently. That way, the new pianist and bass player could work themselves into the band before Tony Williams eventually left.

Filles de Kilimanjaro straddles the period of these personnel changes, three tracks ('Petits Machins', 'Tout de Suite' and 'Filles de Kilimanjaro') being recorded in June with Ron Carter (bass guitar) and Hancock (electric piano), and two tracks ('Frelon Brun' and 'Mademoiselle Mabry') being recorded with Holland (double bass) and Corea (electric piano) in the last week of September, just before Miles's marriage to Betty Mabry. 'Kilimanjaro', incidentally, was the name of a coffee company in Tanzania which Miles owned jointly with the black actor, Jim Brown. He and Brown also owned an animated cartoon business at this time.

168

All the pieces on *Filles* are attributed to Miles Davis, but it is certain that Gil Evans helped to compose at least one ('Petits Machins'). Years later, recalling his work on albums of Miles's, Evans said, 'The last one I really worked on was *Filles de Kilimanjaro* – I really should have had a credit on that one.'[5] There are an extraordinary number of fresh ideas and devices on this album. Although the acoustic piano is featured from time to time, the emphasis is on the electric keyboard which is very prominent throughout. Tonally, it colours the ensemble sound, and it is also used to point up the bass figures; the bass notes of the electric keyboard are very percussive and blend well with bass guitar or string bass. Miles understood this perfectly, saying later: 'Standard (i.e. acoustic) piano is what it says – it's standard. You can't blend any notes or double up with the bass on certain figures, or get those clusters.'[6] And on live gigs, when there was a Steinway grand piano available, Chick Corea would try to sneak it in somewhere, but Miles would stop him saying, 'The piano is over. It's an old-fashioned instrument. I don't want to hear it any more. It belongs to Beethoven. It's not a contemporary instrument.'

Miles was wrong

On *Filles*, not only is the role of the bass circumscribed like that of the drums, but Miles also writes much more for the bass than he had done at any other time. But, just as the earliest rock rhythms the band used had occurred spontaneously in the middle of performances, so, according to Herbie Hancock, did the circumscription of the drums (and presumably of the bass also) have its germ in live performances: 'Tony was real sensitive. If something didn't go right, or if he was upset about something, sometimes he wouldn't play anything. He would just play the cymbal all night. I would be thinking, "Oh, shit!"...but maybe out of that, because we would compensate in some way for it...maybe out of that he kind of *purposely* started doing that at a certain point...it just changes your roles.'

Throughout this album, the bass lines are rhythmically varied and vital, and at no point does either bass player ever revert to the time-honoured jazz habit of playing four straight crotchets to the bar. In other words, there is nothing at all of the conventional jazz time-feel which had characterized nearly all of Miles's work to date, except for some parts of *Miles in the Sky* and *ESP*. Even in a piece like 'Petits Machins' which implies a brisk 4/4 pulse, the bass sticks to the half (or two-in-the-bar) feel, thus creating a deeper trough for the pulse, a greater rhythmic pivot.

The opening piece on side one, 'Frelon Brun', starts with a strong rock beat and a spacey, biting riff played by bass and keyboard. After a brief theme with a slight tinge of African Kwela, Miles plays a solo which is a wild dialogue with the drums. This violent interplay is given point and coherence because the bass riff and fairly static

169

chording on the piano are sustained throughout. Thus the atmosphere and the creation and release of tension are done in a fresh and exhilarating way; the trumpet/drum dialogue can either inhabit the continuum set up by bass and piano, reinforcing its rhythms, or play over it or against it.

The second piece, 'Tout de Suite', has a central structural idea which harks back to 'Saeta' on *Sketches of Spain* where a sort of rough street marching band plays and then stops, and over a droning tremulo, Miles makes his haunting muezzin calls. Here, on 'Tout de Suite', the theme is used literally as an introduction and ending, but the improvised section in the middle has very little relationship to it. The actual tune is in 3/4, and is superbly melodic, developing all the time, unlike the usual jazz piece which is based on the popular song and tends to repeat sections. The horn line is sinuous, floating and evocative (much of it is in harmony), and the atmosphere is charged with the romantic but funky chording of the electric piano. But as soon as the theme has been played, the rhythm section shifts into 8/8 time with a steady cymbal beat from the drums and some syncopated figures on tom-toms and snare. The bass and keyboard play broken rhythmic figures which are given point by the steady continuity of the cymbal beat. It is this feel, with drum *ostinato* and broken figures from the other instruments, that Miles was to explore so brilliantly the following February on *In A Silent Way*. Miles's rhythmically biting solo on 'Tout de Suite' is followed by a Wayne Shorter solo which has an urgency and muscularity which are worlds away from the effete melancholy which pervades some of his work on *Sorcerer* and *Nefertiti*.

'Petits Machins' has a fragmentary theme with evocative ascending bass figures. Miles takes the first solo, and this is a beauty – his best on the album.(Appendix A, Fig.9.) It is a brilliant example of thematic and chromatic improvisation, and is a kind of abstration of the old blues in F. The main motif of the solo is a phrase (see the first four bars) which alternates the major and minor 3rd in a three-note figure going down to the tonic. This insinuates the whole blues tradition, and Miles returns constantly to this motif, approaching it from all angles and playing it many ways with greatly varying inflexions. Tension is created by chromatic runs and convoluted phrases, and it is released by references back to that simple, bluesy motif. The solo is superbly constructed, rising to one climax (bars 60–69) and then to an even greater one (bars 94–98) before concluding with an almost exact restatement of the opening motif.

The title track, 'Filles de Kilimanjaro', has another developing melody, and again a slight feeling of Kwela in its rhythms. The tune is so strong that the horns repeat it three times with little interludes from the rhythm section in between each one. This long theme statement harks back to 'Stuff' on *Miles in the Sky*, and to 'Nefertiti'

170

before that, and it implies many different harmonies, but is played over a bass riff on pedal G (the tonic) throughout, thus presaging what Miles was to do with the title track of *Silent Way* eight months later. On 'Filles', Miles and Wayne Shorter improvise very thematically, constantly referring back to the melodic and rhythmic shapes of the main theme which is not restated after the solos.

The last piece, 'Mademoiselle Mabry', has no written theme at all for the horns, but is a completely composed eighteen-bar structure. Not only the voicing of the chords, but the way they were to be played rhythmically, and the actual rhythmic value of the bass notes, were all written out. It was thus a totally composed piece with a little freedom within the structure. The drums did not really play time so much as colour the movement of bass and keyboard. This is a complete reversal of the usual jazz procedure wherein most of the writing is for the horns, and only chord symbols are given to the rhythm section. The structure of 'Mabry' is a marvellous fusion of elements from the ballad and soul music traditions; it is laid-back, unhurried, full of tenderness and yet extremely funky. It is also full of internal (written) movement, and the structure itself is so interesting that it is repeated three times before Miles starts the first solo.

This was Dave Holland's first time in the recording studio with Miles, and he described both Miles Davis's method of recording and the way the music was organized:

> The pieces were very spontaneous. We'd rehearse a pile of music the day before and not do any of it in the studio – and have a set of new things. And I realize that a lot of reason for the approach that comes across on those things is just because everybody is holding back a lot more, and a lot of space is happening and we're working with the simple elements of the piece...His charts were like sketches. You'd often get a piece of paper with a thing written up here then another thing written halfway down the page...a little bit of a vamp figure, or a bass line, or a set of three-note chords that might be written in a rhythmic figure. And he might say, 'OK Dave, you play this bass line here. Chick, that's your figure up there. You play that against that.'...And at the end of the session Miles might have taken an extract from this take and put it together with this one and then added this one...All the recording I did with him was very edited.

In 1968, Miles's concert and club performances were still based on the jazz/swing idea, and there were, as yet, no implications of rock. For six months after Dave Holland joined the band, they were still mainly using material from *Miles Smiles* and *Nefertiti*, but that may have been because Holland and Chick Corea were new to the group. In public, the band was playing sets of continuous music, and

171

Tony Williams, eternally dialoguing with the soloists, was so loud that Dave Holland, who was still playing acoustic bass, often couldn't hear himself. Also, at this time, the musicians were wearing black suits, and Miles was wearing sharp, but relatively conservative clothes such as striped suits. Throughout that year, Miles and the group were praised lavishly by critics, with ecstatic reviews of live performances from Ralph J. Gleason and Leonard Feather. But despite all the critical recognition, audiences were dwindling and Miles's popularity declining.

But there were some signs of change; Columbia had gone further in their attempts to alter Miles's image, and *Miles in the Sky*, which was beginning to get excellent reviews, was packaged in the more flamboyant rock manner. The title came straight from the Beatles' 'Lucy in the Sky with Diamonds', and the front cover was a psychedelic abstract design using all the colours of the rainbow. On the back, was a large photograph of Miles in striped pants, high leather boots and a casual jacket. He is looking directly at the camera with a slightly wrinkled brow and a rather sardonic expression as if to say, 'OK! If this is how you want it!' He is sitting astride the stuffed head of a lion with gaping jaws and a clear glass eye which both seem to be emanating from Miles's crutch. In addition, the album was beginning to receive some radio play on rock programmes; this was a real breakthrough.

In the late 1960s, Miles Davis was very friendly with Jimi Hendrix, the black superstar of the rock scene. Hendrix's image was flamboyant and wild, and he went in for such excesses as playing guitar solos with his teeth. The two spent much time together, and Dave Holland is convinced that Hendrix influenced Miles in many ways – even in the way he created his music. They were both very tense, charismatic people who had a way of focussing the energy around them through themselves. Holland had recorded with Hendrix and said that he worked just like Miles – setting up a figure and playing on it for a while, and then moving on to another figure. However, it is possible that Hendrix was influenced both musically and in other ways by Miles, though not in so far as electronics were concerned; in that field, Hendrix was the trailblazer.

In November 1968, Miles was once more in the recording studio trying out some new ideas. This time he was experimenting with the instrumentation of his group. His thoughts were now obviously turning more to textural matters, and on this occasion he augmented his quintet (Shorter, Corea, Holland, Williams) with the two ex-members, Herbie Hancock and Ron Carter. Years later, the two tracks from this session ('Two-Faced' and 'Dual Mr Tillman Anthony') were released on an album called *Water Babies*. The use of the two keyboards is strongly in evidence on 'Dual', a fourteen-bar structure with a bluesy/gospel flavour. But although the musicians are clearly having fun, the experiment was a failure. One reason is that if superimposed textural layers are to be effective, they require minimal vertical harmonic movement, and 'Dual' had a chord sequence and at one point a rising bass line which sounds like a parody of gospel music. The pianos muddle along cheerfully, while Tony William plays an eight-to-the-bar cymbal beat, and the resulting sound smacks of early Charles Lloyd – embryonic rock and roll grafted somewhat arbitrarily on to a structure. But this ensemble, though with only one bass player (Holland), was to be the nucleus of the group which made *In A Silent Way* the following February.

From *Miles in the Sky* to *Filles de Kilimanjaro* was a fairly logical progression. Although there is a homogeneity of vision on *Filles* which gives it a unity which the more transitional *In The Sky* lacks, nevertheless, the music of both LPs was, broadly speaking, still based on the old jazz format of theme-solos-theme. Only the pieces, 'Country Son' on the earlier album and 'Mademoiselle Mabry' on the later one, had veered from this in that neither had a written theme for horns. In each case, the underlying structure was all that was posited as a basis for improvisation. The old relationship with popular or standard songs – no matter how tangential – had disappeared. It was out of the trumpet phrases on 'Country Son' (Appendix A, Fig.8) and out of the broken keyboard figures and steady cymbal *ostinato* on 'Tout de Suite' *(Filles de Kilimanjaro)* that the conception of *In A Silent Way* arose. It took insight of real genius to conceive *Silent Way*, and an examination of the way it differs from Miles's previous recording methods will throw much light on the way his imagination works.

Miles's recording ideas now began to mirror the way his group functioned in concerts. The concept of continuous sets which were not tied down to western ideas of form, began to emerge. In his recordings from now on, Miles wouldn't start with the idea of set pieces; instead he would simply explore some fragmentary elements and edit them into a cohesive piece of music afterwards. Teo Macero, who collaborated closely with Miles, described the new method of procedure:

> The earlier thing were pretty much set...but now there's no 'take one' etc. The recording machine doesn't stop at the sessions, they never stop, except only to make the play back. As soon as he gets in there, we start the machines rolling. Everything that's done in the studio is recorded, so you've got a fantastic collection of everything done in the studio. There isn't one thing missed. Probably, he's the only artist in this whole world, since I've handled him, where everything is intact. Normally we used to

173

make master reels, but then I stopped with the advent of three-track and four-track and so forth. We don't do that any more; I just pull out what I want and copy what I want, and then the original goes back into the vaults *untouched*. So whoever doesn't like what I did, twenty years from how they can go back and re-do it.

Miles seems to have gone about the organization of the recording of *Silent Way* in his usual casual manner. Once again, he seemed to be delaying all final decisions until the last possible moment. The session was arranged for 18 February 1969, and Miles's current group plus Herbie Hancock were booked for it. At this time Tony Williams was getting ready to leave Miles Davis and start his own group, Lifetime. He had heard a tape of the British guitarist, John McLaughlin, and was so impressed that he asked McLaughlin to come over to the USA to join his group. The guitarist arrived in New York early in February 1969, and after some rehearsals with Williams they had an audition at Columbia Records – which, ironically, they failed. The day after, Tony Williams took him round to Miles's house, and though Miles had never heard the guitarist, he said, 'We're doing a date tomorrow. Bring your guitar.' It was a momentous occasion for them both; for McLaughlin, because the exposure with Miles made him world famous; and for Miles, because the guitarist was exactly the right musician for him at this time. McLaughlin had a superb harmonic sense and melodic flair, and his playing was notable for both sensitivity and power; also, he was steeped in the jazz and the rhythm and blues traditions.

If the addition of McLaughlin to the ensemble was an after-thought, the recruiting of Joe Zawinul was almost an oversight. Miles telephoned him very early in the morning on the actual day of the recording, and said, 'Hey, man, I have a record date today at one o'clock. Why don't you come over?' Zawinul said he would come to the session. A little while later, the phone rang again, and Miles added, 'And bring some music.' Zawinul took the music of 'In A Silent Way' with him. On the session, Zawinul played both electric piano and organ and so the ensemble with its three electric keyboards and guitar, was a completely new sound in jazz. Miles's deployment of the instruments was crucial to this fresh sound. In general, the drums were confined to a steady repetition of figures, and the bass was similarly circumscribed, though Dave Holland was allowed a little more freedom. The centre of the ensemble – the three key-boards and the guitar – was where most of the dynamism and interplay occured, and over this backcloth the solos were played.

When the session was over, Miles and Teo had about two hours of

174

music, which Macero cut down to eighty minutes, forty minutes per album side. At that point Miles joined him in the editing room and they cut each side down to about nine minutes. Then, Teo recalled Miles saying, 'This is an album'. But Macero knew that this was only half or less of the normal playing time on an album side. They ultimately solved the problem of duration by repeating certain sections on each side of the album, and although this may have begun as a makeshift attempt to lengthen the music, it ended as an artistic triumph.

The first side is one long piece entitled, 'Shhh/Peaceful'. This stays in the tonality of D throughout, and the tonic is always being played by the bass, while the drums play an insistent semi-quaver rhythm on hi-hat cymbals – four beats to each crotchet, sixteen beats to the bar. Over this, organ, keyboards and guitar play little rhythmic and melodic figures. So fresh and interesting was this sound that the whole piece starts off with just that; rhythm and textures. After a while, the ensemble pauses, then starts again and Miles plays an open horn solo. This is followed by more pauses and solos by John McLaughlin and by Wayne Shorter on soprano sax. After another pause, the early section with Miles's solo is edited in to end the side, which makes it a sort of theme for the piece. There is great delicacy and finesse in the solos, great subtlety in the keyboards (everybody is *listening* to everyone else), and the music is pervaded by Miles Davis's unique atmosphere of buoyant though melancholy reflection. Perhaps paradoxically, the total impression is powerful and seductive because the steady time with its occasional pauses (as if the music were actually breathing) creates the non-western climate of timelessness – and in a sense, it is music which should be *inhabited* rather than merely listened to.

The second side begins with a rendition of Joe Zawinul's tune 'In A Silent Way' – the title-piece of the album. John McLaughlin recalled how this version came about:

It was really fancy with a lot of chords – you know, a really heavy tune. We played it and Miles didn't like it. He wanted me to play it solo...Finally he said the first of his many cryptic statements to me, and that was, 'Play it like you don't know how to play the guitar.' I didn't know what he was talking about, I was nervous, anyway, shaking...here was this guy I'd idolized for I don't know how many years – a lot of years...Anyway, so I started playing the melody and I looked at him and he was like...yeah, right...so I carried on doing it. I didn't know they actually recorded it. That was the take. I played the melody twice, then Wayne played it, then Miles and Wayne together...I couldn't believe Miles's version...We played it on *one chord* which is how I started it – E

175

chord, the tune is in E – one simple, really simple chord, open strings, and he really dug it...He transformed it into something that was really special.[7]

This seems to be the first time that anyone has mentioned Miles Davis's 'cryptic comments', and it is significant that it was someone from a different cultural background who noticed and named them. Americans, and particularly black Americans, would perhaps be more used to the non-verbal tradition. And yet, some of the younger American musicians seemed to have difficulty relating to Davis's working methods. Chick Corea, for example, appears to have found no inspiration in the 'cryptic comments', and said: 'After I left him I had a whole reflection about my time in the band, and I told him I really wished he'd told me when it was good and when it was bad, what he wanted and didn't want, getting better, getting worse...I think that's what real leadership is. Miles never even got close to doing that.'[8] However, Miles knew how to inspire and direct his musicians as these comments from the two Britishers, McLaughlin and Holland, show. First McLaughlin: 'Miles always spoke very cryptically, but at the same time you knew what he was saying was really *it* ...He plays and you just know, and that's what he *likes*. He makes you creative. He puts your creativity on the line. He'll make you do something that's *you*, but also in tune with what he wants. That's hard, but it's an incredible challenge that everyone should have because it makes you aware of areas you can go that you wouldn't normally get into.'[9] And Dave Holland: 'What he means is...he's saying "Don't play what's there. Play what's *not* there"... He's saying, "Don't play what your fingers fall into. Don't play what you would play on an E minor 7th. Don't play that. Play something else. Don't play what you go for. Play the next thing." He was always trying to put you in a new space all the time where you weren't approaching the music from the same point of view all the time, or from a preconceived point of view. Usually, he would say those things just to put you in that space. It was almost like a *Haiku* thing – or a *Zen* thing where the master says a couple of words and the student gets enlightened.'

For the whole of the second side of *Silent Way*, Miles Davis expands the concept of 'Saeta' and 'Tout de Suite'. A theme (Zawinul's tune) is played at the beginning of the side, then the solos take place in a basically unrelated context, after which the original theme is repeated. There are no solos on Zawinul's tune 'In a Silent Way'. Miles reduces the performance to stark essentials: the melody is simply played four times over an arco bass pedal note, and shimmering sounds from the keyboards. It is all done *colla voce* – with no set pulse – and this with the droning bass and ruminative keyboards creates a hypnotic, spellbound atmosphere. This same performance is edited on to end the side after the central event which is called 'It's About That Time'.

'It's About That Time' has a tightly controlled formal structure. Again, there is no written melody for the horns; the writing is all in the figures played by bass, drums and keyboards. The drums are confined to a steady eight quavers per bar on closed hi-hat cymbal and four crotchets per bar on snare-drum rim. This creates a clear, short, percussive beat. Over this, three sections are repeated for each soloist: the first section builds up tension with broken base and keyboard figures (cf. 'Tout de Suite'). The bass plays three consecutive semi-quavers per bar, the third one falling on any one of the crotchets in the bar, and the keyboards play either with this figure or against it. In the next section the tension is slightly eased by the keyboards playing repeated *legato* descending chords in a three-bar cycle. The third section provides further release of tension with a flowing, unbroken, two-bar bass riff. There are three solos over this structure – by guitarist, John McLaughlin, by Wayne Shorter on soprano, and finally by Miles himself.

In fact, the piece starts with a brief, almost perfunctory solo by Miles which sets up the atmosphere. The rest of the performance is a gradual build-up to Miles's main solo which occurs at the end. The ensemble is held back on a tight rein during the delicate and thoughtful guitar solo. The more active soprano increases the tension, but even during the marvellously buoyant third section of the structure with the flowing, two-bar riff, the drums do not respond but stick to the mechanical, skeletal beat. Our expectations are aroused, but remain unsatisfied. Then, Miles's solo begins over the broken bass figure, and *at last*, when the two-bar bass riff is played, the drums break out and play a wild accompaniment to the trumpet. This is a totally satisfying climax to the piece, and adds another dimension to the album which has been controlled and understated up to this point.

Though the various elements of the piece are simple, they are used to create extremely subtle and sophisticated music. Once again, Miles Davis has reduced his ideas to the bare essentials and then extracted the maximum amount of music from them. 'It's About That Time' is in the tonality of F, and once again, it is like a gigantic abstraction from the old blues in F, even to the extent of having a three-part structure; the 'call', then the repeat of the 'call', and then (the two-bar bass riff) the response. Although the piece is in F, there is always the suggestion of polytonality, and the soloist is free to use any notes he wishes. Although the bass and drums have fairly static roles, in fact, as one reviewer noted, the mere time-keeping of Tony Williams on this piece and on the first side of the album, is so fine and subtle as to make his cymbal work a star part of the whole performance. And the steady pulse set up by bass and drums contrasts brilliantly with the restless movement of the keyboards.

The homogeneity of the imagination of the eight men involved in this music is extraordinary. The economy is sustained, no one over-plays, and every note is made to tell. Once again, Miles Davis had come up with something fresh, and he had done so, not by turning his back on the jazz tradition, but by finding new ways of expressing some of its basic elements. By confining the role of the drums, he had rescued the pulse from abstraction, and by having three keyboards and guitar all improvising figures, he had reworked the traditional New Orleans jazz idea of collective improvisation behind a leading solo/melody voice. Miles was also finding new ways of reconciling several of the contrary elements in his musical experience: precomposition with improvisation; freedom with control; the static and the dynamic; the blues vocabulary with harmonic abstraction; the small group with the larger ensemble. At the age of forty-two, he was once more in the middle of a brilliantly creative period. And only six months after recording this landmark, Miles would again go into the studio to invade yet more new territory on a double-album called *Bitches Brew*.

Miles knew exactly how important an achievement *Silent Way* was. He rarely enthused about his own albums, but almost as soon as the sessions for *Silent Way* were over, he was excitedly telling people about the album. He even telephoned Joe Zawinul to say how marvellous he thought it was. And he was so pleased with the multiple keyboard sound that he tried, unsuccessfully, to persuade Herbie Hancock to return permanently to team up with Corea. To one journalist, in March, Miles enthused about the album and the three keyboard players, saying, 'They sound like a full orchestra, and we wrote some things with a rock beat.'[10] And another journalist who interviewed Davis at the end of February – only a few days after the recording session – reported: 'He's high on a new record album the group cut for Columbia.'[11]

14
Miles Runs the Voodoo Down

'Hell, if you understand everything I said, you'd be me.'[1]
Miles Davis

Filles de Kilimanjaro was the last album on which Gil Evans worked with Miles, and the two men were not to attempt to collaborate again until the late 1970s. Although it introduced many new ideas, *Filles* still harked back in some ways to the quintet music of the earlier sixties – largely because the group *was* a five-piece unit. *Silent Way*, with its three keyboards and varied textures, presented a new sound, and immediately after recording it Miles Davis seemed exhilarated. From this point on, he was very much on his own and didn't appear to need the consultations with Gil Evans. It is significant that, on the sleeves of *Filles, Silent Way* and the following album, *Bitches Brew,* was printed in small letters: *Directions in Music by Miles Davis*. He had found new musical perspectives, and acquired a clearer idea of his own position in the music scene. He criticized certain aspects of rock music, saying, for example: 'Those cats haven't done much yet. It's very easy to take a riff and vamp for three minutes, but when they get out there to solo, they ain't got nothing to say.'[2] But at the same time, he saw vital connections between rock and jazz, and expressed the opinion that rock wouldn't fade away, 'because, like jazz, it's folk music'.[3]

Miles also fell in love with the trumpet all over again at this time, and his need to play was very great. To one journalist he stated that it would be enough, financially, for him to play only six months a year, because anything over that went entirely in taxes to the government, but nevertheless, he kept on performing because, 'I just dig playing the trumpet... The trumpet is a sacred instrument.'[4] And even in this, the pattern of the earlier great period (1958-1961) was repeating itself in that, after the exquisite expression of the understated, reflective side of his nature (*Kind of Blue* and *Silent Way*), there was to be a period of phenomenal trumpet playing. Even the way Miles described his ideas in the earlier period is mirrored closely in the later one. In 1958 (Chapter 9), when he

179

discovered the subtleties of modal/scalar improvisation, he said: 'There will be fewer chords but infinite possibilities as to what to do with them... You go this way, you can go on for ever.'[5] And in 1970, he says: 'With a C going on in the bass, you can play anything against it... Then we can go on for hours.'[6]

His renewed vision had had its germ in *Miles in the Sky*, and had been steadily increasing in intensity since then. It resulted in great energy and optimism. Dave Holland said that his time with the band (1968-70) seems to have been a very special period in many ways. Miles was always in a very positive frame of mind and did not miss a single engagement; also, he put out very warm feelings to all the musicians who worked with him during that period. Holland added: 'It seemed like he was very healthy... There were no drugs. He ate no meat. He kept off the booze. We were all very much into health things... It was, like, the cleanest band in America.'

Always obsessive about exercise, Miles was now becoming equally fanatical about what he ate. As well as his personal manager, Harold Lovett, who usually accompanied him on tours, Miles now also had a trainer called Bobby Allah who always travelled with him. Allah was an ex-boxer who, according to Miles, had shown Muhammed Ali the punch with which he had knocked out Sonny Liston. Davis was still deeply interested in boxing, and was proud of his son Gregory who had won four boxing titles when he was in the army during the sixties. In March 1970, Bobby Allah told *Newsweek*: 'I'd like to have had Miles as a fighter when he was twenty. Even at forty-three he acts like twenty-five. He's quick, he's got the reflexes – and the imagination, like a chess player seeing the moves ahead. People come in here who don't recognize him and ask me who my new fighter is.'[7] Allah, a Muslim, was a very gentle person who persuaded Miles to be more careful about his diet. The two men seem to have met during the period of recuperation after Miles's illness of the mid-sixties, and Allah not only managed to stop the trumpeter eating chilli and spaghetti and drinking things like tequila, but also went to the gym almost every day and worked out with him. In 1968, when the quintet was in West Germany, Miles said that because they couldn't find an accessible gym, the Olympic stadium was opened so that he and Allah could work out.

In February 1969, Miles Davis weighed one hundred and thirty-five pounds and was eating only one meal a day. In July of the same year, he described his eating habits as follows:

> I just got through eating a soybean salad and vegetable broth. But I don't call it a diet. I just don't eat any meat. I don't even eat fish. I've been off meat for about four months, but even before that I didn't eat meat very much; I used to fix all kinds of Mexican dishes and Italian dishes – chilli and stuff. Sometimes I eat all

fruit. When I go to the gym I drink some vegetable broth and have fruit salad with wheat germ on it, and that's enough for me. If I can go all night without eating, that's great, because I feel light in the morning and I can do more. And actually, it makes you stronger. I figure if horses can eat green shit and be strong and run like motherfuckers, why shouldn't I?[8]

During that year, Miles gave many interviews to the press, and in all of them he seems to be bubbling over with high spirits. Several of the interviews concentrate on his boxing and its relationship to his trumpet playing; and 1969 culminated in a massive feature article on him in *Rolling Stone*. His photograph was on the front cover of the magazine, and of the four photos of him inside, three were of him sparring or working out in vest and shorts. One journalist reported: 'Miles Davis danced lightly on the balls of his feet, his lithe body swaying rhythmically to and fro as he shot punches in rapid-fire combinations – "Uhn, uhn, uhn, uhn, uhn. You see, man, he comes in here and I shift this way and get him *there*, uhn, and *there*, uhn, uhn. When I'm sharp I can just drop a guy...like this!! Uhn, uhn... I do ten rounds a day...like today. I did four rounds in the ring...just moving all round the ring. Then I boxed two rounds with a friend. Then I worked with the floor bag. Forty sit-ups, five of these, five of these, five of these and ten of these..!"'[9] Miles also described the direct relationship between physical fitness and trumpet playing: 'Playing trumpet is hard work. You have to feel strong. I play a lot of notes and sometimes have to hold a note for eighteen bars on one breath, which is tough on the lungs, stomach and legs. But my workouts help my breath control and I can play in spots that no one else can. It's not the note you play, it's what you do with it. And it takes strength to bend notes and to keep from breaking phrases in fast tempos. If you breathe in between, you lose what you're trying to do.'[10]

After the recording of *In A Silent Way*, there began a period of trumpet playing in which Miles revealed more breath control, more power, more sustained use of the highest register, longer melodic lines and more audacious rhythms than ever before. His playing in some of the live sessions of the following two years or so borders on the superhuman. In 1969, there were still no implications of rock in the live performances; the pulse was still jazz-based, and the continuous sets still featured harmonic abstraction though the polyrhythms were often very powerful. The sets had definite changes of mood and thematic material, but the overall control was centred in Miles's trumpet playing. It was this which directed the music. Only musicians of exceptional talent and sensitivity could function under such demanding conditions. Miles said: 'The trick is to surround yourself with musicians who don't play the regular run-of-the-mill clichés. I don't have trouble getting them, but I don't think it's me who attracts them. They just like playing together.'[11] But even to his outstanding musicians, Miles's control seemed magical and inexplicable. Dave Holland said:

He would always come in and change direction at a certain point – take it into a new place – just by a few notes, and everybody would respond because everybody was waiting for that. It's that kind of alertness that he creates in his musicians that I think makes the music so exciting. As soon as he walks into a room, everybody sits up straight... Each tune, there'd be a characteristic phrase Miles would play and we would all know immediately that it would go to that area. So it was this edge that he put you on all the time... As soon as you heard him play – what's happening? Where's it going? And the music changes straightaway. And it seemed like magic to a lot of people. It seemed like magic to me.

This presence which is felt by all musicians working with Miles Davis, and which communicates intuitive musical directions, is inexplicable. It seems very unlikely that he even understood it himself. During 1969 and 1970, he made great efforts to describe to curious journalists how he achieved his music, but nothing is really explained. The cellist and composer, Paul Buckmaster, has said that a mere glance from Miles Davis makes a musician play in a certain way: 'I noticed that he would just look at somebody and something would happen. The mastery that he has is that he is aware all the time of every note and every beat...every minute thing that's happening.'

It was only after the move towards greater abstraction that Miles's telepathic control of the music came into full play. Within the more formal structures of his pre-1967 music it was less necessary and therefore less obvious. After the old structures (harmonies and chorus-lengths) were abandoned, an almost extrasensory perception was needed to hold the music together and give it direction. Although there is much editing on *Bitches Brew*, the music arose largely from this telepathic playing situation with the fairly large ensemble functioning, under Miles's direction, with the flexibility of a small group. *Bitches Brew* starts, as it were, where *Silent Way* left off, and is altogether more complex, more abstract, freer and yet funkier, than the earlier album. It comes out of the fundamental paradox of Miles's aspirations at this time, which were described by Tony Williams: 'He's trying to get further out (more abstract) and yet more basic (funkier) at the same time.'[12]

Once again, the choice of instruments for this recording is absolutely crucial to the music. With most jazz musicians, no matter how many instruments they add to or subtract from their groups, the music remains similar. With Miles Davis, the number and the kind of musicians have a profound effect on the identity of the music. By July 1969, Tony Williams had left, and Jack DeJohnette had joined the group on drums. One reviewer commented: Holland and DeJohnette don't often set up the stop-and-go interludes of Carter and Williams. Instead, they burn straight ahead, creating a deep, luxurious groove for the soloists.'[13] Dave Holland felt a greater affinity with DeJohnette than he had with Tony Williams. He said: 'I had a very frustrating time with Tony, because I hadn't been able to make the kind of musical contact that I would like to make with a drummer when I play with him. Tony was a sort of immovable object to me: he had his place where he played and I was either to play with him, or on my own. But...I never felt that he came over to my space too much. When Jack came in the band, a whole new feeling happened for me because I had played with Jack before and I'd felt this affinity with him; so when he came into the band, the whole feeling of the music changed for me.'

For *Bitches Brew*, Miles added to his quintet two more drummers, a percussionist, bass guitar, bass clarinet, guitar, and two electric keyboards. Again, Wayne Shorter played only soprano sax. With this huge textural palette, Miles was at last following up some of the ideas first touched on in *Sketches of Spain*, and indeed, one of the pieces on the August 1969 sessions, was actually called 'Spanish Kcy'. The strength of this large ensemble lay in the fact that at least one drummer and the bass guitarist would always be stating a basic pulse when that was necessary – some of the sections are *colla voce* – which left the other drummers and the percussionist free to create polyrhythms and textures. The keyboards and guitar could function much as thcy had done on *Silent Way*, but here they have much greater freedom of activity and expression. The most brilliant touch of all, and the ingredient which gives the album much of its particular flavour, is the deployment of the bass clarinet which spends much of the time playing along with the keyboards – not soloing, but creating dark, brooding textures. With so many musicians in the studio and so many electronic instruments, it was essential for Miles to be able to hear himself clearly without having to overblow, so Teo Macero amplified the trumpet, putting a speaker directly in front of Miles.

It is not only in the denser textures that *Bitches Brew* differs from *Silent Way*. The latter album had been tightly controlled, and pervaded by the more urbane side of Miles's introspective self. There had been just one moment of dynamic explosion on the whole album, and this was fitting: *Silent Way*, within the limits of its rather narrow emotional range, is artistically flawless. But the emotional and artistic scope of *Bitches Brew* is altogether broader than that of the earlier album, and there is a very perceptible deepening of the vision. There are dark undertones in many parts of the music which is full of dynamically exploding passages. It was in

183

1967 that the idea of Miles as the 'Prince of Darkness' had first arisen. That was the title of a piece on *The Sorcerer*, and the sleeve note made a direct connection between Miles and the album title. This idea and this feeling were not at all present in the music of *Silent Way*, but now with *Bitches Brew*, a more ominous note enters the music. At times, it seems to relate to certain elements in ethnic music; there is a strong feeling of invocation, of seeking for the state of possession – which is so closely connected with the rapt state of inspired improvisation. But the actual intensity of the performances on these sessions, the almost demonic power of the group's improvisations, were perhaps sparked off by some happenings in the studio.

The first session for the album was prefaced by an almighty row between Miles and Teo Macero, and the latter said:

I think *Bitches Brew* came out of a bitter battle that Miles and I had in the studio over my secretary. He wanted me to fire her, and I said absolutely under no condition would I do so. I told him, 'You're not my boss and I'm not going to take your bullshit any longer. I don't give a goddam whether you like her or not. If you can't get along with her, you don't have to talk to her, you have to talk to me.' And he kept on and on and on and on, until the point where he and I almost had a fistfight in the studio. And I told him, I says, 'Take you and your fucking trumpet' (these were my exact words) 'And your fucking musicians, and get outa here! I want you out of this building! Get your ass outa here!'... I turned black and he turned white! And he was, like, coming at me, and I said, 'You sonofabitch, I'm coming over there! And they were hauling him back...It was like something out of a movie. There were several people sitting around and everybody was dumbfounded. Then finally, Miles came over [they were in the control room] and he pushed the key down [intercom to the studio] and says, 'I want you to know what the fuck Teo said about you motherfucker musicians – Get the fuck outa here... He doesn't want you'... I says, 'Well, take your goddam trumpet and go!' He took his trumpet, and as he started to go out of the door he made a left turn. He went into the studio, took out his trumpet, and I said, 'Put the machines on.'... At that point I could have said, 'Everybody out! – Home!' Right? But I wasn't about to be that stupid, because...you know, it was like having a good fight with your wife...but you didn't really mean it...you'd probably been tired and he just edged you up... He went out there...and from then on during that whole session, he kept saying, 'Come on out! Come on out! I'm going to get you! I'm going to kill you!' So I pushed the key [intercom] and I says, 'You make me sick! If I come out, I'm going to throw up all over you! You're a miserable bastard, that's what you are!' He made another take in there, then finally he kept motioning to me, right? With his hand, like, 'Come out motherfucker!' So I said, 'I'll go out.' I went out, stood right next to him, and didn't move. And he made all those fantastic tracks. This is not the first time I've done this … just about the whole album in two sessions … it was just one thing after another … bam, bam, bam, bam. I said, 'You sonofabitch, you should be this way all the time – mean and miserable!'

This elaborate charade may well have been Miles Davis's way of getting the adrenalin flowing. [But this interchange was not merely a charade; Miles was, perhaps, wilfully stirring things up in order to invoke the dynamism necessary for his best performances]. In a way, it was yet another variation on the old Charlie Parker trick of doing the unexpected and the outrageous, which shocks everyone else and oneself, dislocating habitual thought patterns and releasing a lot of creative energy. In the clinical environment of the recording studio such ploys are often necessary. At the same time, certain aspects of Miles's relationship with Teo Macero seem to have been almost ritualistic. Herbie Hancock said of Teo: 'He's a really nice guy. But when we're recording, sometimes Miles calls him all kinds of names…all these racial slurs and things. That was Miles's way – he doesn't mean any of that stuff…he just kind of says it – 'cause it's dynamic and strong.' But clearly, Macero understands Davis very well, because he too pushed the charade to the limit – to the point where Miles might very well have walked out of the studio and gone home. It was a legitimate risk and a fruitful one: Miles stayed and played, and the music is often very powerful indeed.

Despite their ups and downs over the years, Miles Davis certainly trusts Teo Macero. The latter once said of their relationship, 'It's like a marriage!' And the stormy beginning to *Bitches Brew* was something of a freak event. Normally things were much quieter and calmer in the studio, and hardly a word would be exchanged during the sessions. From time to time, Miles might call Macero to one side, because, as Macero said, 'He never talks in front of anybody.' The two might sit together for ten minutes without a word being exchanged, then Miles would ask Macero what he thought of the take. After a brief discussion, they'd sit on in silence for a few more minutes, then Miles would go back into the studio and probably produce some definitive music.

Bitches Brew is a double album with a total playing time of just over ninety-three minutes. In general, the music is very abstract and chromatic, but there is often a powerful rock beat. The old idea of a string of solos has been completely jettisoned now and the basic elements are Miles's trumpet and the whole of the rest of the ensemble. The main drama and interest lies in how these two factors (Miles and the ensemble) interact. If there is another solo by, say, soprano or bass clarinet, it is usually more a part of the ensemble texture than a solo *per se*. Miles dominates the proceedings throughout.

The first track, 'Pharaoh's Dance', provides some continuity with *Silent Way*, because it opens with a brisk, shallow beat and some textures from keyboards and guitar. Only the low doodling of the bass clarinet hints at more ominous areas of experience. The ensemble pauses, then starts again, and Miles plays a few phrases and then stops. The ensemble plays on. Miles enters again, producing insistent little phrases using the same few notes. The ensemble responds. The roots hover around B and E, but there is strong chromaticism and polytonality; Miles uses other keys and scales. Once more, he stops while the ensemble plays on with the bass clarinet acting as a sort of leader of the responses. After an interlude in which the keyboards dominate, Miles plays some sparse phrases with pronounced echo, and the ensemble activates much more. Miles is again tacit while the bass clarinet and the ensemble interact. The soprano enters, taking over the role of leader of the responses (to Miles). The ensemble activity subsides a little, while drums and percussion play a more solid rock feel. Miles plays again with a huge sound and much echo (reverb) – slow phrases over a boiling and bubbling ensemble which threatens to engulf him. Then it simmers down and he repeats the sparse phrases he'd played at the beginning, only this time it is over a deeply rocking groove. This pattern is typical of most of the double album. It is yet another variant on the old 'call-and-response' ritual, with Miles doing the calling and the entire ensemble responding. He plays a lot of trumpet, both in terms of actual duration, and in terms of how much he says. He is bursting with fresh ideas, and in each piece he plays several times, developing and extending his phrases, and inciting the ensemble into new areas of exploration.

Only two pieces on the album are not composed by Miles, 'Pharaoh's Dance' which is by Joe Zawinul, and 'Sanctuary' by Wayne Shorter. But in fact, both of these were virtually recomposed by Davis to fit in with his new conceptions. Dave Holland said that, in his experience, Miles never played anyone's tune the way it was written, but always moulded the material towards his musical concept. 'Sanctuary' was originally a very straight piece in 3/4 with a definite tempo and specific chord changes, but it ended up being mostly out-of-time and over a drone (sustained pedal note).

The title piece, 'Bitches Brew', harks back to 'Saeta' on *Sketches of Spain* in that it begins with some out-of-time 'muezzin' calls by Miles. After each powerful trumpet 'call' the keyboards, basses and percussion improvise *colla voce* responses. Either Davis is using an echoplex in the studio, or else his sound is being treated with flutter echo, because his phrases re-echo, seeming to ricochet round the

186

room. His 'chops' are obviously in magnificent shape, because not only does he bend and squeeze notes upwards, but he also plays some sustained and strong high Fs. This whole section, with its soaring and 'preaching' trumpet and raggedly rolling responses, has an eerie, hypnotic atmosphere. It is wilder and deeper than 'Saeta', and its trancelike quality takes it nearer to the archetypal priest/congregation relationship. After this, Miles snaps his fingers to bring in the bass riff, and is clearly cuing in the rest of the instruments. At one point during the rest of the performance, he can be heard calling to John McLaughlin to play, and at times one gets the impression that the musicians are not sure what is expected of them. But this track is a very good example of Miles at work, creating music on the spot, and he himself plays magnificently throughout.

With the second record of this double-album, the rock beat becomes much more pronounced. 'Spanish Key' has a fairly heavy offbeat (or backbeat) on the drums, and the rhythm section produces an inspired 'boogaloo', gaining impetus as the piece progresses. Here again, there is much trumpet work, and a continually shifting point of view and emphasis. Also, there is a series of tonal centres which occur on cue – D–G–E–A, but the harmonic freedom in each area is very great indeed.

With 'Miles Runs The Voodoo Down', we have, once more, the key of F and an abstraction from the blues, so this can be compared with 'It's About That Time' on *Silent Way*. The basic material on 'Voodoo' is even more skeletal than that of the earlier piece. Now the tonality, a simple bass riff and a slow pulse are enough for Miles and the ensemble to create fourteen minutes of compelling music. The slow, totally coherent beat is filled out and broadened by congas, and the bass clarinet's sinister brooding is deployed to greatest effect. The atmosphere of invocation, of ritual dances and of possession, is sustained brilliantly throughout. 'It's About That Time' is memorable as much for the precomposed sections as for the solos, but in 'Voodoo', the music is virtually *all* created by the ebb and flow of the improvising ensemble under the spell of Miles's phenomenal trumpet playing. Form and content are one and the same thing.

Once the slow, ominous pulse is set up, Miles plays some phrases in the middle register which yet again alternate major and minor 3rds, thus implying the whole blues tradition. His tone is more vocalized than ever – a human, crying sound. After this quiet start, he develops his ideas with swooping phrases which alternately use the blues scale and then chromaticism. He makes some death-defying forays into the upper register, and his playing is alive with slurs, smears, spaces, screams, long lines, short tense phrases. It is trumpet playing at a fantastic level, not least for the blazing feeling which he seems barely able to control. After his first solo, the

187

ensemble bubbles along relieving the tension a little, and then the soprano plays a hot, hoarse-toned, bluesy solo with the bass clarinet noodling darkly underneath. After some time, the trumpet plays again with falling broad and bent phrases in the middle register. Then suddenly, Miles digs in rhythmically, the ensemble responds immediately with a harder drive and more activity, and the trumpet screams and trills. Then Miles goes back to brooding with more space, quiet phrases, and long, low notes. The ensemble winds down and almost stops, but Miles raises it up again by whipping up the tension with repeated short stabbing notes and displaced accents, until he finally releases the tension with a long, loping phrase to the lower register. The ensemble then simmers down and halts. It is the end of the brew. 'Miles Runs the Voodoo Down' is the most perfect performance on the album. The following year, it was put out by CBS as a double-sided single, and actually got played on jukeboxes around New York.

15
Jazz Into Rock *Will* Go

'Now you can get black people who've been conditioned
by white teachers so that they can't think and they just
know straight music – they don't know anything about
no freedom in music.'[1]

Miles Davis

Even after the recording of *Bitches Brew*, there were still no real
implications of rock in the live performances by Miles Davis's
group. In September, Miles was top of the bill at the Monterey Jazz
Festival, but drew only mild applause and some booing after a
superb performance. The greatest ovations of the weekend went to
the French violinist, Jean Luc Ponty and the Buddy Rich orchestra;
two artists who were still playing jazz which was rooted in diatonic
harmony, with clearly recognizable melodic lines and obvious rhythms. Leonard Feather remarked:

> All this, ironically, took place among an audience that was any-
> where from fifty per cent to seventy five per cent black...The
> thrust at every festival until recently was toward the presentation
> of music as music. If the events of 1969 can be taken as a yardstick,
> that era is now ended...the audience have been radically changed
> by the inclusion of rock acts in what were purportedly jazz concerts.
> The crowds at Monterey last month were representative of the
> trend. Music *per se* has become gradually less relevant year by
> year while the being there, the act of making a scene, has taken
> precedence. During the last three or four years at Monterey a
> tradition has arisen for the audience to become the show.[2]

Despite its clear rhythmic grooves, *Bitches Brew* was not by any
means an 'easy-listening' album; the music is difficult and abstract.
But in live performances during the latter half of 1969, the group's
music was even less accessible to listeners because there were no
rock rhythms to offset the harmonic and linear abstraction.
Although they were still working with some of the musical areas
from both *Filles de Kilimanjaro* and *Bitches Brew*, these were
treated so radically as to lose all relationship with the original
recorded performances. The energy level of the band was high,
everyone was bursting to play, and when Miles had finished his solo,

189

the rhythm section as an entity usually ignored the piece completely, playing an open improvisation until Miles brought everything back under control. The trumpeter was giving his musicians as much freedom as possible within the confines of his conception. Dave Holland described how this happened:

> He would sometimes come on in the middle of something that I felt shouldn't have been interrupted. Sometimes he'd come in at a peak of some kind and, with a couple of notes, would bring it right down again. But the drama in that kind of thing was something else which I might not have understood in the heat of the moment; but he did, and I heard that later. His understanding of the music was often very much more objective than mine...The harmony we were dealing with was chromatic harmony where there were no notes which didn't work with any other notes...Miles was able to set the music up so that there was complete space harmonically, and you could go in whatever way you wanted.

But the trouble was that Miles's music was too far out for the old jazz audience who were, as usual, extremely conservative and reactionary in their tastes; and at the same time, his live performances had not the rhythmic coherence which would gain him an audience among rock enthusiasts. He was thus losing the old jazz audience, but not yet gaining a new one. In particular, he was not gaining one among blacks. The band's image had changed radically by mid-1969, and everyone was wearing the casual and colourful gear associated with the rock scene. Miles had forsaken his sober suits and was now sporting leather or snakeskin pants, elaborate belts, brightly coloured scarves and shirts, and leather waistcoats with trailing thongs.

In October, Miles and the group went to Europe and appeared on the British Jazz Expo bill in London. They created music at an extraordinarily brilliant level of intensity, but the rhythmic feeling was the rolling, multiple groove more associated with the 1960s jazz avant-garde than with rock, and they offered long sets of continuous music. Miles played magnificently that night, but the Hammersmith Odeon was only at seventy-five per cent capacity, and the audience gave him only a lukewarm reception. Many people were seen to walk out.

In America, Miles was still playing clubs for most of the time. At Shelly's Manne Hole, Los Angeles, in late 1969, the band was playing three sets, each one lasting about ninety minutes. According to one witness, the group played a coherent pulse for Miles, but went wildly free after he'd finished his solos. When one of his musicians was asked about this curious dichotomy, he said, 'Miles hasn't found his freedom yet.' Which suggests that there was a certain amount of internal tension in the group; a disagreement

190

about its direction. Miles himself made an attempt to describe his own interests and intentions at this time:

> In my group we play a lot of polyrhythms and everything, you know, a lot of different keys off keys and scales off scales...A lot of what we have in the group has been developed in clubs. I love the possibility of just freaking off on your horn in a night club. In Shelly's I really found out something. Actually it was a learning period in there, when I played everything and made the band play everything they could possibly play. That's what's good about working in clubs. You play a first set, OK; a second set, OK; third set, OK – and they're playing what they know, right? Then the last set they start playing what they *don't* know; which is out of sight! They start thinking, which is worth all the money in the world to me. Thrills me.³

But despite the poor reception at some concerts, there were signs in the latter part of 1969 that Miles was going to break through to a new audience. *In A Silent Way* was released in September and received a huge amount of press coverage, all of it favourable, and most of it ecstatic. The album seemed to point to an alternative direction to the two-horned dilemma: back to conventional jazz on the one hand, or far-out with the avant-garde on the other. There was a general sigh of relief that Miles Davis had found a fresh approach which was neither a retrograde step nor anything like the established avant-garde.

Silent Way also received much acclaim from rock journalists and was hailed as something which, while being full of subtlety and art, could appeal directly to rock audiences. One writer pointed out that it had a double function in that it could be listened to intently and repaid repeated hearings, or on the other hand, like much rock music, it could be used as pleasant background music. After some years of declining press interest, Miles Davis was now regularly making headlines again, and at the end of 1969, he swept the board in the *Down Beat* readers' poll, winning first place on trumpet, first for small group, Jazz Album of the Year (*Filles de Kilimanjaro*; *Silent Way* was third), and being voted Jazzman of the Year. He was 2,000 votes ahead of Dizzy Gillespie in the trumpet poll, and 1,200 votes ahead of Elvin Jones in the small-group category. But even these victories and their huge margins were most probably insignificant when set beside the coverage *Rolling Stone* gave him in December. This enormous feature article reviewing his whole career and quoting his views on the current American scene at length, combined with his photograph on the front cover, established Miles once again as a member of the contemporary American music scene.

Early in 1970, Miles and the group played at a Columbia business convention in the Bahamas, and Clive Davis, when announcing the group, made a speech describing how he had invited Miles to his office one day to discuss the trumpeter's career. The gist of it was that, in looking at the record sales and so on they decided that the music needed to reach a younger audience and a larger one, and that Miles had come up with these new musical ideas. Clive Davis was glad to say that the campaign was very successful. The implication was that the president of Columbia Records had initiated the change in the music. Clive Davis, of course, had no musical influence on Miles whatsoever, but was instrumental in getting the record company to promote the trumpeter as strongly as they did their rock groups. He was also responsible for persuading Miles to appear at big rock concert stadiums which exposed his music to thousands instead of only hundreds per night. Both Clive Davis and Columbia promoted Miles brilliantly in 1970, and it is to the record company's great credit that they succeeded in widening the audience for the trumpeter's difficult music.

Teo Macero flatly denies that Clive Davis had any influence on the actual music. 'Clive was talking about *Bitches Brew* which came out in 1969. Well, there were other things that were done long before that...1965, 1967, 1968...which all preceded *Bitches Brew*. There was a whole lot in there of which I never released anything. And that was because we were groping ourselves. This was the introduction of the electric piano. Clive, I think, takes credit for it...but go back and you'll see the source, and you'll see it in the music.' It had been Macero's job, as producer of Miles's albums, to make sure that all the latest recording techniques were at his disposal. In addition, he kept Miles informed about any new equipment or electronic gear. The motives and forces which lay behind Miles's many musical changes had always been multiple and complex, but at the centre there was always a basic logic which was essentially to do with music. His consistency has been unique; all the strands and themes postulated in his early period up to about 1950, and the later ones up to, say, 1960, have been explored, developed, taken to their ultimate conclusion – and some have even been taken to the point of disintegration.

1970 was a momentous and turbulent year for Miles. By the end of it, only Jack DeJohnette remained from the old group. Around the beginning of the year Miles and Betty were divorced but stayed on friendly terms. There were always several girls in Miles's life, though usually he seemed to have an extra-close relationship with one in particular. In the autumn of 1969, he had a regular companion who even travelled to Europe with him. Dave Holland said of her: 'There was a very special lady who was having a baby of his, but I don't know if it was born or not. She was a very beautiful lady. She was like the Mona Lisa; she had a smile on her face the whole time...she was sort of Indian looking...very beautiful and very

192

peaceful, and Miles, I know, got a lot of peace from this lady because he told me that a couple of times.'

Throughout 1970, Miles Davis revealed an incredible appetite for work, not only by playing concerts and doing exhaustingly long evenings in clubs, but also by filling his leisure hours with activity. He was constantly thinking about music and working out new ideas, and he was constantly giving interviews to the press and talking about everything from race, politics and sex, to music, sport and food. His image appeared in one publication after another. And one magazine, *Zygote/lZygote*, which was read on the college circuit, devoted a whole issue (12 August 1970) to Miles Davis. The reporter spent, literally, days with Miles: in the gym, in restaurants, at concerts, in his house, at Columbia listening to his own tapes, and had mammoth conversations which he quoted at length. So keen was Miles to co-operate with the writer (who does not sign his article), that when the latter failed to turn up one day, he phoned him and said: 'This is Miles. What are you doing? You were supposed to meet me today...Meet me at Columbia at 2.00p.m.'[4]

Obviously, Miles's old habits and attitudes of the sixties had been discarded.Formerly a patrician of few words, he now wished to hog the limelight and dominate the musical press. Also, instead of being a rather anonymous part of the successful American establishment, he was now beginning to be identified with the younger generation as someone beyond the pale of normal bourgeois society. His outlandish clothes, flashy cars and flamboyant lifestyle were making him a more prominent figure than ever before; and he was once more being harassed by the police – a sure sign that he was on the younger, rocky road, a rebel and an outsider.

The first intimation of new troubles with the law came with a bizarre happening in late 1969. Miles and his band were playing a club engagement at the Blue Coronet, Brooklyn, New York, and for four days Davis received telephone calls threatening that 'something would happen to him' if he appeared at the club unless he paid the caller part of his earnings. It was an attempt by some small-time gangsters to extort some protection money. Miles continued working at the club, and after one session, he drove a girlfriend to her home. The two of them were sitting in Miles's parked Ferrari outside her house when they were fired on. The car was holed and Miles's left hip was grazed by one of the bullets, but his companion, Marguerite Eskridge, was not injured. One paper recounted: 'Reportedly, during the police examination of the auto, a small quantity of marijuana was found. Miss Eskridge and Davis were booked for possession. Later, the Manhattan D.A.'s [District Attorney] office refused to press charges and a criminal court judge dismissed them.'[5] Miles put up $10,000 reward for information leading to the capture and conviction of the assailants, but it was never claimed, though he reported in January 1970 that the two gangsters had both been killed. When he was asked how bad the flesh wound was, he replied: 'It wasn't as bad as getting hit over the head by a white cop.' He was referring to the beating-up he'd experienced outside Birdland ten years previously, and he added, 'Funny thing: the cop was killed, too, in a subway.'[6]

Then, early in March 1970, he was arrested again. On this occasion, he was wearing a turban, a white sheepskin coat, and snakeskin pants, and was sitting in his red Ferrari which was parked in a 'no-waiting' area on Central Park South near Fifth Avenue in New York City. A policeman went to the car to ask him to move, noticed that the car had no inspection sticker, and asked to see Miles's driving licence and registration documents. Davis searched for the papers in his shoulder bag and a set of metal knuckledusters fell out of it. In New York State law, these were classified as a deadly weapon. Miles insisted he was carrying them for self-protection, but the policeman booked him on a weapons charge and for driving an unlicensed, unregistered and uninspected vehicle. Miles spent the night in jail, and the next day had to pay a fine of $100 and a further $200 in legal fees to his lawyer. The fine was for being an unlicensed driver; he was cleared of the other charges.

This experience brought home to him, yet again, the futility of the Negro's plight in American society, though he was beginning to realize that the younger, non-conformist rock generation were experiencing similar treatment at the hands of the American establishment. After recounting the story of his own arrest to *Zygote*, Miles added:

It's just the whole attitude of the police force...It's not so much the way black people are treated any more. It's the way they treat all the young people that think the same way, so no matter what colour you are, you get the same shit. That's what the black people have been trying to say for years...The country is so far gone that you can't change it, you can just fuck with it 'til they change certain laws in the city. First thing they should do is legalize marijuana and all drugs. Then you go from there. There's so much graft and shit, like, you wouldn't believe the shit going down with dope. The dope goes in and the judges know about the dope, so subsequently the dope comes up to Harlem and the Spanish people. Both of my sons are hooked because there's nothing else for them to do. There's nothing for them to go to school for 'cause they're gonna get fucked over by the system. The system is so fucked up that by the time they get out of school, they'll be in their late twenties. The whole system is fucked up and the board of education doesn't want to change it.

Miles Davis was identifying with the younger generation of

194

Americans who were rejecting and questioning many of the values of their society, who demonstrated against the continuation of the Vietnam war, and among whom drugs such as marijuana and LSD were very popular. So far as drugs in general are concerned, Miles seems to be drawing a parallel with the Prohibition era and suggesting that the enormous profits of undercover dealing ensure the continuation of the traffic and, at the same time, prevent any kind of control. He knew, as the younger generation was finding out, that governments which refuse to concede anything to reason can be made to concede by force if the collective will is strong enough. A few months previously he had stated baldly: 'Man, you know whites are going to hold on to the power and the money. The white man leaning back smoking his cigar, he's not going to move. He wants everything just the same. That's what makes our music different. It comes from people who have had to learn how to make the white man move.'[7]

For blacks in America at the end of the sixties, it was clear that where reasoned requests for civil rights had failed, the urban riots and the resolution of the Black Panther movement were resulting in concessions. Wars had always resulted in an improvement in the black man's status, and the Vietnam war was no exception. Young blacks and whites alike fought in it; and black and white alike demonstrated against it. And it was not only politics which provided new links between young blacks and whites; it was also the rock music which had grown out of rhythm and blues. During the sixties, a whole generation of young white people came to know and love the blues – the music of the rural and urban Negro.

This idea of black and white fusion pervades the packaging of *Bitches Brew* which was released around the beginning of April 1970. The outside cover has a sort of psychedelic painting of black figures in a hallucinatory landscape of sea and sky and a large pink flower exuding yellow flames. The centrepiece, which hinges on the spine of the double-album jacket, has a black hand and a white hand with long, intertwined fingers, and two fingers growing into a Janus-like pair of black and white heads. The white head stares across the back of the jacket; the black one stares across the front. Inside the cover on the left there is a large colour photograph of Miles who is, once again, smiling; and on the right side, there is a smaller black and white photograph of Miles and Teo Macero standing together during the actual recording of the album. The sleeve note is by the ever-faithful Ralph J. Gleason who wrote it in the fashionable 'stream-of-consciousness' style.

As packaging, it was superlative. Everything about the artwork of the album spoke to the current generation: the psychedelic front cover with black and white fusions; the inside portrait of a new and smiling Miles; the long, rambling sleeve note which struck exactly the conversational style of the age. And Columbia backed up this superb packaging with an energetic promotional campaign right across the country, with such success that, by May, the album had sold 70,000 copies and was the fastest selling record Miles had ever released. It was getting top radio play in key cities, and this was a particular triumph for Columbia's campaign as the actual music is not even remotely 'easy-listening'.

Just how difficult the music seemed at the time, can be judged from the reactions of one of Miles's early associates, Dizzy Gillespie. The latter, one of the most powerful talents in jazz and himself an innovator at the time of the bebop movement, had great difficulty in understanding the basis of Miles's music in the late sixties and early seventies. Dizzy did not seem to grasp how the music was put together or how it worked, and yet he had such respect for Miles that he kept on persevering. During a blindfold test, Leonard Feather played the Miles 1954 recording of 'It Never Entered My Mind', and Gillespie said: 'As for his music, Miles has a deep, deep, deep, spiritual value to it. It's far deeper than mine...But this album is very different to how Miles is playing today [1970] and I personally prefer it, because I can understand better what he's doing. Miles and I played several times together at the Village Gate, and a place in Harlem, and the last time he came up to me afterwards and said, "How'd you like?" So I said, "What is it? Explain it to me." Well, it seems they have a basic melody and they work around that. I guess you have to know the basic tune.' Feather commented: 'It's not so much the tune as a mode, isn't it?' Dizzy replied: 'I don't know; whatever it is. But I'd really like to spend some time having him explain it to me, because I'd like to know what it is he's doing.'[8]

Leonard Feather, one of the most intelligent critics, and an excellent musician and composer himself, shows by his comment, that he too, at that time, had not grasped the essence of the music Miles Davis was making. It was not modal music; it was chromatic improvisation and the basis was a skeletal theme or bass figure. Dizzy Gillespie commented at even greater length:

> I have listened to those recent albums time after time, until I started getting cohesions. The guy is such a fantastic musician that I know he has something in mind, whatever it is. I know he knows what he's doing, so he must be doing something that I can't get to yet. He played some of it for me, and he said, 'How do you like that shit?' I said, 'What is it?' and he said, 'You know what it is; same shit you've been playing all the time,' and I said, 'Have I?' I said, 'Look, I'm going to come by your house and spend several hours and you're going to explain to me what it is.' But we never did get together. I'm sure he could explain it to me musically, though of course you can't explain anything emotionally.'[9]

196

The music on *Bitches Brew*, which was giving such trouble to highly literate musicians, could nevertheless make an impact on several levels. First, there was the general sound of the group which was fairly electronic with the keyboards and guitar. Also, the clear rock pulses created a continuum which was familiar to young audiences.

Columbia also increased Miles's exposure to audiences by putting him on the same bill as their various successful rock acts. During the year, Miles and his group were the supporting attraction on concerts with Blood, Sweat and Tears, The Band, singer Laura Nyro, and other rock stars. This kind of exposure is so valuable that often, supporting groups are paid only a minimal fee, and in some cases, the support group has to *pay* in order to appear on the same bill as the stars. In order to comply with this, Miles had to go against his short-term financial principles, and instead of getting as much money as he could for each concert, he had to accept much reduced fees. This harsh reality became apparent when he did his first big concert to a rock audience. This took place at the Fillmore East in New York City, during March 1970. Miles said later: 'The only reason I played Fillmore, was because Clive Davis, president of Columbia Records, asked me to. He bends backwards for me. All I have to do at Columbia is produce and they try and sell me like they would a white idol with a head of blond hair. That means the next black man that comes up will get the same treatment.'[10] It was, therefore, more than a mere concern for record sales which made Miles play at the Fillmore. The predominantly white rock movement had tended to isolate black music and musicians, and, as one observer put it, Miles was at the Fillmore to 'prove that black artists could speak to whites again and not just to themselves',[11] as they had been doing.

The Fillmore East and the Fillmore West (San Francisco) were run by a man called Bill Graham, who had put on the Charles Lloyd Quartet in 1967. Graham was a fan of Miles Davis's, but he was first and foremost a promoter of rock concerts, and possibly the most successful such promoter in America at that time. The two Fillmores were the key rock establishments, and to put Miles and his group on at either of them required some courage on Graham's behalf. It took courage also, on Miles's part, to agree to play there, and to refuse to change his music in any way, despite considerable pressure.

Miles's usual fee for a big concert performance was around $5,000, and he had to accept a huge cut because Bill Graham refused to pay him more then $1,500. As a result, the two men were barely on speaking terms during Miles Davis's two-night appearance (6 and 7 March) at the Fillmore East. The trumpeter was billed as an 'extra added attraction' on a programme which included the Steve Miller Blues Band, and Neil Young with Crazy Horse, and the young audience was totally attuned to vocal music. Some of Miles's white friends had advised him to reproduce some parts of *In A Silent Way*,

197

and to finish his set with a strong backbeat – the heavy offbeat so familiar to rock audiences. But Miles ignored this advice. His group was now a sextet; the percussionist, Airto Moreira had joined, but the music was still uncompromisingly abstract – exactly the same sort of thing Miles would have done at Shelly's Manne Hole.

By Fillmore standards, Miles's first set there 'bombed out' completely. There was only a smattering of applause and no calls for an encore. His second set that same Friday night was even more severe musically, and the audience reaction was similar: mystified silence leavened by sparse claps. On the Saturday night, there were again no calls for an encore after the first set, and Miles's friends once more pleaded with him to make the music more accessible. He said he would, but didn't. One observer wrote: 'If Miles was going to be accepted by this audience, he was going to be accepted on his own terms. He weaved in front of the microphone. He crouched and he blew from above, from below, from the side. He lifted the bell of his trumpet high in the air to cut off each bent, wailing note at just the perfect time. He blew so hard, he split his lip. And the audience roared. It stood on its feet. It called for more. Miles sauntered offstage with his eyes straight ahead and his chin cocked at a tilt. 'It was an easy gig,' he said afterwards. Of course, he didn't play an encore.'[12]

Shortly after this, Wayne Shorter left the band, and the white saxophonist, Stephan Grossman joined it. In April, they played one long set at the Fillmore West in San Francisco, and this was well received by an attentive audience which included the 'Beat' poet, Allen Ginsberg. Bill Graham said, 'That one set was better than all four at the Fillmore East.' Miles smiled and said, 'I know it.'[13] The two men had obviously patched up their financial quarrel, and after the engagement, Miles sent Graham a telegram saying that he had always wanted to play a club or place where the audience could relax while the musician did his thing and that Graham had made it possible. Miles hoped that he and his band had added something to match the contribution Bill Graham had made to the music scene, and hoped that this event would be a pattern for the future. He finished by saying that he liked the apple juice and sound system but was most unhappy with the air conditioning!

The Fillmore West set was recorded and later released under the title *Black Beauty*. Miles's next engagement at the Fillmore East, four nights in June supporting Laura Nyro, was also recorded. This time he had further augmented the band with Keith Jarrett on organ and keyboards, so the group was now a septet, and more heavily electronic than ever. The money was again too low for Miles's liking, and he made a great deal of fuss about it. Having done it once, he felt that for subsequent concerts his fee should be increased. He said: 'I mean they're gonna make a lot of money for those four nights. What are they gonna do, give me a set of clothes, a watermelon? They'll be kissing me and bringing me coke and offering me a reefer and all that shit. What do I get out of this? Miles is a good nigger. Miles is all right. Right on Miles. What is it with that shit? And then, when you mention it to them, they say we are all in it for the art.'[14]

The sheer complexity of Miles Davis's position in American society and the various psychological pressures with which he had to deal, were described in a perceptive paragraph written by the *Zygote*/*Zygote* author:

> Miles Davis doesn't step aside for or pander to anyone. The old house nigger sickens him. It is part of his heritage that he has been fighting against all his life. His house, his car, his women, his clothes, all his possessions state, 'I'm not as good as you are, I am better.' It is almost as if Miles would be emasculated if he accepted the past. He rebels against it, and it has not been an easy thing. He comes from middle class parents, and cannot claim the poor, street upbringing copout. He is educated and literate, and rather than making it easier for him, these things have made it harder. More than anything, Miles wants to relate to the brother in the ghetto. He does mentally, but because of his past, he can't fully because he hasn't lived it. Miles, beyond all things, is black and he is proud of it. He doesn't want to be anything else.

During the year, Miles improved his personal possessions. His red Ferrari was full of bullet holes after the shooting incident, so he got rid of it and bought a new battleship-grey Lamborghini. It was priced at $20,000, but he paid cash and got it for only $14,000. He also had his house completely redecorated. He had always been extremely houseproud, but even this seems to have increased to epic proportions. Whenever a journalist went to his home to do an interview, the visitor would be subjected to the same ritual: he or she would be left alone listening to tapes of Miles's latest recordings then Davis would appear and at some point there would be a tour of the house. But, like Miles's music, the house redecoration was a spontaneous rather than a premeditated event.

A set designer called Lance Hay, who lived in Los Angeles and was a fan of Miles's, just happened to be around New York when Miles's bathroom ceiling began to crumble and fall down. Miles recalled: 'Lance said to me, "Let me do something. I'll fix you a bathroom that'll be out of sight."'[15] Hay made the bathroom a three-level affair with half-circle steps, a porthole-shaped window and a ceiling, also in three levels, where lighting was concealed between each layer. The large sunken bathtub was circular and had a frame of ersatz marble done in reverse curves. It was separated from the toilet by a curved half-wall. Miles was so pleased with this room that he asked Lance Hay to carry on and do the whole place: 'I wanted everything round. I said, "Lance, you know who I am. I don't like corners. I don't like furniture. And you don't either."'[16]

Each room (and the entrance hall) was given a floor with two or three different levels, and every visible inch of floor space was covered with blue carpet. There were more porthole windows, and a trapezoid bed with rounded corners. In a floor-to-ceiling cylinder near the bedroom, Hay installed a kitchenette, and there was also a full-sized kitchen on the main floor directly below. There were built-in spaces for books, records and hi-fi equipment, and the living-room wall was faced with wood which was cut into three arches where the windows were. The only standing furniture was one round table in the living room, one round ottoman in the foyer and one curvaceous Charles Eames lounge chair in the bedroom. The decor on the lower floor had been done earlier in the year by a Valencian-born craftsman called Manuel Mauri, and there were white plaster walls and arches and wood beams across the ceiling. The façade of the house was Moorish, with wood, tiles and plaster. Miles particularly wanted the North African effect. He said: 'I got tired of living in a George Washington kind of house.'[17] The only photograph in Miles's living room was a colour shot of a pensive John Coltrane, taken during his time with Davis's group.

With all the promotion and publicity, and his exposure to large rock audiences in big auditoriums, Miles was, by mid-1970, beginning to make a strong impact on the jazz and rock scenes, not only in America, but also globally. In a sense, the two main releases of the period worked like a boxer's knock-out combination; *Silent Way* was the blow which set up the public for the KO which was delivered by *Bitches Brew*. At the same time, albums from other periods of Miles's career were still being released. A composite album, *Miles Davis's Greatest Hits*, came out fairly early in the year and was followed a few months later by the release of the 1964 Tokyo concert with Sam Rivers on sax. However, superficial observers of the scene accused Miles of 'selling out' to the younger generation. One or two of the more perceptive jazz critics made great efforts to understand what he was doing and why. As usual, Leonard Feather looked more deeply than most: 'Casual listeners might assume that he had been taken over by the youth movement rock, stock and barrel. The diagnosis would be dangerously over-simplistic. As can be deduced from his current album (*Bitches Brew*), he is creating a new and more complex form, drawing from the avant-garde, atonalism, modality, rock, jazz and the universe. It has no name, but some listeners have called it "Space Music".'[18] And Miles himself commented: 'We play music for you to learn and listen. The kids, they are so great they can dig what we're giving them. The rest of the people give them shit. They give them the same old fucking thing to

200

be comfortable. That's the reason we are playing – not to be pop stars. What does it mean to sell out to the kids? I haven't sold out to the fucking kids. I don't sell out to nobody.'[19]

But Miles was also attacked by the black press for playing 'second fiddle' to white rock groups, and for employing white musicians as well as his black associates. In July 1970, *Jet* magazine stated: 'Not only is the Great One listed in small print as an "extra added attraction", but he comes on first instead of holding down the star's spot.' And the saxophonist, Eddie Harris, whose tune 'Freedom Jazz Dance' Miles had recorded some four years previously, gave a press conference and attacked Miles bitterly for having a 'new white image', and added that the same non-black musicians currently playing with Miles would soon be cutting black brothers out of gigs they should have. Joe Zawinul – a white man, of course – commented: 'They used to attack him for using John McLaughlin. I just talked to him about that and he said, "OK, man, I'd hire one of them brothers if he can play as good as John McLaughlin – I'd hire them both!" They used to say, "Why you got that white boy playing on the guitar?" And he'd say, "Shit! Nobody can play as good as him. You give me one of them niggers and I'll hire him *and* McLaughlin." You see, Miles is very racial, but he is fair. He has the greatest sense of humour.'

Miles Davis was, almost singlehandedly, putting jazz back on the map in America. After he had proved it was possible to get through to audiences at the Fillmores, other jazz musicians, including Dizzy Gillespie and his group, were booked to play there. And Miles was also showing that it was possible for a jazz musician to achieve big record sales without diluting his music or trying to 'play down' to the public. John Hammond of Columbia Records, when asked what things revived interest in jazz at the beginning of the 1970s, replied: 'One is *Bitches Brew* by Miles Davis, which has had fantastic sales for a jazz LP – unprecedented for Miles as well.'[20]

Along with the new decor in his home and his fresh sartorial style, Miles was also experimenting with the colour of his trumpets. He had, at various times, a green one, a blue one, a black one, and a two-toned russet and black one. He explained somewhat obscurely: 'I don't want to play a gold horn... You look at a brass horn and all you see is the horn. When you play a green horn, it sort of disappears and all you are aware of is the music.'[21] He was also experimenting at home with an electronic bug fixed into his mouthpiece and fed through a wah-wah pedal, but it was a month or two before he felt confident enough to use it with the band in public. In fact, his black trumpet lay plugged in and on top of an amplifier on several gigs before he eventually plucked up courage to use it.

In July, a performance at the Schaefer concerts in Central Park showed just how difficult it was to control this new electronic environment. The small stage was already two-thirds full of a second group's equipment when Miles and the band had to go on and play. There was nowhere for Miles to stand except in front of the group, and when he turned to move away after playing his opening statement, he tripped over the mass of wires and leads, almost falling off the bandstand. Keith Jarrett, who'd arrived and plugged in five minutes after the group started its set, was having difficulty with the modulation and fuzz of the organ. Miles had no monitor speaker with which to hear himself or check the sound balance of the group, and the amplifier from the electric piano was too close – which meant that he heard nothing except the electric piano. During the interval, he tried to get these problems sorted out, and his road manager said that he would try to do something about it if the interval was long enough; but he didn't offer much hope and told Davis that these things happen with electrical instruments at outdoor concerts, and that Miles would just have to learn to live with it.

The music on the live albums from Fillmore West (April) and Fillmore East (June) is full of extraordinary invention, but shows a schizophrenia which threatened to tear the band apart – and which ultimately did. The music see-sawed between the rhythmic grooves for Miles and the completely abstract interplay of the rhythm section when it was functioning on its own. On the earlier album, the actual time-playing of the section is often so busy that it fails to provide an adequate contrast with the totally abstract interludes. The tension is built up but rarely satisfactorily released because the pulse is continually disturbed. This facet of improvisation harks back to the European 'free' jazz of the sixties, which in turn has a certain relationship to the avant-garde 'straight' music syndrome. John McLaughlin once remarked that it's only in Europe that musicians are afraid of, or embarrassed by, funk; and it is precisely funk which differentiates the whole jazz tradition from European music. However, Chick Corea, particularly in the abstract passages, is brilliantly inventive, coming up again and again with fresh lines and figures. The new saxophonist, Stephan Grossman, though much maligned by reviewers, was an excellent choice for this music, playing at white heat and creating a flow of interesting melodic lines. Miles brings in at various times some pieces from the recent albums – 'It's About That Time', 'Sanctuary', 'Spanish Key', 'Bitches Brew' – but they rarely ever settle into satisfying rhythmic coherence.

The Fillmore East music is much superior. Not only does everyone, including Miles, play better, but also the rhythm section does occasionally settle so that tension is built up and released in a more satisfactory way. By this time, Keith Jarrett had joined the group on organ, and his profoundly funky feeling and pulse helped the rhythm section to cohere. Miles had been trying for some time to persuade Jarrett to work with him, but the pianist had always refused because

202

he was running his own band and wanted to give that priority. Jarrett recalled: 'He would show up at places we were playing and he'd be sitting in a corner, and he'd say, "You want to play with the band?" And I said, "No". And it kept going like that, and finally I had an open period of time with no work, and I said, "I'll play with the band if I can leave whenever..." It wasn't really joining the band, it was just playing with it.' Jarrett did not really want to play electric keyboard because he much preferred the acoustic piano, but he understood perfectly the requirements of Miles's music and thought he could make a contribution to it: 'The music that he had wouldn't have worked with acoustic piano. You couldn't play chords (functional harmony) – it wasn't chordal at all. It was just...sounds... I thought the band was the most egocentric organization I had heard musically...except for Miles. Miles was still playing nice, beautiful things, and the rest of the band was in boxes. So in a way...I just wanted to do something a little bit to change the feeling. And I knew Jack DeJohnette was there, so we play well together.'

Throughout the Fillmore East double album, Miles Davis plays with tremendous intensity, but the absolute highspot was the Friday night session. Here everyone seems to have been inspired and the music reached great heights. Miles not only utilizes the whole range of the trumpet from the lowest notes to sustained screams, but he also produces series after series of completely fresh melodic lines. The band's reception was also much better than it had been in April on the West Coast. In June, the audience was now responding to many events in the music and there was liberal applause. But in general, although Keith Jarrett's presence improves the music, it is still characterized by the same schizophrenia – a see-sawing between the abstract and the concrete.

Miles himself was delighted with his band's music on all the Fillmore sessions. He went to Columbia to listen to the tapes, and the *Zygote* writer observed:

Miles listened to tapes for about three hours, discussing the merits of one tape, the lack of clarity on another, where a cut should be made, what changes should take place. He was extremely satisfied with his and his group's performances, and joked, bobbed to some of the music, raised his eyebrows in disbelief at some of the intricacies of passages, and rocked back on his heels, his face uplifted, at some of his dynamic trumpet solos... Miles was so excited about the music that he wanted every set, every note made available to the public... Miles had been so productive that Teo [Macero] has one gigantic headache. He has six months worth of editing and enough material to produce albums for the next three years. No one quite knows what to do with all the material at hand.

203

In fact, Miles's fecundity was becoming a bugbear for Columbia. As well as the live albums, he was also recording in the studio, and a backlog was piling up. He would phone Clive Davis or someone else at Columbia such as Bob Altshuler, and play long passages over the phone. He would say that *this* was the album to release. If there had been a release in December, he would record in January and want the results released immediately. Columbia would protest, talk about marketing, about time needed for sales and promotion. Then Miles would call again a month or two later and tell them to forget about the January album because he'd just made another one which was *the* one. From August 1969 to August 1970, Miles had recorded enough material for two live double-albums (the Fillmores), a studio double-album (*Bitches Brew*), a studio single album (*Jack Johnson*), three sides of another studio double-album (*Big Fun*), and four tracks from another double-album (*Live-Evil*). It had been the most productive year of his career.

By August, Stephan Grossman had left the band and Gary Bartz, the (black) saxophonist had joined. In October, both Dave Holland and Chick Corea left the band. In Dave Holland's case, the reason for leaving was not the usual one of 'Join Miles Davis...become a star...leave and lead your own band.' The reason was primarily that Holland had come from one strong music scene in Europe, and his present role with Miles did not fit in with the musical ideals he had at that time. Miles was forty-four years old and had been through many, many musical experiences of all kinds. Holland was twenty-three, and there were very many musical areas which he had not yet explored. The crunch came when he took round to Miles's house a tape he'd made with some of the leading British avant-garde musicians of the 1960s. Holland recalled: 'I played it to him and he listened to it and said he dug it, you know. He liked the way it sounded, but said: "If you want to play that, well, get your own band... I'm not going to play that. That's not what I want to do." That's the point where I realized that I was hitting my head against a wall. I was either going to go along with Miles's music, or leave the band.'

When Holland told Miles that he wanted to leave, Davis asked, 'Why? Why are you leaving?' Holland said, 'Miles, I can't function in this role any more. I need to have more space.' Miles replied, 'But you can do anything you want. I'm not stopping you from doing anything you want. You can play any way you want.' But Dave Holland felt, quite rightly, that the music did demand certain things, and that certain prescribed roles – particularly for the bass and drums – were necessary for it.

So by October 1970, the phase which had begun in 1968 with *Filles De Kilimanjaro* was over. Miles had to find new musicians, and his choice would be crucial to the direction of the music. He had rejected the European, western, approach to improvisation; now he would strengthen the non-western elements in his work.

204

16
Live–Evil

'Jazz today is closer to classical music than it is to
folklore music, and I'd rather stay closer to
folklore music.'[1]
Miles Davis

To replace Dave Holland, Miles chose nineteen-year-old Michael
Henderson who had played with Aretha Franklin and Stevie
Wonder. This was a significant choice; Henderson played with
superb feeling and rhythmic drive, and was happy to produce
hypnotically repeating *ostinati*. His role was to be exactly the one
which Dave Holland had not wanted – that of creating the 'drone'
and solid rhythmic foundation for the music. Henderson also had
a marvellous flair for creating bass figures – something at which
Joe Zawinul also excelled. This faculty was extremely important
to Miles in the late sixties and the seventies. He actually told
Zawinul, 'You're the greatest bass line writer there is.' In Michael
Henderson, Miles had found a similar playing, as
opposed to writing, talent. He said of Henderson: 'He's incredible. He can play lines when there's nothing there but air.'[2] But
Henderson had difficulty at first in hearing how the oblique notes
Miles played related to the bass lines. In 1973 Miles described
some of the delicate aspects of this relationship: 'I never look
down or talk down to any musician because he's nineteen or
something. I don't sell nobody short. I'm always listening. Yester-
day's dead...Michael's got a funky sound, you know, and I been
teaching him for a while. Like if he's in E flat and I play an A chord
or maybe a C or D, he doesn't get ruffled any more like he used
to. He sticks where he is. He's used to all my stuff by now.'[3]

Miles did not bother to replace Chick Corea, because by this
time Keith Jarrett was playing enough for two men, and often
using two keyboards simultaneously – one with either hand. With
the departure of Corea and Holland, and the arrival of
Henderson, all the chittering European 'free jazz' elements
disappeared, and even when Miles soloed out of time with free
accompaniment, the feeling was quite different from the two
Fillmore albums. This tremendous change in the music, from a

205

disruptive schizophrenia to a homogeneity with a new solidity at the core, can be heard on the two sets of recordings which come from the later 1970 period: the studio album *Jack Johnson*, and the live tracks on *Live-Evil*.

In 1970, Miles was asked to make the background music for a long documentary on the great heavy-weight boxer Jack Johnson. This superbly made film also contains footage of live film of Johnson's key fights early in the century. Jack Johnson was the first black heavy-weight champion of the world, and a magnificent man in every sense, showing supreme moral and physical courage. He was also a flamboyant character with many women – several of them white – and a love for fast cars. Miraculously, Johnson lived through all the violent scenes he stirred up, only dying, at the age of sixty-eight in 1946, when he crashed the fast car he was driving. Miles not only created the music, but also wrote the album sleeve note himself. The music was edited by Teo Macero from tapes recorded in the late summer of 1970, and some earlier tapes including excerpts from the *Silent Way* session. In fact, Miles wanted to use the title track from that album, and phoned Zawinul saying, 'I'm going to do the score for *Jack Johnson* and we'd like to use 'In A Silent Way'...can I put my name to it as joint composer?' Zawinul flatly refused, and so the piece was never used on this album.

The music on *Jack Johnson* is worthy of the great champion. The first side, 'Right Off', has a sardonic grandeur. Miles plays acoustic trumpet with a massive sound, biting attack, screaming high notes and some breathtaking chromatic lines which are very oblique to the tonality of B flat (concert). The rhythm section – Henderson, John McLaughlin, Billy Cobham on drums and Herbie Hancock on organ – keep up a hypnotically rocking pulse which, because it is a kind of variation on the 12/8 feel, is nearer to rhythm and blues than to rock and roll. McLaughlin, in particular, handles a confined space and a heavy beat with grace and subtlety. His 'comping' always arises organically out of the basic pulse, enhancing the rhythmic power and the emotional intensity of the piece. Herbie Hancock creates a massive, barbaric sound on the organ. He said of this session: 'By that time we weren't into playing instruments as instrumentalists – we were more into just getting a kind of sound out...I'm not an organ player at all, but there was a sound that maybe I could fit in in some kind of way. So that's why I did it.' At the end of the first side, McLaughlin plays guitar lines with plenty of fuzz, which is a real rock sound – nothing like the polite sound of the traditional jazz guitar. Billy Cobham tried to explain why this session was such a good one:

206

He would tell me what he wanted. He would even sit down and try to play. And it was not in an obnoxious way. It was not meant to degrade. I always felt that he always got the most out of the cats that worked with him because everybody loved him, if only for the musician that he is and what he stands for. He said, like in *Jack Johnson*, 'I want this and I want that,' and I said, 'Oh yeah? OK.' And I didn't do it the way he wanted me to do it, and then he just let me alone...It was really a relaxed session...It's just that on a Miles Davis session, everybody's very reserved. Sort of a cloud-cover comes over, and business gets taken care of![4]

The track 'Yesternow' on side two, is remarkable for its economy and the brilliant use of space. The first third or so is very sparse but is held together and given unity by an intermittent yet insistent bass figure. All kinds of events take place within this eerily empty framework, until eventually the spaces, the holes in the music, close up, and a tight continuous groove is created while a soprano sax solo by Steve Grossman bites deeply. There is some cross-fading on this side, and also some abstract electronic sounds by the guitarist, Sonny Sharrock, towards the end. The side ends with actor, Brock Peters, reciting Jack Johnson's words: 'I'm black. They never let me forget it. I'm black all right. I'll never let *them* forget it.'

Live-Evil is a double album, and the live tracks on it – 'Inamorata', 'What I Say', 'Sivad', 'Funky Tonk' – were recorded in a club during December 1970. Miles phoned John McLaughlin and asked him to play on the session, so the group was once more a septet with guitar and keyboard, drums and percussion, bass guitar, saxophone and trumpet. The sounds and the atmosphere are quite unlike the previous albums; the whooping, barking percussion, the persistent bass *ostinati*, the raving keyboards and wailing guitar, the insistent drum rhythms, the wild saxophone sound, and the acoustic and amplified trumpet with its wah-wah and extreme tonal distortion, all give the impression of total possession...the inspired state of rapt improvisation in which the individual and the ensemble are one, and the player becomes his instrument. The whole atmosphere on these tracks is unlike anything else in jazz, although it relates perhaps to some of Ellington's jungle music. The music on these live tracks is, nevertheless, quite varied, ranging from the ruminative feel of the slow section of 'Sivad' to the ferocity of 'What I Say'. The former passage is based on a slow, spacey riff with a cunningly displaced accent which makes it seem asymmetrical, though it is not. Over this lopsided figure, Miles improvises with wah-wah,

207

while Airto Moreira adds some wordless singing. Then McLaughlin plays a powerful solo. There is all the time a sense of dark contemplation.

'What I Say' is the most extreme track of all. Once again it is in B flat, and the rhythm is a furiously fast rock beat. The bass guitar anchors the piece by sticking to a repetitive figure, and the drums are purely supportive, playing motor rhythms. The groove is phenomenal. Jarrett, playing two keyboards, matches the energy and momentum of bass and drums, and after setting up the whole demonic atmosphere, he prepares the way for Miles's entry which is exceptionally dramatic. The latter stabs out some high trumpet Es which give yet more momentum to the already headlong rhythm, and then hits some notes which are so high that they approach bat frequencies. Everything is taken to its ultimate extremity: the sheer physical range of the trumpet, the speed of the phrases, the intensity of the rhythms. Miles seems to be beating almost despairingly at the limits of his abilities in his shrieking notes and his chromatic scurrying around. However, he swings madly along, and the whole ensemble reacts wildly to his phrases, because he is pushing the other musicians to the limits of their own abilities. There is an extraordinary collective violence in this music. After Miles, Gary Bartz plays an excellent soprano solo, and is followed by John McLaughlin, after which Keith Jarrett solos at length. This exhilarating keyboard solo metamorphoses into a long drum solo by Jack DeJohnette which changes the pulse into a looser, rolling, triple feel. This relaxation of the tension is logical and necessary, but it doesn't occur until the original ferocious pulse has been sustained for almost fifteen minutes. This is one great difference between the present group and the one which made the two Fillmore albums: the earlier group would never have sustained the groove for more than two or three minutes.

The music on *Live-Evil* is the antithesis of the highly arranged, understated pieces on the 1949/50 recordings of the *Birth of the Cool* band. It is also the opposite end of the spectrum from the 1959 *Kind of Blue* album. 'What I Say' relates more to the live albums of the early 1960s; they swung perhaps more viciously than any previous jazz music. 'What I Say' swings in a different way and even more viciously, but in essence it is the same kind of performance. According to Keith Jarrett, however, the *Live-Evil* tracks were not entirely representative of the band at that time. He said: 'Unfortunately with *Live-Evil*, John McLaughlin just happened to be in town, and he wasn't playing (regularly) with the band. He just sat in, and the band sound wasn't the same because there was now...a different voice.' In Jarrett's opinion, the band (without the guitar) had been at its best sometime earlier, during a week-long engagement in Boston. The Norwegian saxophonist, Jan Garbarek, had been in the audience, and he verified Jarrett's opinion. Keith Jarrett recalled: 'I talked to Miles the second night and said, "Can we record here? Can you call CBS and have them send..." And he said he already had. You know, everyone knew how good it was. He'd already talked to them [Columbia] and they couldn't do it that quickly ...maybe next week! And I said, "It's not going to be next week, it's going to be these six days." Anyway, Jan (Garbarek) was there and he has the same opinion about the music then.'

The following year, 1971, Jack DeJohnette left the group, and when Miles played the Berlin Festival and the London Festival Hall in November, he had Leon Chancler on drums, and two percussionists, Don Alias and James Foreman: one reinforcing the pulse with congas and the other producing colours and textures. Jarrett, Bartz and Henderson were still with the group, and the Berlin Festival concert in particular has some of the most deeply satisfying music of the post-Fillmore period. The music is not as frenetic as that of *Live-Evil*; the long stretches of beautifully rocking rhythm are a sheer delight; the *colla voce* passages are full of colour and feeling; and the key soloists – Miles, Jarrett and Bartz – are in peak form. This session was a joy throughout. Although the non-western elements had been intensified, there was still a delicate balance and the music was not marred by an over-emphasis on physical pulse.

Miles's was the first jazz group to top the bill at the Fillmore West, which they did for three nights in May. Miles was also on the bill with Nina Simone at the Shrine Auditorium, Los Angeles, in April. Voluminous review space was given to *Live at the Fillmore* and *Jack Johnson* when they were released, and although the former received some indifferent notices from mystified writers, *Jack Johnson* was given many ecstatic reviews. At the same time, the fascination with Miles continued in the general press, and he was again mentioned in *Time* magazine. Also, there were other articles, such as the one in *Essence* in March, about his legendary wardrobe, his flair for clothes designing, and his own private hairdresser, Finny the Scorpio, who is described as, 'a far-out, free spirit who gave up his private hairdressing practice to travel with Miles. And as Finny says, "It's a trip"...While we sipped Galliano and listened to Gladys Knight and the Pips, Miles would become concerned with his hair and summon Finny to touch up his curls. Miles sometimes wears his hair in tight, hot curls which give the effect of an extremely full, kinky Afro.'[5] At the end of the day with the journalists, Miles amazed them by preparing a meal from ancient French recipes – fish, potatoes, and salad.

209

In January 1971, Miles received a letter from Chick Corea saying that working with Miles Davis for the previous two years had been 'one of the most beautiful experiences of my whole life'. The trumpeter was so gratified that he showed the letter to a complete stranger who had come to interview him, saying, 'Here, I got this letter from Chick the other day. It's one of the nicest letters I've ever received.'⁶ Perhaps the departure from his group of Holland and Corea had disturbed Miles more deeply than he liked to admit. After leaving, they had formed a group together – presumably to create the kind of music they felt was missing in Miles's band. That is clearly why it was such a relief when Corea's letter arrived and reaffirmed that it had been good working with Davis.

But a little later in the year, a catalogue of disasters, some minor and some fairly weighty, really upset Miles. The great status symbol, his Lamborghini sports car, which he now claimed was worth $30,000, had been damaged and was off the road. The rear end had been dented in one accident, and then a couple of weeks later, someone had forced Miles up on the pavement and into a brick wall on 79th Street, denting a headlamp and the grille. He took the car to a body repair shop, expecting his insurance company to pay for the repairs, but the bill came to $11,000, and Miles reported: 'They fixed the car, sent me the bill, then the insurance company was supposed to pay, but it went out of business. And I'm not going to pay.'⁷ Meanwhile, he was spending a fortune on hired cars. Also, a Philadelphia deejay had sued Davis for $13,000, alleging that he failed to show up for a concert with Aretha Franklin a year previously. Miles pleaded illness as the reason for his default, but the man continued to press his suit for compensation. And in July, Davis played four concerts at the Beaco Theatre in New York as a favour to a friend, but, as one journalist pointed out: 'Miles doesn't get the kind of airplay in New York that he needs to fill a 2,600-seat house for four shows in two nights. He would have done better booking himself for one concert and enough ticket buyers would have knocked on the box office window for him to turn away a couple of thousand.'⁸ In fact, the theatre was never more than forty per cent full on any night, and only 4,000 in all attended the concerts. It must have been a shock to Miles to realize that despite all his recent publicity, acclaim and record sales, his drawing-power was still fallible; a modicum of advertising plus the word-of-mouth grapevine, were not enough to get him full houses.

In addition, rumours began to fly around that Miles Davis was thinking of quitting jazz because he was being harassed by the United States Bureau of Internal Revenue. Miles was quoted as

210

saying: 'The hell with it...I'm not going to work for "the man" or anyone else. The Internal Revenue people have been messing with my bank acount so often that the bank finally got sick and tired of it and closed out my account. Imagine them bothering me after I paid $40,000 in taxes last year alone. To hell with them all – they can kiss my ass. I'm through.'⁹ But by the end of the year, Davis had re-signed with Columbia, and this time it was a three-year, $300,000 contract: *Live-Evil* had been released to astonished and delighted notices, and Miles and the group had had a resounding success at the Berlin Festival.

1972 saw another decisive change in Miles Davis's music, and this came about in a very curious way. It crystallized in the album *On The Corner* which was recorded at a time when Miles was listening intently to some European avant-garde music (Stockhausen in particular), and having long musical discussions with a young, academy educated British musician, Paul Buckmaster. The latter had studied the cello both privately and at the Royal Academy of Music, but his interests ranged from the classics and twentieth century composers such as Roberto Gerhard and Humphrey Searle to Indian classical music and jazz. As well as being able to compose for large ensembles, Buckmaster also had a remarkable feeling for rhythm and was completely at home improvising with small jazz or rock groups. He also had an awed regard for Miles Davis's work from the fifties on.

Paul Buckmaster was managed by Tony Hall who had been an ardent Miles Davis fan since the late 1940s, and who had become friendly with the trumpeter during one of his trips to Europe in the fifties. In 1969, when Miles came to Britain to play at the Hammersmith Odeon, he had met Paul Buckmaster at Tony Hall's house. Buckmaster recalled: 'He'd heard a tape that I'd got together. It consisted of a twenty-five-minute jam (session). All I'd supplied was a drum rhythm and a bass figure which could mutate from one form to another shape. And the thing went through a lot of mood changes – light, heavy, dark, intense – definitely space music. He liked this.' The following day, Buckmaster had accompanied Miles on a shopping spree, taking in some of the most fashionable clothes designers in London.

But it wasn't until 1972 that Paul Buckmaster received a telephone call from Miles asking him to fly over to New York and work on some music at Davis's house. Buckmaster stayed with the trumpeter for about six weeks in May and June of that year. Every morning, Miles and his protégé, who was exactly twenty years younger and also a Gemini, would talk about various aspects of music, and sometimes Davis would simply listen to Buckmaster practising the cello. At other times, Miles would sit down at the piano and play something, then he would ask

Buckmaster to sit down and play. The latter recalled: 'And I would play a phrase that was maybe based on a chord or scale that he'd used and he'd say, "Right! Hold it there. Write that down." So I'd jot it down.'

At the time, Buckmaster was practising some of Bach's unaccompanied suites for cello; every morning he would read through and study them, and Miles would listen and discuss them. Sometimes he singled out particular phrases or passages and said, "Why don't you write a piece around that?" He became very enthusiastic about Bach. But Buckmaster also introduced Miles to Stockhausen's work. He'd brought with him a record of 'Mixtur' and 'Telemusik' – music for acoustic orchestra which was also miked up through ring modulators and was transformed in that way. Miles sat upstairs for a whole day listening to this record, and had it blaring through the whole house. Subsequently, he bought a number of cassettes of Stockhausen which he played in his car. But although Miles found the German composer's music very interesting, it is unlikely that he would have willingly moved his own music towards Stockhausen's conception, because he was groping for a fresh direction which would take him nearer to the black audience in America – an audience to whom the sounds of Stockhausen were foreign.

Some four days after Paul Buckmaster arrived at Miles's house, in May 1972, he learned that there was to be a recording session in two or three weeks time. When Miles asked him what ideas he had about the music they were going to record, Buckmaster said he would like to see what would happen if they utilized the non-regular temporal music (out-of-time passages) which was already indicated in some of Miles's recent work and which was typical of certain pieces by Stockhausen. The idea would be to try and combine that approach with some sort of street-music concept (city street), at the same time combining it with the space concept. As the recording date drew nearer, Buckmaster felt less sure of what Miles wanted, and more nervous about the occasion. It was not until they actually arrived at the studio that it became certain what the exact personnel for the session was going to be. Miles had phoned around and booked musicians, but a couple of the people he'd booked brought along other musicians who were then introduced to Davis. According to Buckmaster, that seemed to be how Harold Williamson, who played keyboard on one track, got on the session...and how the drummer, Al Foster, did too; it was the first time Miles had met Foster. The total personnel comprised two drummers, bass guitar, three keyboard players, two percussionists and a tabla player, sitar, guitar, two reed players and Miles himself.

Paul Buckmaster described how Miles extracted what he

212

needed from the material they had prepared, and how the music was created in the studio:

> There would be a bass figure, a drum rhythm that was notated, tabla and conga rhythm and a couple of keyboard phrases which fitted. In fact, I would write out a whole tune, but what actually happened in the studio was that the keyboard players related to these phrases and transformed them. They played them more or less accurately to begin with and transformed them in the Stockhausian sense – making them more unrecognizable until they became something else. I had written places where changes would occur, but these changes weren't rehearsed and they didn't occur. I made photostat copies of these parts and gave them to the musicians, and Miles asked me to sing the bass part and sing the drum part and check the keyboard phrases with the players. And I'd barely done this when he said, 'OK. That's enough of that!' and started clicking his fingers, beating time, and the thing would start and go on for half an hour until he'd say, 'OK. That's enough of that. Let's go and hear it.'...If he wanted it to be more bouncing or raunchy rhythmically, he would signify by a characteristic shrugging of the shoulders. He would also indicate coming down with body movements...arm gestures.

It is ironical that after his discussions with Paul Buckmaster, and after his immersion in the music of Stockhausen, Miles should have produced an album (*On The Corner*) so alien to the European tradition. Although the instrumentation is related to that on *Bitches Brew*, the music is very different. There is some vital interplay, particularly between the chordal instruments (Herbie Hancock and John McLaughlin were on this session) and the horns, but the rhythm section roles are very much proscribed. The sitar provides the perpetual drone, and the brilliantly conceived intermeshing of the two drums, the congas and tabla, the bass line, and various other riffs, owes more to Africa and India than the music on *Bitches Brew*. The German critic and musician, Manfred Miller, described it as: 'Music based on the principles of West African ritual dances, with a multi-woven rhythmical line (drum-choir) as a basis for a "soundstream" and a collective choir which, instead of fragmented solos, takes the place of the lead singer.'[10] Miles plays amplified trumpet with wah-wah – never acoustic trumpet – and he is the leading voice of the ensemble which interweaves with flashing rhythms and rich textures. His trumpet is well down in the mix, and most of the time is more like a dominant texture than a solo voice. Indeed, for long sections of the album, Miles does not play at all, but simply directs the ensemble.

There can be no doubt that Miles Davis was radically reasses-

213

sing his own work at this time. In a *Playboy* interview, he dismissed all of his work before 1970. He may, of course, have been trying to shock the readers into re-evaluating his recent work, but nevertheless there must have been a deep-seated unease behind his outburst. The white audience who loved his earlier music of the fifties and sixties had probably been attuned to it by exposure to the French impressionists and to the Spanish influences which lay behind the Miles Davis/Gil Evans orchestral music and much of the Davis small-group music of that time. The ghetto blacks, of course, did not have this conditioning, and therefore Miles's earlier music had largely escaped them. Perhaps the realization of this lay behind Miles's assertion in that interview that he wanted to be accepted by black audiences on the same terms as the Temptations. And from this point onwards, his music showed a much greater emphasis on rhythm – on a steadily incessant 'soundstream' in which audiences could find familiarity and reassurance. Later his thoughts were to crystallize on this subject: 'I like when a black boy says "Oohh! Man, there's Miles Davis." Like they did with Joe Louis. Some cats did me like that in Greensboro. They said, "Man, we sure glad you came down here." That thrilled me more than anything that happened to me that year...I don't feel like I'm doing anything. I mean, so what, so I play music but, my race don't get it. You know what I mean, it's cause they can't afford it, man.'[11]

During 1972, Miles attacked the record industry's 'Grammy' awards because, he said, they usually went to white artists who had made their careers out of copying black artists. Miles wanted to initiate some awards for blacks only, and to call them 'Mammy' awards. He said:

The Mammy's are going to be different. I got the idea watching this programme on TV: *Soultrain*. It's an all-black show and it's better...than all other shows on the stage. Kids are dancing and moving, taking off, you know. And it's no African boonga, bonga, boonga; just black Americans doing their thing... That is what Mammys are going to be like: fun...What we could do...is give them an award and then have them tear it up right on TV, and them give them a film clip of that as the real award. Hell, it's just going to be fun; like it should be. None of this Grammy shit of being prim and proper so the President can see it.[12]

Miles also refused, at the last moment, to play the Newport Festival because he thought his fee of $7,500 was for one show only, but discovered that he had to play twice for that money. He claimed that he once previously worked for George Wein (organizer of Newport) for a reduced fee in order to help the promoter out, and then found that other promoters wanted to pay him the same low price. Davis

214

said: 'We're past that stage of a Newport jazz artist, which is like an Uncle Tom version of a slave musician working for his master, George Wein...He'll pay me what I want...but I just don't want to do it. I can't cheapen myself by being one of the Newport boys. He keeps sending me telegrams saying, "You can't do this to me", but look what he's doing to me.'[13]

There had been another brush with the law in July, when Miles was charged with unlawfully imprisoning and menacing a woman in his own house. One of his former tenants, Mrs Lita Merker, charged that on 9 July Miles verbally abused her, slapped her and prevented her from leaving his apartment. A detective who examined her said he found no signs of injuries at all, but described her as being 'emotionally upset'. Miles, wearing a blue-striped shirt, flared blue pants and red shoes, pleaded innocent before the judge. The case was adjourned until 22 August, with Davis put on parole in his own custody. Miles had told this woman: 'You respect my name...Look at these trophies and awards. Don't you *ever* scream at a black man. You don't know what your ancestors have done to him.'[14] The papers were full of headlines alleging that Miles Davis had molested a white woman etc., but Miles later recalled: 'They neglected to say that she lived upstairs, that my woman was standing right there when it all went down, and that the white woman had got caught smuggling hashish into this country. She was upset about that and apologized for trying to take her frustrations out on me. No, the news media didn't pick that up and run with it.'[15]

Miles's health was not quite so good this year. In April he had been rushed to hospital with gall-stone trouble. He was also having trouble with his breathing, although he was still working out in the gym two or three times a week and usually in three-hour stints. Paul Buckmaster noted that when Miles was asleep the rasping breath of the trumpeter could be heard all over the house. And almost as if Miles were courting disaster, he crashed his car into a traffic island on Manhattan's West Side Highway at 8.00 a.m. on 9 October. He had felt restless and decided to take a morning drive. It was a costly whim; both his legs were broken, and he suffered facial cuts which required twelve stitches. This effectively stopped him from working for the rest of the year. When a reporter asked him about the accident, he said: 'I'm all right...I'll just have to stop buying those little cars.'[16]

After recording *On the Corner*, Miles had got together a band to play that music in live performance. It included drummer Al Foster, and conga player M'tume who was, in fact, the son of Miles's old associate saxophonist Jimmy Heath. The instrumentation also included tablas (Badal Roy), sitar, guitar and saxophone. Miles rehearsed them at his home for some days before they went out on the road. After some five or six concerts, they played the Philharmonic Hall, New York, on 29 September, and this was recorded by Columbia (*Miles Davis in Concert*). The music has the rhythmic 'soundstream' of *On the Corner* but it also refers back to some of the bass figures of *Jack Johnson* and *Live-Evil*. Davis plays with wah-wah throughout and seems to be in very good lip for the occasion. Although there are some excellent moments, the performance as a whole is too diffuse to bear comparison with his best work.

On the Corner was released in the autumn, and Miles wanted to tour with his new band to promote the album. They were scheduled to open at Harlem's Apollo Theatre on 24 October, but his car accident put a stop to that. This was very bad luck because *On the Corner* received excellent reviews and sold more than 50,000 in the first week, so there was every chance of it achieving really big sales if Miles promoted it properly. The art work showed a different departure in that it consisted of caricature drawings of blacks in platform shoes, hotpants (the girls) and flared pants, all standing in various postures on the street. There are one or two token whites in the scene, but the general impression is that Columbia were attempting to make a folk hero of Miles. This was certainly what he wanted. And there was another new departure with this album: the names of the musicians were not credited on the sleeve. One reason was certainly because Miles felt that the new direction would incur the misapprehension and wrath of the usual jazz critics. He said: 'There's no critic in that world that knows as much about my music as I do. There's no but, period...I didn't put those names on *On the Corner* specially for that reason, so now the critics have to say, "What's that instrument, and what's that?"..the critics have to listen.'[17] But it also seemed that Miles might be phasing out the period when musicians climbed to stardom on his back. He was very pleased with *On the Corner* and said: 'People have to respect *me*, I know they respect me, there's no doubt about it because they can't do it themselves. Otherwise there'd be five *On the Corners*.'[18]

17
Manhattan Jungle
. Symphony

'I don't care who buys the records as long as they get to
the black people, so I will be remembered when I die.'[1]
Miles Davis

Miles Davis began 1973 on crutches and with one of his legs still in
plaster, but despite his injuries, he was determined to work and did
so throughout that year. On stage, he sat on a tall stool in front of
the band and exercised much more control than he had done over
his previous ensembles. Despite the large salaries he had paid his
musicians since 1970, most of the jazz virtuosi had left, and Miles
was now producing an essentially collective music with multiple
rhythms and textures. Early in 1973, saxophonist Dave Liebman,
who had played on the first side of *On The Corner*, joined Miles's
touring band, but even though Liebman was a virtuoso soloist, his
talents were used collectively; he was not a solo star supported by an
ensemble, but a part of the colour and texture of that ensemble. The
rest of the line-up comprised Michael Henderson, Al Foster (drums),
Badal Roy (tabla), James M'tume (percussion), Bala Krishna (sitar),
Reggie Lucas (guitar) and Cedric Lawson (organ).

From this period on, Miles usually rehearsed his musicians
individually at his home, showing each man the kind of rhythmic
patterns he could create for different pulses and at various tempos.
Miles now directed his ensemble both by playing and by using
bodily signals; with a flick of his wrist the whole ensemble would
slide smoothly from one complex rhythmic pattern to another. It
was done so perfectly, and was such a dramatic change, that one
critic who had heard it only on record, thought that it was an edited
tape-splice. On attending a concert, he was astonished to witness it
happening on stage. Attempting to explain his new approach, Miles
said: 'It's just about three bands in one, just feeling out different
rhythms. We have African drums, an eastern section and melodies,
although the melodies are shorter and most times the things I play
are based on rhythm because most of the melodies you can possibly
hear have been recorded by the record companies and exploited. In
melody you have usually heard it somewhere before, so I use

217

polyrhythms, and things I write might be in the bass or drums.'[2]

Dave Liebman, who had previously worked with Elvin Jones and Pete LaRoca among others, learned a great deal from Miles during the eighteen months he spent with the band. Recalling this period, Liebman said:

> You can play lines . . . that flow over the time and rhythm. But if you point off your lines by stopping and going with a particular kind of rhythmic figure, maybe a staccato figure, you tie in the rhythm section in a very quick way. You make them come together very quickly. Miles is a master at this. He plays one note and everybody gathers to that note, or he plays something and lets the band take it from there. He said, 'Don't finish your idea; let them finish it'; and 'End your solo before you're done.' . . . Before, I would always take it through a cycle, up and down like Coltrane. But Miles creates an overall mood where each solo is just a little part of a larger picture . . . So the thing is to give the essence to the musicians without creating their parts for them . . . Even with electronic instruments, Miles still used colour to differentiate one note from another. Even playing E flat for four hours, which is what we did most of the time, even within the context of that very limited area and beat, and four guitars and an amazing amount of sound – even within that I was able to discern the subtleties of Miles's playing.[3]

From Liebman's description, it can be seen that even though Miles's music had apparently changed radically, many of the old criteria still applied. Areas of subtlety and lyricism did exist, though now they took on rather different forms. However, Miles's new band and its music presented great problems for some critics – particularly jazz critics, one of whom was seen openly weeping at one of Davis's concerts. Many critics who had made Herculean efforts to understand Miles's previous changes of direction, now began dismissing the music.

If many jazz critics gave up at this point, many other critics were stimulated and excited by the music, using terms such as 'sonic jungle' and 'Manhattan jungle symphony' to describe their impressions. One reviewer wrote excitedly:

> Miles, still suffering the after-effects of an abrupt meeting between his car and a wall, hobbled in a walking cast, and was in a genuinely good mood. Swinging about on a stool, he conducted the band, altering the texture with brief signals, guiding soloists in and out and often changing the beat completely with a single wave of his hand. And he soloed beautifully, dominating the music with a lot of open horn, some amazing wah-wah pedal trumpet, and brief patches of mute. Sometimes his sudden leaps

218

into the upper register would leave me gasping for breath. He used sharp phrases that tugged at the rhythm, and as always his improvisation suggested and hinted much more than it actually came right out and said . . . Miles began hushing the band up at intervals and dropping poignant *Kind of Blue* lines, his trumpet pointed downward toward the floor of the stage, as if raising the spirits of his past. The dialogues with Liebman's sax were fascinating. The two men would spit lines back and forth at each other, blend them together in unison, blare them out like a wild fanfare, and then team up together on some shrieking high note until it disappeared into the heavens.[4]

This was the first time Miles had regularly utilized the dialogue technique with his saxophonist, though there had been at least one isolated example in the past (a version of 'The Theme' on *Live At Plugged Nickel* Vol.2, December 1965). Miles and Liebman were working on yet another variation of the call-and-response device and it was natural that the instrumental sounds were extremely vocalized. Since 1969, Miles's groups had been creating music which was veering further and further away from the orthodox notational system of western music. At the time of *Bitches Brew*, only a fraction of the music was conventional enough to make transcription a possibility; by 1973, his music was almost totally beyond transcription. It was not just that the subtle rhythms and inflexions were outside the scope of western notation, but that there were no precise symbols for the kinds of sounds Davis was using. The non-western elements (African and oriental) in his music were becoming ever more predominant. Reviewing a 1974 concert in the *Washington Post*, writer Gene Williams compared Miles with someone who was:

leading his exploring party through a dense electronic rain forest. Sensing a clearing, Davis extends his fingers in a signal and his group halts motionless as a soprano sax or electric guitar or even the leader's trumpet slips ahead alone, reporting what he sees. The leader listens, choosing a path. He arches his body, nodding his head to the desired pulse, beckoning the rhythm guitar, and his group falls in, resuming their journey. Echoing, reverberatingly, electronically shaped notes and phrases form the strange beautiful foliage and strong life rhythms of Davis's musical world.[5]

By this time, Miles had severed the business relationship with Harold Lovett, his black lawyer/manager. His new manager was white and Jewish, a man called Neil Reshin, who specialized in representing 'difficult' artists. Lovett had idolized Miles, but Reshin's strength was his ability at his job, his hard-headedness and his unsentimental approach to the business of protecting the interests

219

of his clients. In February 1973, Reshin managed to rescue Miles from a very awkward situation. Once again, the trumpeter had a brush with the law, and this time it could have become a very serious matter. Davis was arrested at his own address on 23 February on charges of possession of cocaine and of possessing a dangerous weapon (a .25 calibre automatic pistol).

According to Reshin, Miles and a girlfriend got back to Miles's house around 1.00 a.m. and the trumpeter couldn't find his keys and began banging on his own front door. One of his tenants upstairs heard someone trying to break down the door, and phoned the police. A sergeant and a patrolman arrived on the scene, and as soon as she saw them, Miles's girlfriend threw her handbag into a corner. The two policemen saw the bag on the ground and asked to whom it belonged. Miles and his girlfriend said they didn't know, so the policeman opened it and found some cocaine and a loaded pistol, whereupon they arrested Miles and the girl. At 3.00 a.m., Reshin got a phone call from the police precinct saying, 'We have Miles Davis here and he's using you as his one phone call.' Miles got on the phone and said, 'Neil, get me outa here, they're treating me like a nigger.'[6] Reshin called a lawyer and then went back to sleep. But at 5.00 a.m., there was another phone call, and Miles said, 'Neil, get me outa here, wake up a fucking judge or something.'[7] In the morning, Reshin talked to the district attorney who said that it was impossible to drop a gun charge on a black man in New York when policemen were getting shot on the streets every day. On 1 March Miles was fined $1,000 on the weapons charge and was given two months to pay, but the judge said that there was insufficient evidence to convict him of charges of possessing three small packages of cocaine.

Police harassment had become so familiar to Miles that he soon got over this incident, but there were other problems which struck home deeply. Despite his apparent self-sufficiency ('I don't live for my family, I live for myself')[8] he had family problems which saddened and troubled him. He was proud of his eldest son, Gregory, who had been an army boxing champion, and kept Gregory's three trophies – each of a little gold fighter leading with his right – by his bed. But Gregory was in trouble at that time, and Miles, pointing to the boxing trophies, told a reporter:

> See these trophies? They're my son's. He was a champion boxer in the army in Germany. He comes back, a white guy pokes fun at him because of his colour, and the first thing my son does is try to break his neck, you know? And I tried to tell him about this shit . . . But he's a Black Muslim, and he says 'What do you think I'm supposed to do, father, let the guy stand up and say that to me? They send me into the army to kill somebody I don't even know,

220

then they won't give me a job, they make fun of me.' . . . He's in jail now . . . in St Louis. I got to get him out fast.'⁹

By 1973, several of Miles's recent ex-sidemen were world-famous superstars in their own right. Chick Corea's *Return to Forever* was extremely popular and successful, and his records came out on the Polydor label. But three groups were recording for Miles's own company, Columbia, and outselling their former boss: John McLaughlin's Mahavishnu Orchestra, Zawinul and Wayne Shorter's Weather Report, and Herbie Hancock and his group. The last two were already beginning to make a big impact on black audiences – the very thing that Miles wanted so much to do. In 1973, Hancock's *Headhunters* was released and became the biggest and fastest selling album in jazz history. Miles actually felt in danger of being over-shadowed by his ex-musicians, and phoned Neil Reshin demanding that the latter get him a publicity agent. Reshin called the publicity department at Columbia and told them how unhappy Miles Davis was. So Columbia began contacting writers and setting up a series of interviews.

Miles's alarm – or actual jealousy as some writers called it – must be seen in perspective. First of all, his ex-associates were all making very accessible music for which there seemed to be ready-made markets. In the case of the Mahavishnu Orchestra, there was the white, eastward-looking, rock audience which had been built up in the sixties by the cult of the guru and the interest in Indian religion started mainly by the Beatles; in the case of Herbie Hancock and Weather Report, their secular, intensely funky sounds were very acceptable to rock fans, but also appealed to the black market whose ears were attuned to Sly Stone and Stevie Wonder. Although Miles Davis was exploring rhythms which were accessible to these audiences, the extremely African elements in his current music were as foreign to American blacks as they were to whites. In particular, the absence of organic harmony (chord sequences) and of diatonic melody made his music forbidding, even alien, to ears attuned to the European tradition. Furthermore, to quote the German writer, Manfred Miller, Miles was no longer sharing 'the tonal system of any "white" middle class tradition.'¹⁰ Also, he had never really tried to create music for a particular market. On this subject, he said:

I tell the guitar player that if he likes Hendrix or Sly, to play something like that, just to open it up. It can't sound exactly like them because it'll have a little more music . . . in it. What we play on top wouldn't be like what Hendrix'll play on top; what Sly and them need is a good soloist . . . I ain't thinking about no fucking market . . . Hendrix had no knowledge of modal music; he was just a natural musician, you know, he wasn't studied, he wasn't into no market, and neither am I. Columbia tries to get me into that shit but I won't let them do it.[11]

Columbia's three 'acolyte' groups all functioned in the usual way, releasing albums only at fairly wide intervals, and promoting each album by touring and playing pieces from it. Miles, on the other hand, was prodigal with his record releases; there were usually at least two new albums a year, either or both of which, after 1970, might be double-albums. And every year saw the reissue of some gem or other from his past, or of a composite LP of some of his most famous pieces. Even when he agreed to make a 'single' (a 45 RPM disc which might get top forty airplay), the one he made in 1969 was in no sense tailored for any market; even the musicians on the session didn't know what to make of the music. It was called 'Little Blue Frog' and it lasted two minutes and thirty-seven seconds – the only concession Miles made to the industry's requirements. The instrumentation for this brief piece included tabla, tambour, electric bass, acoustic bass, guitar, three keyboards, three saxophones, three drummers. Herbie Hancock, who played one of the keyboards, recalled: 'We must have come out of the studio and scratched our heads wondering what the heck was that about? It was interesting, but we had no idea whether it was good or bad. It was just so different.'

There was always a great difference between Miles's music and that of almost all his ex-associates. Teo Macero commented:

Of all the people that have played with him...sooner or later, they start out being a little aggressive and all of a sudden they revert back and they establish themselves in a groove, and there they stay. But unlike those, Miles has transposed himself from here to here, and has moved constantly. And all the other people are moving backwards...and you can go back and listen to any of them...You can listen to Bill Evans, and Cannonball when he was alive, they didn't do anything experimental... Coltrane was the only one. I think Coltrane had more sense of Miles in direction... But all the other players...you listen to them and you say 'What are they doing? I heard all that before.' But Miles...you never heard it before...The source was Miles Davis. Herbie, Wayne Shorter, Joe Zawinul, Chick Corea, Bill Evans – all these people, they all come from one group...McLaughlin too – he developed into something unique with Miles...With Miles, they play at their very best all of the time.

The music created by Miles's bands from 1973 onwards was much more forbidding and severe than that of his ex-associates. His habit of staying on one root for very long periods of time ('E flat for four hours' as Dave Liebman put it) was rather like taking, say one bar or

222

one chord of a tune and putting it under a microscope: examining in extreme close-up its melodic, rhythmic, textural, spatial implications. At the same time, this process could also contain the essence of other eras, styles and themes, hence Miles's (cryptic) comment: 'All the clichés are so condensed that you can play 'Body and Soul' in two bars.'[12] The result of such austerity was that people often went to his concerts more because of the mystique surrounding Miles than because of their interest in his music. Rock fans could relate to his rhythms, but were often baffled by and complained about the 'disorganization' of the music. At the Berlin Festival, Miles and the group played a wildly exciting set and his trumpet playing (with wah-wah) was extraordinarily powerful. The feeling of invocation, of possession, was enhanced by the ritualistic way Miles bobbed up and down and sweated, a hypnotic, demonic figure in dark glasses that curved round his face like the huge eyes of an insect. He was also wearing robes that looked African, and seemed to be exulting in the 'Prince of Darkness' image. Before going on stage, he snarled at a young fan who was standing in the wings, and flipped his cigarette end contemptuously over her head. When a female journalist went to his hotel to interview him, he opened the door and was brutally rude to her whereupon she retired in confusion. In 1975, when he was asked why he wasn't playing so much trumpet, Miles said: 'I play my trumpet long enough, but some people don't notice it because they are busy looking to see what I have on, how tight my pants are in the crotch, how much I'm sweating, and all that. Then there are those who just look, how you are taking care of yourself, how you are using the money you make, what kind of girls you like. But all the serious listeners in the audience want for me to do is to play. And I just give it all I got, and that's it.'[13]

However, Miles gained some recognition at the end of 1973 and during the following year, which he must have found gratifying and reassuring. The Japanese quarterly magazine, *Ad Lib*, devoted its entire autumn (1973) edition to Miles Davis. In this glossy and expensive issue, there were 318 pages, hundreds of photographs, critical analyses, and discographies. It was a unique act of homage. In America, the 18 July 1974 issue of *Down Beat* (the magazine's fortieth anniversary issue), contained a very long interview with Miles, and a tribute to him complete with framed adulatory quotes from people representing all aspects of the music industry. And there were particularly generous quotes from Miles's recent ex-associates – Herbie Hancock, Joe Zawinul, John McLaughlin and Chick Corea.

When Miles and his band played a concert at the Avery Fisher Hall in September, he surprised everyone by starting exactly on time, waving a fist at the audience as he walked on stage, flashing smiles at everyone, and actually fooling around with M'tume –

223

playing on the congas and then offering his horn for M'tume to play. The latter seemed taken aback and was reluctant to respond, but Miles insisted and even seemed disappointed when the percussionist blew only a few notes and tried to hand it back. At the end of the set, Miles picked up a black cane and strolled offstage, waving to the audience as he did so. During the interval, he actually reappeared on stage to touch hands with the crowd milling round the apron, and even allowed an MC (Master of Ceremonies) to read out the personnel. One critic noted, however: 'Significantly, his present audience has a higher percentage of blacks than the white-dominated clubs he used to work...for the first time in more than a decade, his music seems static...Davis seems locked in a cul de sac: he has become predictable.'[14]

At this time, Miles seemed suddenly to miss his older friends – contemporaries who appeared to be alienated from him by his new music and new life-style. When Paul Buckmaster was staying with him, Miles had gone out to see only one musical event; he had taken Buckmaster to hear Ahmad Jamal, and had still enthused about the pianist. But, apart from this isolated example, Miles rarely saw any of the old associates to whom he had once been so close. It was after hearing that Thad Jones had walked out of one of his concerts that Miles felt pangs of rejection and a certain loneliness. He said:

> You know, Thad's always around, and he doesn't come to see me. All the young musicians do, but Thad and all the friends that I like never do. Dizzy asks me to teach him. I say, 'Yeah, come by. I'll show you everything we're doing. It'll be my pleasure. You tell me when.' And he don't come by. Herbie Hancock always comes by when he's in town. Chick does...No, Chick doesn't come to hear me...Chick wouldn't be interested in my band...Damn it, I'm gonna throw a party. Do you think they'll come? Max, Mingus, Gil, Dizzy, Thad?...That's what I'm gonna do, I'm gonna throw a party.'[15]

Around the middle of the year the double-album, *Big Fun*, was released, and most of the tracks were performances from the 1969/70 period. Only one, 'Ife', came from the later *On The Corner* sessions. Of *Big Fun*, Miles commented: 'I'll be tired of *this* music before today is over. *That's* four years old!'[16] But the end of the year saw the release of *Get Up With It* which was more representative of Miles's current work. on 24 May, the day before Miles's forty-eighth birthday, Duke Ellington had died of lung cancer. *Get Up With It* was dedicated to Ellington who had done so much for jazz and for twentieth century music in general. Miles said: 'I loved and respected Duke. He was one of my idols. He sent me a letter before he died, to say goodbye.'[17] Side one of this double-album is Miles Davis's tribute to Duke – his elegy for him. It is a long (thirty-

224

minute) piece called 'He Loved Him Madly', and begins out-of-time with sparse, lamenting electronic sounds and broken phrases from one of the guitars. It moves imperceptibly into C minor and a time-feel, finishing with a long grooving pulse which transforms all the grieving into something positive and even optimistic. Dave Liebman plays some lyrical flute, and Miles with wah-wah shows all the glory of his acoustic tone even though he is amplified and using repeated echo. It is a superb tribute, and one which Ellington would have deeply appreciated.

The rest of the album is very uneven in quality, and some pieces are simply dull. The first part of 'Maiysha' for example, with its claves, its smooth latin rhythm and comfortable chord sequence, gets very near to 'easy listening' night club music, rather in the way that some pieces on *Quiet Nights* had done twelve years previously. 'Red China Blues' is also a very ordinary bit of 12/8 soul music. The fantastic spate of creative activity which started in 1968 and cut a large wedge into the seventies, was now dwindling, and encroaching illness may have had something to do with this. A decade earlier, he had been hospitalized with calcium deposits in his hip joints, and in 1974 the ailment returned in a very much worse form. The hip joint seemed to be disintegrating, and apart from the pain this caused, Miles also complained that he could not exercise properly because his leg simply went out of its socket if he tried. By mid-1974 he was having to take about eight pain-killing pills a day. He had suffered from insomnia for years and, for example, in the late fifties when he was on tour and couldn't sleep, he often used to wake up drummer, Jimmy Cobb, and talk to him. Now the pain from his hip joint was making it even more difficult for him to sleep.

In February 1975, while touring Japan, his health worsened. He said: 'I kept throwing up in every city. I had to have pills for my leg, codeine and morphine. But you have to work, you have to make the date.'[18] Then back in the States in March, his ulcer flared up again, but he forced himself to appear at concerts that had already been booked. His road manager, Chris Murphy, said: 'Miles hates to cancel gigs. I've seen him play – like the gig he did in March with (i.e. supported by) Herbie Hancock in St Louis, Miles came off the stage and was sick to his stomach, violently sick. And I said, "Come on, go lie down in the dressing room." And he said, "Fuck that shit," and went back on stage and finished the set, played beautifully. The next morning he was admitted to hospital with an ulcer.'[19] While he was in hospital, he also had thirty polyps or nodules removed from his vocal chords. He was visited there by an old friend who always stayed faithful – Clark Terry, who was in St Louis at the time with George Wein's mini Newport package tour. Terry said in 1976: 'Ironically, the last time I saw him was in an East St Louis hospital...Gerry Mulligan and I were doing a radio show, with my small group, Gerry's group and Gary Burton's group. Mulligan and I were sitting around talking after the show and I had a phone call from Miles's doctor who says, "I'm Miles's doctor and I know he's a good friend of yours and he thinks a lot of you and I just thought you'd like to know that he's in hospital"...so we, my nephew and I, went right over there.'

When he got out of hospital, Miles carried on playing concerts with his band. His live performances had always been variable in quality, but from the spring to the summer of 1975, there were times when, musically, the band seemed to reach an absolute nadir. This occurred when the theatrical side of a performance – the physical, non-musical, events on stage – took precedence over the actual music. One such performance was witnessed by the British trombonist and arranger, Derek Wadsworth, in San Francisco. Miles and the band were appearing in a fairly shabby, smoky, cellar-club which held about three hundred people. The place was packed and the audience was mainly black.

On this occasion, Miles was wearing a superbly-cut chamois leather suit with cowboy tassels and thongs hanging from it, a Dior silk neckerchief, and a shirt with sequins. The usual huge sunglasses completely masked his eyes. He strode out on stage first, and the band followed him, scuffling subserviently to their places. Almost at once, a heavy rhythm began on one chord. The whole audience was waiting for Miles to play his trumpet, but in front of him was an organ, and after the rhythm had been building up for a good ten minutes, he leaned over to play this organ. However, he didn't deign to use his fingers or to make any coherent chord or phrase on it; he simply leaned his elbow on the keyboard and produced a violent, dissonant sound. Then he leaned back and glared at the audience. And so it went on for what seemed like a very long time; elbow on organ, then leaning back and glowering at the audience. Then he wandered over and stood in front of the conga player, staring at him, and with his back to the audience began to wiggle his bottom to the rhythm.

After a while he blew a couple of notes on his trumpet, then put it down again and went back to elbowing the organ keyboard. Almost an hour had gone by, and the key and the pulse had remained constant. The interest had been entirely visual, entirely theatrical. It was reminiscent of the Archie Shepp concert at the British Expo in 1967; in each case, the artist seemed to be attempting to rile the audience to get a reaction. By now, even the black people in the San Francisco audience were becoming disenchanted with their hero. One shouted out: 'Sketches of Spain!' Another one yelled: 'Give us a song!' And then, Miles started taking off his chamois leather jacket in a very deliberate manner, and the audience began shouting and jeering as if he were a strip-tease artist. In fact, he had made a

226

sort of ritual of taking off his jacket at concerts for some years now. At the 1971 Festival Hall concert in Britain, he had held the entire audience riveted as he slowly removed his black velvet jacket. But on that occasion, he had also played superb trumpet. At the 1975 concert, all his mannerisms and rituals and the non-musical aspects of his performance (which he knew had drawn audiences to his concerts for years, and had thus helped to finance his whole operation), had reached macabre proportions. It was as if he were saying by his actions: 'OK. If this is what brings you to my music, then this is what I'm going to give you!' Whatever the reasons, the ritual of removing his coat, as his bottom-wiggling had done, took on grotesque comic dimensions because, when the jacket was half off, the thongs and tassels became tangled in the sequins of his shirt, and Miles was stuck with it. He could not get it back on; nor could he take it off. His four white, long-haired road managers scuttled on stage and, two at either side of Davis, began disentangling the sequins and thongs. It was a ludicrous sight; a kind of black comedy. And after almost two hours, Miles had still not played any trumpet. At that point, Derek Wadsworth and the British contingent left the club in disgust.

The only recordings of the Miles Davis band during his final period, were two live double-albums made during their Japanese tour earlier in the year. On 1 February, their afternoon and evening concerts were recorded and later released on Japanese CBS under the respective titles of *Agharta* and *Pangea*. Both albums offer long stretches of powerful rhythm, plenty of trumpet playing, and some excellent saxophone from Sonny Fortune. But they are diffuse, and would have been improved by rigorous editing. Also, *Agharta* in particular, suffers from a monotony of sound caused mainly by the perpetual 'freaking-out' of the lead guitarists, Pete Cosey and Reggie Lucas. Even so, the album is almost redeemed by the indomitable jazz virtuosity of Sonny Fortune whose playing is full of vitality. But the most telling factor in both albums is the emotional climate of Miles's own trumpet playing. Although he is in good lip, and often creates strong rhythms, his sound is intensely mournful – almost weary. It is characterized by sadness which seems all-pervasive, and even the bursts of energy seem to have a certain desperation. There is nothing of his old buoyancy, that 'joy with a melancholy edge' which typified his best work. And his lamenting sound is at strange odds with the band's heavy and driving rhythms.

Miles Davis played the Newport Festival in July, and a concert in Central Park, New York City, in August, and then disbanded because he needed to sort out his health problems. With typically ghoulish humour, he organized what he called a 'doctor party'. By this time, he had a hernia as well as his other ailments, as did his old friend Gil Evans, and Gil's wife, Anita. So Miles laid on some

French salads at his house and invited all his friends who had physical ailments. The guest of honour was Muhammad Ali's doctor, and after partaking of the refreshments, he examined each of the guests. This was, perhaps, Miles's way of helping his less affluent friends. Gil Evans said, recalling this event: 'Don't believe all the things you read about Miles: he's one of the nicest, gentlest men.'

In September, however, Miles's operation was delayed because he again contracted pneumonia and had to be rushed to hospital by ambulance. His general health in 1975 was so bad that it gave cause for concern to everyone. There was a general feeling of mortality in the jazz world after the many premature deaths in recent years. In 1975 Miles's old friend, Cannonball Adderley, died at the age of only forty-six. Thirteen years previously, Cannonball had been told that he had only ten years more to live because he had sugar diabetes and was over-weight. So when Miles left hospital after being cured of pneumonia and went home to recuperate and gather his strength for the major hip surgery, he was at last visited by some of the old friends who had been shunning him. In the late summer, Percy Heath with his brothers Jimmy and Tootie, bulldozed their way in to visit Miles. When they were asked at the door what they wanted, they said, 'We've come to see him because we know he's sick and lonely, and we know he wants to see us.' And in they went.

In December 1975, Miles was at last strong enough to undergo surgery, and a prosthetic ball-and-socket was implanted in the hip. He spent the whole of 1976 recuperating, and during this time renewed his association with Gil Evans. The two men, after a gap of eight years or so, began to consider another collaboration, and it was rumoured that they might record excerpts from the opera 'Tosca'. Miles said: 'I would just play a couple of arias on my trumpet. Some very emotional arias in "Tosca". I wouldn't know if I could equalize it or not, I wouldn't want to drag it, you know – cut it short or play under it. I like the nothing parts, the parts that ramble...I can think of a *lot* of things to do, man, that'd be great. I can do a nine-piece brass section that plays like we play now, and it'd be a motherfucker. I'd write ten or twelve arrangements. You see, the thing about an arrangement is not to stretch it out so that it gets to be a bore.'[20] But these plans came to nothing.

In June 1976, Miles's record contract with Columbia came up for renewal, but the company did not want to pay Davis the advance he was asking as part of the re-signing deal. Miles's lawyer began negotiations with United Artists, and just as Miles was about to sign with them, Columbia matched United Artists' offer. So early in December 1976, Miles Davis renewed his contract with CBS. At this point, his account was 'in the black' with Columbia, his record sales having paid off the large advances he'd had. The following year it was rumoured that he was thinking of forming a group with

Gil Evans on keyboards, but again nothing transpired. In fact, since his concert in Central Park in the summer of 1975, up to the time of writing (September 1980) Miles Davis has not appeared in public. During the intervening years he has been plagued by ill-health: bursitis (a kind of arthritis) in the shoulders and hands, and pain in his leg and feet. In the early summer of 1980 he was again in hospital with an infected leg which the doctors managed to save from amputation.

Nor have there been any more recordings since 1975. Since he re-signed with Columbia, the company seem to have regarded him as a permanent affiliate and have created a 'Miles Davis Fund' which pays him on a regular basis. Only one other Columbia artist has this status – the concert pianist, Vladimir Horowitz. However, in 1979, Miles was still only fifty-three (Horowitz was in his seventies), and Columbia felt, not unreasonably, that they could expect some fresh recordings. After some discussion, Davis phoned Paul Buckmaster in London and asked him to go over to New York to work on a new album. Buckmaster arrived in May 1979, to find that George Butler, the CBS A and R man, had got a group of young musicians together and rehearsals were in progress – without Miles. Eventually, the trumpeter turned up to listen to the band, didn't like it, and phoned Pete Cosey in Chicago asking him to come to New York and form a band. Gil Evans, as well as Paul Buckmaster was involved with the project, but when, after several weeks, Evans had received no money for his involvement, he left in disgust. Although Miles attended a rehearsal he played no trumpet at all, and in July, after almost three months of effort, CBS cut their losses and abandoned the project.

However, the following year (1980), Dave Liebman visited Miles in hospital and found the trumpeter in good spirits, enthusiastic about a new recording project and keen to get on the road and do some concerts. He was planning five or six concerts in major cities in America, Europe and the Far East. The projected band was made up of musicians from Chicago who were friends of a cousin of Miles's, and they were a self-contained unit writing their own original compositions. According to Dave Liebman, the music was black-disco-funk, and 'much more commercial than anything I heard him do even after I left.' So far, the band had recorded seven or eight pieces and Miles had played only a little trumpet on one of them. For all his enthusiasm, Davis seemed a little concerned about how the public would react to the music. Liebman commented: 'It's definitely air-play material...There's a definite effort by him and Teo and Columbia to get the stuff happening, because the record business in the States is not so good, and they want something heavy from him for commercial use...But after Miles puts his touches to it I'm sure it'll come out being really special.'

229

18
Postscript

'I just bring out in people what's in them.'[1]
Miles Davis in 1974

Duke Ellington once compared Miles Davis with Picasso, in the multiplicity of his genius. Some idea of his huge output on record was given in July 1979, when the New York FM jazz station (WKCR), which transmits twenty-four hours a day every day, played the whole of Miles's recorded work in chronological order. The programme began on the afternoon of Sunday, 1 July and ended on the morning of Friday, 6 July. This amounted to over one hundred hours of music. (Stravinsky's works, if played consecutively, would last for about twenty-four hours).

A pattern emerges over the years in the way Miles's creative vitality curves upwards and downwards, matched by similar fluctuations in his general health. In two decades the pattern was almost identical. In the early fifties he was seriously ill with drug addiction. After kicking the habit and making himself fit again, there was a tremendous spate of creativity over the years 1954-61. From 1954 to, say, 1957, he was playing magnificently and perfecting a whole new approach to the trumpet with a fresh vocabulary of phrases; then from 1957 onwards there were major conceptual innovations – the introduction of modal improvisation and the great orchestral works with Gil Evans. In the sixties, Miles again became seriously ill and was out of action for most of 1965, after which he slowly began another equally creative phase. Again, from 1963 to 1967 there was some fine playing which brought to peaks of perfection another fresh and more abstract approach to improvisation: 'time – no changes'. Then from 1968 to the early seventies there were more innovations: he changed his instrumentation, his group sound, the continuum and the relationship of soloist with ensemble. In 1975, he once again became seriously ill and was forced into semi-retirement. He reached his fiftieth birthday in 1976, old for a jazz musician (average life-span is about forty-two), but young for a practitioner in most of the other arts. However, the renewed creative

230

activity which had characterized the two previous decades, did not happen in the seventies. He had already opened up so much new ground that it was becoming progressively more difficult each decade to find fresh sounds and modes of procedure.

Furthermore, his physical condition seemed much more serious than in the previous decades. By the late seventies, although his new hip was functioning adequately, he was still suffering from bursitis in the shoulders and wrists. It was a recurrence of the same problem he'd had in 1965, and may perhaps have been caused by over-exercise – all those three-hour work-outs when he was well into his forties. Sufferers from bursitis are forbidden to exercise, and in 1978 Miles was putting on weight – something which he abhorred. He'd always tended to poke fun at overweight people. Gil Evans suggested that it was the bursitis and the hip complaint which explained Miles's behaviour on stage just before his total incapacitation. With painful wrists and shoulders it was agonizing to hold the trumpet up to his lips, and it was because of this that he began playing organ. Later, the complaint inhibited him from practising when he was recuperating after surgery.

Part of Miles Davis's uniqueness in the jazz world stems from the fact that he matured slowly into a self-conscious artist with an acute awareness of the progress and development of his music. By the middle 1950s he was already showing a reluctance to re cover ground he had opened up and explored. Jazz musicians in general have little knowledge of the past of their own art; when they come into the music they take up the current language (a few of the more gifted ones may invent a new vocabulary) and more or less stick with it for the rest of their active life. Miles acquired a knowledge of the music's history and a sense of his own past, and over the years his personal language as a soloist developed and changed, as did the sound and approach of his various groups. The continuity in his work and the steady evolution of his music from its faltering beginnings in the 1940s to the supreme artistry of his middle and later periods have been matched by few other jazz musicians.

Also unique is his sustained (though sometimes strained) relationship with Columbia. Most jazz musicians change their record companies with bewildering frequency, but Columbia and Miles have been together since 1956 – though not without occasional struggles in which Davis has redefined his relationship with the company and insisted on adjustments and changes. Undoubtedly, the presence of Teo Macero, the brilliant musician whom CBS assigned as Miles's producer, has been a major factor in the continuing dynamism of the relationship. Macero always understood the duality: music as music, and music as product. Occasionally, the two factors were at loggerheads. When Miles felt barren of ideas and had nothing to say, he didn't wish to record. But with music as product, the albums had to keep coming out as part of the record company's sales plan. Thus in the 1962-3 period, *Quiet Nights* came out against his wishes and his relationship with Macero was strained. Similarly, in the late 1970s, after some years of inactivity, Columbia were anxious to release more 'product', and Davis was subjected to more pressure.

The sense of the organic development of his music inhibited Miles from recording anything which did not meet his own high standards of artistic necessity. He could still have done what most jazz musicians do: make a whole career out of one phase. Unlike other jazz musicians (except perhaps for the late John Coltrane), Miles had about five phases from which to choose: the middle fifties quintet music with its popular songs, blues and sprinkling of original compositions; the late fifties sextet modal music; the more abstract music of the middle sixties; the electronic, rock-influenced music of the late sixties and early seventies; the various bigger ensembles with Gil Evans. Miles could have made a career out of any one of these. The fact that he has always chosen not to do so is a mark of his greatness. His dilemma at the end of the 1970s was that he would not go back and retrace his steps, but he had not yet found a fresh direction, and so he did nothing. Paul Buckmaster remarked after the abortive attempt at recording in 1979, 'He's done more than enough, anyway!'

This scrupulous refusal to record for the sake of it (or the record company) explains, perhaps, why so many albums in his illustrious career have become classics – touchstones of quality for other musicians and for the jazz public. They were made when, and only when, he had something to say: and the results expanded the jazz language and its emotional scope, opening up avenues of exploration for legions of musicians. There were various recordings with Charlie Parker in the 1940s, which showed a whole new concept of trumpet playing. At the end of that decade, came the first orchestral chamber-jazz music, *Birth of the Cool*, which also defined new territory and spawned a host of followers. Then there was the miraculous year 1954, with its spate of superb and influential music: the sextet recording of 'Walkin'' and 'Blue 'n' Boogie', the quintet with Sonny Rollins, the Christmas Eve session with Thelonious Monk and Milt Jackson. The middle fifties quintet with John Coltrane created a whole way of playing which stimulated musicians all over the world with the five classic LPS: *Workin', Steamin', Cookin', Relaxin', Round Midnight*. Then came the great orchestral recordings with Gil Evans: *Miles Ahead, Porgy and Bess, Sketches of Spain*. At the same time there were two masterpieces by the sextet with Coltrane and Adderley: *Milestones* and *Kind of Blue*. In the early sixties, several recordings of live performances were released, the key ones being *Miles Davis in Europe* and *My Funny Valentine*.

232

Then came the move towards greater harmonic abstraction with *ESP* and *Miles Smiles*, both studio albums with his new group, followed by the period of experimentation with instrumentation, electronics and structure. This produced *Filles de Kilimanjaro, In a Silent Way, Bitches Brew* and *Jack Johnson*.

It was Gil Evans who said, 'Every form, even though it becomes traditional and finally becomes academic, originally came from someone's spirit who created the form. Then it was picked up and taught in schools after that. But all forms originated from spirit.'[2] Miles Davis's best work always comes directly from his spirit; it forces us to hear with fresh ears because it challenges all our received ideas. There is a heroic quality about the way he has always maintained the highest standards in an unsympathetic artistic and social climate. He has had no help from the state-subsidized American musical establishment. He has, throughout his career, worked in a totally *laissez-faire* situation without handouts or academic sinecures of any kind. The fact that he has not only survived, but also made consistently great music and even prospered, is a triumph made possible by the strength of his vision, willpower and intelligence, and also by the talents of his associates, all of whom have been magnified by their relationship with Miles Davis.

African music, broadly speaking, is based on repetition, whereas Indo-Arabic music is based on variation. Because much of the dynamism of Miles Davis's music has always come from the interaction of these two approaches, it is more accurate to refer to these elements in his work as non-western rather than specifically African. However, the phase which began with *On The Corner* and ended with *Agharta* and *Pangea*, was notable for the greater Africanization of his whole approach. African dances can have a total structure which divides into as many as five or six master patterns, and these are initiated by the master drummer who also determines their duration. In other words, drum patterns are repeated until the master drummer signals the change to another set of inter-related patterns. It is precisely this 'master drummer' role that Miles played during the final period (1972-75) before his incapacitation. He determined the duration of interlocking rhythms, signalled for changes to new rhythmic patterns, and sometimes halted the entire ensemble while one instrument played an unaccompanied interlude. But this greater Africanization of his music made it much less acceptable to western ears – hence the weeping jazz critic and the general dismay of fellow musicians and audiences.

Throughout his career, his music has been at its finest when there was a delicate balance between western and non-western elements: between on the one hand, ideas of structure, harmony, texture, and of a sequence of events taking place in time which passes; and on the other, of improvisation with subjective tonal inflexions and repeated motor rhythms so perfectly executed that they invoke the state of possession which takes the listener beyond time. And his music has been less effective when there was an imbalance on either side. Thus in the great albums of the later 1950s there was a perfect balance between repetition and variation, between soloist and ensemble, between pre-composition and improvisation. This was followed by a period of faltering vision with schizophrenic albums such as *Some Day My Prince Will Come* and *Seven Steps to Heaven*. Then came another period of balance with some of the live albums, and the studio recordings *ESP* and *Miles Smiles*. In 1967, *The Sorcerer* and *Nefertiti* suffered from a tendency towards western abstraction, after which a marvellous fusion is attained in *Filles de Kilimanjaro, In a Silent Way, Bitches Brew* and *Jack Johnson*. With the two live double-albums of 1970 at the Fillmores East and West came another bout of schizophrenia resulting in music which created tension but rarely satisfactorily released it with flowing rhythms. After these, there was an over-emphasis on heavy rhythmic *ostinati* and the two live albums of 1975, *Agharta* and *Pangea,* seemed to have all the mannerisms of 'possession' without much of the substance.

Miles Davis's importance and his influence are so great that an account of his career from 1945 to 1975 amounts to a history of the main events which have taken place in jazz during that period. His music has been known and loved by a public many of whom knew little of other kinds of jazz, yet at the same time he has been admired, even idolized, by key musicians of three decades. The three major post-war saxophonists, Charlie Parker, Sonny Rollins and John Coltrane, all had close relationships with Miles Davis, and some of their best recorded work was done with him. And like a magnet, he drew to his music some of the key musicians from other generations: Tony Williams, Jack DeJohnette, Herbie Hancock, Chick Corea, Joe Zawinul, Keith Jarrett, John McLaughlin, Wayne Shorter, Dave Liebman, Dave Holland, Ron Carter and others. Miles has been a catalyst and a liberating force for other musicians who, under his influence, have achieved greater self-realization and fulfilment. It is arguable that Gil Evans's greatest work has been done in collaboration with Miles Davis. He has been one of the great leaders in jazz, welding disparate personalities into homogeneous groups and bringing out the creativity and the individual identity of each member. He is a master at making music breathe – creating and releasing tension; and he is a master of economy of means and expression. And each of these masteries is not only in playing as a soloist, but also in creating group music. His interpretation of existing material and his own original compositions have vastly enriched the jazz repertoire; very many of the themes he has recorded have been played afterwards by other musicians all over the world. He has shown that instrumental virtuosity alone is not

234

sufficient: it is possible to play a lot of instrument and very little music. Conversely, he has proved time and again that when allied to real imagination and emotional depth, economy of means can produce music of the highest quality.

The greatest and most influential jazz musicians have not only played supremely well; they have also found new structures and opened up fresh ways of tackling improvisation. But usually, they have done this only once: Louis Armstrong in the late 1920s; Basie, Lester Young and others in the 1930s; Charlie Parker and Dizzy Gillespie in the 1940s. Only Duke Ellington, Charles Mingus, John Coltrane and Miles Davis have introduced new concepts and methods throughout their working lives. Aside from Ellington, Miles has made the longest, most sustained and most influential contribution. Throughout his thirty-year career (1945-75), at roughly five-year intervals, the sound, approach and emphasis of his music have subtly evolved, and this sustained adventure in musical ideas is minutely documented in his magnificent body of recorded work. Whether or not he rises phoenix-like from the ashes of his spent phases, he has done more than enough and we have inherited a legacy of music which will delight and inspire future generations of players and listeners.

References

1 – *Miles Dewey Davis III*   pages 1–11

1   Leonard Feather, *From Satchmo to Miles*, Stein and Day, New York, 1972, p.230
2   Marc Crawford, 'Miles Davis: Evil Genius of Jazz', *Ebony*, January 1961
3   *Ibid.*
4   Nat Hentoff, 'Miles Davis – Last Trump', *Esquire*, March 1959
5   *Melody Maker*, 9 January 1971
6   Interview, *Playboy*, September 1962
7   Down Beat, 6 March 1958
8   *Ibid.*
9   Hentoff, *Esquire*, March 1959
10 Stephen Davis, 'Miles Davis: An Exclusive Interview', *The Real Paper*, 21 March 1973
11 *Down Beat*, 6 March 1958
12 Marc Crawford, *Ebony*, January 1961
13 *Playboy*, September 1962
14 *From Satchmo to Miles*, p.231
15 Sy Johnson, 'Sparring with Miles Davis', *Changes*, 1974, p.32
16 *The Real Paper*, 21 March 1973
17 *Down Beat*, 2 July 1964
18 *Down Beat*, 6 March 1958
19 *The Real Paper*, 21 March 1973
20 *From Satchmo to Miles*, p.231
21 *Encore*, 21/28 July 1975
22 Don Demichael, *Rolling Stone*, 13 December 1969
23 *Down Beat*, 2 July 1964
24 *Down Beat*, 6 March 1958
25 *Ibid.*
26 *Melody Maker*, 4 September 1954
27 *International Musician*, November 1972

2 – *Bird Land*   *pages 12–30*

1 *Down Beat*, 6 March 1958
2 *Ibid.*
3 *Changes*, 1974, p.32
4 *The Real Paper*, 21 March 1973
5 *Esquire*, March 1959
6 *Down Beat*, 6 April 1967
7 *Ibid.*
8 *Esquire*, March 1959
9 Ira Gitler, *Jazz Masters of the 40s*, Macmillan, 1966, p.208
10 *Down Beat*, 22 April 1946
11 Ross Russell, *Bird Lives!* Quartet Books Limited, 1973, pp.208–9
12 *Down Beat*, 6 April 1967
13 *Esquire*, March 1959
14 *Down Beat*, 13 June 1968
15 *The Real Paper*, 21 March 1973
16 *Esquire*, March 1959
17 *Ibid.*
18 *Ibid.*
19 Wilfrid Mellers, *Music in a New Found Land*, Barrie and Rockliff, London, 1964, p.341
20 *Down Beat*, 16 February 1961
21 *Bird Lives!*, p.267
22 *Jazz Masters of the 40s*, p.34
23 Gilbert Millsteen, 'Jazz Makes it Up the River', *New York Times Magazine*, 1958

3 – *The Birth of the Cool*   *pages 31–40*

1 *Playboy*, September 1962
2 *Down Beat*, 2 July 1964
3 *Music in a New Found Land*, p.355
4 Sleeve note
5 Sleeve note
6 Nat Hentoff, *The World of Jazz*, The Ridge Press Inc., 1976, pp.103–5
7 *Down Beat*, 2 July 1964
8 *Ibid.*
9 Sleeve note
10 Mike Zwerin, 'Miles Davis: A Most Curious Friendship', *Down Beat*, 10 March 1966
11 Sleeve note
12 *Down Beat*, 2 July 1964
13 *Down Beat*, 23 March 1951
14 *Down Beat*, 6 April 1967

4 – *Cold Turkey*   *pages 41–52*

1   Nat Hentoff, *The Jazz Life*, Panther Books, 1964, p.77
2   *Down Beat*, 6 March 1958
3   *Down Beat*, 18 July 1974
4   *Down Beat*, 23 March 1951
5   *Melody Maker*, 30 September 1950
6   Babs Gonzales, *Movin' on Down De Line*, Expubidence Publishing Corp., 1975, pp.63–4
7   *Jazz Masters of the 50s*, p.70
8   *The Jazz Life*, p.77
9   *Ibid.*
10 *From Satchmo to Miles*, p.236
11 *The Jazz Life*, p.77
12 *Melody Maker*, 23 February 1952
13 *Jazz Masters of the 40s*, p.50
14 Sleeve note
15 *Ebony*, January 1961
16 *Down Beat*, 18 July 1974
17 *Ebony*, January 1961
18 *Ibid.*

5 – *The First Great Quintet*   *pages 53–67*

1   *Playboy*, September 1962
2   *Esquire*, March 1959
3   *Ibid.*
4   *Down Beat*, 30 November 1955
5   Nat Hentoff, 'An Afternoon with Miles Davis', *Jazz Review*, December 1958
6   *Ibid.*
7   *Ebony*, January 1961
8   *Esquire*, March 1959
9   *Jazz Masters of the 50s*, p.73
10 *Down Beat*, 21 September 1955
11 *Ibid.*
12 *Esquire*, March 1959
13 *Down Beat*, 2 July 1964
14 Sleeve note
15 *The World of Jazz*, p.136
16 *The Jazz Life*, p.181

6 – *Miles Ahead*   *pages 68–81*

1   *Playboy*, September 1962
2   *The Jazz Life*, p.77
3   *Down Beat*, 29 September 1960
4   *Jazz Masters of the 50s*, p.76
5   *The Jazz Life*, pp.179–80

6 *The Jazz Review*, December 1958
7 *Ibid.*
8 Sleeve note
9 Alun Morgan, 'Miles Davis: Miles Ahead', *These Jazzmen of Our Time*, edited by Raymond Horricks, The Jazz Book Club, 1960, p.49
10 *Chasin' the Trane*, p.65
11 *Ibid*, p.69
12 *Melody Maker*, 16 March 1957
13 André Malraux, *L'Espoir*, Grove Press, p.396
14 *Down Beat*, 2 July 1964
15 *Down Beat*, 16 February 1961
16 Quoted by Charles Fox, *These Jazzmen of Our Time*, p.96
17 *Jazz Monthly*, February 1960
18 *New York Times*, 12 January 1958
19 *Ibid.*
20 *Jazz Monthly*, February 1960

7 – The First Great Sextet   pages 82–94

1 *Ebony*, January 1961
2 *Esquire*, March 1959
3 *Time*, 20 January 1958
4 *Life International*, 11 August 1958
5 *Down Beat*, 2 July 1964
6 Cannonball Adderley, 'Paying Dues: The Education of a Combo Leader', *Jazz Panorama*, edited by Martin Williams, Cromwell-Collier Press, 1962, pp.260–61
7 Mike Zwerin, 'Miles Davis – A Most Curious Friendship', *Down Beat*, 10 March 1966
8 *Jazz Hot*, June 1960
9 '30 Ans De Cinema', *Jazz Magazine*, May 1961
10 *The Jazz Review*, January 1958
11 *Down Beat*, 29 September 1960
12 *Jazz Panorama*, p.261-2
13 *Esquire*, March 1959
14 *The Jazz Life*, p.181
15 *Ibid.* p.43
16 Sleeve note
17 *Playboy*, September 1962
18 *Ebony*, January 1961
19 *Music in a New Found Land*, p.367

8 – *Porgy and Bess*   *pages 95–103*

1   *Fontana*, June 1959
2   *Jazz Review*, December 1958
3   *Jazz Panorama*, p.262
4   *Jazz Review*, December 1958
5   *Music in a New Found Land*, p.367
6   Sleeve note
7   Kenneth Tynan, 'Miles Apart', *Holiday*, February 1963
8   *Down Beat*, 10 March 1966
9   *Holiday*, February 1963
10 *Fontana*, June 1959
11 *Ibid.*
12 Richard Williams, 'Sketches of Gil', *Melody Maker*, 4 March 1978

9 – *Is It Jazz?* *pages 104–116*

1   *Ebony*, January 1961
2   *Jazz Review*, December 1958
3   *Ibid.*
4   *Ibid.*
5   *Ibid.*
6   *Ibid.*
7   Sleeve note
8   *San Francisco Sunday Chronicle*, 7 June 1959
9   *Ibid.*
10 Sleeve note
11 Brian Priestley, 'Cleanhead's Comeback', *Melody Maker*, 3 June 1972
12 *Down Beat*, 6 March 1968
13 Jack O'Brien says: 'Bob Herridge Does it Again!' *New York Journal – American*, 22 July 1960
14 *Melody Maker*, 12 September 1959
15 *Melody Maker*, 5 September 1959
16 *Down Beat*, 18 February 1960
17 *Melody Maker*, 24 October 1959
18 Nat Hentoff, *Hi Fi Review*, February 1960
19 Sleeve note
20 *Ibid.*
21 *Down Beat*, 27 October 1960
22 *Ibid.*
23 Leonard Feather, 'Jazz Beat', *New York Post*, 26 April 1964
24 *Down Beat*, 27 October 1960
25 *Jazz News*, 15 October 1960
26 *New York Times*, 11 September 1960
27 Barbara J. Gardner, 'The Enigma of Miles Davis', *Down Beat*, 7 January 1960

10 – *After Coltrane   pages 117–128*

1   *Ebony,* January 1961
2   *Playboy,* September 1962
3   'Jazzmen Not Vaudevillians', *New York Journal–American,* 26 March 1960
4   'Pourquoi Si Méchant Miles?', *Jazz Magazine,* October 1960
5   *The Jazz Life,* p.196
6   *Chasin' The Trane,* p.85
7   *San Francisco Sunday Chronicle,* 6 March 1960
8   Quoted by Art Farmer, *Melody Maker,* 25 March 1960
9   *Chasin' The Trane,* p.84
10 Paul Ackerman, 'Davis Sets Vanguard Fans Jumping', *Billboard,* 8 August 1960
11 Leonard Feather, 'The Real Miles Davis', *Melody Maker,* 17 September 1960
12 *Jazz Monthly,* December 1960
13 *New York Post,* 16 October 1960
14 *Playboy,* September 1962
15 *Down Beat,* 16 February 1961
16 Sleeve note
17 *Playboy,* September 1962
18 Sleeve note   ·
19 *Ebony,* January 1961
20 *New York Times,* 29 May 1961
21 Bill Coss, *Down Beat,* 6 July 1961
22 George T. Simon, *New York Herald Tribune,* 20 May 1961
23 *New York Post,* 21 May 1961
24 *Ibid.*
25 *Ibid.*

11 – *In and Out of the Doldrums   pages 129–147*

1   *Playboy,* September 1962
2   *Melody Maker,* 18 March 1961
3   *Down Beat,* 17 August 1961
4   *Ibid,* 20 July 1961
5   *Ibid,* 25 April, 1963
6   *Ibid,* 21 October 1965
7   Sleeve note
8   Leonard Feather, 'The Modulated World of Gil Evans', *Down Beat,* 23 February 1967
9   *Playboy,* September 1962
10 *Down Beat,* 10 September 1964
11 *Down Beat,* 14 July 1977
12 *Ibid.*
13 *Ibid.*
14 *Melody Maker,* 1 February 1964
15 *Down Beat,* 18 June 1964
16 *Ibid.*

242

12 – *Miles in the Sky*   *pages 148–164*

1   Hollie I. West, 'Black Tune', *The Washington Post*, 13 March 1969
2   Clive Davis, *Clive: Inside the Record Business*, William Morrow, 1974, p.260
3   *The Louisville Times*, 9 December 1967
4   *Down Beat*, 13 June 1968
5   *Ibid.*
6   *Ibid*, 23 February 1967
7   *Ibid*, 13 June 1968
8   *Ibid*, 21 October 1965
9   *Ibid*, 13 June 1968
10 *Melody Maker*, 20 April 1968
11 Sleeve note
12 *From Satchmo to Miles*, p.242
13 *Clive: Inside the Record Business*, p.260
14 *Melody Maker*, 20 January 1973
15 *Jet*, August 1966
16 *Clive: Inside the Record Business*, p.260
17 *Washington Post*, 13 March 1969

13 – *Play What's Not There!*   *pages 165–178*

1   *Rolling Stone*, 13 December 1969
2   *Playboy*, September 1962
3   *Down Beat*, 18 June 1974
4   *Ibid*, 14 November 1968
5   *Melody Maker*, 4 March 1978
6   *The Washington Post*, 13 March 1969
7   *New Musical Express*, 1 February 1975
8   *Ibid*, 8 February 1975
9   *Ibid*, 1 February 1975
10 *Washington Post*, 13 March 1969
11 *Time Out, The Times Union*, 28 February 1969

14 – *Miles Runs the Voodoo Down*   *pages 179–188*

1   *Newsweek*, 23 March 1970
2   *The Washington Post*, 13 March 1969
3   *Ibid.*
4   *Time Out, The Times Union*, 28 February 1969
5   *Jazz Review*, December 1958
6   *Down Beat*, 3 September 1970
7   *Newsweek*, 23 March 1970
8   *The Village Voice*, 31 July 1969
9   *Ibid.*
10 *Time Out, The Times Union*, op. cit.
11 *Ibid.*
12 *Melody Maker*, 17 January 1970
13 Larry Kart, *Down Beat*, 7 August 1969

15 – *Jazz Into Rock* Will *Go*   *pages 189–204*

1   *Rolling Stone*, 13 December 1969
2   *Los Angeles Times Calendar*
3   *From Satchmo to Miles*, pp.246–7
4   *ZygoteIIZygote*, 12 August 1970
5   *Afrostar*, 6 November 1969
6   *New York Post*, 6 January 1970
7   *Newsweek*, 23 March 1970
8   *Down Beat*, 23 July 1970
9   *From Satchmo to Miles*, p.240
10 *Newsweek*, op. cit.
11 Al Aronowitz, *'Go' Magazine*, June 1970
12 *Ibid.*
13 *San Francisco Chronicle*, 13 April 1970
14 *ZygoteIIZygote*, op. cit.
15 *New York Times*, 18 July 1970
16 *Ibid.*
17 *Ibid.*
18 *The Sunday Denver Post*, 14 June 1970
19 *ZygoteIIZygote*, op. cit.
20 *Down Beat*, 4 March 1971
21 *New York Times*, 18 July 1970

16 – *Live–Evil*   *pages 205–216*

1   *New York Post*, 3 July 1972
2   *Melody Maker*, 9 January 1971
3   *The Real Paper*, 21 March 1973
4   Interview with Brian Priestley, *Down Beat*, 14 March 1974
5   *Essence*, March 1971
6   *Melody Maker*, 9 January 1971
7   *Ibid*, 31 July 1971
8   *New York Post*, 23 July 1971
9   *Melody Maker*, 31 July 1971
10 *Stereo – Das Deutsche Hi-Fi und Musik Magazin*, Number 17/75
11 *Down Beat*, 18 July 1974
12 *The Herald,* 7 April 1972
13 *New York Post*, 3 July 1972
14 *Encore*, 21/28 July 1975
15 *Ibid.*
16 *Down Beat*, 1972
17 *Melody Maker*, 20 January 1973
18 *The Real Paper*, op. cit.

17 – *Manhattan Jungle Symphony*   *pages 217–229*

1   *Melody Maker*, 20 January 1973
2   *Sounds*, 19 March 1973
3   *Down Beat*, op. cit.

4   Eugene Chadbourne, *The Herald*
5   Quoted in Hentoff's *The World of Jazz*, pp.135–6
6   *The Real Paper*, 21 March 1973
7   *Ibid.*
8   *From Satchmo to Miles*, p.255
9   *The Real Paper*, op. cit.
10 *Stereo-Das Deutsche Hi-Fi und Musik Magasin,* Number 17/75
11 *The Real Paper*, op. cit.
12 *From Satchmo to Miles*, p.246
13 *Encore*, op. cit.
14 Gary Giddins, *New York Magazine*, 13 September 1974
15 *Changes,* 1974
16 *Ibid.*
17 *Melody Maker*, 7 September 1974
18 *Rolling Stone*, 11 March 1976
19 *Ibid.*
20 *Ibid.*

18 – *Postscript   pages 230–235*

1   *Down Beat*, 18 July 1974
2   *International Musician*, November 1972

Bibliography

Books

Bogle, Donald *Toms, Coons, Mulattoes, Mammies & Bucks: An Interpretive History of Blacks in American Films*, The Viking Press, New York, 1973
Cleaver, Eldridge *Soul on Ice*, Jonathan Cape, London, 1969
Cole, Bill *Miles Davis: A Musical Biography*, William Morrow, New York, 1974
Davis, Clive *Clive: Inside the Record Business*, William Morrow, New York, 1975
Feather, Leonard *Inside Be-bop*, J.J. Robbins & Sons, New York, 1949
Feather, Leonard *The Book of Jazz*, Arthur Barker, London, 1961
Feather, Leonard *The Encyclopedia of Jazz in the Sixties*, Horizon Press, New York, 1966, Quartet Books, London, 1978
Feather, Leonard *From Satchmo to Miles*, Stein and Day, New York, 1972, Quartet Books, London, 1975
Gitler, Ira *Jazz Masters of the 40s*, Macmillan, New York, 1966
Gleason, Ralph J. *Jam Session*, Peter Davies, London, 1961
Goldberg, Joe *Jazz Masters of the 50s*, Macmillan, New York, 1965
Gonzales, Babs *Movin' On Down De Line*, Expubidence Publishing Corp., New York, 1975
Harrison, Max *A Jazz Retrospect*, David and Charles, Newton Abbot, 1976
Hentoff, Nat *The Jazz Life*, Peter Davies, London, 1962
Hentoff, Nat *The World of Jazz*, Ridge Press, New York, 1976
Hodeir, Andre *Jazz: Its Evolution and Essence*, Grove Press, New York, 1956
Horricks, Raymond *These Jazzmen of our Time*, Victor Gollancz, London, 1960
James, Michael *Miles Davis*, Cassell, London, 1961
Jazz Improvisation: Miles Davis, Vol I and II, Nichion Publications Inc., Japan
Jones, LeRoi *Blues People*, William Morrow, New York, 1963
Mellers, Wilfred *Music in a New Found Land*, Barrie and Rockliff, London, 1964

Middleton, Richard *Pop Music and the Blues*, Victor Gollancz, 1972
Reisner, Robert *Bird: The Legend of Charlie Parker*, Quartet Books, London, 1974
Russell, Ross *Bird Lives!*, Quartet Books, London, 1973
Schuller, Gunther *Early Jazz: Its Roots and Musical Development*, Oxford University Press, New York, 1968
Stearns, Marshall *The Story of Jazz*, Oxford University Press, New York, 1956
Thomas, J.C. *Chasin' the Trane*, Elm Tree Books, London, 1976
Williams, Martin (ed.) *Jazz Panorama*, Crowell-Collier Press, 1962
Wilmer, Valerie *Jazz People*, Allison and Busby, London, 1970

Articles

Ackerman, Paul 'Davis Gets Vanguard Fans Jumping', *Billboard*, 8 August 1960
Crawford, Marc 'Miles Davis: Evil Genius of Jazz', *Ebony*, January 1961
Davis, Miles 'Self-Portrait', *Down Beat*, 6 March 1958
Davis, Stephen 'Miles Davis: An Exclusive Interview', *The Real Paper*, 21 March 1973
Demichael, Don 'Miles Davis', *Rolling Stone*, 13 December 1969
Feather, Leonard 'The Real Miles Davis', *Melody Maker*, 17 September 1960
Feather, Leonard 'Jazz Beat', *New York Post*, 26 April 1964
Feather, Leonard 'Miles and the Fifties', *Down Beat*, 2 July 1964
Feather, Leonard 'The Modulated World of Gil Evans', *Down Beat*, 23 February 1967
Gardner, Barbara J. 'The Enigma of Miles Davis', *Down Beat*, 7 January 1960
Gleason, Ralph J. 'Miles Davis', *Rolling Stone*, 13 December 1969
Gleason, Ralph J. 'Miles Davis: 3 Hours to Unwind', *New York Post*,
Grove, Gene 'The New World of Jazz', *New York Post*, 16 November 1960
Hall, Gregg 'Miles: Today's Most Influential Contemporary Musician', *Down Beat*, 18 July 1974
Hentoff, Nat 'An Afternoon with Miles', *Jazz Review*, December 1958
Hentoff, Nat 'Miles Davis – Last Trump', *Esquire*, March 1959
Hentoff, Nat 'Miles Davis', *Hi-Fi Review*, February 1960
Hentoff, Nat 'The New York Jazz Scene', *New York Herald Tribune*, 7 April 1963
Hoefer, George 'Early Miles', *Down Beat*, 6 April 1967
Johnson, Sy 'Sparring with Miles', *Changes*, 1974
Kolodin, Irving 'Miles Ahead or Miles' Head', *Saturday Review*, 12 September 1959
Malle, Louis 'Le Problème de la Musique de Film', *Jazz Hot*, June 1960
'Miles Davis', *Playboy*, September 1962
Miller, Manfred 'Miles Davis', *Stereo – Das Deutsche Hi-Fi und Musik Magazin*, 17 November 1975
Millstein, Gilbert 'Jazz Makes It Up The River', *New York Times Magazine*, 1958

248

Morgenstern, Dan 'Sippin' at Miles', *Metronome*, May 1961

Murphy, Frederick D. 'Miles Davis: The Monster of Modern Music', *Encore*, 21–28 July, 1975

'Pourquoi si Méchant Miles?', *Jazz Magazine*, October 1960

'Pourquoi si Gentil Miles?', *Jazz Magazine*, November 1960

Priestley, Brian 'Cleanhead's Comeback', *Melody Maker*, 3 June 1972

'The Prince of Darkness also brings Light', *Zygote/Zygote*, 12 August 1970

Tynan, Kenneth 'Miles Apart', *Holiday*, February 1963

Vartan, Eddie 'Miles Davis', *Jazz Magazine*, March 1960

Watts, Michael 'Miles Davis', *Melody Maker*, 20 January 1973

Williams, Richard 'Sketches of Gil', *Melody Maker*, 4 March 1978

Zwerin, Mike 'Miles Davis: A Most Curious Friendship', *Down Beat*, 10 March 1966

Appendix A
Musical Examples

A Note on the Solo Transcriptions

These transcriptions of solos by Miles Davis are only approximations. I have tried to be as accurate as possible, but western notation is inadequate to codify precisely the subtleties of rhythm and pitch inflexion which characterize jazz. In all cases the reader is urged to go to the recordings and listen to the solos in context.

Figure 1

'Godchild' by George Wallington from *The Birth of the Cool*.

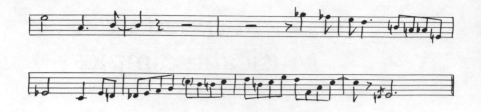

Figure 2

'Walkin' by Richard Carpenter from *Walkin'*.

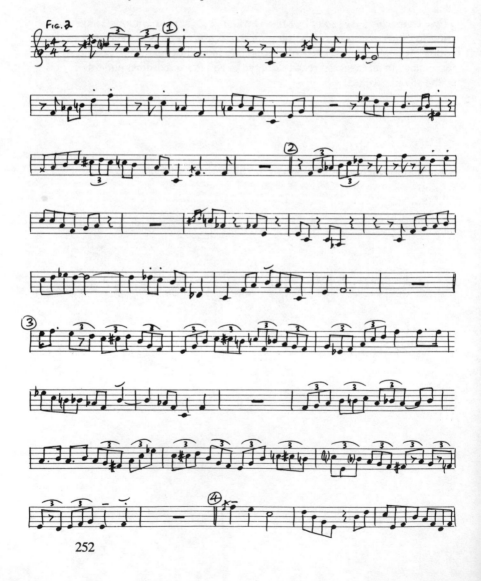

253

Figure 3

'Bag's Groove' by Milton Jackson from *Bag's Groove*.

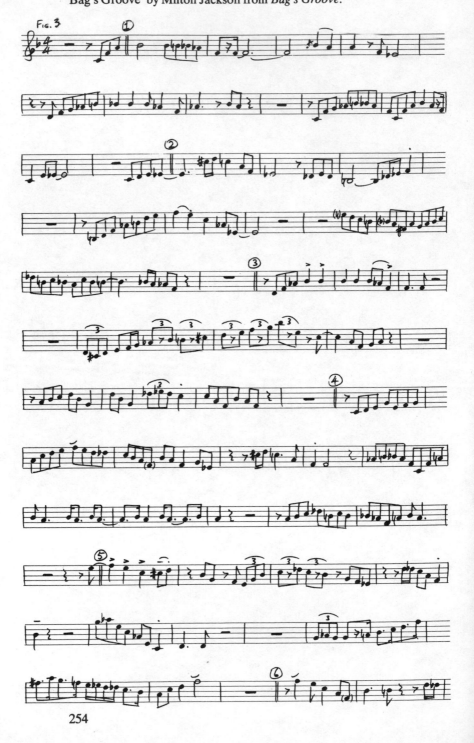

255

Figure 4

'My Funny Valentine' by Richard Rodgers from *Cookin'*.

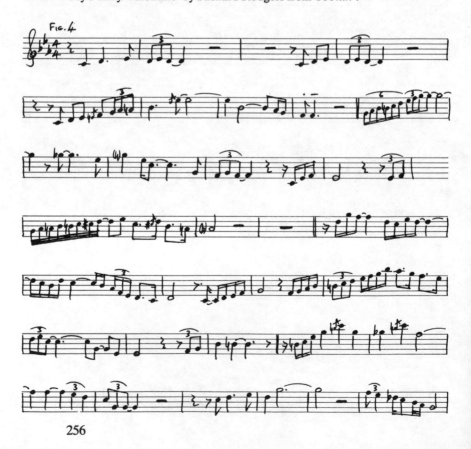

Figure 5a

'Florence sur les Champs Élysées' by Miles Davis from *Jazztrack*.

Figure 5b

'Chez le Photographe du Motel' by Miles Davis from *Jazztrack*.

Figure 6

'Sid's Ahead' by Miles Davis from *Milestones*.

Figure 7

'My Funny Valentine' by Richard Rodgers from *My Funny Valentine*.

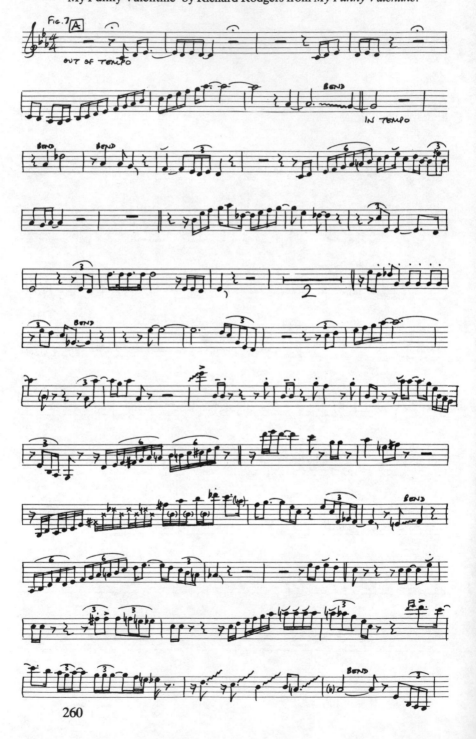

260

Figure 8

'Country Son' by Miles Davis from *Miles in the Sky*.

Figure 9

'Petits Machins' ('Little Stuff') by Miles Davis from *Filles de Kilimanjaro*.

263

Appendix B
Notes on Repertoire

Brian Priestley provided the following list of songs which were recorded by Frank Sinatra and which crept into Miles Davis's repertoire during the 1950s:

Sinatra recorded   'There's No You' (November 1944)
                    'I Fall In Love Too Easily' (December 1944)
                    'Stella by Starlight' (March 1947)
                    'S'posin'' (October 1947)
                    'It Never Entered My Mind' (twice: November 1947
                        with Bobby Hackett and March 1955)
                    'Spring is Here' (twice: March 1949 and May 1958)
                    'My Funny Valentine' (October 1953)
                    'I Thought About You' (January 1956)

The last two came respectively from the albums, *Songs For Young Lovers* and the even more influential *Songs For Swinging Lovers*.

I am indebted to Trevor Timmers for the following list of comparative recordings by Ahmad Jamal and Miles Davis:

	Jamal	*Davis*
'Surrey with the Fringe on Top'	25 October 1951	11 May 1956
'Will You Still Be Mine?'	25 October 1951	7 June 1955
'Ahmad's Blues'	25 October 1951	11 May 1956 (rhythm section)
'Gal in Calico'	25 October 1951	7 June 1955
'But Not For Me'	January 1954	29 June 1954
'New Rhumba'	23 May 1955	23 May 1957
'All of You'	25 May 1955	10 September 1956
'Autumn Leaves'	25 May 1955	9 March 1958 (*Somethin' Else*)
'Love For Sale'	25 May 1955	9 March 1958 (*Somethin' Else*)
'Green Dolphin Street'	27 September and 4 October 1956	26 May 1958

Appendix C
Discography

This lengthy appendix is nevertheless a mere synposis since, in most cases, only the original catalogue number is listed for each title. The exceptions occur where different versions of the same material, for instance mono and stereo or LPs and 45s (and, in the early fifties, 78s), were released more or less simultaneously, although in practice it has been difficult to draw a line between such instances and 45RPM *reissues*, often some years later and prompted by Miles's increasing popularity.

The fact that some of the Dial items with Charlie Parker have appeared on up to 50 separate issues should be enough to show why a synopsis was thought necessary, but an attempt has also been made to cross-reference with an index of current album numbers from (1) to (80), demonstrating that over 90% of Miles Davis's issued output is available at the time of going to press. As to private recordings and air-shots, everything thus far issued commercially has been listed, plus known unissued material up to and including 1960, after which date the proliferation of private recorders eventually renders this task impossible.

Where location recordings have been issued under incorrect titles, these have been placed in parentheses after the original title, while retitled *studio* items have the issued title first with the title of any subsequent issue (or, distinguished by the prefix 'i.e.', the title of other known recordings) shown in parentheses.

Other innovations include the use of asterisks after catalogue numbers to indicate performances which are (*) incomplete on the record or (**) edited on the issue in question; however, these are dropped for album tracks after 1968, since Miles's recording practices render such descriptions applicable to all his later studio work. The more standard legend 'breakdown' refers to a performance which was terminated in mid-stream but was issued complete as it stands, while 'theme' describes a radio signature-tune, often played for no more than a few bars. The following standard abbreviations have also been used:

alt	alternative take
arr	arranger
as	alto saxophone
b	bass

bar-h	baritone-horn
bars	baritone saxophone
bcl	bass clarinet
bgo	bongo
btb	bass trombone
cga	conga
cl	clarinet
cond	conductor
d	drums
dir	director
Du	Dutch
E	English
el	electric
F	French
fl	flute
flh	flugelhorn
fr-h	french-horn
G	German
g	guitar
hca	harmonica
J	Japanese
keyb	keyboards
mc	master of ceremonies
narr	narrator
org	organ
p	piano
perc	percussion
ss	soprano saxophone
synth	synthesizer
tb	trombone
tp	trumpet
ts	tenor saxophone
tu	tuba
tymp	tympani
vcl	vocal
vib	vibraphone
vtb	valve trombone

Brian Priestley

268

1945:

<table>
<tr><td>*April 24*</td><td colspan="2">RUBBERLEGS WILLIAMS & ORCHESTRA</td></tr>
<tr><td>*New York City*</td><td colspan="2">FEATURING HERBIE FIELDS</td></tr>
<tr><td></td><td colspan="2">Miles Davis (tp); Herbie Fields (as,ts); Teddy Brannon (p); Leonard Gaskin (b); Eddie Nicholson (d); Rubberlegs Williams (vcl)</td></tr>
<tr><td>S5805</td><td>**That's the stuff you got to watch**</td><td>Savoy 564</td></tr>
<tr><td>S5806</td><td>**Pointless mama blues**</td><td>—</td></tr>
<tr><td>S5807</td><td>**Deep sea blues**</td><td>Savoy 5516</td></tr>
<tr><td>S5808</td><td>**Bring it on home**</td><td>—</td></tr>
</table>

<table>
<tr><td>*November 26*</td><td colspan="3">CHARLEY PARKER'S REE BOPPERS</td></tr>
<tr><td>*New York City*</td><td colspan="3">Miles Davis (tp); Charlie Parker (as); 'Hen Gates' (Dizzy Gillespie) (p); Curley Russell (b); Max Roach (d)</td></tr>
<tr><td>S5850-1</td><td>**Billie's bounce**</td><td>(1)</td><td>Savoy MG12079</td></tr>
<tr><td>S5850-2</td><td>**Billie's bounce** (breakdown)</td><td>(1)</td><td>—</td></tr>
<tr><td>S5850-3</td><td>**Billie's bounce**</td><td>(1)</td><td>—</td></tr>
<tr><td>S5850-4</td><td>**Billie's bounce** (breakdown)</td><td>(1)</td><td>—</td></tr>
<tr><td>S5850-5</td><td>**Billie's bounce**</td><td>(1)</td><td>Savoy 573</td></tr>
<tr><td>S5851-1</td><td>**Now's the time** (breakdown)</td><td>(1)</td><td>Savoy MG12079</td></tr>
<tr><td>S5851-2</td><td>**Now's the time** (breakdown)</td><td>(1)</td><td>—</td></tr>
<tr><td>S5851-3</td><td>**Now's the time**</td><td>(1)</td><td>—</td></tr>
<tr><td>S5851-4</td><td>**Now's the time**</td><td>(1)</td><td>Savoy 573</td></tr>
<tr><td></td><td colspan="3">Sadik Hakim (p) replaces Gillespie</td></tr>
<tr><td>S5852-1</td><td>**Thriving on a riff**</td><td>(1)</td><td>Savoy MG12079</td></tr>
<tr><td>S5852-2</td><td>**Thriving on a riff** (breakdown)</td><td>(1)</td><td>—</td></tr>
<tr><td>S5852-3</td><td>**Thriving on a riff**</td><td>(1)</td><td>Savoy 903</td></tr>
<tr><td></td><td colspan="3">Note: Davis and Hakim out on remaining titles from this session</td></tr>
</table>

1946:

<table>
<tr><td>*c.early March*</td><td colspan="3">CHARLIE PARKER QUINTET</td></tr>
<tr><td>*Finale Club*</td><td colspan="3">Miles Davis (tp); Charlie Parker (as); Joe Albany (p);</td></tr>
<tr><td>*Los Angeles*</td><td colspan="3">Addison Farmer (b); Chuck Thompson (d)</td></tr>
<tr><td></td><td>**Anthropology**</td><td>(2)</td><td>Queen-Disc Q-017</td></tr>
<tr><td></td><td>**Billie's bounce**</td><td>(2)</td><td>—</td></tr>
<tr><td></td><td>**Blue 'n' boogie**</td><td>(2)</td><td>—</td></tr>
<tr><td></td><td>**All the things you are**</td><td>(2)</td><td>—</td></tr>
<tr><td></td><td>**Ornithology**</td><td>(2)</td><td>— *</td></tr>
</table>

<table>
<tr><td>*March 28*</td><td colspan="3">CHARLIE PARKER SEPTET</td></tr>
<tr><td>*Los Angeles*</td><td colspan="3">Miles Davis (tp); Charlie Parker (as); Lucky Thompson (ts); Dodo Marmarosa (p); Vic McMillan (b); Roy Porter (d)</td></tr>
<tr><td>D1010-1</td><td>**Moose the mooche**</td><td colspan="2">(3) Dial DLP201</td></tr>
<tr><td>D1010-2</td><td>**Moose the mooche**</td><td colspan="2">(3) Dial 1003, 1004</td></tr>
<tr><td>D1010-3</td><td>**Moose the mooche**</td><td colspan="2">(3) Spotlite 105, 101</td></tr>
<tr><td></td><td colspan="3">Arv Garrison (g) added</td></tr>
<tr><td>D1011-1</td><td>**Yardbird suite**</td><td colspan="2">(3) Dial DLP201</td></tr>
<tr><td>D1011-4</td><td>**Yardbird suite**</td><td colspan="2">(3) Dial 1003</td></tr>
<tr><td>D1012-1</td><td>**Ornithology**</td><td colspan="2">(3) Dial DLP208</td></tr>
<tr><td>D1012-3</td><td>**Bird lore (Ornithology)**</td><td colspan="2">(3) Dial 1006</td></tr>
<tr><td>D1012-4</td><td>**Ornithology**</td><td colspan="2">(3) Dial 1002</td></tr>
<tr><td>D1013-1</td><td>**Famous alto break**</td><td colspan="2">(3) Dial DLP905 *</td></tr>
<tr><td>D1013-4</td><td>**Night in Tunisia**</td><td colspan="2">(3) Dial DLP201</td></tr>
<tr><td>D1013-5</td><td>**Night in Tunisia**</td><td colspan="2">(3) Dial 1002</td></tr>
<tr><td></td><td colspan="3">Notes: **D1010-2. D1011-4, D1012-4** and **D1013-5** have also been reissued as by MILES DAVIS; **D1012-1** originally issued as by DODO MARMAROSA SEXTET</td></tr>
</table>

March 31	BENNY CARTER	
Streets of Paris,	Miles Davis (tp); Al Grey (tb); Benny Carter (as); Bumps	
Los Angeles	Myers (ts); Sonny White (p); Jimmy Cannady (g); prob.	
	Tommy Moultrie (b); prob. Percy Brice (d)	
	Just you, just me	Air-shot
	Don't blame me	—
	Sweet Georgia Brown	—

c. May/June	BENNY CARTER AND HIS ORCHESTRA	
Los Angeles	As above plus 3 tp, 3 tb, 3 sax – unknown	
	Just you, just me	(4) AFRS Jubilee 186
	Jump call	(4) —
	untitled original	(4) AFRS Jubilee 191

October 5	BILLY ECKSTINE AND HIS ORCHESTRA	
Los Angeles	Hobart Dotson, Leonard Hawkins, Miles Davis, King Kolax	
	(tp); Walter Knox, Chips Outcalt, Gerry Valentine (tb);	
	Sonny Stitt, John Cobbs (as); Gene Ammons, Arthur	
	Sammons (ts); Cecil Payne (bars); Linton Garner (p);	
	Connie Wainwright (g); Tommy Potter (b); Art Blakey (d);	
	Billy Eckstine (vcl-1, vtb-2)	
NSC164	**Oo bop sh'bam** -1,2	(5) National 9125
NSC164(alt.)	**Oo bop sh'bam** -1,2	(5) CBS-Sony (J) SOPL-54
NSC165	**I love the loveliness** -1	(5) National 9030
NSC166	**In the still of the night** -1	(5) National 9037
NSC167	**Jelly jelly** -1,2	(5) National 9021
NSC167(alt.)	**Jelly jelly** -1,2	CBS-Sony (J) SOPL-54

c. Autumn	EARL COLEMAN/ANN HATHAWAY	
Los Angeles	Miles Davis (tp); Gene Ammons (ts); Linton Garner (p);	
	Connie Wainwright (g); Tommy Potter (b); Art Blakey (d);	
	Earl Coleman-1, Ann Hathaway-2 (vcl)	
	two unknown titles -1	Sunset unissued
	two unknown titles -2	—

1947:

March	ILLINOIS JACQUET AND HIS ORCHESTRA	
New York City	Marion Hazel, Miles Davis, Fats Navarro, Joe Newman (tp);	
	Gus Chappel, Ted Kelly, Eli Robinson, Dickie Wells (tb);	
	Ray Perry, Jimmy Powell (as); Illinois Jacquet, Big Nick	
	Nicholas (ts); Leo Parker (bars); Bill Doggett (p); Al Lucas	
	(b); Shadow Wilson (d); Tadd Dameron-1, Jimmy Mundy	
	(arr)	
94-4	**For Europeans only** -1	Aladdin 180
95-3	**Big dog** -2	—
96-4	**You left me alone**	Aladdin 179
97-2	**Jivin' with Jack the bellboy**	—
	2- Leonard Feather (p) replaces Doggett	

May 8	CHARLIE PARKER ALL STARS	
New York City	Miles Davis (tp); Charlie Parker (as); Bud Powell (p);	
	Tommy Potter (b); Max Roach (d)	
S3420-1	**Donna Lee** (breakdown)	(1) Savoy S5J5500
S3420-2	**Donna Lee**	(1) Savoy MG12001
S3420-3	**Donna Lee**	(1) —
S3420-4	**Donna Lee**	(1) Savoy MG12009
S3420-5	**Donna Lee**	(1) Savoy 652
S3421-1	**Chasin' the Bird**	(1) Savoy MG12001
S3421-2	**Chasin' the Bird** (breakdown)	(1) Savoy S5J5500
S3421-3	**Chasin' the Bird**	(1) Savoy MG12009
S3421-4	**Chasin' the Bird**	(1) Savoy 977
S3422-1	**Cheryl** (breakdown)	(1) Savoy MG12001
S3422-2	**Cheryl**	(1) Savoy 952

270

S3423-1	**Buzzy**	(1) Savoy MG12009
S3423-2	**Buzzy** (breakdown)	(1) Savoy MG12001
S3423-3	**Buzzy**	(1) —
S3423-4	**Buzzy** (breakdown)	(1) Savoy MG12000
S3423-5	**Buzzy**	(1) Savoy 652

Note: **S3421-4** originally issued as by MILES DAVIS ALL STARS

June
New York City

COLEMAN HAWKINS ALL STARS
Miles Davis (tp); Kai Winding (tb); Howard Johnson (as); Coleman Hawkins (ts); Hank Jones (p); prob. Curley Russell or Tommy Potter (b); prob. Max Roach (d)

215	**Bean-a-re-bop**	Aladdin 3006
216	**Isn't it romantic**	Aladdin EP516
217	**The way you look tonight**	Aladdin 3006
218	**Phantomesque**	Aladdin EP516

August 14
New York City

MILES DAVIS ALL STARS
Miles Davis (tp); Charlie Parker (ts); John Lewis (p); Nelson Boyd (b); Max Roach (d)

S3440-1	**Milestones** (breakdown)	(1) Savoy S5J5500
S3440-2	**Milestones**	(1) Savoy 934
S3440-3	**Milestones**	(1) Savoy MG12001
S3441-1	**Little Willie leaps** (breakdown)	(1) —
S3441-2	**Little Willie leaps**	(1) —
S3441-3	**Little Willie leaps (Wailing Willie)**	(1) Savoy 977
S3442-1	**Half Nelson**	(1) Savoy MG12001
S3442-2	**Half Nelson**	(1) Savoy 951
S3443-1	**Sippin' at Bells** (breakdown)	(1) MG12009
S3443-2	**Sippin' at Bells**	(1) Savoy 934
S3443-3	**Sippin' at Bells** (breakdown)	(1) Savoy S5J5500
S3443-4	**Sippin' at Bells**	(1) Savoy MG12001

Note: All issues except 78s as by CHARLIE PARKER

October 28
New York City

CHARLIE PARKER QUINTET
Miles Davis (tp); Charlie Parker (as); Duke Jordan (p); Tommy Potter (b); Max Roach (d)

D1101A	**Dexterity**	(6) Dial DLP203
D1101B	**Dexterity**	(6) Dial 1032
D1101C	**Dexterity**	unissued, presumed lost
D1102A	**Bongo bop (Blues)**	(6) Dial 1024
D1102B	**Bongo bop (Parker's blues)**	(6) Dial 1024
D1103A	**Prezology (Dewey Square)** -1	(6) Dial 1056 *
D1103B	**Dewey Square**	(6) Dial DLP203
D1103C	**Dewey Square**	(6) Dial 1019
D1104A	**The hymn (Superman)**	(6) Dial 1056
D1104B	**Superman**	(6) Dial DLP212
D1105A	**Bird of paradise (All the things you are)**	(6) Dial 1032
D1105B	**Bird of paradise**	(6) Dial 1032
D1105C	**Bird of paradise**	(6) Dial 1032
D1106A	**Embraceable you**	(6) Dial 1024
D1106B	**Embraceable you**	(6) Dial 1024

November 4
New York City

D1111C	**Bird feathers (Schnourphology)**	(7) Dial 1058
D1112A	**Klactoveedsedstene (Klact-oveeseds-tene)**	(7) Dial 1040
D1112B	**Klactoveedsedstene (Klact-oveeseds-tene)**	(7) Dial DLP904
D1113B	**Scrapple from the apple**	(7) Dial DLP203
D1113C	**Scrapple from the apple**	(7) Dial 1021

D1114A	**My old flame**	(7) Dial 1058
D1115A	**Out of nowhere**	(7) Dial DLP207
D1115B	**Out of nowhere**	(7) Dial DLP904
D1115C	**Out of nowhere**	(7) Spotlite 105
D1116A	**Don't blame me**	(7) Dial 1021

1- opening ensemble edited out on most issues
Notes: **D1105C, D1106A, D1113C, D1114A** and **D1115A** have also been reissued as by MILES DAVIS; **D1104B** originally issued as by MILES DAVIS QUINTET

December 17
New York City

CHARLIE PARKER SEXTET
As last plus J.J. Johnson (tb)

D1151B	**Giant swing (Drifting on a reed)**	(8) Dial 1056
D1151D	**Drifting on a reed**	(8) Dial DLP904
D1151E	**Drifting on a reed**	
	(Air conditioning)	(8) Dial 1043
D1152A	**Quasimodo**	(8) Dial DLP203
D1152B	**Quasimodo (Trade winds)**	(8) Dial 1015
D1153B	**Charlie's wig**	(8) Dial DLP905
D1153D	**Bongo bop (Charlie's wig)**	(8) Dial DLP203
D1153E	**Charlie's wig**	(8) Dial 1040
D1154B	**Dexterity (Bird feathers)**	(8) Dial DLP904
D1154C	**Bird feathers (Bongo beep)**	(8) Dial DLP207
D1155ABX	**Crazeology II**	(8) Dial 1034**
D1155C	**Crazeology**	(8) Dial DLP905
D1155D	**Crazeology**	(8) Dial 1034,1055
D1156A	**How deep is the ocean**	(8) Dial 1055
D1156B	**How deep is the ocean**	(8) Dial DLP211

Note: **D1155ABX** is a montage of the opening and the alto solo of take A, the alto solo of take B, and the alto solo and remainder of take C

December 21
Detroit

CHARLIE PARKER ALL STARS
As last except Johnson out

D830-1	**Another hair-do** (breakdown)	(1) Savoy MG12000
D830-2	**Another hair-do** (breakdown)	(1) —
D830-3	**Another hair-do** (breakdown)	(1) Savoy S5J5500
D830-4	**Another hair-do**	(1) Savoy 961
D831-1	**Bluebird**	(1) Savoy MG12000
D831-2	**Bluebird** (breakdown)	(1) Savoy S5J5500
D831-3	**Bluebird**	(1) Savoy 961
D832-1	**Klaunsen's vansan's (Klaunstance)**	(1) Savoy 967
D833-1	**Bird gets the worm**	(1) Savoy MG12000
D833-2	**Bird gets the worm** (breakdown)	(1) Savoy S5J5500
D833-3	**Bird gets the worm**	(1) Savoy 952

1948:
c.January
prob. New Savoy
Ballroom, Chicago

CHARLIE PARKER QUINTET
As last plus Kenny Hagood (vcl-1)

	unknown title	Private recording
	Drifting on a reed	—

c.March
Three Deuces,
New York City

	Dizzy atmosphere	(9) Spotlite SPJ141
	My old flame	(9) — *
	All the things you are -1	(9) — *
	Half Nelson	(9) — *
	Drifting on a reed (Big foot)	(9) —
	52nd street theme (3 versions)	(9) —

c.Spring
Onyx Club,
New York City

	52nd street theme	(10) Jazz Workshop
		JWS501**
	Shaw nuff	(10) — **

Out of nowhere	(10) —	**
Hot house	(10) —	**
This time the dream's on me	(10) —	**
Night in Tunisia	(10) —	*
My old flame	(10) —	**
52nd street theme (2 versions)	(10) —	*
The way you look tonight	(10) —	**
Out of nowhere	(10) —	**
Chasin' the Bird	(10) —	*
This time the dream's on me	(10) —	
Dizzy atmosphere	(10) —	**
How high the moon	(10) —	**

c. Autumn		
Three Deuces,	**How high the moon**	Private recording
New York City	**52nd street theme**	—

September 4	MILES DAVIS AND HIS ORCHESTRA	
Broadcast,	Miles Davis (tp); Mike Zwerin (tb); Junion Collins (fr-h); Bill	
Royal Roost,	Barber (tu); Lee Konitz (as); Gerry Mulligan (bars,arr-1), John	
New York City	Lewis (p,arr-2); Al McKibbon (b); Max Roach (d); Gil Evans	
	(arr-3); Kenny Hagood (vcl-4); Symphony Sid (mc)	
	Move -2	Air-shot
	Why do I love you -1,4	(11) Ozone 2
	Godchild -1	(11) —
	S'il vous plait -2	(11) —
	Moon dreams -3	(11) —
	Hallucinations -2	(11) — *

Same broadcast	CHARLIE PARKER ALL STARS	
	Miles Davis (tp); Charlie Parker (as); Tadd Dameron (p);	
	Curley Russell (b); Max Roach (d)	
	52nd street theme	(11a) Savoy MG12186
	Ko-ko	(11a) Le Jazz Cool LJC101
	52nd street theme (theme)	Air-shot

September 18		
New York City	As last except John Lewis (p) replaces Dameron	
B900-1	**Barbados**	(1) Savoy MG12000
B900-2	**Barbados** (breakdown)	(1) Savoy MG12009
B900-3	**Barbados**	(1) —
B900-4	**Barbados**	(1) Savoy 936
B901-1	**Ah-leu-cha** (breakdown)	(1) Savoy MG12000
B901-2	**Ah-leu-cha**	(1) Savoy 939
B902-1	**Constellation** (breakdown)	(1) Savoy S5J5500
B902-2	**Constellation**	(1) Savoy MG12000
B902-3	**Constellation** (breakdown)	(1) —
B902-4	**Constellation** (breakdown)	(1) Savoy MG12009
B902-5	**Constellation**	(1) Savoy 939
	Note: Davis out on **Parker's mood** from this session	

September 18	MILES DAVIS AND HIS ORCHESTRA	
Broadcast,	As for September 4 except poss. Ted Kelly (tb) replaces Zwerin	
Royal Roost,	**Darn that dream** -1,4	(11) Alto AL701
New York City	**Move (Mood)** -2	(11) —
	Moon dreams -3	(11) —
	Hallucinations -2	(11) —

September 24	CHARLIE PARKER ALL STARS	
New York City	As for September 18	
B908-1	**Perhaps**	(1) Savoy MG12014
B908-2	**Perhaps** (breakdown)	(1) Savoy MG12009
B908-3	**Perhaps**	(1) —
B908-4	**Perhaps** (breakdown)	(1) Savoy S5J5500

B908-5	**Perhaps** (breakdown)	(1) Savoy MG12000
B908-6	**Perhaps**	(1) —
B908-7	**Perhaps**	(1) Savoy 938
B909-1	**Marmaduke** (breakdown)	(1) Savoy S5J5500
B909-2	**Marmaduke** (breakdown)	(1) Savoy MG12000
B909-3	**Marmaduke** (breakdown)	(!) Savoy S5J5500
B909-4	**Marmaduke** (breakdown)	(1) —
B909-5	**Marmaduke**	(1) Savoy MG12000
B909-6	**Marmaduke** (breakdown)	(12) Savoy SJL1129
B909-7	**Marmaduke** (breakdown)	(12) Savoy MG12001
B909-8	**Marmaduke** (breakdown)	(12) —
B909-9	**Marmaduke**	(12) —
B909-10	**Marmaduke** (breakdown)	(1) Savoy S5J5500
B909-11	**Marmaduke** (breakdown)	(1) Savoy MG12009
B909-12	**Marmaduke**	(1) Savoy 938
B910-1	**Steeplechase** (breakdown)	(1) Savoy S5J5500
B910-2	**Steeplechase**	(1) Savoy 937
B911-1	**Merry-go-round**	(1) Savoy MG12000
B911-2	**Merry-go-round**	(1) Savoy 937

September 25
Broadcast,
Royal Roost,
New York City

MILES DAVIS
Miles Davis (tp); Lee Konitz (as); John Lewis (p); Curley Russell (b); Max Roach (d); Kenny Hagood (vcl-1); Symphony Sid (mc)

52nd street theme (Broadway theme)	Session Disc 101
Half Nelson	—
You go to my head -1	—
Chasin' the Bird	—

December 11
Broadcast,
Royal Roost,
New York City

CHARLIE PARKER ALL STARS
Miles Davis (tp); Charlie Parker (as,vcl-1); Al Haig (p); Tommy Potter (b); Max Roach (d); Symphony Sid (mc)

Jumpin' with Symphony Sid (theme)	Air-shot
Groovin' high	(13) Le Jazz Cool LJC101*
Drifting on a reed (Big foot)	(13) Le Jazz Cool LJC102
Ornithology	(13) Le Jazz Cool LJC101*
Slow boat to China	(13) ESP ESP-BIRD-1

December 12
Broadcast,
Royal Roost,
New York City

Hot house	Le Jazz Cool LJC101, LJC103
Salt peanuts -1	Le Jazz Cool LJC102

December 18
Broadcast,
Royal Roost,
New York City

Chasin' the Bird	(14) Meexa 1776
Out of nowhere	(14) Le Jazz Cool LJC102
How high the moon	(14) —

1949:
January 3
New York City

METRONOME ALL STARS
Dizzy Gillespie, Fats Navarro, Miles Davis (tp); J.J. Johnson, Kai Winding (tb); Buddy DeFranco (cl); Charlie Parker (as); Charlie Ventura (ts); Ernie Caceres (bars); Lennie Tristano (p,arr-1); Billy Bauer (g); Eddie Safranski (b); Shelly Manne (d); Pete Rugolo (cond,arr-2)

D9-VB-0021-1	**Overtime** -2	Victor 20-3361
D9-VB-1000-2	**Overtime** -2	(15) Victor EPBT3046, LPT3046

D9-VB-1001-3 **Victory ball** -1 (15) — —
Note: Davis, Navarro, Johnson and Caceres out on two other
issued takes of **Victory ball**

January 21 MILES DAVIS AND HIS ORCHESTRA
New York City As for September 4, 1948 except Kai Winding (tb); Al Haig (p);
Joe Shulman (b) replace Zwerin, Lewis and McKibbon

3395-3	**Jeru** -1	(16) Capitol 60005
3396-3	**Move** -2	(16) Capitol 15404
3397-2	**Godchild** -1	(16) Capitol 60005
3398-1	**Budo** (i.e. **Hallucinations**) -2	(16) Capitol 15404

February 19 TADD DAMERON BIG TEN
Broadcast, Miles Davis (tp); Kai Winding (tb); Sahib Shihab (as); prob.
Royal Roost, Benjamin Lundy (ts); Cecil Payne (bars); Tadd Dameron
New York City (p,arr); John Collins (g); Curley Russell (b); Kenny Clarke (d);
Carlos Vidal (bgo); prob. John Lewis (arr-1); Symphony Sid
(mc)

Focus	(17)	Jung Cat RBD948
April in Paris	(17)	—
Good bait	(17)	—
Webb's delight	(17)	—

February 26
Broadcast,
Royal Roost,

Milano (Miles) -1	(17)	—
Casbah	(17)	—

New York City

March 5
Broadcast,
Royal Roost,

Good bait		Air-shot
The squirrel		—

New York City

April 21 As for February 19 except J.J. Johnson (tb) replaces Winding;
New York City Lundy definite; Kay Penton (vcl-1) added

3760	**John's delight**	Capitol 60015
	What's new -1	Capitol (Du) 5C052. 80852
	Heaven's doors are open wide -1	—
3763	**Focus**	Capitol 60015

April 22 MILES DAVIS AND HIS ORCHESTRA
New York City Miles Davis (tp); J.J. Johnson (tb); Sandy Siegelstein (fr-h);
Bill Barber (tu); Lee Konitz (as); Gerry Mulligan (bars,arr-1);
John Lewis (p,arr-2); Nelson Boyd (b); Kenny Clarke (d);
Gil Evans-3, John Carisi-4 (arr)

3764	**Venus de Milo** -1	(16) Capitol 1221
3765	**Rouge** -2	(16) Capitol EAP2-459,H459
3766-2	**Boplicity** -3	(16) Capitol 60011
3767-2	**Israel** -4	(16) —

May 8 MILES DAVIS – TADD DAMERON QUINTET
Broadcast, Miles Davis (tp); James Moody (ts); Tadd Dameron (p);
Salle Pleyel, Barney Spieler (b); Kenny Clarke (d); Frank Tenot, Maurice
Paris Cullaz (mc)

Rifftide	(18)	Columbia JC34804
Good bait	(18)	—
Don't blame me -1	(18)	—
Lady bird	(18)	—

May 9,12,14,15
Broadcasts,
Salle Pleyel,
Paris

Wahoo (Wah hoo)	(18)	—
Allen's alley	(18)	—
Embraceable you	(18)	—
Ornithology	(18)	—

275

	All the things you are	(18)	—
	The squirrel	(19)	Phontastic NOST7602
	Wahoo	Air-shot	
	Crazy rhythm	—	
	All the things you are	—	
	1-Moody out		

May 15
Broadcast,
Salle Pleyel,
Paris

JAM SESSION
Aime Barelli, Bill Coleman, Miles Davis, Kenny Dorham, Hot Lips Page (tp); Russell Moore (tb); Hubert Rostaing (cl); Pierre Braslavsky, Sidney Bechet (ss); Charlie Parker (as); Don Byas, James Moody (ts); Hazy Osterwald (vib); Al Haig (p); Toots Thielemans (g); Tommy Potter (b); Max Roach (d)

Blues (Farewell blues)   (20) Bird in Paris CP3*

December 24
Broadcast,
Carnegie Hall,
New York City

JAM SESSION
Miles Davis (tp); Bennie Green (tb); Sonny Stitt (as); Serge Chaloff (bars); Bud Powell (p); Curley Russell (b); Max Roach (d); Symphony Sid (mc)

Move	(21) VOA JC6
Hot house	(21) IAJRC 20
Ornithology	(21) — *

1949-50
c. Winter
Harlem(?),
New York City

JAM SESSION
Miles Davis (tp); Charlie Parker (as); unknown p, b, d

Drifting on a reed   Private recording

1950:
February 10
Broadcast,
WNYC Studio,
New York City

MILES DAVIS SEXTET
Miles Davis (tp); J.J. Johnson (tb); Stan Getz (ts); Tadd Dameron (p); Gene Ramey or Tommy Potter (b); Max Roach (d)

Conception	Ozone 1
Ray's idea	—
Max is making wax	—
Woody'n you	—

Note: Davis and Johnson play final chord only of **That old black magic** from this session

March 9
New York City

MILES DAVIS AND HIS ORCHESTRA
As for September 4, 1948 except J.J. Johnson (tb); Gunther Schuller (fr-h) replace Zwerin and Collins

4346	**Deception**	(16) Capitol EAP1-459,H459
4347	**Rocker** -1	(16) Capitol EAP2-459, —
4348	**Moon dreams** -3	(16) Capitol EAP1-459, —
4349	**Darn that dream** -1,4	Capitol 1221

May 18
New York City

SARAH VAUGHAN WITH JIMMY JONES'S BAND
Miles Davis (tp); Bennie Green (tb); Tony Scott (cl); Budd Johnson (ts); Jimmy Jones (p,arr); Freddie Greene (g); Billy Taylor (b); J.C. Heard (d); Sarah Vaughan (vcl)

CO43825	**Ain't misbehavin'**	Columbia 38896
CO43826	**Goodnight my love**	Columbia 38897
CO43828	**It might as well be spring** -1	Columbia 38899

May 19
New York City

Mundell Lowe (g) replaces Greene

CO43829	**Mean to me**	Columbia 38899
CO43830	**Come rain or come shine**	Columbia 38898
CO43831	**Nice work if you can get it**	Columbia 38897

1-Johnson and Greene out
Note: Davis out on two remaining titles from these sessions

276

June 30	BIRDLAND ALL STARS	
Birdland,	Miles Davis (tp); J.J., Johnson (tb); Brew Moore (ts); Walter	
New York City	Bishop (p); Curley Russell (b); Art Blakey (d)	
	Eronel (Overturia)	(22,23) Session Disc 102
	52nd street theme	(22) — *
	Conception (Poobah) -1	Alto AL701
	Tadd Dameron (p) replaces Bishop	
	Wee (Rambunctious rambling)	(22) —
	Hot house (Miles's midnight	
	breakaway)	(22,23) Session Disc 101*
	Embraceable you	(22) —
	Brew's blues	Private recording
	For you my love	—

1-Fats Navarro (tp); Charlie Parker (as) join in on last chorus
Note: Davis out on **September in the rain** and **Chubbie's blues**
from this session

1951:

January 17	CHARLIE PARKER AND HIS ORCHESTRA	
New York City	Miles Davis (tp); Charlie Parker (as); Walter Bishop (p);	
	Teddy Kotick (b); Max Roach (d)	
C489-2	**Au privave**	(24) Verve MGV8010
C489-3	**Au privave**	Mercury/Clef 11087
C490-3	**She rote**	(24) Verve MGV8010
C490-5	**She rote**	Clef 11101
C491-1	**K.C. blues**	(24) —
C492-2	**Star eyes**	(24) Mercury/Clef 11087

January 17	MILES DAVIS BAND	
New York City	Miles Davis (tp); Bennie Green (tb); Sonny Rollins (ts); John	
	Lewis (p,arr-1); Percy Heath (b); Roy Haynes (d)	
128A	**Morpheus** -1	(25) Prestige 734
129B	**Down**	(25) Prestige 742
130B	**Blue room** -2	(25) Prestige PRLP140**
130BB	**Blue room** -3	(25) Prestige 734
131B	**Whispering**	(25) Prestige 742

2-Green out; consists of one take and part of another spliced
together (Davis prob. plays p on second part)
3-Green and Rollins out

Same session	SONNY ROLLINS QUARTET	
	As last except Green and Lewis out; Davis plays p	
132	**I know**	(25) Prestige 757

January 24	METRONOME ALL STARS	
New York City	Miles Davis (tp); Kai Winding (tb); John LaPorta (cl); Lee	
	Konitz (a (ts); Serge Chaloff (bars); Terry Gibbs	
	(vib); George Shearing (p,arr-1); Billy Bauer (g); Eddie	
	Safranski (b); Max Roach (d); Ralph Burns (arr-2)	
6252	**Early spring** -2	Capitol 1550
6253	**Local 802 blues** -1	—

February 17	MILES DAVIS ALL STARS	
Broadcast,	Miles Davis (tb); J.J. Johnson (tb); Sonny Rollins (ts); Kenny	
Birdland,	Drew (p); Tommy Potter (b); Art Blakey (d); Symphony	
New York City	Sid (mc)	
	Evans	Air-shot
	Half Nelson	—
	Tempus fugit	—
	Move	—
	Jumpin' with Symphony Sid	
	(theme)	—

March 8	**LEE KONITZ SEXTET**		
New York City	Miles Davis (tp); Lee Konitz (as); Sal Mosca (p); Billy Bauer (g); Arnold Fishkin (b); Max Roach (d)		
140B	**Odjenar**	(25) Prestige 753	
141B	**Ezz-thetic**	(25) Prestige 843	
142B	**Hi Beck**	(25)	—
143B	**Yesterdays** -1	(25) Prestige 755	

1-Roach out
Note: Davis and Roach also out on further take of **Yesterdays**

June 2	**MILES DAVIS ALL STARS**		
Broadcast,	As for February 17		
Birdland,	**Move (Moo)**	(26) Session 102,Ozone 7	
New York City	**Half Nelson**	(26)	—	—
	Down (Mick's blues)	(26)	—	—
	Jumpin' with Symphony Sid (theme)		—

September 29	Miles Davis (tp); Lockjaw Davis, Big Nick Nicholas (ts); Billy		
Broadcast	Taylor (p); Charles Mingus (b); Art Blakey (d); Symphony		
Birdland,	Sid (mc)		
New York City	**Move (Mod)**	(26) Ozone 7	
	The squirrel	(26)	—
	Lady bird	(26)	—*

October 5	As for February 17 except Jackie McLean (as); Walter Bishop	
New York City	(p) replace Johnson and Drew	
228	**Conception**	(25) Prestige 868, PREP1349,PRLP124
229	**Out of the blue** (i.e. **Evans**) **Pts.1 and 2**	(25) Prestige 876, PREP1361,PRLP140
230	**Denial**	(25) Prestige PREP1361
231	**Bluing Pts.1,2 and 3**	(25) Prestige 846/868, PREP1355,PRLP140
232	**Dig Pts.1 and 2**	(25) Prestige 777, PREP1339,PRLP124
233	**My old flame Pts.1 and 2** -1	(25) Prestige 766, PREP1339,PRLP124
234	**It's only a paper moon Pts.1 and 2** -1	(25) Prestige 817, PREP1339,PRLP124

1-McLean out

1952:

c.Spring	**MILES DAVIS**	
Club Barrelhouse,	Miles Davis (tp); Jimmy Forrest (ts); Charles Fox (p); John	
St Louis	Hixon (b); Oscar Oldham (d); unknown bgo-1, vcl-2	
	All the things you are	Jazz Showcase 5004
	Wahoo	—
	Our delight -1	—
	Ow! -2	—*
	Lady bird -1	—
	What's new	Private recording

May 2	Miles Davis (tp); Don Elliott (mellophone-1,vib); Jackie	
Broadcast,	McLean (as); Gil Coggins (p); Connie Henry (b); Connie	
Birdland,	Kay (d)	
New York City	**Evans**	Ozone 8
	Confirmation -1	—

May 3		
Broadcast,	**Wee dot** -1	—
Birdland,	**The chase**	—
New York City	**It could happen to you** -2	—

| | **Evans (Opmet)** | — |
| | 2-McLean out | |

Similar period	As for May 2 except Beryl Booker (p); Chuck Wayne (g) replace
Broadcast	Coggins and McLean
	The squirrel	(27) Stash ST113
May 9	As for May 2 except J.J. Johnson (tb); Oscar Pettiford (b);
New York City	Kenny Clarke (d) replace Elliott, Henry and Kay
BN428	**Dear old Stockholm**	(28) Blue Note 1595,
		BLP5013
BN429	**Chance it (**i.e. **Max is making wax)**(28) Blue Note 1596,
		BLP5013
BN430	**Donna (**i.e. **Dig)**	(28) Blue Note 1595,
		BLP5013
BN430(alt.)	**Donna**	(28) Blue Note 45-1633
BN431	**Woody'n you**	(28) Blue Note 1596,
		BLP5013
BN431(alt.)	**Woody'n you**	(28) Blue Note BLP1501
BN432	**Yesterdays** -1	(28) Blue Note 1597,
		BLP5013
BN433	**How deep is the ocean** -1	(28)	—
	1-Johnson and McLean out	

June	JAZZ INC.
New York City	At last except Zoot Sims (ts); Milt Jackson (vib,p); Percy Heath
	(b) replace McLean, Coggins and Pettiford
	unknown titles	unissued

1953:

January 30	MILES DAVIS
New York City	Miles Davis (tp); Sonny Rollins, 'Charlie Chan' (Charlie
	Parker) (ts); Walter Bishop (p); Percy Heath (b); Philly Joe
	Jones (d)
450	**Compulsion**	(25) Prestige PRLP7044
451-1	**Serpent's tooth**	(25)	—
451-2	**Serpent's tooth**	(25)	—
452	**Round midnight**	(25)	—
	Well you needn't -1	unissued, presumed lost
	1-Parker (or Rollins?) out	

February 19	Miles Davis (tp); Sonny Truitt (tb); Zoot Sims (ts); Al Cohn
New York City	(ts,arr); John Lewis (p); Leonard Gaskin (b); Kenny Clarke (d)
423	**Tasty pudding**	(25) Prestige PRLP154
424	**Willie the weeper**	(25)	—
425	**Floppy**	(25)	—
426	**For adults only**	(25)	—

April 20	Miles Davis (tp); J.J. Johnson (tb,arr-1); Jimmy Heath (ts,
New York City	arr-2); Gil Coggins (p); Percy Heath (b); Art Blakey (d)
	Tempus fugit	(28) Blue Note 1618,
		BLP5022
(alt.)	**Tempus fugit**	(28) Blue Note 45-1649
	Enigma -1	(28) Blue Note 1618,
		BLP5022
	Ray's idea	(28) Blue Note 1619,
		BLP5022
(alt.)	**Ray's idea**	(28) Blue Note BLP1502
	I waited for you -3	(28) Blue Note 1619,
		BLP5022
	Kelo -1	(28) Blue Note 1620,
		BLP5022
	C.T.A. -2	(28) Blue Note 1620,
		BLP5022

(alt.)	**C.T.A.** -2	(28) Blue Note BLP1501	
	3-Johnson and J. Heath out		

Similar to next
Broadcast,
Birdland,
New York City

DIZZY GILLESPIE QUINTET
Dizzy Gillespie, Miles Davis (tp); Charlie Parker (as); Sahib Shihab (bars); Wade Legge (p); Lou Hackney (b); Al Jones (d); Joe Carroll (vcl-1)

The bluest blues -1	Klacto MG102

May 16
Broadcast,
Birdland,
New York City

MILES DAVIS
As last except Gillespie and Parker out; Candido Camero (cga-2) added

I got rhythm -1,2	Chakra CH100MD
Move	Air-shot
Tenderly	—
Night in Tunisia -2	—
Dig -2	—
Lullaby of Birdland (theme)	—

May 19
New York City

Miles Davis (tp); John Lewis (p); Percy Heath (b); Max Roach (d)

479	**When lights are low**	(25) Prestige 902, PREP1326,PRLP161
480	**Tune up**	(25) Prestige 884, PREP1326,PRLP161
481	**Miles ahead**	(25) Prestige 902, PREP1326,PRLP161
482	**Smooch (i.e. Weird nightmare)** -1	(25) Prestige 884, PREP1326,PRLP161

1-Charles Mingus (p) replaces Lewis

1954:
March 6
Hackensack, N.J.

As last except Horace Silver (p); Art Blakey (d) replace Lewis and Roach

	Well you needn't	(28) Blue Note 45-1633, BLP5040
	Lazy Susan	(28) Blue Note 45-1649, BLP5040
	Weirdo	(28) Blue Note 45-1650, BLP5040
	The leap	(28) — —
	Take-off	(28) Blue Note BLP5040
	It never entered my mind	(28) —

March 15
New York City

556	**Four**	(25) Prestige 898, PREP1360,PRLP161
557	**Old devil moon**	(25) Prestige 898 PREP1360,PRLP161
558	**Blue haze Pts. 1 and 2**	(25) Prestige 893, PREP1360,PRLP161

April 3
Hackensack,N.J.

Miles Davis (tp); Dave Schildkraut (as); Horace Silver (p); Percy Heath (b); Kenny Clarke (d)

559	**Solar**	(25) Prestige PRLP185
560	**You don't know what love is** -1	(25) —
561	**Love me or leave me**	(25) Prestige PRLP7076
562	**I'll remember April**	(25) Prestige PRLP185

1-Schildkraut out

April 29 *Hackensack, N.J.*		As last except J.J. Johnson (tb); Lucky Thompson (ts,arr-1) replace Schildkraut	
	unknown titles -1		unissued, presumed lost
568	**Blue 'n' boogie Pts. 1 and 2**	(25) Prestige PREP1358, PRLP182	
569	**Walkin' Pts. 1 and 2**	(25) Prestige PREP1357, PRLP182	
June 29 *Hackensack, N.J.*		As last except Sonny Rollins (ts) replaces Johnson and Thompson	
590	**Airegin**	(25) Prestige PRLP187	
591	**Oleo**	(25) —	
592	**But not for me Pts. 1 and 2**	(25) Prestige 915,PRLP187	
592(alt.)	**But not for me**	(25) Prestige PRLP7109	
593	**Doxy**	(25) Prestige PRLP187	
December 24 *Hackensack, N.J.*		As last except Milt Jackson (vib); Thelonious Monk (p) replace Rollins and Silver	
676	**Bag's groove**	(25) Prestige PRLP196	
676(alt.)	**Bag's groove**	(25) Prestige PRLP7109	
677	**Bemsha swing**	(25) Prestige PRLP200	
678	**Swing spring**	(25) Prestige PRLP196	
679	**The man I love**	(25) Prestige PRLP200	
679(alt.)	**The man I love**	(25) Prestige PRLP7150	

1955:

June 7 *Hackensack, N.J.*		Miles Davis (tp); Red Garland (p); Oscar Pettiford (b); Philly Joe Jones (d)	
745	**I didn't**	(25) Prestige PRLP7007	
746	**Will you still be mine**	(25) —	
747	**Green haze Pts. 1 and 2**	(25) Prestige 45-103, PRLP7007	
748	**I see your face before me**	(25) —	
749	**Night in Tunisia Pts. 1 and 2**	(25) Prestige 45-114, PRLP7007	
750	**A gal in calico**	(25) —	
July 9 *New York City*		Miles Davis (tp); Britt Woodman (tb); Teddy Charles (vib); Charles Mingus (b); Elvin Jones (d)	
	Nature boy	(29) Debut DEB120	
	Alone together	(29) —	
	There's no you	(29) —	
	Easy living	(29) —	
August 5 *Hackensack, N.J.*		Miles Davis (tp); Jackie McLean (as-1); Milt Jackson (vib); Ray Bryant (p); Percy Heath (b); Art Taylor (d)	
781	**Dr. Jackle** -1	(25) Prestige PRLP7034	
782	**Bitty ditty**	(25) —	
783	**Minor march** -1	(25) —	
784	**Blues changes (Changes)**	(25) —	
October 18 *Broadcast,* *Basin St. East,* *New York City*	MILES DAVIS QUINTET As for June 7 except John Coltrane (ts) added; Paul Chambers (b) replaces Pettiford		
	Max is making wax	Air-shot	
	It never entered my mind	—	
October 27 *New York City*			
CO54130	**Ah-leu-cha**	(30)	Columbia CL949
	Little Melonae	(31a,32)	Columbia KC32025
	Two bass hit	(33)	Columbia KC2 36278
CO54133	**Budo**	(31a)	Columbia CL1020

November 16
Hackensack, N.J.

814	**Stablemates**	(25)	Prestige PRLP7014
815	**How am I to know**	(25)	—
816	**Just squeeze me**	(25)	—
817	**There is no greater love** -1	(25)	—
818	**Miles's theme (The theme)**	(25)	—
819	**S'posin'**	(25)	—

December 8
Broadcast,
Blue Note,   **Tune up**   (34) Teppa 76
Philadelphia   **Walkin' (Royal garden blues)**   (34) —

1-Coltrane out

Note: The October 27 **Little Melonae** has also been claimed as being a March 1958 recording

1956:

March 16   Miles Davis (tp); Sonny Rollins (ts); Tommy Flanagan (p);
Hackensack, N.J.   Paul Chambers (b); Art Taylor (d)

864	**In your own sweet way**	(25)	Prestige PRLP7044
865	**No line** (breakdown)	(25)	—
866	**Vierd blues** (i.e. **John Paul Jones**)	(25)	—

c.1956
Broadcast,   As for October 18, 1955
unknown location   **Bye bye blackbird**   Air-shot

May 11
Hackensack, N.J.

888	**In your own sweet way**	(25)	Prestige PRLP7166
889	**Diane**	(25)	Prestige PRLP7200
890	**Trane's blues** (i.e. **Vierd blues**)	(25)	Prestige PRLP7166
891	**Something I dreamed last night** -1	(25)	Prestige PRLP7200
892	**It could happen to you**	(25)	Prestige PRLP7129
893	**Woody'n you**	(25)	—
894	**Ahmad's blues** -2	(25)	Prestige PRLP7166
895	**The surrey with the fringe on top**	(25)	Prestige PRLP7200
896	**It never entered my head** Pts. 1 and 2	(25)	Prestige 45-165, PRLP7166
897	**When I fall in love Pts. 1 and 2** -1	(25)	Prestige 45-195, PRLP7200
898	**Salt peanuts**	(25)	—
899	**Four**	(25)	Prestige PRLP7166
900	**The theme I**	(25)	—
901	**The theme II**	(25)	—

June 5
New York City

CO56090	**Dear old Stockholm**	(30)	Columbia CL949
CO56091	**Bye bye blackbird**	(30)	—
CO56092	**Tadd's delight** (i.e. **Webb's (Sid's) delight**)	(30)	

September 10
New York City

CO56584	**All of you**	(30)	Columbia B9491, CL949
CO56585	**Sweet Sue** -3	(31, 31a)	Columbia CL919*
CO56586	**Round midnight**	(30,31)	Columbia B9491, CL949

1-Coltrane out, except for last chord of 896
2-Garland, Chambers and Jones only
3-Teo Macero (arr); end of last chorus faded on original issues

October 20 New York City	BRASS ENSEMBLE OF THE JAZZ AND CLASSICAL MUSIC SOCIETY Miles Davis (tp-1,flh-2); Bernie Glow, Art Stratter, Melvin Broiles, Carmine Fornarotto, Joe Wilder, John Ware (tp); J.J. Johnson (tb,arr-3); Urbie Green, John Clark (tb); Jim Buffington, Ray Alonge, Joe Singer, Art Sussman (fr-h); Ron Ricketts, John Swallow (bar-h); Bill Barber (tu); Milt Hinton (b); Osie Johnson (d); Dick Horowitz (tymp,perc); John Lewis (arr-4); Gunther Schuller (cond)	
	Three little feelings -1,2,4	Columbia CL941
October 23 New York City	**Poem for brass** -2,3	—
	Note: Davis, Hinton and O. Johnson out on **Pharoah** from this session	

October 26 Hackensack,N.J.	MILES DAVIS QUINTET As for October 18, 1955	
995	**If I were a bell Pts. 1 and 2**	(25) Prestige 45-123, PRLP7129
996	**Well you needn't**	(25) Prestige PRLP7200
997	**Round midnight**	(25) Prestige PRLP7150
998	**Half Nelson**	(25) Prestige PRLP7166
999	**You're my everything**	(25) Prestige PRLP7129
1000	**I could write a book**	(25) —
1001	**Oleo**	(25) —
1002	**Airegin**	(25) Prestige PRLP7094
1003	**Tune up**	(25) —
1004	**When lights are low**	(25) —
1005	**Blues by five**	(25) —
1006	**My funny Valentine** -1	(25) —
	1-Coltrane out	

November 19 Concert, Zurich	MILES DAVIS Miles Davis (tp); Rene Urtreger (p); Pierre Michelot (b); Christian Garros (d)	
	unknown titles	Private recording
November Broadcast, Freiburg	**Tune up**	(35) Unique Jazz UJ14
	What's new	(35) —
Same broadcast	Miles Davis (tp); Lester Young (ts); Milt Jackson (vib); John Lewis (p); Percy Heath (b); Connie Kay (d); unknown big band personnel; Kurt Edelhagen (cond)	
	Lester leaps in	(35) Unique Jazz UJ14

1957: May 6 New York City	MILES DAVIS WITH ORCHESTRA UNDER THE DIRECTION OF GIL EVANS Miles Davis (flh); Bernie Glow, Ernie Royal, Louis Mucci, Taft Jordan, John Carisi (tp); Frank Rehak, Jimmy Cleveland, Joe Bennett (tb); Tom Mitchell (btb); Willie Ruff, Tony Miranda (fr-h); Bill Barber (tu); Lee Konitz (as); Romeo Penque, Sid Cooper (woodwinds); Danny Bank (bcl); Paul Chambers (b); Art Taylor (d); Gil Evans (arr,cond)	
CO57917	**The maids of Cadiz**	(36) Columbia B10412, CL1041
CO57918	**The Duke**	(36) Columbia B10413, CL1041
May 10 New York City		
CO57933	**My ship**	(36) Columbia B10411, CL1041

CO57934	**Miles ahead**	(31,36) Columbia B10413, CL1041

May 23
New York City

CO58017	**New rhumba**	(36) Columbia B10411, CL1041
CO58018	**Blues for Pablo**	(36) Columbia B10412, CL1041
CO58019	**Springsville** -1	(36) Columbia B10413, CL1041

May 27
New York City

CO58171	**I don't wanna be kissed**	(36) Columbia B10412, CL1041
CO58172	**The meaning of the blues**	(36) Columbia B10413, CL1041
CO58173	**Lament**	(36) Columbia B10411, CL1041

1-unknown p heard for a few bars
Note: Jim Buffington (fr-h); Eddie Caine (woodwinds) replace Miranda and Cooper for one session each, but it is not known which one(s)

July 13
Broadcast,
Café Bohemia,
New York City

MILES DAVIS QUINTET
Miles Davis (tp); Sonny Rollins (ts); Red Garland (p); Paul Chambers (b); Art Taylor (d)

Four (Four squared) (Roy's romp)	(37) Ozone 18,Chakra CH100MD
Bye bye blackbird	(37) Ozone 18*,Chakra CH100MD*
It never entered my mind -1	(37) — *
Walkin' (Roy's nappin' now)	(37) — *

December 4
Paris

Miles Davis (tp); Barney Wilen (ts-1); Rene Urtreger (p-2); Pierre Michelot (b); Kenny Clarke (d)

Generique -1,2	(38) Fontana(F)460.603ME, 660.213MR
L'assassinat de Carala -2	(38) —
Sur l'autoroute -1	(38) Fontana(F)460.603ME, 660.213MR
Julien dans l'ascenseur -2	(38) —
Florence sur les Champs-Elysées -1,2	(38) Fontana(F)460.603ME, 660.213MR
Diner au motel	(38) —
Evasion de Julien -3	(38) Fontana(F)460.603ME, 660.213MR
Visite du vigile -4	(38) —
Au bar du petit Bac -1,2	(38) Fontana(F)460.603ME, 660.213MR
Chez le photographe du motel -2	(38) —
Blue 'n' boogie -1	unissued (see note)

3-Michelot only
4-Michelot and Clarke only
Note: The riffs from **Blue 'n' boogie** (actually borrowed from **Disorder at the border**) used on the 'Ascenseur pour l'echafaud' soundtrack sound like part of the same performance as **Diner au motel**

1958:
March 9
Hackensack,N.J.

JULIAN 'CANNONBALL' ADDERLEY
Miles Davis (tp); Cannonball Adderley (as); Hank Jones (p); Sam Jones (b); Art Blakey (d)

Autumn leaves Pts. 1 and 2	(39) Blue Note 45-1737,	
	BLP1595,BST81595	
Love for sale	(39) —	—
Somethin' else Pts. 1 and 2	(39) Blue Note 45-1738;	
	BLP1595,BST81595	
One for Daddy-O Pts. 1 and 2	(39) Blue Note 45-1739,	
	BLP1595,BST81595	

Note: Davis out on **Dancing in the dark** from this session

April 2
New York City

MILES DAVIS

Miles Davis (tp-1,flh-2); Cannonball Adderley (as); John Coltrane (ts); Red Garland (p); Paul Chambers (b); Philly Joe Jones (d)

CO60199	**Two bass hit -1**	(40) Columbia CL1193
CO60200	**Billy boy -3**	(40) —
CO60201	**Straight no chaser -1**	(40) —
CO60202	**Milestones (Miles) -2**	(40) Columbia B11931,
		CL1193

April 3
New York City

CO60203	**Dr.Jekyll (i.e. Dr.Jackle) -1**	(40) Columbia B11931,
		CL1193
CO60204	**Sid's ahead (i.e. Weirdo) -1,4**	(40) —

3-Garland, Chambers and Jones only; has been reissued as by
RED GARLAND
4-Garland out; Davis also plays p

prob. May 17
Broadcast,
Café Bohemia,
New York City

Bill Evans (p) replaces Garland		
Bye bye blackbird -1,5	(37) Chakra CH100MD	
Walkin' (Rollin' and blowin') -1,5	(37)	—
Four (Four plus one more) -1,5	(37)	—

May 26
New York City

Jimmy Cobb (d) replaces Jones		
CO61165	**One Green Dolphin Street -1**	(31,32) Columbia CL1268
CO61166	**Fran-dance -1**	(32)
CO61167	**Stella by starlight -1,5**	(31,32)
	Love for sale -1	(31a,32,33) Columbia
		PG33402

5-Adderley out
Note: This version of **On Green Dolphin Street** not on 4-33059
(see April 1961)

June 25
New York City

MICHEL LEGRAND AND HIS ORCHESTRA

Miles Davis (tp); Phil Woods (as); John Coltrane (ts); Jerome Richardson (bars,cl); Herbie Mann (fl); Eddie Costa (vib); Bill Evans (p); Paul Chambers (b); Kenny Dennis (d); Betty Glamann (harp); Michel Legrand (arr,cond)

CO61067	**Wild man blues**	Columbia CL1250,
		CS8079
CO61068	**Round midnight**	– —
CO61069	**Jitterbug waltz**	– —
CO61070	**Django -1**	– —

1-Woods, Coltrane and Richardson out
Note: An earlier Legrand album (CL1139, Paris 1957), often alleged to feature Davis, in fact has Miles-ish trumpet solos played by Fernand Verstraete

July 3
Freebody Park,
Newport,R.I.

MILES DAVIS
As for May 26

285

CO81844	**Ah-leu-cha** -1	(41)	Columbia CL2178, CS8978
CO81845	**Straight no chaser** -1	(41)	—
CO81846	**Fran-dance** -1	(31,41)	—
CO81847	**Two bass hit** -1	(41)	—
	Bye bye blackbird -1	unissued	
	The theme -1		—

July 22
New York City

MILES DAVIS WITH ORCHESTRA UNDER THE DIRECTION OF GIL EVANS
Miles Davis (tp-1,flh-2); Bernie Glow, Ernie Royal, Louis Mucci, Johnny Coles (tp); Frank Rehak, Jimmy Cleveland, Joe Bennett (tb); Dick Hixon (btb); Willie Ruff, Julius Watkins, Gunther Schuller (fr-h); Bill Barber (tu); Cannonball Adderley (as); Phil Bodner, Romeo Penque (woodwinds); Danny Bank (bcl); Paul Chambers (b); Philly Joe Jones (d); Gil Evans (arr,cond)

CO61300	**My man's gone now** -2	(42)	Columbia B12741, CL1274,CS8085
CO61301	**Gone, gone, gone** -2	(42)	Columbia CL1274,CS8085
CO61302	**Gone** -2	(42)	Columbia B12741, CL1274,CS8055

Note: Jimmy Cobb has claimed that **CO61301**, which is certainly spliced from more than one take, includes part of a version from one of the later sessions on which he is present

July 29
New York City

Jimmy Cobb (d) replaces Jones

CO61359	**Here comes de honeyman** -1	(42)	Columbia CL1274, CS8085
CO61360	**Bess, you is my woman now** -2	(42) –	—
CO61361	**It ain't necessarily so** -2	(42)	Columbia JJ1,JS1, CL1274,CS8085
CO61362	**Fisherman, strawberry and devil crab** -2	(42) –	—
CO67547	**It ain't necessarily so** -2 (edited from **CO61361**)		Columbia 3-42057**, 4-42057**,3-42069**, 4-42069**

August 4
New York City

As for July 29 except Jerome Richardson (woodwinds) replaces Bodner

CO61366	**Prayer** -2	(42)	Columbia CL1274, CS8085
CO61367	**Bess, oh where's my Bess** -2	(42) –	—
CO61368	**Buzzard song** -2	(42) –	—

August 18
New York City

CO61421	**Summertime** -1	(42)	Columbia B12471, CL1274,CS8085
CO61422	**There's a boat that's leaving soon** -2	(42) –	—
CO61423	**I loves you Porgy** -1	(42)	Columbia 3-42069*, 4-42069*,CL1274, CS8085

September 9
Plaza Hotel,
New York City

MILES DAVIS
As for May 26

If I were a bell -1,3	(43)	Columbia PC32470
Oleo -1	(43)	—
My funny valentine -1,4	(43)	—

286

	Straight no chaser (Jazz at the Plaza) -1	(43)	—
	3-Adderley out		
	4-Adderley and Coltrane out		

c. Summer
Broadcast,
unknown location

Walkin' -1	Air-shot
All of you -1,3	—
Sid's ahead -1	—
Round midnight -1	—
3-Adderley out	

1959:
January
Broadcast,
Jazz Unlimited,
Washington
c. early 1959
Broadcast,
Birdland,
New York City
March 2
New York City

Sid's ahead -1	Air-shot	
Bye bye blackbird -1	— *	
Walkin' -1,3	Air-shot*	

CO62290	**Freddie freeloader** -1,3	(44) Columbia CL1355, CS8163
CO62291	**So what** -1	(44) –	—
CO62292	**Blue in green** -1,4	(44) –	—
	3-Wynton Kelly (p) replaces Evans		
	4-Adderley out		

April 2
TV recording,
New York City

MILES DAVIS QUINTET
Miles Davis (tp); John Coltrane (ts); Wynton Kelly (p); Paul Chambers (b); Jimmy Cobb (d) WITH GIL EVANS AND HIS ORCHESTRA: Ernie Royal, Louis Mucci, Clyde Reasinger, Johnny Coles, Emmett Berry (tp); Frank Rehak, Jimmy Cleveland, Bill Elton (tb); Rod Levitt (btb); Julius Watkins, Bob Northern (fr-h); Bill Barber (tu); Romeo Penque, Eddie Caine (woodwinds); Danny Bank (bcl); unknown harp; Gil Evans (arr,cond)

So what -1	(23) Ozone 18
The Duke -2	(23) —
Blues for Pablo -2	(23) —
New rhumba -2	(23) —
1-Quintet plus 3 tb only	
2-Coltrane plays as; Kelly out	

April 22
New York City

MILES DAVIS
As for May 26, 1958

CO62293	**Flamenco sketches** -1	(44) Columbia CL1355, CS8163
CO62294	**All blues** -1	(44) – —
CO67548	**All blues** -1	Columbia 3-42057**, 4-42057**

Note: On original European issues, **CO62293** and **CO62294** listed in reverse

November 15
New York City

MILES DAVIS WITH ORCHESTRA ARRANGED AND CONDUCTED BY GIL EVANS
Personnel similar to next

Concierto de Aranjuez	unissued

November 20

Miles Davis (tp-1,flh-2); Bernie Glow, Ernie Royal, Louis

New York City	Mucci, Taft Jordan (tp); Frank Rehak, Dick Hixon (tb); John Barrows, Jim Buffington, Earl Chapin (fr-h); Jay McAllister (tu); Albert Block, Eddie Caine, Harold Feldman (woodwinds); Danny Bank (bcl); Paul Chambers (b); Jimmy Cobb (d); Elvin Jones (perc); Janet Putnam (harp); Gil Evans (arr,cond)	
CO63791	**Concierto de Aranjuez** -1,2	(45) Columbia CL1480, CS8271

1960:
March 10
New York City   Johnny Coles (tp); Joe Singer, Tony Miranda (fr-h); Bill Barber (tu); Romeo Penque (woodwinds); Jack Knitzer (bassoon) replace Mucci, Jordan, Barrows, Chapin, McAllister and Caine

CO64558	**The pan piper** -1	(45) Columbia CL1480, CS8271

March 11
New York City   Louis Mucci (tp) added

CO64560	**Solea** -1	(45) Columbia 4-33037*, CL1480,CS8271
CO64561	**Will o' the wisp** -1	(45) Columbia 4-33037, CL1480, CS8271
CO64562	**Saeta** -1	(45) Columbia CL1480, CS8271
	Song of our country -1	(46) Columbia KC2 36472

March 21
Broadcast,
Olympia,
Paris

MILES DAVIS QUINTET
As for April 2, 1959

All of you	Air-shot*
Round midnight	—
Oleo	—
The theme	—

March 22
Broadcast,
Koncerthuset,
Stockholm

So what	Air-shot*
Walkin'	Bird Notes unnumbered*
So what	Air-shot
Fran-dance	—
All blues (Somethin' else)	Bird Notes unnumbered**

March 24
Broadcast,
Tivoli,
Kþbenhavn

So what	Air-shot
On Green Dolphin Street	—
All blues	—*

April 9
Broadcast,
Kurhaus,
Scheveningen

On Green Dolphin Street	(47) Unique Jazz UJ19	
So what	(47)	—
Round midnight	(47)	—
Walkin'	(47)	—
The theme	(47)	—

October 13
Broadcast,
Koncerthuset,
Stockholm   Sonny Stitt (ts-1,as) replaces Coltrane

Walkin' -1	Bird Notes unnumbered*

1961:
March 7
New York City   Hank Mobley (ts) replaces Stitt

CO66235	**Drad-dog**	(30) Columbia S7 31379*, GB9*,GS9*, CL1656**,CS8456**
CO66236	**Pfrancing**	(30) Columbia CL1656, CS8456
CO69815/6	**Pfrancing Pts. 1 and 2**	Columbia S7 31378**

288

March 20
New York City

CO66500	**Some day my prince will come** -1	(30) Columbia S7 31377*, CL1656,CS8456
CO66501	**Old folks**	(30) Columbia S7 31377*, CL1656, CS8456

March 21
New York City

CO66505	**Teo** -1,2	(30) Columbia CL1656, CS8456
CO66506	**I thought about you**	(30) Columbia S7 31379*, CL1656,CS8456
	Blues no. 2 -3	(33) Columbia KC2 36278
CO69817/8	**Teo Pts. 1 and 2** -1,2	Columbia S7 31380**

1-John Coltrane (ts) added
2-Mobley out
3-Philly Joe Jones (d) replaces Cobb

April 21,22
The Black Hawk,
San Francisco

CO67458	**Walkin'**	(48) Columbia C2L20, C2S820,CL1669, CS8469
CO67459	**Bye bye blackbird**	(48) Columbia S7 31381*, C2L20,C2S820, CL1669,CS8469
CO67460	**All of you** -1	(48) Columbia C2L20**, C2S820**,CL1669**, CS8469**
CO67461	**No blues** (i.e. **Pfrancing**)	(48) Columbia C2L20**, C2S820**,CL1669**, CS8469
CO67462	**Bye bye** (i.e. **The theme**)	(48) Columbia C2L20, C2S820,CL1669, CS8469
CO67463	**Love, I've found you** -2	(48) Columbia C2L20, C2S820,CL1669, CS8469
GO67464	**Well you needn't**	(48) Columbia C2L20**, C2S820**,CL1670**, CS8470**
CO67465	**Fran-dance**	(48) Columbia C2L20, C2S820,CL1670, CS8470
CO67466	**So what**	(48) Columbia C2L20, C2S820,CL1670, CS8470
CO67467	**Oleo**	(48) Columbia C2L20, C2S820, CL1670, CS8470
CO67468	**If I were a bell** -1	(48) Columbia S7 31381*, C2L20**,C2S820**, CL1670**,CS8470**
CO67469	**Neo** (i.e. **Teo**)	(48) Columbia C2L20, C2S820,CL1670, CS8470
CO69451	**On Green Dolphin Street**	(31a) Columbia 7-8565**, 4-33059*,CL1765**, CS8565**

	Round midnight	(46)	CBS-Sony (J) 36AP1409-10

1-Mobley not heard, as a result of editing of these tracks
2-Kelly only
Note: **CO67466** ends with a few bars of an alternative take of **No blues**

May 19
Carnegie Hall,
New York City

MILES DAVIS QUINTET
Miles Davis (tp); Hank Mobley (ts-1); Wynton Kelly (p-2); Paul Chambers (b); Jimmy Cobb (d) WITH GIL EVANS AND HIS ORCHESTRA: Bernie Glow, Ernie Royal, Louis Mucci, Johnny Coles (tp); Frank Rehak, Dick Hixon, Jimmy Knepper (tb); Julius Watkins, Paul Ingraham, Bob Swisshelm (fr-h); Bill Barber (tu); Jerome Richardson, Romeo Penque, Eddie Caine, Bob Tricario, Danny Bank (reeds,woodwinds); Bobby Rosengarden (perc); Janet Putnam (harp); Gil Evans (arr,cond)

CO69842	**So what** -1,2	(49) Columbia CL1812, CS8612
CO69843	**Spring is here** -2	(49) – —
CO69844	**No blues** -1,2,3	(49) – —
CO69845	**Oleo** -1,2,3	(49) Columbia 7-8612*, CL1812*,CS8612*
CO69846	**Some day my prince will come** -2,3	(49) Columbia CL1812, CS8612
CO69847	**The meaning of the blues/Lament/ New rhumba**	(49) Columbia 7-8612, CL1812,CS8612
CO76258	**New rhumba** (excerpt from above)	Columbia 3-42583,4-42583
	I thought about you -1,2,3	unissued
	Concierto de Aranjuez	—
	Saeta	—
	Solea	—

3-orchestra out
Note: The **New rhumba** portion of **CO69847** has been shown as re-recorded on July 27, 1962, but the album was in fact shipped before this date

c. December
New York City

No personnel details
unknown titles   Columbia unissued

1962:
July 27
New York City

MILES DAVIS WITH ORCHESTRA ARRANGED AND CONDUCTED BY GIL EVANS
Miles Davis (tp-1,flh-2); unknown big band personnel including Steve Lacy (ss); Gil Evans (arr,cond)

CO75683	**Corcovado** -1,2	(50) Columbia 4-33059, CL2106,CS8906
CO76257	**Slow samba (Aos pes da cruz)** -2	(50) Columbia 3-42583*, 4-42583*,CL2106, CS8906

Note: **CO75683** (lasting 2′41″) consists of 1′18″ of **Corcovado** spliced to 1′23″ of an alternative take of **Slow samba**, starting at the equivalent of 44″ from the beginning of **CO76257**

August 13
New York City

Similar personnel

CO75678	**Song no.1** -1	(50) Columbia CL2106, CS8906
CO75837	**Wait till you see her** -1	(50) – —

August 21
New York City

MILES DAVIS
Miles Davis (tp); Frank Rehak (tb); Wayne Shorter (ts); Paul Chambers (b); Jimmy Cobb (d); Willie Bobo Correa (cga); Bob Dorough (vcl-1,arr)

| CO75734 | Blue Xmas -1 | (31a) Columbia CL1893, CS8693 |
| CO75735 | Nothing like you -1 | (51) Columbia CL2732, CS9532 |

August 23
New York City

| CO76323 | Devil may care | (31,31a) Columbia CL1970, CS8770 |
| CO78873 | Devil may care | Columbia 4-42853** |

November 6
New York City

MILES DAVIS WITH ORCHESTRA ARRANGED AND CONDUCTED BY GIL EVANS
Similar to July 27 including Ernie Royal (tp); Frank Rehak (tb); John Barrows, Jim Buffington (fr-h); Jimmy Cobb (d); Elvin Jones (perc); Janet Putnam (harp); Gil Evans (arr,cond)

| CO77119 | Once upon a summertime -1 | (50) Columbia CL2106, CS8906 |
| CO77120 | Song No.2 -1 | (50) –   — |

1963:
April 16
Los Angeles

MILES DAVIS
Miles Davis (tp); Victor Feldman (p); Ron Carter (b); Frank Butler (d)

HCO71337	I fall in love too easily	(52) Columbia CL2051, CS8851
HCO71338	Baby, won't you please come home	(52) – —
HCO71340	Basin Street blues	(52) – —

April 17
Los Angeles

George Coleman (ts) added

| | So near, so far | (46) Columbia KC2 36472 |
| HCO71342 | Summer night-1 | (50) Columbia CL2106, CS8906 |

Same sessions

| | Seven steps to heaven | unissued |

May 14
New York City

As last except Herbie Hancock (p); Tony Williams (d) replace Feldman and Butler

CO78342	Seven steps to heaven	(52) Columbia CL2051, CS8851
CO78343	So near, so far	(52) – —
CO78344	Joshua	(52) – —
CO78872	Seven steps to heaven	Columbia 4-42853**

June
Jazz Villa,
St. Louis

	All blues	(53) VGM 0003
	I thought about you-1	(53) —
	Seven steps to heaven	(53) —

July 26,27,29
Pinede Gould,
Juan-les-Pins

As last; Andre Francis (mc)

CO81817	Autumn leaves	(54) Columbia CL2183, CS8983
CO81818	Milestones	(54) – —
CO81819	Joshua	(54) – —
CO81820	All of you	(54) – —
CO81821	Walkin'	(54) – —
	So what	unissued
	If I were a bell	—
	Stella by starlight	—
	My funny valentine	—

1-Coleman out

c. Autumn Los Angeles	MILES DAVIS WITH GIL EVANS AND HIS ORCHESTRA		

Miles Davis (tp); Dick Leith (btb); Richard Perissi, Bill
Hinshaw, Art Maebe (fr-h); Paul Horn, Buddy Collette (fl);
Gene Cipriano (oboe); Fred Dutton (bassoon); Herbie
Hancock (p); Ron Carter (b); Tony Williams (d); Gil Evans
(arr,cond)
unknown titles (prob.incl. **General
assembly** and **Hotel me**)   Columbia unissued

1964:
February 12
Philharmonic Hall, MILES DAVIS
New York City As for May 14, 1963; Mort Fega (mc)

CO81836	So what	(55)	Columbia CL2453, CS9253
CO81838	Walkin'	(55) –	—
CO81839	All of you	(56)	Columbia CL2306, CS9106
CO81840	Stella by starlight	(56) –	—
CO81841	All blues	(56) –	—
CO81842	My funny Valentine	(56) –	—
CO81843	I thought about you	(56) –	—
CO88696	Four	(55)	Columbia CL2453, CS9253
CO88697	Seven steps to heaven	(55) –	—
CO88698	Joshua/Go-go (i.e. **The theme**)	(55) –	—
CO88699	There is no greater love/Go-go	(55) –	—

July 14
Kohseinenkin, Sam Rivers (ts) replaces Coleman; Teruo Isono (mc)
Tokyo

	If I were a bell	(57)	CBS-Sony(J) SONX60064-R
	My funny Valentine	(57) —	
	So what	(57) —	
	Walkin'	(57) —	
	All of you	(57) —	
	The theme	(57) —	
	Stella by starlight	unissued	

c. September
TV recording, Wayne Shorter(ts) replaces Rivers
Los Angeles **No blues**   (34) Teppa 76*
September 25
Philharmonie, Milestones   (58) CBS(G) S62976
Berlin

	Autumn leaves	(58)	—
	So what	(58)	—
	Walkin'	(58)	—
	The theme	(58)	—

1965:
c. January
The Hungry i,
San Francisco **unknown titles**   Columbia unissued
January 20
Los Angeles

HCO72230	E.S.P.	(59)	Columbia CL2350, CS9150
HCO72231	R.J.	(59) –	—

January 21
Los Angeles

HCO72232	Eighty-one	(59) –	—
HCO72233	Little one	(59) –	—

292

January 22
Los Angeles

HCO72234	**Iris**	(59) –	—
HCO72235	**Agitation**	(59) –	—
HCO72236	**untitled -1**	unissued	
HCO72237	**Mood**	(59) —	
	1-Williams only		

December 22
Plugged Nickel,
Chicago

If I were a bell	Columbia unissued
Stella by starlight	—
Walkin'	—
I fall in love too easily/The theme	—
My funny Valentine	—
Four	—
When I fall in love	—
Agitation	—
Round midnight	(60) CBS-Sony(J) 25AP291
Milestones/The theme	unissued
All of you	—
Oleo	—
I fall in love too easily	—
No blues	—
I thought about you/The theme	—

December 23
Plugged Nickel,
Chicago

If I were a bell	—
Stella by starlight	(60) CBS-Sony(J) 25AP291
Walkin'	(61) CBS-Sony(J) 25AP1
I fall in love too easily/The theme	unissued
All of you	—
Agitation	(61) CBS-Sony(J) 25AP1
My funny Valentine	unissued
On Green Dolphin Street	(61) CBS-Sony(J) 25AP1
So what/The theme	(61) — *
When I fall in love	unissued
Milestones	—
Autumn leaves	—
I fall in love too easily	—
No blues/The theme	—
Stella by starlight	—
All blues	(60) CBS-Sony(J) 25AP291
Yesterdays -1	(60) — **
The theme	(60) — **
1-Shorter not heard, as a result of editing	

1966:
October 24
New York City

CO91173	**Circle**	(62) Columbia CL2601, CS9401	
CO91174	**Orbits**	(62) –	—
CO91175	**Dolores**	(62) –	—
CO91176	**Freedom jazz dance**	(62) –	—

October 25
New York City

CO91177	**Gingerbread boy**	(62) –	—
CO91178	**Footprints**	(62) –	—

1967:
May 9 | Buster Williams (b) replaces Carter
Hollywood | **Limbo** | (46) Columbia KC2 36472

May 16		
New York City	Ron Carter (b) replaces Williams	
CO93122	**Limbo**	(51) Columbia CL2732, CS9532
CO93123	**Vonetta**	(51) – —
May 17		
New York City		
CO92211	**Masqualero**	(51) – —
CO92212	**The sorcerer**	(51) – —
May 24		
New York City		
CO92218	**Prince of darkness**	(51) – —
CO92219	**Pee wee** -1	(51) – —
June 7		
New York City		
CO92239	**Nefertiti**	(63) Columbia CS9594
June 22		
New York City		
CO92250	**Madness**	(63) —
June 23		
New York City		
CO92249	**Hand jive**	(63) —
June		
New York City	**Water babies**	(64) Columbia PC34396, A2S323
	Capricorn	(64) —
July		
New York City	**Sweet Pea**	(64) —
July 19		
New York City		
CO92289	**Fall**	(63) Columbia CS9594
CO92290	**Pinocchio**	(63) —
CO92291	**Riot**	(63) —
December 4		
New York City	**Circle in the round** -2,3	(33) Columbia KC2 36278
December 28		
New York City	**Water on the pond** -2	(46) Columbia KC2 36472
	1-Davis out	
	2-Joe Beck (g) added	
	3-Davis also plays chimes, bells; Hancock plays celeste	

1968:

January 11		
New York City		
	Fun	(46) Columbia KC2 36472
January 16		
New York City	George Benson (g-1) added	
	Teo's bag	(33) Columbia KC2 36278
	Paraphenalia -1	(65) Columbia CS9628
February 13		
New York City	**Side car I**	(33) Columbia KC2 36278
	Side car II -1	(33) —
February 15		
New York City	**Sanctuary** -1	(33) —
March	MILES DAVIS WITH GIL EVANS AND HIS ORCHESTRA	
New York City	Miles Davis (tp,el-tp); unknown band personnel; Gil Evans arr,cond)	
	unknown titles	Columbia unissued

May 15	MILES DAVIS	
New York City	Miles Davis (tp); Wayne Shorter (ts); Herbie Hancock (p-1, el-p-2); Ron Carter (b-1,el-b-2); Tony Williams (d)	
	Country son -1	(65) Columbia CS9628
May 16		
New York City	**Black comedy** -1	(65) —
May 17		
New York City	**Stuff** -2	(65) —
June 19		
New York City	**Petits machins** -2	(66) Columbia CS9750
June 20		
New York City	**Tout de suite** -2	(66) —
June 21		
New York City	**Filles de Kilimanjaro** -2	(66) —
CO100069	**Filles de Kilimanjaro Pts. 1 and 2** -2	Columbia 4-44652*
September 24	Chick Corea (el-p); Dave Holland (b) replace Hancock and	
New York City	Carter	
	Frelon brun	(66) Columbia CS9750
	Mademoiselle Mabry	(66) —
November	As last plus Herbie Hancock (el-p); Ron Carter (el-b)	
New York City	**Two faced**	(64) Columbia PC34396
	Dual Mr. Tillman Anthony	(64) — **
November 25	As last except Joe Zawinul (p) replaces Carter	
New York City	**Splash**	(33) Columbia KC2 36278
November 27	As last except Jack DeJohnette (d) replaces Williams	
New York City	**Directions I**	(46) Columbia KC2 36472
	Directions II	(46) Columbia KC2 36472
	Ascent	(46) Columbia KC2 36472

1969:

February 18	As for November 25 except Shorter plays ss; Zawinul el-p,org;	
New York City	John McLaughlin (g) added	
	Shhh/Peaceful	(67) Columbia CS9875
	In a silent way/It's about that time (67)	—
CO103511	**In a silent way/It's about that time Pts. 1 and 2**	Columbia AE13*
August 19	Miles Davis (tp); Wayne Shorter (ss); Chick Corea (el-p); Dave	
New York City	Holland (b); Jack DeJohnette (d); Jumma Santos, Charles Don Alias (perc)	
	Sanctuary	(68) Columbia GP26
	As last plus Bennie Maupin (bcl); Joe Zawinul (el-p); John McLaughlin (g); Harvey Brooks (el-b); Lenny White (d)	
	Bitches brew	(68) Columbia GP26
August 20	As last plus Larry Young (el-p)	
New York City	**Spanish key**	(68) Columbia GP26, G30121*
CO107194	**Spanish key**	Columbia 4-45171*
	As last except Zawinul out	
	Miles runs the voodoo down	(68) Columbia GP26
CO107204	**Miles runs the voodoo down**	Columbia 4-45171*
August 21	As last except Davis and Shorter out	
New York City	**John McLaughlin**	(68) Columbia GP26
	As for CO107194	
	Pharaoh's dance	(68) —
	Note: Billy Cobham (d) has claimed to be present on one or more of the above three sessions, and the attribution of the keyboard players to each of the last five items may well be unreliable	

November 19	Miles Davis (tp); Steve Grossman (ss); Bennie Maupin (bcl);	
New York City	Chick Corea, Herbie Hancock (el-p), John McLaughlin (g);	
	Khalil Balakrishna, Bihari Sharma (el-sitar,tambura,etc.); Ron	
	Carter (b); Harvey Brooks (el-b); Billy Cobham (d); Airto	
	Moreira (perc)	
	Great expectations/Mulher laranja	
	(i.e. **Orange lady**)	(69) Columbia PG32866
CO103282	**Great expectations**	Columbia 4-45090*,
		4-46074*

November 28	As last except Joe Zawinul, Larry Young (el-p) replace Corea;	
New York City	Jack DeJohnette (d) added	
CO103290	**The little blue frog**	Columbia 4-45090

1970:

January 27	As last except Wayne Shorter (ss); Chick Corea (el-p); Dave	
New York City	Holland (b) replace Grossman, Hancock, Young and Carter;	
	McLaughlin and Sharma out	
	Lonely fire	(69) Columbia PG32866
	Guinnevere	(33) Columbia KC2 36278
February 6	As last except John McLaughlin (g) replaces Maupin; Holland	
New York City	plays el-b replacing Brooks	
	Gemini/Double image	(70) Columbia KC30954
	Note: Shorter and Balakrishna not heard on issued excerpt	
	(though listed)	

February 17	Miles Davis (tp); Wayne Shorter (ss); Bennie Maupin (bcl);	
New York City	John McLaughlin (g); Dave Holland (el-b), Billy Cobham (d)	
	Duran	(46) Columbia KC2 36472

February18	As last except Sonny Sharrock (g); Jack DeJohnette (d) replace	
New York City	Shorter and Cobham	
	Yesternow 'Pt.3'	(71) Columbia KC30455

February 27	As last except Steve Grossman (ss) replaces Maupin; Sharrock	
New York City	out	
	Willie Nelson	(46) Columbia KC2 36472

March 30		
New York City	**Go ahead John**	(69) Columbia PG32866
CO103283	**Go ahead John**	Columbia 4-46074*

April 7	Miles Davis (tp); Steve Grossman (ss); Herbie Hancock (org);	
New York City	John McLaughlin (g); Mike Henderson (el-b); Billy Cobham (d)	
	Right off 'Pt.1'	(71) Columbia KC30455
	Right off 'Pt.3'	(71) —
	Right off 'Pt.4' -1	(71) —
	Yesternow 'Pt.1' -2	(71) —
CO109409	**Right off Pt.1** (excerpt from	
	'Pt.1' above)	Columbia 4-45350
CO109410	**Right off Pt.2** (excerpt from	
	'Pts.1 & 3' above)	—

Same period		
New York City	As last plus Keith Jarrett (keyb); Airto Moreira (perc)	
CO103883	**Honky tonk**	(74) Columbia KG33236
	1-Davis out	
	2-unknown second el-b (Dave Holland?) added on this segment	
	Note: The segments of **Right off** and **Yesternow**, delineating	
	them from the session below, obscure the fact that **Right off**	
	'Pts.4,1 & 3' are (in that order) probably from a single take	

Similar period	Miles Davis (tp) accompanied by pre-recorded backgrounds:
New York City	1-synth; 2-excerpt from **Shhh/Peaceful** rec. February 18, 1969;
	3-unknown brass, b, d; 4-Brock Peters (narr); Teo Macero (arr)

Right off 'Pt.2' -1	(71) Columbia KC30455,	
	Teo Macero 99045-1A	
Yesternow 'Pt.2' -2	(71)	—
Yesternow 'Pt.4' -3,4	(71)	—
Yesternow 'Pt.4' -3	Teo Macero 99045-1A	

Note: Davis's solo on these three segments is identical; the two segments on the Teo Macero LP are edited together as one piece titled **Jack Johnson**

April 10
Fillmore East,   Miles Davis (tp); Steve Grossman (ss); Chick Corea (el-p);
San Francisco   Dave Holland (el-b); Jack DeJohnette (d); Airto Moreira (perc)
Black beauty Pts.1,2,3 and 4   (72) CBS-Sony (J)
                                               SOPJ39-40

May 21   Miles Davis (tp); Keith Jarrett (el-p); John McLaughlin (el-g);
New York City   Airto Moreira (perc)
Konda   (46) Columbia KC2 36472

June 3   Miles Davis (tp); Steve Grossman (ss); Hermeto Pascoal (el-p-1,
New York City   vcl-2,whistling-3); Chick Corea, Keith Jarrett, Herbie Hancock
                  (keyb); Ron Carter (el-b); Jack DeJohnette (d); Airto Moreira
                  (perc)
Nem um talvez -2   (70) Columbia KC30954
Selim -2,4   (70)   —

June 7   As last plus John McLaughlin (g); Dave Holland (el-b) replaces
New York City   Carter
Little church -1,3   (70) Columbia KC30954
4-Moreira out
Note: **Nem um talvez** and **Selim** are alternative takes of the same piece

June 17
Fillmore East,
New York City   As for April 10 plus Keith Jarrett (org)
                  Wednesday Miles   (73) Columbia KG30038
June 18
Fillmore East,
New York City   **Thursday Miles**   (73)   —
June 19
Fillmore East,
New York City   **Friday Miles**   (73)   —
         CO109337 **Friday Miles**   Columbia 4-45327*
June 20
Fillmore East,
New York City   **Saturday Miles**   (73) Columbia KG30038
         CO109336 **Saturday Miles**   Columbia 4-45327*

August 29   Miles Davis (tp); Gary Bartz (ss-1,as-2,fl-3); Keith Jarrett, Chick
Isle of Wight   Corea (keyb); Dave Holland (el-b); Jack DeJohnette (d); Airto
                  Moreira (perc)
Call it anythin' -1   Columbia G3X30805**
December 18   John McLaughlin (g); Mike Henderson (el-b) replace Corea
The Cellar Door and Holland
Washington   **Sivad**   (70) Columbia KC30954
                  What I say -1,3   (70)   —
                  Funky tonk -1   (70)   —
                  Inamorata -2,4   (70)   —
4-Conrad Roberts (narr) added on issued version
Note: **Funky tonk** and **Inamorata** may in fact be Pts.1 and 2 of the same performance

1971:
November 26   Don Alias, James M'tume Foreman (perc) replace
Philharmonic Hall, McLaughlin and Moreira

| New York City | **Bwongo** -1 | Session Disc 123 |
| | **Ananka** -1,2 | — |

1972:
June 1
New York City
Miles Davis (tp); Dave Liebman (ss); Bennie Maupin (bcl); Herbie Hancock, Chick Corea, Harold Williams (keyb); John McLaughlin (g); Colin Walcott (sitar); Mike Henderson (el-b); Jack DeJohnette (d); Billy hart (d,perc); Don Alias, M'tume (perc); Badal Roy (tabla)

	On the corner/New York girl/		
	Thinkin' one thing and doin'		
	another/Vote for Miles	(75) Columbia KC31906
CO113952/3	**Vote for Miles Pts.1 and 2**	Columbia 4-45822*

June 6
New York City
Carlos Garnett (ss,ts) replaces Liebman

	Black satin	(75) Columbia KC31906
	One and one	(75) —
	Helen Butte	(75) —
	Mr. Freedom X	(75) —

June 12
New York City
Sonny Fortune (ss,fl) added; Lonnie Liston Smith (keyb); Al Foster (d) replace Hancock, Corea and DeJohnette; Williams plays keyb and sitar; McLaughlin, Walcott and Alias out

| | **Ife** | (69) Columbia PG32866 |

July 7
New York City
Personnel similar to last or next session

| CO112691/2 | **Molester Pts.1 and 2** | Columbia 4-45709 |

September 6(?)
New York City
Miles Davis (tp-1,org-2); Carlos Garnet (ss); Cedric Lawson (keyb); Reggie Lucas (g); Khalil Balakrishna (el-sitar); Mike Henderson (el-b); Al Foster (d); Mtume (perc); Badal Roy (tabla)

| CO112591 | **Rated X** -2,3 | (74) Columbia KG33236 |
| CO112994 | **Billy Preston** 1,3 | (74) — |

September 29
Philharmonic Hall,
New York City

	20.45 -1	(76) Columbia KG32092
	25.23 -1	(76) —
	18.12 -1	(76) —
	20.21 -1	(76) —

3-Garnett not heard on issued excerpts of these tracks

1973:
poss.January
New York City
Miles Davis (tp) accompanied by (prob.pre-recorded) unknown brass (poss.incl.Joe Newman (tp)); Wally Chambers (hca); Cornell Dupree (g); Mike Henderson (el-b); Al Foster, Bernard Purdie (d); Mtume (perc); Wade Marcus, Billy Jackson (arr)

| | **Red China blues** | (74) Columbia KG33236 |
| CO118934 | **Red China blues** | Columbia 3-10110* |

February 13
New York City
Prob. as for September 29, 1972 except Dave Liebman (ss) replaces Garnett

| | **unknown titles** | Columbia unissued |

September
New York City
Similar to next

| CO117260 | **Big fun** | Columbia 4-45946 |
| CO117261 | **Holly-wuud** | — |

Similar period

New York City
Miles Davis (tp-1,org-2); Dave Liebman (fl); John Stubblefield (ss); Reggie Lucas, Pete Cosey (g); Mike Henderson (el-b); Al Foster (d); Mtume (perc)

| CO117296 | **Calypso Frelimo** -1,2 | (74) Columbia KG33236 |

1974:

March 30
Carnegie Hall,
New York City

Liebman plays ts,ss; Azar Lawrence (ts) replaces Stubblefield; Dominique Gaumont (g) added

Dark Magus-Moja -1   (77) CBS-Sony (J)
          40AP741-742

Dark Magus-Wili -1,2   (77) —
Dark Magus-Tatu 1,2   (77) —
Dark Magus-Nne 1,2   (77) —

late May
New York City   Liebman plays fl; Lawrence out
      CO118537   **He loved him madly** 1,2   (74) Columbia KG33236

June 19
New York City   Sonny Fortune (fl) replaces Liebman
      Maiysha -1,2   (74) —
      CO121653   **Maiysha**   Columbia 3-10110*

June 20(?)
New York City   Gaumont out
      CO121652   **Mtume**-1,2   (74) Columbia KG33236
      Note: Fortune not heard on issued excerpt

1975:

February 1
Festival Hall
Osaka

As last except Fortune plays ss-3, as-4, fl-5; Cosey plays g. synth, perc

Prelude Pts.1 and 2 1,2,3,4   (78) CBS-Sony(J)
          SOPJ92-93

Maiysha 1,2,5   (78) —
   CO123133   **Maiysha** -1,2,3,5   Columbia AS214**
        Theme from Jack Jackson -1,2,4,5 (78) CBS-Sony(J)
          SOPJ92-93

   CO123144   **Theme from Jack Johnson** -1,2   Columbia AS214*
        Interlude -1,2,5   (78) CBS-Sony(J)
          SOPJ92-93

        Zimbabwe Pts.1 and 2 -1,2,3,4   (79) CBS-Sony(J)
          SOPZ96-97

        Gondwana Pts.1 and 2 -1,2,5   (79) —

Note: **Theme from Jack Johnson** and **Interlude** reversed on labels of all album issues, hence **CO123144** is actually an excerpt from **Interlude**; **CO123133** contains excerpts from both **Prelude Pt.2** and **Maiysha**

c. 1975
New York City

BETTY DAVIS
Fred Mills (keyb); Carlos Morales (g); Larry Jackson (el-b); Nicky Neal (d); unknown brass; Gil Evans (brass,arr,cond); Miles Davis (dir); Betty Davis (vcl)

You and I   Island ILPS9329
Note: Neither Evans nor M.Davis is implicated in other tracks on this album

1978:

c. February
New York City

MILES DAVIS
Miles Davis (org); Masabumi Kikuchi, George Pavlis (keyb); Larry Coryell (g); T.M. Stevens (el-b); Al Foster (d); unknown brass; Bobby Scott (brass arr)

unknown titles   Columbia unissued

1980:

c. May-July
New York City

Miles Davis (tp,el-p); Bill Evans (saxes,woodwinds); Robert Irving (keyb); Randy Hall (g,vcl); Felton Crews (el-b); Vince Wilburn (d); Sammy Figueroa (perc); unknown vcl group

Spider's web   Columbia unissued
Solar energy   –

	Space	–
	Burn	–
	I'm blue	–
	Mrs. Slurpey	–
	Thanksgiving	–
	1980s	–
	The man with the horn	(80) Columbia FC36790
	Shout	–

1981:

c. March   Miles Davis (tp), Bill Evans (ss), Barry Finnerty (g), Marcus
New York City   Miller (el-b). Al Foster (d), Sammy Figueroa (perc).

	Ursula	(80) Columbia FC36790
	Aida	—
	Back seat Bertha	—

Mike Stern (g) replaces Finnerty

| | Fat time | — |

Acknowledgments: As well as previous Davis discographers Jørgen Jepsen, Jan Lohmann and Michel Ruppli, I should like to thank Hugh Attwooll (CBS), Johs Bergh, Brian Davis, Mike Doyle, Charles Fox, Graham Griffiths (Mole Jazz), Ian Kendall, Michel Legrand, Alun Morgan and David Yates (RCA) for assistance at various stages in the compilation of this listing.   B.P.

300

Index to Discography

(1)   Savoy S5J5500
(2)   Spotlite SPJ123
(3)   Spotlite 101
(4)   Spotlite SPJ148
(5)   Savoy SJL2214
(6)   Spotlite 104
(7)   Spotlite 105
(8)   Spotlite 106
(9)   Spotlite SPJ141
(10) Prestige PR24009
(11) Cicala BLJ8003
(11a) ESP ESP-BIRD-2
(12) Savoy SJL1129
(13) ESP ESP-BIRD-1
(14) Meexa Discox 1776
(15) RCA (F) PM42408
(16) Capitol(E) CAPS1024
(17) Beppo BEP503
(18) Columbia JC34804
(19) Phontastic NOST7602
(20) Spotlite SPJ118
(21) IAJRC 20
(22) Cicala BLJ8023
(23) Beppo BEP502
(24) Verve(F) 2610.042
(25) Prestige P-012
(26) Beppo BEP501
(27) Stash ST113
(28) United Artists UAS9952
(29) Prestige PR24022
(30) CBS(Du) 88029
(31) Columbia PC32025
(31a) Columbia JP13811
(32) CBS-Sony(J) 20AP1401
(33) CBS(E)88471
(34) Teppa 76
(35) Unique Jazz UJ14
(36) Columbia PC8633
(37) Bopera 2-100
(38) Philips(E) 6444.507
(39) BN-LA169-G

(40) Columbia PC9428
(41) Columbia PC8978
(42) CBS (E) SBPG62108
(43) Columbia PC32470
(44) CBS (E) SBPG62066
(45) CBS (E) SBPG62327
(46) CBS (E) 88514
(47) Unique Jazz UJ19
(48) Columbia C2S820
(49) Columbia PC8612
(50) Columbia PC8906
(51) Columbia PC9532
(52) Columbia PC8851
(53) VGM 0003
(54) CBS (Du) EMB31103
(55) Columbia PC9253
(56) Columbia PC9106
(57) CBS-Sony(J) 25AP762
(58) CBS-Sony(J) 25AP763
(59) CBS-Sony(J) 25AP764
(60) CBS-Sony(J) 25AP291
(61) CBS-Sony(J) 25AP1
(62) Columbia PC9401
(63) Columbia PC9594
(64) Columbia C34396
(65) Columbia PC9628
(66) Columbia PC9750
(67) CBS(E) 63630
(68) CBS(E) 66236
(69) CBS-Sony(J) SOPW5-6
(70) Columbia CG30954
(71) Columbia PC30455
(72) CBS-Sony(J) SOPJ39-40
(73) ColumbiaCG30038
(74) CBS(Du) 88092
(75) Columbia C31906
(76) CBS-Sony(J) SOPJ37-38
(77) CBS-Sony(J) 40AP741-742
(78) CBS(Du) 88159
(79) CBS-Sony(J) SOPZ96-97
(80) CBS 84708

301

Index

Adam Lambert's Six Brown Cats, 10
Adderley, Julian 'Cannonball', 84, 87, 88, 90-2, 95-8, 106, 109, 110, 112, 124, 132, 158, 162, 222, 228, 232
Adderley, Nat, 84
Agharta, 227, 233, 234
'Agitation', 143
'Ah-Leu-Cha', 66
'Airegin', 57
Albany, Joe, 22
Ali, Muhammed, 180, 228
Alias, Don, 209
Allah, Bobby, 180
'All Blues', 107, 134, 138
'All Of You', 72, 136, 137, 143
'All The Things You Are', 42
A Love Supreme, 144
Alton, Illinois, 1, 102
Altshuler, Bob, 204
Ammons, Gene, 23
Amsterdam, 75
Anderson, Buddy, 10, 11
Andrews Sisters, 38
'Anthropology', 18, 22, 23
Antibes Festival, 136, 137
Archie Shepp in Europe, 152
Arkansas, 1
Armstrong, Louis, 3, 13, 31, 32, 44, 45, 57, 64, 71, 74, 81, 89, 104, 117, 153, 158, 235
Atlantic Records, 119, 158
'Autumn Leaves', 136, 137
Avakian, George, 69, 70, 113, 158
Ayler, Albert, 141, 151, 152

Babbitt, Milton, 83
'Baby Won't You Please Come Home', 133, 141
Bach, J.S., 212
Bacharach, Burt, 155
Backlash, 152
Baez, Joan, 149
'Bag's Groove', 59, 60
Baker, Chet, 39, 51
Baker, Harold, 3, 6

Baldwin, James, 90
Balliett, Whitney, 104
Band, The, 197
Barber, John 'Bill', 36, 38
Bartok, Bela, 154
Bartz, Gary, 204, 208, 209
Basie, William 'Count', 4, 9, 13, 35, 36, 72, 157, 167, 168, 235
'Basin Street Blues', 133, 141
Beatles, The, 149, 154, 172, 221
Bechet, Sidney, 41, 66, 77
Beethoven, Ludwig von, 169
Beiderbecke, Bix, 31, 61
'Bemsha Swing', 59
Bennett, Tony, 154, 155
Benson, George, 162
Berlin, 136, 140, 209, 211, 223
Berman, Sonny, 51
Bernstein, Leonard, 32, 98, 112, 115, 119
'Bess, Oh Where's My Bess', 101
'Bess, You Is My Woman Now', 101
Big Fun, 204, 224
'Billie's Bounce', 17, 18, 20
'Billy Boy', 72, 91
'Bird Gets The Worm', 27
Birth of the Cool, 38, 39, 77, 78, 208, 232
Bishop, Walter, Jnr., 47-9
Bitches Brew, 115, 116, 165, 178, 179, 182-9, 192, 195-7, 200, 201, 204, 213, 219, 233, 234
'Bitches Brew', 186, 187, 202
Black Beauty, 165, 198
'Black Comedy', 162, 163
Blackhawk, Friday & Saturday Night At The, 165, 166
Blakey, Art, 37, 43, 47, 48, 50, 53, 54, 83, 88, 124, 140
Blanton, Jimmy, 8
Bley, Paul, 141
Blood, Sweat and Tears, 150, 160, 197
Blue Devils, Eddie Randall's, 6, 7
'Blue Haze', 54
'Blueing', 47, 48
'Blue In Green', 107-9

'Blue n' Boogie', 55, 57, 232
Bluenote (record label), 49, 50, 58
'Blue Room', 46
'Blues for Pablo', 79, 80, 110
Bolden, Buddy, 3
'Boplicity', 39, 40, 42
Bostic, Earl, 65
Boyd, Nelson, 26, 37
Bradshaw, Tiny, 8, 9
Brass Ensemble, 77, 83
Brooks, Emmanuel St Clare 'Duke', 8
Brown, Clifford, 51
Brown, James, 154
Brown, Jim 168
Brown, Oscar, 132
Brubeck, Dave, 70, 83, 84, 144
Bryant, Ray, 64, 65
Buchanan, Elwood, 3, 4, 6, 7
Buckmaster, Paul, 182, 211-3, 215, 224,
    229, 232
'Budo', 66
Burton, Gary, 226
Butler, Frank, 133
Butler, George, 229
'But Not For Me', 57, 72
Butterfield, Billy, 15
'Buzzard Song', 101
'Buzzy', 26
Byrds, The, 154, 155

Caccienti, Guido, 125, 126
Calendar, Red, 8, 23
Capitol Records, 37, 38, 40, 43, 44, 49,
    77
Carisi, John, 33, 39
Carter, Benny, 21-3
Carter, Ron, 133, 134, 143, 144, 155,
    157, 158, 167, 168, 172, 183, 234
Catlett, Big Sid, 17
Chambers, Paul, 64, 67, 70, 73, 75, 87,
    95, 96, 98, 133, 135
Chancler, Leon, 209
'Changes', 64
Charles, Ray, 130
Charles, Teddy, 63
'Chasin' the Bird', 26
'Cherokee', 17
'Cheryl', 26
'Chez Le Photographe Du Motel', 86, 92
Chicago, 5, 10, 11, 23, 41, 43, 44, 65, 66,
    71, 76, 90, 110, 118, 123, 132, 145,
    166, 229
Chicago (rock group), 160
Christian, Charlie, 8, 10
Clarke, Kenny, 13, 37, 41, 49, 53, 55-8,
    60, 85
Cobb, Jimmy, 95-9, 105, 108, 118-20,
    126, 132, 133, 135, 225
Cobham, Billy, 206
Coggins, Gil, 7, 8, 10, 43, 49, 50
Cohn, Al, 49, 50

Cole, Cozy, 17
Cole, Nat, 130
Coleman, George, 133-5, 139
Coleman, Ornette, 119, 140, 153
Collins, Junior, 36
Coltrane, John, 65, 66, 68, 69, 73-6, 84,
    87-9, 91, 92, 96, 98, 99, 105, 106, 110,
    119-21, 125, 127, 132, 140, 141, 144,
    147, 149, 200, 222, 232-5
Columbia (CBS) Records, 66, 70, 72,
    77, 78, 80, 89, 102, 109, 112-4, 127,
    142, 148-51, 158-60, 172, 174, 188,
    191-3, 197, 201, 204, 209, 211, 216,
    221, 222, 227-9, 231, 232
'Compulsion', 49, 203
'Concierto De Aranjuez', 113, 115, 116,
    127
Condon, Eddie, 40
Cookin', 71, 74
Corea, Chick, 168, 169, 171, 172, 176,
    178, 202, 204, 205, 210, 221-4, 234
Cosey, Pete, 227, 229
'Country Son', 161, 163, 173
Crawford, Marc, 123, 131
'Crazy Rhythm', 42
Crosby, Bing, 38

Daisy Mae and the Hepcats, 65
Dameron, Tadd, 14, 37, 40, 41-3, 132
Dance, Stanley, 124
Davis, Cheryl Anne, 9, 21, 129, 148
Davis, Cleo, 2, 3, 8, 12, 102, 148
Davis, Clive, 148-51, 159, 160, 191, 192,
    197, 204
Davis, Dorothy, 1, 2, 9
Davis, Eddie Lockjaw, 15
Davis, Gregory, 21, 129, 131, 180, 220,
    221
Davis, Irene, 9, 21
Davis, Jean-Pierre, 129
Davis, Miles, II, 1-4, 8, 12, 43, 44, 48, 52
Davis, Miles, III, 1, 3
Davis, Miles, IV, 43, 129
Davis, Vernon, 1, 44
Dean, Walter, 159
Debussy, Claude, 96
DeFranco, Buddy, 37
DeJohnette, Jack, 158, 167, 183, 192,
    203, 209, 234
Delibes, Leo, 79
Delmar, Elaine, 167
'Desafinado', 141
Detroit, 29, 51, 64, 90, 144
Dial Records, 21, 22, 26, 27
'Dîner Au Motel', 86
'Django', 89
Dodds, Johnny, 157
Dolphy, Eric, 141
Donovan, 150
'Donna Lee', 26, 27, 33, 109
Dorham, Kenny, 27

304

Dorough, Bob, 132
Dorsey, Jimmy, 158
Dorsey, Tommy, 158
'Down', 46
'Doxy', 57
'Dr Jekyll', 91
'Dual Mr Tillman Anthony', 172, 173
Dylan, Bob, 149, 155

Eager, Allan, 35
East St Louis, 1, 2, 4, 9, 10, 21, 49, 225
'Easy Living', 63
Eckstine, Billy, 10, 11, 14, 23, 24, 33, 43
'Eighty-one', 143, 163
'El Amor Brujo', 113
Eldridge, Roy, 3, 14
Ellington, Edward Kennedy 'Duke', 6,
    8, 9, 36, 45, 64, 66, 102, 117, 141,
    142, 158, 207, 224, 225, 230, 235
'Embraceable You', 42, 81
Eskridge, Marguerite, 193
ESP, 142, 143, 145, 163, 166, 169, 233,
    234
Evans, Anita, 227
Evans, Bill, 65, 96-9, 106-8, 123, 165,
    222
Evans, Gil, 11, 27, 32-6, 39, 44, 45, 54,
    57, 60, 71, 77-9, 84, 98, 100-2, 106,
    107, 110-14, 116, 117, 123, 124, 127,
    132-4, 136, 137, 143, 147, 153, 154,
    161, 164, 165, 169, 214, 224, 227-34

'Fall', 146
Falla, Manuel de, 113
Farmer, Addison, 22
Farmer, Art, 51
Feather, Leonard, 43, 45, 49, 64, 76,
    117, 118, 121, 130, 140, 141, 148,
    152, 154, 172, 189, 196, 200
Feldman, Victor, 133
Fields, Herbie, 15
Fifth Dimension, 152, 154, 155, 159
Filles de Kilimanjaro, 116, 164-6, 168-
    71, 179, 189, 191, 204, 233, 234
'Filles de Kilimanjaro', 168, 170, 171,
    173
Finny the Scorpio, 209
'Flamenco Sketches', 107
Flanagan, Tommy, 70, 84
'Florence Sur Les Champs-Élysées', 92
'Footprints', 146
Foreman, James, 209
Forest, Jimmy, 49
Fortune, Sonny, 227
Foster, Al, 212, 215, 217
'Four', 109, 145
Four and More, 138
'Fran Dance', 97, 98
Franklin, Aretha, 154, 205, 210
'Freddie Freeloader', 106-8
'Freedom Jazz Dance', 146, 201

'Frelon Brun', 168, 169
Friedman, Don, 90
'Funky Tonk', 207

'Gal In Calico', 72
Garbarek, Jan, 209
Garland, Red, 63, 65, 67, 73-5, 87, 91-3,
    95-7, 132, 135
Garner, Erroll, 72, 83
Garrison, Arvin, 22
Garros, Christian, 75
Gary, Indiana, 166
Gaskin, Leonard, 49
Gates, Hen, 17
Gaulle, General Charles de, 165
Gerhard, Roberto, 211
Gershwin, George, 17, 59, 77, 100, 101
Get Up With It, 224
Getz, Stan, 120, 141
Gilberto, Joao, 141
Gillespie, John Birks 'Dizzy', 5, 6, 9-11,
    13, 14, 16-18, 20-5, 27, 29, 31, 34,
    36-8, 41, 46, 50, 63-5, 71, 80, 82, 84,
    124, 130, 142, 153, 191, 196, 201,
    224, 235
Ginibre, Jean-Louis, 86
Ginsberg, Allen, 198
Gitler, Ira, 124
Gladys Knight and the Pips, 209
Gleason, Ralph J., 73, 117-9, 136, 172,
    195
'Godchild', 39
Golson, Benny, 66
'Gone', 102
'Gone, Gone, Gone', 100
Gonzales, Babs, 37, 44, 45
Goodman, Benny, 8-10, 158
Gordon, Dexter, 16, 37
Graham, Bill, 158, 197, 198
Grantz, Norman, 120
Gray, Wardell, 37
Green, Benny, 46
Greensboro., 214
Grossman, Stephan, 198, 202, 204, 207
'Gruppen Fur Drei Orchester', 79
Guiffre, Jimmy, 77, 83
Gustav, 6
Guy, Joe, 14, 15

'Hackensack', 62
Hackett, Bobby, 3, 64
Hagood, Kenneth, 36
Haig, Al, 16
'Half Nelson', 26
Hall, Tony, 211
Hallberg, Bengt, 65
Hamburg, 82
Hamilton, Chico, 60, 84
Hammond, John, 201
Hampton, Lionel, 51
Hancock, Herbie, 134, 138, 140, 142,

143, 145-7, 154, 155, 163, 164, 167-9, 172, 174, 178, 185, 206, 213, 221-5, 234
Harper, Michael, 76
Harris, Eddie, 146, 201
Harrison, Max, 79, 122
Harvey, Laurence, 136
Hawkins, Coleman, 15, 16, 35, 65
Hay, Lance, 199, 200
Haynes, Roy, 37, 46
Headhunters, 221
Heath, Jimmy, 49, 50, 124, 215, 228
Heath, Percy, 46, 49, 50, 53-5, 57, 58, 60, 62, 64, 228
Heath, Tootie, 228
'He Loved Him Madly', 225
Henderson, Michael, 205, 206, 209, 217
Hendrix, Jimi, 172, 221
Henry, Cleo, 39
Hentoff, Nat, 59, 69, 71, 89, 97, 104, 109, 117, 124
'Here, There and Everywhere', 158
Herman, Woody, 34
Herridge, Robert, 109
Hines, Earl 'Fatha', 9
Hodeir, Andre, 68
Hodges, Johnny, 65
Holiday, Billie, 15, 102, 104, 155
Holland, Dave, 99, 157, 161, 165-7, 171-4, 176, 180, 182, 183, 186, 190, 192, 204, 205, 210, 234
Hollywood, 22, 136
Hope, Bob, 32
Horne, Lena, 99
Horowitz, Vladimir, 151, 229
Horricks, Raymond, 68
'How Am I To Know', 66
Hubbard, Freddy, 152

'I Don't Wanna Be Kissed', 78
'I Fall In Love Too Easily', 133
'Ife', 224
'If I Were A Bell', 73
'I Got Rhythm', 17, 26, 57, 66
'I Loves You Porgy', 106
'Inamorata', 207
In A Silent Way, 20, 116, 164, 165, 170, 173-9, 181-4, 186, 187, 191, 197, 200, 206, 233, 234
'In A Silent Way', 175, 176
'Indiana', 26
Inkspots, 38
'In Your Own Sweet Way', 70
'Israel', 39
'It Ain't Necessarily So', 100, 101
'It Might As Well Be Spring', 43
'It Never Entered My Mind', 54, 196
'It's About That Time', 177, 187, 202
'It's Only A Paper Moon', 47

Jack Johnson, 116, 165, 204, 206, 207,

209, 216, 233, 234
Jackson, Bull Moose, 65
Jackson, Larry, 9
Jackson, Milt, 37, 49, 58, 59, 64, 232
Jacquet, Illinois, 10, 24
Jamal, Ahmad, 71, 72, 78, 91, 105
Jarrett, Keith, 158, 198, 202, 203, 205, 208, 209, 234
Jasper, Bobby, 84
Jazz Goes To College, 70
Jefferson, Thomas, 10
'Jeru', 39
'Jitterbug Waltz', 88, 89
Johnson, Jack, 51, 206, 207
Johnson, J.J., 43, 49, 50, 54-6, 70, 77, 124, 131, 132
Johnson, James P., 77
Jones, Elvin, 63, 191, 218
Jones, Hank, 88
Jones, Philly Joe, 49, 50, 63-6, 73-5, 87, 92, 93, 95-7, 99, 124, 132, 134, 135, 167
Jones, Sam, 88
Jones, Thad, 224
Joplin, Janis, 150
Jordan, Duke, 24, 25
'Joshua', 134

Kansas City, 5, 10, 13, 109
Kay, Connie, 62
Kay, Monte, 35
Kelly, Wynton, 97, 105, 106, 125, 126, 132, 133, 135
Kennedy, Jack, 138
Kennedy, Bobby 165
Kenton, Stan, 34
Kentucky, 48
Khatchaturian, Aram, 104
Kind Of Blue, 20, 96, 97, 104-9, 113, 116, 121, 134, 142, 149, 165, 179, 208, 219, 232
King, Martin Luther, 165
Kirk, Andy, 6
Kirk, Roland, 144
'Koko', 17, 18, 20
Kolax, King, 65
Konitz, Lee, 27, 33, 34, 36, 38, 39, 44, 47, 98, 99
Krishna, Bala, 217

La Faro, Scott, 123
Lambert, Dave, 37
LaRoca, Pete, 218
Lawrence, Baby, 16
Lawrence, Elliot, 40
Lawson, Cedric, 217
Leadbelly, 41, 104
Legrand Jazz, 88, 89
Legrand, Michel, 88, 89
Lennon, John, 158
Levey, Stan, 16

Lewis, John, 26, 34, 36, 39, 44, 46, 49, 58, 77, 83, 89, 91, 105, 119
Lieberson, Goddard, 113, 114
Liebman, Dave, 99, 217, 218, 222, 225, 229, 234
Lifetime, Tony Williams's, 174
Lift to the Scaffold, 85-7, 91, 93, 105, 116
Liston, Sonny, 180
'Little Blue Frog', 222
'Little Willie Leaps', 26
Live At Fillmore, 165, 209
Live at Plugged Nickel, 219
Live–Evil, 116, 165, 204, 206-9, 211, 216
Lloyd, Charles, 158, 159, 173, 197
Lombardo, Guy, 4
London, 82, 111, 155, 190, 209
Los Angeles, 21, 23, 132, 133, 142, 155, 190, 199, 209
Louis Armstrong Hot Five, 69
Louis, Joe, 214
'Love For Sale', 98
Lovett, Harold, 62, 63, 70, 89, 90, 111, 112, 140, 180, 219
Lucas, Reggie, 217, 227
'Lucy in the Sky with Diamonds', 172
Lunceford, Jimmy, 9

Mabern, Harold, 133
Mabry, Betty, 166-8, 192
McCartney, Paul, 158
Macero, Teo, 112-14, 119, 126, 137, 142, 161, 173, 175, 183-5, 192, 195, 203, 206, 222, 229, 231, 232
McGhee, Howard, 23, 37, 41, 46
McKibbon, Al, 36
McKinney's Cotton Pickers, 10
McLaughlin, John, 99, 165, 174-7, 187, 201, 202, 206, 208, 213, 221-3, 234
McLean, Jackie, 47-9, 64, 91
McMillan, Vic, 22
McRae, Carmen, 54
McShann, Jay, 9
Maddison, Levi, 6
'Mademoiselle Mabry', 166-8, 171, 173
Mahavishnu Orchestra, 221
'Maids of Cadiz', 79, 80
'Maiysha', 225
Malle, Louis, 85-7, 92
Malraux, André, 77
Mantler, Mike, 141
Marmarosa, Dodo, 22, 23
Mauri, Manuel, 200
'Meandering', 17
Mellers, Wilfrid, 27, 94, 97
'Mercy Mercy', 162
Merker, Lita, 215
Mexico City, 162
Michelot, Pierre, 41, 75, 85
Miles Ahead, 78-80, 82, 84, 85, 91, 100, 102, 110, 113, 116, 158, 232
Miles Davis at Carnegie Hall, 127, 165

Miles Davis in Concert, 216
Miles Davis in Europe, 137, 232
Miles Davis's Greatest Hits, 200
Miles In The Sky, 161-4
'Miles Runs The Voodoo Down', 187, 188
Miles Smiles, 145, 146, 150, 156, 171, 233, 234
'Miles's Theme', 66
Milestones, 91-5, 102, 104, 116, 137, 165, 232
'Milestones', 26, 91, 93, 94, 105, 107
Miller, Glenn, 12, 45
Miller, Manfred, 213, 221
Miller, Mitch, 149
Milwaukee, 110, 159
Mingus Ah Um, 112
Mingus, Charles, 23, 59, 63, 83, 112, 119, 224, 235
'Mixtur', 212
Mobley, Hank, 99, 124, 132
Modern Jazz Quartet, 39, 58, 75, 90, 132
Monk, Thelonious, 13, 14, 16, 49, 58-60, 62, 65, 76, 87, 89, 91, 124, 232
Monterey Festival, 150, 151, 158, 189
Moody, James, 41
'Moon Dreams', 39
Moore, Archie, 7
Moreau, Jeanne, 85
Moreira, Airto, 198, 207
Morgan, Alun, 68, 75
'Morpheus', 46
Morrissey, Jim, 151
Morton, Jelly Roll, 89
Motian, Paul, 123
M'tume, James, 215, 217, 224
Mulligan, Gerry, 27, 33-6, 38, 39, 44, 51, 62, 99, 124, 128, 225, 226
Murphy, Chris, 225
My Funny Valentine, 138, 232
'My Funny Valentine', 74, 137, 139, 143, 156
'My Old Flame', 47

'Nature Boy', 63
Navarro, Fats, 23, 27, 37, 51
Nefertiti, 145, 146, 150, 166, 170, 171
'Nefertiti', 146, 170
Neil Young with Crazy Horse, 197
New Jazz Records, 44
New Miles Davis Quintet, 66
New Orleans, 5, 10, 44, 122
Newport Jazz Festival, 62, 63, 66, 70, 112, 214, 215, 227
'New Rhumba', 78, 110
New York, 8, 10, 11-14, 16, 21, 23, 24, 31, 41-5, 64, 68, 75, 78, 80, 87, 102, 110, 111, 119, 121, 123, 124, 127, 131, 134, 136, 137, 142, 144, 145, 174, 188, 193, 194, 197, 199, 210, 216, 227, 229, 230

307

Nice, 41
Nijinsky, Vaslav, 85
Nixon, Richard, 165
Noble, Ray, 17
'Now's the Time', 17-22, 26, 57, 62, 93, 104
Nyro, Laura, 150, 197, 198

Oklahoma City, 5
'Old Devil Moon', 54
'Oleo', 57, 58
Oliver, Joe 'King', 44, 45, 157
'On Green Dolphin Street', 97, 98
On The Corner, 211, 213, 215-17, 224, 233
'On the Que-Tee', 152
Orchestra USA, 83

Page, Hot Lips, 41
Pangea, 227, 233, 234
'Paraphernalia', 162
Paris, 34, 41, 42, 68, 75, 81, 82, 84, 85, 121, 122, 165
Parker, Charlie 'Bird', 8-11, 13, 14, 16-31, 33-5, 37, 40-3, 45, 48, 49, 53, 55, 61-4, 67, 70, 71, 75, 77, 84, 86, 87, 90, 93, 104, 109, 119, 121, 126, 130, 142, 149, 185, 232, 234, 235
Peacock, Gary, 144
Pearl Harbor, 7
'Pennies From Heaven', 47
Peter, Paul and Mary, 149
Peters, Brock, 207
Peterson, Oscar, 104, 105
'Petits Machins', 168-70
Pettiford, Oscar, 32, 37, 49, 63
'Pharoah's Dance', 186
Philadelphia, 65, 68, 73, 76, 108, 120, 124, 132, 144, 210
Picasso, Pablo, 230
Pittsburgh, 71, 72
Polydor Records, 221
Ponty, Jean-Luc, 189
Porgy and Bess, 100-2, 104, 105, 112-16, 121, 149, 154, 232
Porter, Roy, 22, 23
'Potato Head Blues', 104
Potter, Tommy, 24, 47
Powell, Bud, 16, 25, 37, 45, 75
'Prayer', 100, 101, 115
Prestige Records, 44, 47, 55, 58, 62, 66, 69-72, 75, 77, 81, 129
Preston, Denis, 41
'Prince of Darkness', 184, 223
'Prologue, The Magic Garden', 154

Quiet Nights, 134, 137, 142, 225, 232

Raeburn, Boyd, 23
Randall, Eddie, 5-8, 25
Ravel, Maurice, 123

RCA Victor Records, 37
'Red China Blues', 225
Redman, Don, 6
Relaxin', 71, 73, 232
Reshin, Neil, 219-21
Return to Forever, 221
Rich, Buddy, 9, 189
'Right Off', 206
Rivers, Sam, 139, 140, 200
Roach, Max, 16, 17, 24, 26-8, 36, 46, 64, 124, 127, 128, 224
Robinson, Sugar Ray, 51
Rodgers, Richard, 74
Rodney, Red, 14, 20, 27, 33, 48, 51, 61
Rodrigo, Joaquin, 113
Rollins, Sonny, 32, 37, 44, 46-9, 57, 61, 65, 70, 71, 75, 76, 105, 121, 132, 144, 232, 234
Ronnie Scott Club, 167
Round About Midnight, 73, 102
'Round Midnight', 49, 62, 89, 156, 232
Roy, Badal, 215, 217
Rudd, Roswell, 141
Rugulo, Pete, 38
Rushing, Jimmy, 102
Russell, Curly, 16
Russell, George, 33, 83
Russell, Ross, 21, 22, 24, 29
Russo, Bill, 114

'Saeta', 113-5, 127, 170, 176, 186, 187
St Louis, 5-8, 10, 11, 13, 14, 25, 44, 48, 121, 132, 225
Sanchez, Pat, 148
'Sanctuary', 186, 202
San Francisco, 125, 130, 133, 157, 158, 197, 198, 226
Savoy Records, 16, 17, 25-7, 58
Schildkrant, Dave, 55
Schuller, Gunther, 68, 77, 83, 115, 119
Searle, Humphrey, 211
Seven Steps to Heaven, 133-5, 137, 234
'Seven Steps to Heaven', 134
Shakespeare, William, 153
Shapero, Harold, 83
Sharrock, Sonny, 207
Shaw Artists' Corporation, 63, 89
Shaw, George Bernard, 153
Shepp, Archie, 141, 145, 151, 152, 155-7
'Shhh/Peaceful', 175
Shorter, Wayne, 140, 144-6, 155, 164, 172, 175, 177, 183, 198, 221, 222, 234
Shulman, Joe, 34
'Sid's Ahead', 91, 92
Silver, Horace, 53-7, 61, 64, 65, 83, 124
Simmons, John, 34
Simone, Nina, 209
Sims, Zoot, 49, 50, 62
Sinatra, Frank, 38, 72, 90, 155
'Sippin' at Bells', 26
'Sivad', 207

308

Sketches of Spain, 113-16, 127, 149, 153, 165, 170, 183, 186, 232
Smith, Bessie, 104
Smoky and the Miracles, 154
'Solea', 113, 115, 127
Soloman, Dave, 124
Some Day My Prince Will Come, 125, 165, 166, 234
'Some Day My Prince Will Come', 123, 125, 127
'Somethin' Else', 88, 91
Sorcerer, 145, 146, 151, 166, 170, 184
'So What', 105-7, 109, 110, 134, 137, 140, 156
'Spanish Key', 183, 187, 202
'S'posin'', 66
'Squeeze Me', 72
'Stablemates', 66
Steamin', 71, 129
'Stella by Starlight', 97, 98, 138, 139, 140, 156
Steve Miller Blues Band, 197
Stitt, Sonny, 8, 23, 34, 37, 121, 122, 124
Stockhausen, Karlheinz, 79, 154, 211-13
Stockholm, 75, 121, 122
Stone, Sly, 221
'Stormy Weather', 64
'Straight No Chaser', 91, 92
Stravinsky, Igor, 154, 230
Strayhorn, Billy, 64
Streisand, Barbra, 149
Strozier, Frank, 133, 134
'Stuff', 161-3, 170
Suliman, A.J., 10
'Summer Night', 134
'Summertime', 100, 101, 106
Supremes, 154, 159
'Sur L'Autoroute', 86
'Surrey With The Fringe On Top', 72
'Sweet Sue', 112, 113
'Swing Spring', 59

'Take-Off', 54
Taylor, Art, 64, 70, 84
Taylor, Billy, 124
Taylor, Cecil, 67, 141
Taylor, Frances, 98, 111, 122, 124, 129, 166
'Telemusik', 212
Temptations, 214
Terry, Clark, 4-8, 48, 66, 81, 141, 159, 225
Thad Jones–Mel Lewis Band, 152
'The Duke', 110
'The Funeral', 152
'The Leap', 54
'The Man I Love', 59, 60
'The Pan Piper', 113
'There Is No Greater Love', 66
'The Serpent's Tooth', 49
Thompson, Chuck, 22

Thompson, Lucky, 22, 23, 37, 55, 56
Thompson, Sir Charles, 16
Thornhill, Claude, 27, 32, 33, 34, 35
Thornton, Argonne, 16, 17, 18
'Thriving on a Riff', 17, 18
'Time of the Barracudas', 136, 141
Tokyo, 136, 140, 143, 200
Torin, 'Symphony' Sid, 35, 49
'Tosca', 228
'Tout De Suite', 168, 170, 173, 176, 177
Townsend, Irving, 142
Tristano, Lennie, 24, 37, 39, 61, 142
Truitt, Sonny, 49
Trumbauer, Frank, 31
'Tune Up', 109
'Two Bass Hit', 91
'Two-Faced', 172
Tyson, Cicely, 166

United Artists, 228
Urtreger, Rene, 75, 78

Van Gelder, Rudy, 58, 63
Vaughan, Sarah, 43, 54
Vinson, Eddie 'Cleanhead', 65, 109

Wadsworth, Derek, 226, 227
'Walkin'', 55-7, 60, 83, 85, 121, 137, 142, 156, 232
Waller, Fats, 15, 88
Wallington, George, 64
'Warming up a Riff', 17
Warwick, Dionne, 154, 155
Water Babies, 172
'Watermelon Man', 154
Washington, D.C., 96, 144
Weather Report, 221
Webb, Jim, 154
Webster, Freddie, 14, 19
Wein, George, 214, 215, 225
Weinstock, Bob, 44, 45, 54, 55, 58, 59, 69, 70
'Weirdo', 91
Wells, Mary, 154
'West End Blues', 57
West Point, 131
West Side Story, 98
'What I Say', 207, 208
What Is Jazz?, 112, 113
'When The Saints Go Marching In', 92
'Whispering', 46
Whittemore, Jack, 63, 89, 112, 167, 168
'Wild Man Blues', 89
Wilen, Barney, 85, 99
Williams, Andy, 149
Williams, Gene, 219
Williams, Martin, 124
Williams, Rubberlegs, 15
Williams, Rudy, 15
Williams, Tony, 115, 134, 135, 140, 144, 146, 155, 158, 162, 163, 167, 168,

172-4, 177, 182, 183, 234
Williamson, Harold, 212
'Will You Still Be Mine', 72
Wilson, George, 159
Wilson, John S., 79, 115, 116, 124, 127
Wilson, Teddy, 6
Winding, Kai, 35, 37
Winter, Johnny, 150
Wonder, Stevie, 205, 221
Woodman, Britt, 63
Workin', 71, 232

Workman, Reggie, 144

'Yardbird Suite', 33
'Yesternow', 207
Young, Charlie, 10
Young, Lester 'Pres', 25, 26, 31, 34, 50, 75, 235

Zawinul, Joe, 99, 162, 165, 174-6, 178, 186, 201, 205, 206, 221-3, 234
Zwerin, Mike, 35, 36, 85, 99, 151